C66839
P9-ARC-532

# RECENT MUSIC
AND
# MUSICIANS

Da Capo Press Music Reprint Series
General Editor
FREDERICK FREEDMAN
Vassar College

# RECENT MUSIC
AND
# MUSICIANS

*As Described in the Diaries and Correspondence of*

IGNATZ MOSCHELES

EDITED BY HIS WIFE

*Adapted from the Original German by*
A. D. COLERIDGE

DA CAPO PRESS • NEW YORK • 1970

A Da Capo Press Reprint Edition

This Da Capo Press edition of *Recent Music and Musicians* is an unabridged republication of the first American edition published in New York in 1873.

*Library of Congress Catalog Card Number 73-125057*

SBN 306-70022-0

Published by Da Capo Press
A Division of Plenum Publishing Corporation
227 West 17th Street, New York, N.Y. 10011



Manufactured in the United States of America

# Recent Music and Musicians

*As Described in the Diaries and Correspondence*

OF

IGNATZ MOSCHELES

*EDITED BY HIS WIFE*

*AND ADAPTED FROM THE ORIGINAL GERMAN BY*

A. D. COLERIDGE

NEW YORK
HENRY HOLT AND COMPANY
1873

THIS VOLUME

(ADAPTED FROM THE GERMAN)

IS AFFECTIONATELY DEDICATED

TO

SIR JOHN DUKE COLERIDGE,

*ATTORNEY-GENERAL OF ENGLAND,*

HIMSELF A LOVER OF MUSIC,

AND ON MANY OCCASIONS

ITS ELOQUENT ADVOCATE AND SUPPORTER.

# PREFACE.

THE reader will find in the following pages a truthful record of the life and works of Moscheles, as also a chronicle of the musical history of his time; for from the year 1814 up to the date of his death, he rarely omitted to enter in his diary reflections, more or less minute, on events that interested him. These entries, supplemented by letters from Moscheles and his wife to relatives and friends, are the groundwork of this Biography. Moscheles frequently expressed a wish that his art experiences, ranging over a period of nearly sixty years, as well as his relations to his musical contemporaries, should be published after his death. During his lifetime he entrust ed to his wife the task of remodelling these notes, making many additions with his own hand.

It was his habit to communicate and explain to her his opinions and views on all subjects, so that she has been able to retain in her memory much that was not committed to writing. He hoped, in case she should survive him, by these means to have prepared her for carrying out his favorite object. The wish of a dear one taken from us is sacred, far above all personal feelings and petty considerations; the editor therefore, although not without diffidence, undertakes the arduous task as a duty bequeathed to her. Others might perhaps have done the work better, none with such reverential love.

May this book faithfully and impartially represent to the art-world Moscheles as an artist, and may it recall to his friends the picture of a friend.

CHARLOTTE MOSCHELES.

# NOTE.

My best thanks are due to Felix Moscheles, Esq., not only for the advice and generous assistance he has given me in the revision of the following pages, but for much specific information gathered from his father's manuscripts and valuable collection of autographs, both musical and literary. Among these are such miscellaneous treasures as sketch-books of Beethoven, manuscript music of Sebastian Bach, Mozart, Weber, and Mendelssohn, and a correspondence, as yet unpublished, between Moscheles and Mendelssohn.

For the versions of the two poems by Heine and Castelli, I am indebted to my friend, that distinguished scholar and humorist, Charles Steuart Calverly, Esq.

A. D. Coleridge.

# CONTENTS.

CHAPTER I.

1794—1814.



CHAPTER II.

1814—1816.



CHAPTER III.

1816—1821.

## CHAPTER IV.

1821.



## CHAPTER V.

1822.



## CHAPTER VI.

1823.



## CHAPTER VII.

1824.

## CHAPTER VIII.

1825.



## CHAPTER IX.

1826.



## CHAPTER X.

1827.



## CHAPTER XI.

1828.

## CHAPTER XII.

1829.



## CHAPTER XIII.

1830—1831.



## CHAPTER XIV.

1832.



## CHAPTER XV.

1833.

## CHAPTER XVI.

1834.



## CHAPTER XVII.

1835.



## CHAPTER XVIII.

1836.



## CHAPTER XIX.

1837.

## CHAPTER XX.

1838.



## CHAPTER XXI.

1839.



## CHAPTER XXII.

1840.



## CHAPTER XXIII.

1841.



## CHAPTER XXIV.

1842.

# RECENT

# MUSIC AND MUSICIANS.

## CHAPTER I.

### 1794—1814.

Early Recollections—Musical Instinct—Too Quick for his Music-Master—Indiscreet Friends—Beethoven Fever—A Pupil of Dionys Weber—A Candid Opinion—On the Wrong Road—Tomaschek—First Visit to the Opera-House—Death of Moscheles' Father—First Appearance in Public—Vienna—The Baroness Eskeles—Curious Attestatum—Beethoven—Salieri.

THE time of life preceding the period when Moscheles began to keep a diary (1814) has been described by him in the following memoranda, which are here given verbatim :

"I was born at Prague on the 30th of May, 1794, so that my memory carries me back as far as the beginning of the century. In those days I heard the great French Revolution and all its horrors constantly discussed. Military instincts were uppermost, even in the minds of boys, and there was no end to the playing at soldiers. When the military band performed parade music in front of the guard-house, I was seldom absent. The bandsmen got little boys to hold their music for them, and I was always at hand to undertake the duty. Coming home all enthusiasm from these street concerts, I used to say, 'I too will be a musician' (Spielmann). My mother was kindness, love, and affection itself; she was constantly attentive to the wants of her husband and her five children. The marriage was a happy one. My father, a cloth-merchant by trade, found leisure, with all his business, to keep up his music, which he loved devotedly. He played the guitar, and sang as well. I owe to him my first impulses towards a musical career, for he used constantly to say, 'One of my children must become a thoroughbred musician'—words which made me desire that I might be that one child. My father, however, began with my eldest sister. During her pianoforte lessons, I used to stand, mouth and ears wide open, by the upper C (the extreme limit of the little instrument), watching how my sister worked her way through the little pieces, which she never thoroughly mastered. When by myself I had tried to spell out these same pieces, it seemed to me anything but a difficult matter. My sister's clumsy playing was trying to my temper, and on one occasion I forgot myself so far as to call out, 'Dear me, how stupid! I could do it better myself.' Zadrakha, the old master, chuckled incredulously, but allowed me nevertheless to jump up on the music-stool and play instead of my sister. His report to my father must have been a favorable one, for a few days afterwards I was suddenly informed that a trial should be made with me instead of my sister.

"Who in the world could be happier than I? The pianoforte lessons were started at once, and I made rapid progress—too rapid perhaps for the old music-master, to whose dreary, monotonous exercises I was not disposed to submit. I subscribed out of my own pocket-money to a circulating music-library, and took away as many as half a dozen pieces at a time—pieces by Kozeluch, Eberl, Pleyel, and others, which I scampered through. Whether my master took umbrage at this proceeding, or was dismissed by my father, I know not; anyhow he left off teaching me.

"Our friends thought they were doing my father and myself a service by taking me occasionally with them to the houses of neighbors and acquaintance, where my performances, miserable as they must have been, caused me to be petted and admired as an infant prodigy. Naturally, I enjoyed all the compliments, kisses, and all kinds of endearments heaped on me by the ladies. My father, however, soon put a stop to this mischief, by reprimanding my indiscreet friends. He argued rightly that such practices were not calculated to advance me. The more the musical instinct stirred within me, the more gentle and tender was his treatment; but many a time did I get into trouble when I presumed to slink away from the piano and the odious finger-exercises, to make scabbards, helmets, and other pasteboard armor, to distribute among my troop. After all, I had my duties as a Captain, and felt myself bound to furnish my men with new equipments.

"Meanwhile I had advanced, under my new musical teacher Horzelsky, to the study of more important pieces, which did not however prevent my regularly attending school. Although but seven years old, I actually ventured upon Beethoven's Sonate Pathétique. Imagine if you can how I played it; imagine also the Beethoven fever, to which I fell a victim in those days—a fever which goaded me on to mangle the other great works of the immortal author.

"My father put a check to this mischief by taking me one day to Dionys Weber. 'I come,' he said, 'to you, as our first musician, for sincere truth instead of empty flattery. I want to find out if my boy has such genuine talent that you can make a really good musician of him.' Naturally, I was called on to play, and I was bungler enough to do it with some conceit. My mother having decked me out in my Sunday best, I played my best piece, Beethoven's Sonate Pathétique. But what was my astonishment on finding that I was neither interrupted by bravos nor overwhelmed with praise; and what were my feelings when Dionys Weber finally delivered himself thus: 'Candidly speaking, the boy is on the wrong road, for he makes a hash of great works, which he does not understand, and to which he is utterly unequal. But he has talent, and I could make something of him if you would hand him over to me for three years, and follow out my plan to the letter. The first year he must play nothing but Mozart, the second Clementi, and the third Bach; but only that—not a note as yet of Beethoven, and if he persists in using the circulating libraries, I have done with him for ever.'

"My father agreed to all these terms, and on my way home I received many a golden precept on the subject of my studies, which were now to be begun in sober earnest. I was told that if I went through them conscientiously and thoroughly, I should bring credit to myself, my father, and all the family. Gladly would I have resigned this remote prospect for my beloved Beethoven, and the constant varied enjoyments of my circulating library. But as it was, I had been expelled from Paradise, and must begin to toil in the sweat of my brow. My father, who generally came himself to fetch me home after lessons, questioned Weber very closely on the subject of my progress, and if the report was thoroughly satisfactory, I was invariably rewarded with a visit to the confectioner's.

"Weber and his contemporary Tomaschek were opposed to one another—the former representing the German, and the latter the Italian school. 'Who on earth is there, excepting Mozart, Clementi, and Bach?' said Weber. 'A pack of crazy, hare-brained fools, who turn the heads of our young people. Beethoven, clever as he is, writes a lot of hare-brained stuff, and leads pupils astray.' He would dwell however with enthusiasm on the beauties of Mozart, rejoice in the original intricacies and combinations of Bach, and interpret them by dint of his vast theoretical knowledge. His own compositions were not successful. Not a publisher could be found for them; they were lithographed at his own expense, and lay piled up in his study. When he began to take delight in my progress, he made me play his music in his presence at the houses of Count Clam-Gallas and Schlick, but without much success. Then, as in later years at Vienna, my efforts failed to make his works popular. Tomaschek held a very different art creed. His compositions however equally failed to make their way.

"One day when Weber had given my father repeated assurances that I should do something in the world, I was rewarded by being taken for the first time to the theatre. The opera was that of 'Achilles,' by Paer; it was a new work, and I was particularly delighted with the funeral march. When I came home, I played it correctly from beginning to end, and drew tears from my dear father's eyes. A visit to the Opera House, which was now and then allowed to me, was a source of the greatest enjoyment. Would to God I could have kept for years my excellent and judicious father! He was taken from us suddenly by typhus fever, and, as a boy of fourteen years of age, I stood weeping by the side of the coffin. Time has soothed my sorrow, but never chilled my gratitude and love. His wish, repeated over and over again during his illness, to hear my first composition, was destined never to be fulfilled; but his death, and the not too affluent circumstances in which he left his family, were the reasons of my first public appearance in Prague. Dionys Weber's opinion being that I ought to rely solely on myself, and was quite able to do so, he allowed me to finish the concerto which I had been working at, and then to give a musical soirée, where I was much applauded and earned something for my pains. My mother was greatly comforted by this event, but an old uncle declared I was on the road to ruin, and would end by playing at dancing parties; that if I had taken to business I might have had the good fortune to find my way to the wealthy city of Hamburg, and who could say I might not have married the daughter of some great merchant! Well, I did not become a 'beer-fiddler,' as the good old man used to call me, and I never got a place in a merchant's office. The second half of his wish, however, was realized in after-years: I went to Hamburg, and married a Hamburg lady.

"A short time after the death of my father, my mother sent her young musician to Vienna. It cost her a struggle, but she yielded to the advice of her friends. At Vienna I was to continue my studies, and earn my own bread and independence. I remember with gratitude the hearty welcome and kind attentions I received in the family circles of Lewinger and Eskeles, and in the house of the Italian Artaria, who afterwards published my first compositions. A relation of the Baroness Eskeles gave large musical parties, in which I was allowed to take a part. The daughter of the house was a pupil of Streicher, and a warm supporter of his school. Both master and pupil fancied they alone were genuine and correct pianoforte players. The lady advised me to listen frequently to her daughter's playing, and at the same time to take lessons of Streicher. The first half of this advice seemed to me arrogant on her part, and to follow the latter would have been ungrateful. I owed so much to my old friend Dionys Weber. Should I now, as a deserter, serve under another flag? No, I determined to build for the future only on the groundwork he had constructed with such infinite pains. I would hear and examine everything, and appropriate all that was good according to my best ability, but I would remain his grateful pupil to the last."

Moscheles did not fail to keep up his connection with Streicher, and gladly acknowledged himself indebted to him for many hints, although he would not bind himself down to copy his style of playing. He was a constant attendant at the musical evenings given by the best connoisseurs, with whom the society at Vienna in those days abounded. Many of the Viennese ladies had been admirably taught, and the youthful Moscheles modestly admitted their superiority in delicacy of touch and expression, and soon learned to appropriate these qualities. At the same time he became a laborious student of the theory of music under the Dom-Kapellmeister Albrechtsberger, who on parting gave him the following curiously worded testimonial:—

"ATTESTATUM.

"The undersigned testifies that Ignatz Moscheles has for some months acquired under me such a good knowledge of thorough Bass and Counterpoint that he is capable (as he plays in a masterly way on the pianoforte and organ as well) of earning his bread anywhere with both these arts. And as he now wishes to set out on his travels, I think it only fair to warmly recommend him in all places he may choose to visit.

"Vienna, 28th September, 1808.
"GEORGIUS ALBRECHTSBERGER,
(Seal) "Kapellmeister in der
"Domkirche zu St. Stephan."

"As a matter of course," Moscheles continues, "the great Beethoven was the object of my deepest veneration. Having so exalted an opinion of him, I could not understand how the Viennese ladies just mentioned had the courage to invite him to listen to their musical performances, and play his compositions in his presence. He must have liked it, however, for at that period he was frequently to be met with at these evening entertainments. His unfortunate deafness might have made him reluctant to perform on the piano, so that he entrusted these ladies with the first playing of his new compositions. But how astonished I was one day when calling upon Hofkapellmeister Salieri, who was not at home, to see on his table a sheet of paper on which was written, in large, bold characters, 'The pupil Beethoven has been here.' That set me thinking. What! a Beethoven acknowledges he has yet to learn of a Salieri! How much more then do I stand in need of his teaching! Salieri had been the pupil and most fervent admirer of Gluck, but it was well known that he would not acknowledge Mozart's works. Notwithstanding this, I went to him, became his pupil, was his deputy Kapellmeister at the Opera for three years, and received as such a free pass to all the theatres. Those were happy and busy days in dear old Vienna!"

# CHAPTER II.

## 1814—1816.

Moscheles' Diary—Meyerbeer—Beethoven—Celebration of the Liberation of Germany—Compositions—Sonate Mélancolique—Pupils—Habits of study—Artistic circle—Connection with Beethoven—Congress of Verona—Imperial Festivities—Musical Entertainments—The Countess Hardegg—Alexander Variations—Amusing Incident—Visit to Prague—The Ludlamshöhle—Moscheles and Hummel—Karlsbad—Schumann.

THE diary, which begins on the 1st of April, 1814, opens to us a life full of cheerful activity. The youth, just turned twenty, is dependent entirely on his own exertions, and earns at artistic réunions or at public performances his first laurels as an executant as well as a composer.

On the 8th of April he hears for the first time Meyerbeer, who plays a rondo of his own composition. We quote from the diary :—"Thoroughly convinced of his masterly playing, I was still curious to see what effect it would have on a mixed audience, and remarked that even those passages which possibly were not understood, caused great astonishment—chiefly on account of the mastery shown in overcoming great difficulties."

On the 10th of April Moscheles' diary mentions the great enthusiasm which the intelligence of the taking of Paris produced at Vienna; how the populace, in great excitement, marched through the streets, singing national songs.

"April 11.—At a matinée in the 'Römischen Kaiser,' I heard a new trio by Beethoven. It was no less than the Trio in B flat, and Beethoven himself played the pianoforte part. In how many compositions do we find the little word 'new' wrongly placed! But never in Beethoven's compositions; least of all in this work, which is full of originality. His playing, apart from the spirit prevailing in it, satisfied me less, for it lacks clearness and precision; still I observed several traces of the grand style of playing which I had long since recognized in his compositions."

The great event, the liberation of Germany, was vibrating in the hearts of even the light-minded Viennese, and not only their poets, but their musicians also, vied with each other in celebrating the event. Spohr wrote his "Befreites Deutschland;" Hummel celebrated the return of the Kaiser; Moscheles wrote the "Entry into Paris," and afterwards a sonata entitled "The Return of the Kaiser." The Jewish congregation at Vienna, to which he at that time belonged, commissioned him to write for the occasion a cantata, which was performed very impressively and then re-arranged for the pupils of the famous Guntz Institute, who played it before the foreign princes. He also wrote six Scherzos, "Variations on a Theme by Handel;" his Rondo for Four Hands in A; minuets and trios; Austrian Ländler, for Artaria's Collection of National Dances; the Polonaise in E flat; a Sonata for Pianoforte and Violin; another for Piano and Bassoon, and lastly, the subject of the "Sonate Mélancolique"—thought by himself and competent judges to be one of his best works. The diary proves that this subject, which occurred to him while giving a lesson, was worked out with particular pleasure. Pupils, and those of the highest rank, had become so numerous that he was obliged to refuse any addition to their number. The diary shows that invitations never interfered with his studies, since he tried to make up for lost time by composing during the small hours of the night. In spite of this, by 7 A. M. the day's work was begun with the study of English and both pianoforte and violin exercises. That he judged himself severely is shown by such notes as these:—

"To-day I was much applauded, especially by Count P., who was quite enthusiastic; but I was not satisfied with myself." And again, "The company was enchanted; but I was not. I must do much better than that." And once again, "I was not to be talked over into playing, for I should not have done anything worth hearing to-day, and always see cause to repent, when I have been inveigled to the piano against my inclination."

The unceremonious artistic circle of the family of L., at Dornbach, near Vienna, where Salieri, Meyerbeer, Hummel, and others were to be met with, is described by Moscheles as particularly congenial to his tastes. "On delightful summer evenings walks were taken, tableaux arranged, all sorts of musical trifles composed and performed on the spot."

At this period he came into closer connection with Beethoven. "The proposal is made to me," he writes, "to arrange the great master-piece, 'Fidelio,' for the piano. What can be more delightful?"

We now come across constant short notices in the diary; for instance, he tells how he has taken two numbers at one time to Beethoven, then again two others; next come occasional notes—such as, "he altered little," or "he altered nothing," "he simplified" such and such a passage, or "he strengthened it."

Again: "When I came early in the morning to Beethoven, he was still lying in bed; he happened to be in remarkably good spirits, jumped up immediately, and placed himself, just as he was, at the window looking out on the Schottenbastei, with the view of examining the 'Fidelio' numbers which I had arranged. Naturally, a crowd of street boys collected under the window, when he roared out, 'Now what do these confounded boys want?' I laughed, and pointed to his own figure. 'Yes, yes; you are quite right,' he said, and hastily put on a dressing-gown.

"When we came to the last grand duet, 'Namenlose Freude,' and I had written the words of the text—'Retterin des Gat-ten,' he struck them out and altered them to 'Rett-erin des Gatt-en;' 'for no one,' said he, can sing upon t.' Under the last number I had written 'Fine mit Gottes Hülfe' (the end with the help of God). He was not at home when I brought it him; and on returning my manuscript, the words were added, 'O, Mensch, hilf dir selber' (Oh, man, help thyself)."

We read on the 29th November: "at Beethoven's concert at noon, in the large Redoutensaal. He gave his glorious Symphony in A major, the Cantata 'Der glorreiche Augenblick,' and the 'Battle of Vittoria.' Everything was worthy of him."

In winter Moscheles is commissioned to write the Carrousel music, to be performed in the presence of the foreign princes. He writes: "The Riding School was brilliantly illuminated, and mediæval decorations had transformed it into a kind of arena. Twenty-four knights in armor did their part admirably, and their ladies were in splendid costume. I never saw such a fine pageant." Whenever he visits the classical quartet performances of the Schuppanzig party, he praises the admirable execution, especially of Beethoven's quartets; observing on one of these occasions, "How could Spohr speak against Beethoven and his imitators?"

During the great Congress at Vienna we find Moscheles and his young friends eagerly joining the enthusiastic crowd which surrounds the royal family of Austria, to welcome the Kings of Würtemberg, Denmark, Prussia, and lastly, the Emperor of Russia. The Hiller regiment plays a march composed by Moscheles. The Burgplatz, the Imperial family at the window, the foreign princes below, everybody and everything *en fête*, the theatre in the evening, and the brilliant illuminations excite his admiration.

A few days later he describes a grand Court Ball in the Riding School, "changed into a garden, and the illuminations brilliant as daylight. Our own Emperor personally superintended the arrangements for the comfort of his distinguished visitors. I saw everything and everybody, and remained there until three o'clock in the morning."

Again: "St. Stephen's tower in a blaze of fire-works at the people's fête in the Augarten was most beautiful; the artistic rainbow, the imitations of the Brandenburg Gate, and the column constructed of French cannon left in Russia, well worth seeing. The 'Vestalin,' by Spontini; Rossini's 'Mosé,' and 'Jean de Paris,' as well as Handel's oratorio of 'Samson' were performed before the Princes." "Handel's 'Samson!'" exclaims Moscheles, with youthful enthusiasm, "which always strengthens and elevates my soul! The first time I heard it, I was in ecstasies of delight; since then I have heard every rehearsal and performance of this masterpiece, and always found myself refreshed anew."

Many youthful pranks were played, and many practical jokes devised with his artistic colleagues Merck and Giuliani, the poets Castelli and Campani, and other jovial fellows. The intercourse with Meyerbeer materially benefited the artistic development of Moscheles, who constantly played to and with him and never tired of admiring him. He repeatedly says, "His bravura playing is unparalleled—it cannot be surpassed. I admire his own original manner of treating the instrument."

For hours together they sat extemporizing and improvising on one piano; hence arose the "Invitation to a Bowl of Punch," and other duets. It was a hard matter for Moscheles to part from his friend, when the latter prepared to leave Vienna. Meyerbeer was at that time in his transition period. He began to apply himself to dramatic music, wrote an operetta for Berlin, and soon afterwards went to Paris, where he steadily pursued his career as a great dramatic composer.

The new year opens as busily as its predecessor had closed. The most important event in this new year, and the most momentous in its consequences, was Moscheles' visit to the Countess Hardegg.

"She sent for me," he says, "to ask me if I was willing to play at a concert on Ash Wednesday for the charitable institutions of Vienna. I was not very eager in the matter, because I had no new compositions, but she was not to be denied. 'Write something, Moscheles, as quickly as you can, and let it be brilliant,' she said. 'Yes, but what?' I replied. After much deliberation it was settled that I was to write variations upon the march played by the regiment bearing the name of the Emperor Alexander of Russia."

He began writing the variations on the 29th of January, and finished them on the 5th of February. These are the famous Alexander Variations, of which it was said for many years that Moscheles alone could play them, and which won for him, both at Vienna and elsewhere on his artistic tours, his high reputation as a bravura player. There were certain parts in this composition which (twenty years later) sent a thrill of enthusiasm through the audience; nay, when he would have been glad "to lock them away in some dark corner"—so that his "youthful effort," as he called it, might be entirely forgotten—they were still rapturously called for, and those who had heard him play them in his youth would have him repeat them in his more mature age.

In the diary of the 8th of February we read :—" To-day being Ash Wednesday, I had a rehearsal of my Alexander variations at the Kärtnerthor Theatre; they went very well with the orchestra, and were much applauded. In the evening I played them at the concert given by the committee of noble ladies for the benefit of charitable institutions; all the Allied Princes were present. The variations were unexpectedly well received—they seemed to be the piece best appreciated during the evening."

A concert given jointly with Hummel follows; the art-loving Grand-Duchess of Weimar, who is present, cordially invites him to come to Weimar. "I am most proud," he writes, "at Salieri's attending the concert and being satisfied with my performance." Another note speaks of Moscheles' devotion to this master. "My beloved master, Salieri, is in great danger; he is suffering from inflammation on the lungs. God grant that his illness may take a favorable turn!" After several days of anxiety he is allowed to see him, but not to speak to him, and then follow expressions of joy at his recovery.

An amusing incident occurs on the 7th of May. The friends had taken a walk to Mödling (near Vienna), Moscheles had off-hand arranged the picnic music, and says, "To set every one going, I took the sticks out of the drummer's hands and thundered and flourished, while the violins twittered, the clarionets doodled, the trumpets clanged, and the bassoon growled. It was a wonderful ensemble."

His cheerful mood does not always predominate. Moscheles confides to his diary that, "not being up to the mark, I preferred leaving the company." Again we meet with this remark, "Played and pleased others, not myself." Then he works all the more industriously, and is cheered by the consciousness of uninterrupted progress and an almost invariably unclouded intercourse with his friends.

He is busy composing his Polonaise in E flat major, which became afterwards the last movement of the concert in the same key; but at the rehearsal he complains of the three discordant drums (in E flat, B flat, and C flat,), and this complaint is repeated at nearly every performance, even in later years; so that at last, in the year 1832, when Mendelssohn makes a humorous illustrated sketch of Moscheles' works, he writes underneath, "Respect, sie sind eingestimmt!" ("All honor to them. They are in tune!") Scarcely is the Polonaise finished, when he begins his Sestet. In after years he used to tell of his great anxiety at that time to write something in the style of Hummel's Septet. But he always winds up with the admission, "My ambition resulted in a light youthful effort, not to be compared with Hummel's work."

On one occasion at Dornbach a pelting storm drives a whole party, Moscheles included, to seek shelter in the house, and he is asked to play to the company, to compensate them for the loss of the walk. "I improvised," he said, "but in conjunction with the elements; for with every flash of lightning I brought my playing to a pause, which allowed the thunder to make itself heard independently." During the autumn his mother spends a fortnight with him; he devotes himself to her entirely, and after she leaves, we find him resuming his studies and his frequent attendance at the theatres. He also looks for incentives in the sister arts. Speaking, in the diary, of Oehlenschläger's "Correggio," he says: "I find so many beautiful things in it with reference to painters and painting, that I applied it all to my own art, to impress it indelibly on my mind." There are interesting notices interweaved in his diary at this period with reference to serenades ("Nacht-musiken") practiced at this time. Count Palffy gave six of them this winter in the Botanical Gardens. The performers, besides Moscheles, were Mayseder, Merck, Giuliani, and Hummel. At the first series, the Empress Marie Louise, the Archdukes Rainer and Rudolf, etc. etc., were present, and the programme contains an arrangement of the overture to "Fidelio" (the chief parts by Moscheles and Mayseder); Sonata for piano and horn by Beethoven (Moscheles and Radezki); Polonaise by Mayseder; Rondo by Hummel, with quartet accompaniment played by Moscheles. In the intervals there were jovial "Jodler," echoing merrily through the gardens, and a still more jovial supper. The other five Serenades, as well as one for the Empress Marie Louise, and half a dozen for the name-days of private people, were not less interesting.

The first incident worthy of record in this new year (1816) is a journey to his native town, Prague, where he gave a concert for the poor, the proceeds of which amounted to 2400 florins. At Pesth he met with his usual success. Old friends and new gathered around him, the Batthyany and other noble families invited him to their country seats, and he was never weary of praising the artistic taste and hospitality of this circle. Scarcely had he returned to Vienna when he resumed his former pursuits. In those days he was a constant guest at the Ludlamshöhle, an artists' tavern, where poets, painters, musicians, and actors used to meet to spend an hour in unrestrained conviviality, and wit and wine were the order of the evening. Every member had his nickname; and these Moscheles took as the words of a chorus composed for his jovial comrades. Often in after-years he fondly recalled the happy hours spent in this circle.

Meanwhile Moscheles had, by dint of study and observation of the strong points of others, steadily improved in finish and execution, so that two camps were formed—the one preferring Hummel, the other Moscheles. Trustworthy contemporaries are of opinion that Hummel's legato playing had not at that time been attained to by Moscheles; Hummel's touch, they said, was soft as velvet, his running passages perfect as a string of pearls; whereas Moscheles, with his dashing bravura and youthful enthusiasm, carried away his hearers with irresistible force. There was no kind of personal rivalry between the two artists themselves. We have seen how Moscheles preferred Hummel's Septet to his own composition of the same kind. In return Hummel gave Moscheles tokens of the most sincere acknowledgment, such as entrusting him with a favorite pupil when obliged himself to be absent from Vienna. Moscheles mentions his intercourse with several other artists, among them Reichardt and Czerny, of whom he says: "No one understood better how to strengthen the weakest fingers, or to lighten study by practical exercises, without neglecting to form the taste." While recognizing the merits of others, he cannot forbear saying, "We musicians, whatever we may be, are mere satellites of the great Beethoven, the dazzling luminary."

Moscheles produced about this time his grand Sonata in E flat, for two performers, dedicated to the Archduke Rudolf of Austria, who played it in musician-like style at first sight with him. One concert follows another. Moscheles' reputation is rising, but, in spite of the homage paid him he never relaxes, but energetically devotes himself to his regular studies. His friends urge him to try his fortune in the wide world; he at first opposes their views. No wonder! He felt so perfectly happy in his beloved Vienna, as a favorite of the public and the centre of a large circle of friends. His influential patrons and patronesses however prevail upon him to set out on longer artistic travels, and remove all obstacles attending such a plan. We next find him at Prague, and read, "How delightful it is once more to be with mother and sisters! What pleasure it gives me to play before them; no one listens as they do." And again, "To-day my sisters and I had some of our old childish fun—a regular game of romps; I think mother liked it." He had to play to his truly respected teacher, Dionys Weber, to artists and friends, one and all of whom were surprised and delighted with his progress. Every family which had known him as a boy, and set hopeful store on his future, gave him a hearty reception. Success followed success; merry adventures and pleasant excursions are recorded, and Moscheles accepts an invitation of Count Wallis to pass the summer with him and his family at Karlsbad. This celebrated watering-place was just then the resort of princes and nobles, famous statesmen and artists. Besides King William III. of Prussia, there were Hardenberg and Gneisenau, Wittgenstein, Rostopschin, and others. The Prussian, Austrian, and Russian nobility vied with each other in the magnificence of their entertainments, and a happy fusion of the various ranks proved that the great folk were glad to associate with the artists and make music with them. The Russian Baroness Lunin sang extremely well, and Prince Galitzin, who had devoted himself to composition, wrote for her romances which Moscheles revised and accompanied. Moscheles created quite a furore with his Alexander variations and fantasias; such attentions were lavished on him that years afterwards he would eulogize the favors shown him in that artistic circle, and contrast them with the coolness and indifference of "now-a-days."

It was in Karlsbad that the young Robert Schumann

heard Moscheles for the first time, and lasting were the impressions there produced. Many years later, when Moscheles dedicated to Schumann the Sonata (op. 121) for pianoforte and violoncello, he received from him the following letter :—"I am honored and delighted by the dedication of your Sonata, and I regard it as an encouragement to my own aspirations, in which you took a friendly interest from early days. When I, completely unknown to you, kept for more than twenty years at Karlsbad, as a relic, a concert programme which had been yours, how little I dreamt of being honored in this way by so illustrious a master! Accept my sincerest thanks for your kindness."

An excursion was made from Karlsbad to Eger. Moscheles saw the house in which Wallenstein was murdered, the old fortress with its massive pillars, and lastly the Mordgässchen, "Murderer's Lane," where, in the days of darkness, all the Jews, except the family of Seligsberg, whose descendants still inhabited the same spot, were cruelly put to death. A visit to Franzensbrunn and Mariakulm, and another short stay at Karlsbad, concluded this successful tour.

Meanwhile the Countess Hardegg and other influential admirers had prepared his grand tour for him on his return to Vienna, by providing him with letters of recommendation to every Court he might visit, to every diplomatic or art-loving celebrity, as well as to the "haute finance." These letters were something more than ordinary introductions: the young man was warmly and earnestly recommended, his talents and general bearing placed in the most favorable light, and his successes described as accomplished facts. In those days letters of recommendation had their real value, and this partly explains the social as well as artistic success that almost invariably attended Moscheles. In the first instance confidence inspired by those who had recommended him, was followed by pleasure in his artistic performances. To this must be added the charm of modest, unassuming manners, which made the stranger a welcome guest, then a friend—not for months, or even years, but for life itself. Let us now follow him upon his wanderings, which were the means of carrying his name far and wide, and investing it with a European celebrity.

# CHAPTER III.

## 1816—1821.

Impressions of Leipzig—Conversation with Beethoven—Schicht—Professor Schulze—Gewandhaus Concerts—Classig's Coffee-house—Moscheles' Concert—Concert at Altenburg—Dresden—Spontini's "Vestalin" at the Opera—Introduction to the Artistic World—Goethe and Music—Anecdote of Haydn—Performance before the Court—Intrigues of Polledro—Munich—Excursion to Holland—Musical Life in Brussels—Paris—Spohr.

IN the autumn of 1816 Moscheles bid a sorrowful adieu to the beautiful Imperial city, and went to Leipzig by way of Prague. He travelled in a so-called "Hauderer," a most tedious and cumbersome vehicle, and many ejaculations of impatience did it draw from him, which neither books, nor the dumb row of keys he carried with him, in order to keep his fingers exercised, at least technically, availed to moderate. At last he reaches Leipzig. He says :—"Anxious to see the place, I hastened to the promenades, the ancient market-place, and thence went to the theatre. The students, with their unseemly noise, their furious thumping on the ground with sticks when impatiently calling for the piece to proceed, astonished me, the orderly Austrian. I was destined to be further annoyed. The performance was a parody upon Künstler's 'Erdenwallen,' in which the author, Julius Voss, in biting satire, speaks of all those who had come to the Leipzig fair with some show or other to make money. Was that a hit at me? I quickly laughed away the notion, and thoroughly enjoyed my supper in the 'Joachimsthal.'" Some pages further on we find frequent notices of the crowds in the streets, the foreign costumes, the Polish Jews in the Brühl, and the overcrowded public places. He says afterwards :—"The first concert I heard in Leipzig was given by Mlle. Sessi; the overture was played very steadily. I must make special note of the contrabasso-player Wach, because, with his force and energy, he seemed to keep the whole orchestra together." And again a few days afterwards we read:— "To-day I was with Schicht, the Cantor of the Thomas Schule. We had a long conversation about art and artists, and he gave me the full benefit of his opinions on Beethoven. Among other things he affirmed that 'the Mount of Olives' was not written in the oratorio style, and told the story that when Beethoven had sent the work to the publisher, the latter had thought it right to omit the chorus, 'Welchen Weg fliehen wir?" ('Ah, whither shall we fly?') Beethoven was very indignant, condemned such conduct as arbitrary, and wrote a very strong letter to the publishers. Schicht seemed to think this curious, whereupon I clearly set before him the proper point of view.

"At the house of Schulze, Professor of Music, I heard several choruses and motets without accompaniment, admirably executed by his pupils, and these performances were in the presence of Zelter, the severe critic, who happened to be at Leipzig at the time. I heard also in the Thomas Church eight part motets and fugues sung with much force and precision by pupils under the directorship of my friend Cantor Schicht."

On the 6th of October the Gewandhaus concerts began. Moscheles attended of course. Some interest may attach to a programme of those days; we therefore copy it from the diary:—

PART I.

Symphony . . . MOZART.

Aria . . . . . Madame SESSI.

Pianoforte Concerto, written and played by Zeuner of St. Petersburg.

Duet . . Madame SESSI and Herr BERGMANN.

PART II.

Overture . . ANDREW ROMBERG.

Aria . . . WILD.

Cavatina, with Guitar.

Lied, "Vergissmeinnicht."

Swiss Rondo . . . By ZENNER.

Finale. A chorus from Winter's "Power of Music."

Moscheles finds life in Leipzig extremely pleasant. At Classig's coffee-house he falls in "daily with the most delightful company," hears "arrangements of the best symphonies, overtures, and operas, with an almost complete orchestra, that plays admirably." But the mediæval custom of closing the city gates at dusk (Thorsperre), now abolished, and being admitted only on payment of some few groschen, frequently troubles him when he is returning from visiting the Wiecks (the parents of the famous Clara Schumann).

His own concert was to be given on the 8th of October. "I was in great excitement," he says. "My pressing business began as early as seven o'clock in the morning. In accordance with the local custom, I paid the cashier beforehand a bill receipted by the committee, charging sixty-six thalers, twelve neugroschen, for the room and lights. The rehearsal began at nine A. M. My overture to the ballet, 'Die Portraits,' was admirably performed at the first leading, but the orchestra wished to rehearse it again, and then it exceeded my expectations. I cannot sufficiently praise the horns and trombones, but beyond all the admirable violin of Matthäi, the leader. The small audience collected in the room was unanimous in applauding me, and the Alexander variations allured many of the orchestral players away from their desks towards the piano, where they could watch the execution of the difficult passages. In spite of this success, my nervousness was so overpowering, in expectation of the evening, that I could not swallow a morsel. In the afternoon I found my instrument in the concert-room, well tuned and in good order, when I felt its pulse; my own was anything but quiet. At five o'clock the room was opened and lighted. Everything looked grand and impressive, and half an hour afterwards some ladies elegantly dressed arrived, so as to secure good places. It is not easy to imagine a handsomer room, or one better fitted for its purpose. I also found the seats arranged in a very practical manner, and one which was quite new to me. At half-past six, after I had swallowed a cup of tea with a drop of rum in it, I gave the signal for the concert to begin, and was received with applause on my appearance—a distinction not given to every one in this place. My overture, owing to the hearty co-operation of every one, surpassed my expectations. The public was so enthusiastic and unanimous in its applause, that I look back to this evening as one of the brightest and happiest of my life. A chorus by Schicht followed. My Polonaise, which was shown to the best advantage by the delicate accompaniment of three drums, all admirably tuned, will probably never be more effectively performed than here, or secure me more genuine applause. Between the parts the directors warmly congratulated me.

In the second part we had Romberg's Capriccio for Violin, played by Matthäi; the Alexander Variations, repeated with the same enthusiastic applause; a Hymn by Mozart; then a pause of a few moments, after which I began my Improvisation. The public, feeling more and more interested, came nearer to me, and ended by regularly hemming me in, so that I became the centre of a great and admiring circle."

Such a success, on such difficult ground, was as surprising as it was encouraging to Moscheles.

It was the universal wish that a second concert should soon follow, and the 14th of October was the day fixed on. "I had intended to-day," says the diary, "to introduce no extraneous subject into my Improvisation, when coming to a pause, the melody, "Das klinget so herrlich" (Zauberflöte) involuntarily forced itself upon me. Two rounds of applause rewarded my treatment of this subject."

Next morning Moscheles gave a déjeûner to artists and amateurs; there were plenty of oysters and good wines, supplemented by a musical entertainment. In the following days he strolled about among the booths at the fair, and attended some interesting theatrical performances; he also examined the battle-field, the gardens, streets and villages through which the torrent of war had rolled. Councillor L., of Altenburg, arranged a concert for him at Altenburg, "in which the enthusiasm of the good Leipzig people was loyally repeated." Some new songs, as well as the Sestet, were published by Hofmeister.

Delighted beyond measure with his artistic successes in the musical city of Leipzig he prepared to go on to Dresden. On his arrival there, after a tedious journey, and considerable bodily suffering, in consequence of an affection of the throat, he sought for some relief and forgetfulness of pain by listening to Spontini's "Vestalin" given by an Italian company. "The director is called Polledro, the singers Madame Sandrini, Benelli, etc., etc. Their genuine Italian method and extraordinary power of spontaneous vocalization delighted me extremely, but I was so irritated with their constant ritardando at the finish of each melodious phrase, and the halts and draggings of the band, that I was obliged to brood over my bodily ills, and only got through the three acts by great effort. Myself and my pains I should completely have forgotten had I been present at a classical opera, classically performed. The orchestra, of which I had formed such great expectations, left much to be desired, notably the first horn-player. One passage in the andante of the overture could not be recognized." Moscheles about this time was confined to his room for a month, by order of his medical advisers, and beguiled this somewhat irksome time by arranging his four heroic marches for an orchestra, writing the Andante of the Sonata in E major, which he dedicated to Beethoven, and arranging some other pieces besides reading several of Goethe's works, Mendelssohn's "Phädon," etc.

At last he was restored to health, and utilized the early days of his newly acquired freedom by introducing himself to the artist world of Dresden. In the choir of the Catholic church, during the performance of the mass, he made the acquaintance of Morlacchi, Polledro, Dotzauer, Benelli, and other artists. "I find the effect of the Mass grand" (we read in the diary); "twenty violins, six violas, four basses and violoncellos, with but one only of each of the wind instruments, with the exception of the four bassoons, the leading solos sung by Sassaroli." Further on we read: "I found in August Klengel an interesting acquaintance. He plays in the Clementi style, his toccatas, fugues, and gigues are as solid as they are artistic and thorough. Klengel and Zenner often come to visit me, and play to me alternately."

At the next grand concert, he speaks of "the room as inferior in many respects to that at Leipzig, the programme itself meagre, and the performance rather consumptive."

The diary of this period contains several notes on miscellaneous subjects. We give some few extracts. "Goethe writes in the 'Neuen Melusine' (a periodical), 'I must confess that I have never been able to make much out of music.' A thing I naturally cannot understand," Moscheles added. Further on : "I must note a proof of Haydn's love of justice. Haydn heard that Beethoven had spoken in a tone of depreciation of his oratorio the 'Creation.' 'That is wrong of him,' said Haydn ; 'what has he written then? His Septet? Certainly that is beautiful, nay, splendid!' he added, in tones of earnest admiration, completely forgetting the bitterness of the censure directed against himself." But to revert to Dresden. Here Moscheles met with many obstacles in the way of professional success ; first his own illness, then the intrigues of Polledro, who wanted himself to give concerts, and finally the aggravating Court etiquette. "At last," says Moscheles, "I got my foot firmly in, or rather my hand, for I played, and with approval, first at the house of the Austrian Ambassador, Count Bombelles, then before Oberhofmeister Count Piatti, and Ober Stallmeister Count Vitzthum, ending finally on the 20th of December by a successful performance before the Court itself. The Court actually dined (this barbarous custom still prevails), and the Royal household listened in the galleries, while I and the Court band made music to them, and barbarous it really was, but in regard to truth, I must add that Royalty, and also the lackeys, kept as quiet as possible, and the former actually so far condescended as to admit me to friendly conversation." His success secured for him what he had hitherto in vain striven to acquire, the permission to have the aid of the Royal band at his intended concert ; this permission, invariably refused to all others, was granted to Moscheles in recognition of his special merits. The musicians, too, began to like him better ; Morlacchi and Schubert frustrated the intrigues of Polledro, who wished to give him the weakest players in the orchestra, Count Piatti negotiated with the ungracious landlord of the Hôtel de Pologne for the hire of the room, and the day of the concert was fixed for the 28th of December. "In accordance with local usage," he says, "I gave tickets to each of the members of the orchestra. We rehearsed, and in the evening the concert came off before a brilliant public, profuse in manifestations of applause." Moscheles, in comparing the performance of some pieces given at Leipzig and Dresden, gives the palm to the Leipzig orchestra.

The next place visited was Munich, where Moscheles, after taking part in some grand performances, gave two concerts on his own account. He had letters of introduction to Prince Eugene of Leuchtenberg and the Court; the old King Max was very kind and amiably disposed towards him, and after hearing him play before the royal circle, presented him with a diamond ring. A pin with the letter E, set in diamonds on an enamelled ground (a present from Prince von Leuchtenberg), is still kept as a precious souvenir.

After playing at Augsburg before the ex-Queen Hortense, Moscheles made an excursion to Holland, giving four concerts at Amsterdam, and one at the Hague. There he saw for the first time the glorious sea, and he records the powerful impression made upon him. It was at Amsterdam that he began his concerto in G minor, which he finished on the 4th of August, 1817. He says, "Since I daily heard the chimes of the melancholy church bells, it was natural that I should choose a minor key, and mark the first movement as 'malinconico.'" A first rehearsal of this concerto in the "Liebhaber Gesellschaft" was a great success, but certainly neither the listeners nor the author himself could have foreseen the long life in store for this favorite composition.

He next visited the Rhine and Belguim, and writes, "Brussels is the preparation for Paris, both as regards language and customs." The musical life in that city was one of great activity, and Moscheles' performances were eagerly welcomed.

On the 29th of December he reached Paris, and put up at the Hôtel de Bretagne. He writes thus: "The impression as I drove through the crowded streets, and watched the brilliant shops filled with purchasers, will never be effaced from my memory. Going out for a morning walk on the 30th, whom should I meet but my friend Spohr—a good omen! Our joy on meeting was mutual, we were a long time together, and sauntered on the Boulevard des Italiens. Later in the day I accompanied him to the Palais Royal, and in the evening we heard 'Don Juan' at the Italian Op era, given, to my surprise, in its integrity; Fodor was a charming Zerlina, and all the others good. We had, however, great trouble in getting into the theatre. The crowd was so dense, that we were obliged to engage a man to take tickets for us."

# CHAPTER IV.

## 1821.

Baron Poiféré de Cère—Spohr—Gall the Phrenologist—Diary of a Day—Concert at the Théatre Favart—Soirées with Lafont—Concerts Spirituels—A Curious Bet—An Evening at Ciceri's—The Theatres of Paris—Christening of the Duke of Bordeaux—Mistaken for a Courier—London—A Learned Waiter—Musical Celebrities—Her Majesty's Theatre—Braham—Soirées and Concerts—Visit to Kalkbrenner—The Erards—August Leo.

DURING the first week of his stay in Paris, Moscheles throughly explored the city in every direction, and his delight in the novelty and sights is duly recorded in the diary. Besides this, special mention is made of Spohr, who frequently met Moscheles at the house of Baron Poiféré de Cère. The baron gave morning parties every Sunday, where the aristocracy of artists, as well as the great world of Paris, were numerously represented.

Spohr had entrusted Moscheles at one of his matinées with the pianoforte part of his quintet in E flat (with wind instruments), which was greatly applauded by the audience. In addition to this, Moscheles was called on to improvise, and was particularly happy to find Reicha and Kreutzer for the first time among his audience. Moscheles and Spohr attended the quintet and quartet parties given by Reicha and Sina, and the two Germans delighted in finding our great masters, Haydn, Mozart, and Beethoven, admirably played and admired in the capital of France. The following passage from the diary proves how anxious Moscheles was to see those of his colleagues whom he himself revered, in the enjoyment of full recognition by a French as well as German public.

"Why does Spohr fail to awaken general enthusiasm here? Will the French, from a feeling of national pride, acknowledge none but their own violin school? Or is Spohr too little communicative, too retiring for the Paris fashionable world? Enough that to-day he has been obliged to give up his intended evening concert from want of public interest; this really pains me. Yesterday, at a soirée at the Valentins, he played in his E flat quartet, which passed without the applause it well deserved—a man like Spohr!" Again we read: "At Baillot's, who had got up for Spohr and myself a genuine soirée of artists, he was greeted with real enthusiasm. I also played and improvised. He played, I played, and we each shared in a brotherly way the applause of this select audience."

Applause in this instance means no ordinary recognition, for we read in the diary the following names—Cherubini, Auber, Herold, Adam, Lesueur, Pacini, Paër, Mazas, Habeneck, Plantade, Blangini, Lafont, Pleyel, Ivan Müller, Strunz, Viotti, Ponchard, Pellegrini, the brothers Bohrer, the famous singers Nadermann, Garcia, and others. Nor were the leading journalists, such as Martinville, Mangin, Bertin, wanting on these occasions. There were also present Schlesinger, Boieldieu, Lemoine, the publishers, and Pape, Petzold, Erard, and Freudenthaler, the pianoforte makers, whose rivalries were a constant source of trouble to Moscheles. At that time he preferred Pape's instruments; the Viennese pianos, with their lightness of touch, had rather spoilt him for the slow and heavy action of the Erards of that time.

The leading families in Paris became more and more attracted towards Moscheles, partly to secure him as a teacher, partly from the hope of hearing him at their own musical parties, but here, as in Vienna, he steadily devoted his morning hours to pianoforte practice and composition. "This work done," he says, "I plunge cheerfully into the joys and delights of this great capital." He was loaded with invitations to dinners, balls, and all sorts of fêtes.

The houses most notable for music were those of the Princess Vaudemont, the Marquise de Montgerault (a good pianist herself, and the authoress of a very able work on pianoforte playing), the Princess Ouwaroff, Madame Bonnemaison, who sang prettily, and Monsieur Mesny, to whose daughter Moscheles dedicated his variations on the theme, "Au clair de la lune." Music and dinner parties were frequently given by the Prussian and other ambassadors, and the "haute finance," represented by Lafitte, Rothschild, Fould, and others, vied with each other in hospitable and luxurious entertainments. There were brilliant assemblies also at the d'Hervillys', Matthias', and Valentins'. "There is less grandeur at the Valentins'," says Moscheles, "but for that very reason I feel more at home with them." The first publisher of Goethe in the French language, Monsieur Pankouke and his wife, received Moscheles with the greatest cordiality. "They were so delighted to see me that, when I joined their large party, I was greeted with clapping of hands."

At that time he was brought into contact with Gall, the famous phrenologist. "He did not know me, but, at the suggestion of some friends, examined my skull, and found, in addition to my decided organization for music, the bump of mathematics, a passion for travelling, and a memory for persons and things!"

We extract from the diary the description of a single day (28th January), which may, with its varied occupations, be taken as a correct type of many others during Moscheles' stay in Paris. "This morning, Herr Strunz brought Rigel, the pianoforte player, to my house, to hear me play. At eleven A. M. I rehearsed at Paër's with Baillot for this evening; then I went, or rather ran, with him at full speed to the Court Chapel in the Tuileries, where we heard a glorious mass by Cherubini, admirably performed, as might be expected with the co-operation of such men as Kreutzer, Baillot, Habeneck. Plantade directed, and Cherubini, who talked to me, was among the audience. After this Spohr and I went to the rehearsal of Lafont's concert in the Theatre Favart, and on our return home, we had long and animated discussions on musical matters. Schlesinger and I dined at the famous but expensive Restaurant the Frères Provençaux (I am not always so luxurious). Then I drove with Paër, Levasseur, Rigaud-Pallard and his wife, to the large evening party given by the Duchess of Orleans. There was a large Court circle assembled. Besides the vocal pieces, I played with Baillot my Potpourri, and was obliged to improvise twice. I was received with favor and kindness."

Moscheles, in giving public performances in Paris, had

many difficulties to contend with, and there were constant negotiations with the Marquis Lauriston and M. de la Ferté, before he managed to fix on the 25th of February for his concert in the Theatre Favart. We have the following notice of the concert and matters incidental to it: "I was still busy in the forenoon in adding trombone parts to my concerto, distributing boxes and free tickets; in the afternoon I went to the Theatre Favart to try my piano, one of Pape's. Ever since the rehearsal it had been specially guarded by one of his men, to prevent any trick being played. The concert passed off successfully. The attendance and receipts were all in keeping with the artistic honors showered upon me; but woe to the artist if ever in public he violates the forms of etiquette and politeness. The singer Bordogni was hissed, because, from forgetfulness or intention, he did not offer to conduct Mademoiselle Cinti back to her seat after finishing their duet."

Besides this concert, Moscheles gave another with Lafont, and four soirées with the same artist: the fourth and last was given on the 21st of May, for the benefit of a poor family. The two artists played on this, and on other occasions, a Potpourri on subjects by Gluck, Mozart, and Rossini. It was their joint composition, and, blending as it did the thoughts of three such different schools of art, proved highly interesting. Both artists were so much patronized by the fashionable world of Paris that Count Senzillon had arranged a concert for them at Versailles also. They arrived with their piano and violin, had a rehearsal, walked about the castle and park, played to a very enthusiastic audience, and returned well satisfied. Moscheles remarks upon Lafont: "He was a sentimental artist, not only as a violin player, but also as a vocalist, and knew how to draw many a tear from the eyes of the fair ones by singing the Romanza 'La Larme.' His wife also sang romances. She was as pretty as she was voiceless, and this called for the following pointed remark in a newspaper: 'Madame Lafont a chanté, elle a de beaux yeux.'" Moscheles often entertained parties of jovial artists at his lodgings; music, punch, and supper were going on up to three in the morning. Whoever could play or sing was present, and good music alternated with amusing tricks played upon the respective instruments.

"Altogether," he writes, "it is a happy, merry time! Certainly, at the last state dinner of the Rothschilds, in the presence of such notabilities as Canning or Narischkin, I was obliged to keep rather in the background. The invitation to a large, brilliant, but ceremonious ball appears a very questionable way of showing me attention. The drive up, the endless queue of carriages, wearied me, and at last I got out and walked. There, too, I found little pleasure." On the other hand, he praises the performance of Gluck's opera, at the house of the Erards. The 'concerts spirituels' delight him. "Who would not," he says, "envy me this enjoyment? These concerts justly enjoy a world-wide celebrity. There I listen with the most solemn earnestness." On the other hand, there are cheerful episodes, and jovial dinners with Carl Blum and Schlesinger, at the Restaurant Lemelle. "Yesterday," he writes, "Schlesinger quizzed me about my slowness in eating, and went so far as to make the stupid bet with me, that he would demolish three dozen oysters while I ate one dozen, and he was quite right. On perceiving, however, that he was on the point of winning, I took to making faces, made him laugh so heartily, that he couldn't go on eating; thus I won my bet." We find the following notice on the 20th of March: "I spent the evening at Ciceri's, son-in-law of Isabey, the famous painter, where I was introduced to one of the most interesting circles of artists. In the first room were assembled the most famous painters, engaged in drawing several things for their own amusement. In the midst of these was Cherubini, also drawing. I had the honor, like every one newly introduced, of having my portrait taken in caricature. Bégasse took me in hand, and succeeded well. In an adjoining room were musicians and actors, among them Ponchard, Levasseur, Dugazon, Panseron, Mlle. de Munck, and Mad. Livère, of the Theatre Français. The most interesting of their performances, which I attended merely as a listener, was a vocal quartet by Cherubini, performed under his direction. Later in the evening, the whole party armed itself with larger or smaller 'Mirlitons' (reed pipe whistles), and on these small monotonous instruments, sometimes made of sugar, they played, after the fashion of Russian horn music, the overture to Demophon, two frying-pans representing the drums." On the 27th of March this "Mirliton" concert was repeated at Ciceri's, and on this occasion Cherubini took an active part. Moscheles relates of that evening: "Horace Vernet entertained us with his ventriloquizing powers, M. Salmon with his imitation of a horn, and Dugazon actually with a Mirliton solo. Lafont and I represented the classical music, which, after all, held its own."

We find many an interesting notice of the theatres, nearly all of which Moscheles visited in succession. In Franconi's Cirque Olympique, in the Faubourg du Temple, he saw the harrowing story of Ugolino, a falling tower, and other startling effects, produced by machinery. At the Porte St. Martin, the burlesque of "Les Petites Danaïdes" and Potier's exquisite comic acting created a furore. People laughed in the "Variétés" at Scribe's pieces, written in his earliest best time, such as "L'Ours et le Pacha," "La Champenoise," "Les Voitures Versées," etc. At the Gymnase he was enchanted with the appearance and playing of the lovely actress Esther. Perlet's comedy made him "die of laughing; and," says he, "words cannot be found" to describe Talma's "Mithridates." The "Jeune Femme Colère" of Mademoiselle Mars draws from him the observation; "The acting of this great artiste must live for ever in the memory of any fortunate enough to have seen her." He was greatly interested by a pilgrimage to the graves of Rousseau and Voltaire, and enjoyed with the enthusiasm of youth and a keen susceptible nature the art-treasures of Paris, and the charm of its environs. These delights, however, are only briefly hinted at in the diary. A thorough musician, Moscheles records again and again his musical impressions. Thus, for example: "I drove early with Lafont to the Hotel de Ville, where Cherubini's new Cantata, and the Intermède by Boieldieu and Berton, written for the christening of the Duke of Bordeaux, were rehearsed. The first of these works was under the direction of the great master himself. His squeaky, sharp little voice was sometimes heard in the midst of his conducting, and interrupted my state of ecstasy, caused by his presence and composition. The whole of the magnificent and far-famed Court band was in attendance. The Prefect, Count Chabrol, and his wife, whom I met at this rehearsal, offered me, in the most friendly manner, a ticket for the grand ball to be given in honor of the christening. In the evening I attended the general rehearsal of an opera which Cherubini, Paër, Berton, Boieldieu, and Kreutzer had jointly composed in honor of this same christening. The final chorus by Cherubini made an indelible impression on my mind. Each master conducted his own pieces, and Cherubini was loudly cheered.

"On the morning of 30th of April, present at another rehearsal of the Intermède at the Hotel de Ville, under the direction of the composers, Boieldieu and Berton. Rigaud-Pallard and Boulanger, M.M. Pouchard and Huet, sang. Immense crowds of people and a host of carriages are moving about. To-day is evidently the beginning of the grand festivities."

"May 1.—Christening of the little Duke of Bordeaux. The whole of Paris turned out; the streets were crowded. I could not stay much within doors. I saw the procession on its way to the Church of Notre Dame, then went to the Tuileries, where the Duchess, standing on the balcony, showed her infant to the enthusiastic crowd. In the evening I joined a party of friends to see the illuminations. Those in the Tuileries gardens made the scene one of fairy-land.

"May 2.—The Intermède given in a brilliant manner in the Salle du St. Esprit in the Hotel de Ville.

"May 9.—To-day I played in the Hotel de Ville, where the City of Paris gave a grand banquet to the Provincial Deputies; Cherubini, Boleidieu, and Berton directed the music. The Intermède was repeated. Lafont also played.

"May 13.—I went with friends to the Villette, to witness the inauguration of the Canal St. Denis. The Court party were rowed about in gayly decked gondolas or yachts; the crowd was enthusiastic."

A few days later he writes: "The festivities, and my stay at Paris, are drawing to a close, and I have every reason to feel grateful. As an artist I have had great success, and in a material point of view I can announce to my mother that I have been doing extremely well. She shall enjoy my good fortune with me."

We have already mentioned that, after the early death

of Moscheles' father, the widow and her five young children were left completely unprovided for—it is delightful to record that the constant and beneficent care bestowed by Moscheles on his mother and sisters dates from this success in the French capital. His brother, too, whose weakly health never allowed him to enjoy complete independence, was an object of his tenderest solicitude, and so cheerfully did he render this assistance, that it was a source of happiness to both giver and receiver, it lightened the sense of obligation.

His most intimate Parisian friends having vied with each other in showing him kindness and hospitality, Moscheles gave them in return a dinner at the Frères Provençaux, and finally left Paris on the 23d of May. The coach, owing to unfavorable weather, did not reach Calais until the evening of the 24th. The wind was contrary, no sailing vessel could leave the harbor until the 26th. "A day never to be forgotten by me!" he says. "We spent fully fourteen hours on the stormy sea. I was tormented with all the sufferings of sea-sickness. At last, at midnight, when we were getting near Dover, and the steward asked me for my passage fare, I only had strength to point to my well-filled pocket. 'For shame!' exclaimed the fellow, 'a courier, and so sea-sick!' And whence did I get this title of a courier? At the Austrian Embassy they had stamped the large packet of my music with the Imperial seal, and inscribed it 'Despatches,' so that I might travel free of tax and delay, and the steward of course supposed I was the bearer of dispatches, crossing and recrossing the Channel frequently.

"On arrival at Dover I soon recovered, and the following morning started in the mail-coach, which in twelve hours brought me to London. Little did I think that there I was to find my second home."

"Yesterday evening" (we quote from the diary of the 28th of May), "I arrived at the Golden Cross Hotel, in Charing Cross. Early this morning, when I told the waiter how I admired the 'Platz,' he explained, with a scholar-like air, that the very spot on which we stood had been one of the halting-places at the time when the body of Queen Eleanor was carried to Westminster Abbey for interment, that crosses had then been erected at all the halting-places of the funeral procession, and that this present Charing-Cross took its name from the then village of Charing, which in those days formed the site of the present 'Platz' and its surroundings. All this was new to me with my hazy ideas of England's history and London geography. Little did I think that this strange London was to become my second home."

Launched into the metropolis of the British Empire, Moscheles plunged, full of youthful fire and energy, into the musical and fashionable world, as he had done before at Paris. He wished above all things to hear music and be listened to, and just as many opportunities presented themselves in London as in Paris. Players on his own instrument, such as J. B. Cramer, F. Ries, Kalkbrenner, entered the lists with him, and men like Clementi were the judges. (Moscheles at that time played by preference on Clementi's pianos.)

Moscheles writes of his colleague Cramer: "His interpretation of Mozart, and his own Mozart-like compositions, are like breathings 'from the sweet south,' but nevertheless he shows no hostility to me and my bravura style; on the contrary, in public and private he pays me the sincerest homage, which I requite with heartfelt admiration. Cramer is exceedingly intellectual and entertaining; he has a sharp satirical vein, and spares neither his own nor his neighbor's foibles. He prefers to converse in French, and shows by his manners that he has spent much of his early life in France.

"He is one of the most inveterate snuff-takers. Good housekeepers maintain that after every visit of the great master, the floor must be cleansed of the snuff he has spilt, while I, as a pianoforte player, cannot forgive him for disfiguring his aristocratic, long, thin fingers, with their beautifully-shaped nails, by the use of it, and often clogging the action of the keys. Those thin, well shaped fingers are best suited for legato playing; they glide along imperceptibly from one key to the other, and whenever possible, avoid octave as well as staccato passages. Cramer sings on the piano in such a manner that he almost transforms a Mozart andante into a vocal piece, but I must resent the liberty he takes in introducing his own and frequently trivial embellishments." Further on we read: "His newly composed Sonata in D minor gives me great delight, and our friendly relationship is all the warmer from the sincere admiration I bestow on that work.

"With Ferdinand Ries, too, I pass very happy musical hours, for I eagerly embrace the opportunity of becoming acquainted with a man whose admirable Concerto (in C sharp minor) I had performed in public at Vienna." Each performer wished to hear the earliest and latest compositions of the other, and they tested each other's powers in pieces written for four hands. Kindred sympathies were fostered, and a lasting friendship promoted by their profound veneration for Beethoven, the master of Ries. At that time Ries had ceased to appear in public as a pianoforte player, and lived entirely as a professional teacher and composer; his lessons and writings were both sources of honor and income, so that as early as the year 1824 he retired to Godesberg, in the neighborhood of Bonn, and lived there with his amiable wife and family, a well-to-do and esteemed artist. There he continued to compose music; his pianoforte pieces, and particularly his violin Sonatas, were greatly esteemed in Vienna, as well as other German musical cities. As to his orchestral works, they met with no greater success than those of Clementi. Overtures and symphonies by both of them were performed at the Philharmonic Concerts, but soon disappeared from the programmes in England, as well as in other countries. Moscheles spent the greatest part of his leisure hours with Kalkbrenner, Dizi, the harp-player, and Latour. "Dizi," he says, "has the most charming house at Crabtree, in the neighborhood of London; a pretty drive by the side of the Thames brings me to the place, and as the heavy London atmosphere oppresses me and gives me bad headaches, which I never knew formerly, Dizi and his wife wish me to visit them frequently, and kindly place a bed at my disposal."

Kalkbrenner and Latour being, like Moscheles, regular visitors at the house, music was the order of the day. Kalkbrenner was known in the musical world as a brilliant pianoforte-player. Moscheles admired the power and elasticity of his fingers, enjoyed reading pieces for two performers with him, but condemned his octave passages played with a loose wrist. "It is a bad method," he writes in the diary, "and not a sound one. He took me to hear the young people who study with Logier, but I could not share his admiration of this newly invented system, although I think Logier and his wife a clever and artistic couple. Would I have any one follow this system? I hardly think so. The mind should work more intensely than the fingers, and how can there be a question of *mind* when two pupils play the same piece at the same time?"

Dizi was an excellent artist on his own instrument; Latour also was a painstaking pianoforte teacher and able composer of light pieces, which he published himself. At that time, as now, there was a great influx and variety of artistic celebrities in London. There was Kiesewetter, the admirable violin-player, the superlatively great Mara and still greater Catalani, besides Dragonetti, who for many years together held successfully the foremost place as double-bass player. Dragonetti was an original of the purest water. Moscheles says of him: "In his 'salon' in Leicester Square, he has collected a large number of various kinds of dolls; among them a negress. When visitors are announced, he politely receives them, and says that this or that young lady will make room for them; he also asks his intimate acquaintances whether his favorite dolls look better or worse since their last visit, and similar absurdities. He is a terrible snuff-taker, helping himself out of a gigantic box, and he has an immense and varied collection of snuff-boxes. The most curious part of him is his language—a regular jargon, in which there is a mixture of his native Bergamese, bad French, and still worse English."

In the earliest days of his stay in London, Moscheles visited His Majesty's Theatre (Haymarket), and was not a little astonished that, in conformity with a troublesome custom, people had to appear in evening dress. "It was a fortunate thing for me," he says, "to have to listen to the 'Turco in Italia,' with its light, shallow music, for I could give myself up to entire enjoyment in the excellent singing of a Camporese, an Ambrogetti, and feast my eyes, as I sat in the pit, on the brilliant company in the boxes. This galaxy of charming and beautiful women, with their elegant toilettes and jewels, and the house brilliantly illuminated, formed a splendid scene." The English operas at Drury Lane interested him very much, and he was delighted with Braham, whose wonderfully beautiful tenor voice had been most effectively trained by his friend Madame Camporese. He also found the other singers admirably taught, Miss Wilson, the prima donna, less attractive than the others, and the audience at Drury Lane less elegant and fashionable than the habitués of the Italian Opera.

Descending in the theatrical scale, he visited the Surrey Theatre, where he saw a sensational melodrama, which gave him no kind of pleasure. On the other hand, he was greatly amused with a small French company performing in the Argyle Rooms. This troupe was supported by the nobility for its own entertainment, and at its own expense. Astley's Theatre rivalled that of Franconi in its splendid performance of "Gil Blas." Moscheles says of Hyde Park in those days: "I admire the splendid horses and carriages, their fair occupants, reclining lazily on soft cushions, and the Amazons on their spirited horses. The Park itself is quite bare, without tree or shrub. I have hardly ever seen anything like it, and I couldn't help thinking of Byron's words:

> "Those vegetable puncheons called parks
> With neither fruit nor flower to satisfy
> Even a bee's slight munchings."

In later years he was able to enjoy the Parks decked out with flowers, and so endlessly beautified and improved. In London, as in Paris, the diary refers, generally speaking, to matters essentially musical.

"May 28th.—Beethoven's Pastoral Symphony was very fairly executed under Kiesewetter's direction at the Philharmonic Society's Concert, the drums too noisy. There was some fine singing by Mrs. Salmon and others, and all the concerted pieces went with remarkable precision."

"May 30th.—Heard the famous flute-player Tulon at his own concert in the Argyle Rooms. A medley of vocal pieces sung by Goodall, Vestris, Camporese. Salmon, Signor Ambrogetti, and others. Mademoiselle Buchwald, a very clever pupil of Kalkbrenner, played in his Septet."

"June 1st.—Met Clementi by agreement at his piano.

forte warehouse, and played some things to him, with which he declared himself extremely pleased. Afterwards called on Prince Esterhazy, Prince Leopold, Lords Lowther and Castlereagh. In the evening, at a concert given by Vaughan the singer, I heard Cramer again play with rare delicacy a concerto of Mozart's. The grand choruses and vocal selections from Handel's Oratorios, with the organ accompaniment, impressed me as being given with unusual precision and effect."

"June 6th.—At the ancient concert (in the Hanover Square Rooms), Handel's 'Messiah' was given in all its grandeur and simple majesty. The organ accompaniments were supplemented in the full passages by wind instruments. The chief soloists were Mrs. Salmon, Miss Stephens, and Mr. Vaughan. It seemed strange to me that, instead of boys, elderly men sang the contralto part with the head voice. The famous Hallelujah Chorus was given in very slow time. The obligato trumpet parts attracted my attention."

"June 9th.—In the evening went with Cramer to the dinner of the Royal Society of Musicians."

"June 11th.—Important day. My first appearance at the last Philharmonic Concert. I had great success in my E flat concerto, and the Alexander variations. This piece had been named in England the 'Fall of Paris' (a circumstance which exposed me in after-years to some unpleasant remarks in the French papers)."

"July 4th.—At last, my concert, which cost me such trouble to arrange, came off to day in the Argyle Rooms. The Concerto and the 'Clair de Lune Variations' went well, and were very favorably received; but what pleased most was my extempore playing on the air, 'My lodging is on the cold ground.' Cramei accompanied the vocal pieces on the piano. Mrs. Salmon, Camporese, the Ashes, Corri, Begrez, and Braham were the singers. I was also assisted by the violinist Kori."

"July 11th.—A grand evening musical party at the Rothschilds', at their country house on Stamford Hill, given to the foreign Ministers present in England on account of the approaching coronation of George IV. I was introduced to most of the Ministers, who, with the old Prince Esterhazy, expressed themselves greatly pleased with my playing. In the intervals vocal solos and quartets were given by English singers. Not at home till four o'clock in the morning."

"July 19th.—To-day being the coronation-day, I went early to the vicinity of the Abbey. Saw the brilliant procession, and the banquet in Westminster Hall."

Moscheles, before leaving London, wrote his rondo for piano and horn, arranged the choruses from 'Timotheus" for the piano, heard the *new* Cavatina of "di tanti palpiti," from Rossini's "Tancredi," sung by Catalani, and in the evening was invited to her house. At last the farewell visits were paid, and when it came to Prince Esterhazy's turn, the Prince handed over to him a new passport, with the title of "Kammervirtuos." He took an unwilling leave of the London art-world, but was delighted to get away from the London atmosphere; "the heavy air," he calls it in his diary, "which so often gives me headaches, that I am glad to leave it." Then he made his way back to France, taking Boulogne on his road, and visiting Kalkbrenner, at the Château Pralin. There, until the following October, he led a cheerful, quiet country life, devoting much time to music. Madame Kalkbrenner, a highly intellectual woman, was a most amiable hostess, and he wrote for her, in gratitude for the hospitality he received, his rondo "La Tenerezza." In this rural retreat he composed three "Allegri di Bravura," which he dedicated to Cramer, and a brilliant Polonaise in E flat. Constant pianoforte playing, reading of musical scores, and French studies, filled up the rest of his time.

He had only just returned to Paris when Lafont persuaded him to make a tour with him to Normandy, and give concerts jointly. These were brilliantly successful. In Paris, Moscheles was in constant requisition. Among the soirées at which he assisted, special mention is made of one at the Duchesse de Berry's, which Paër conducted, and where Garcia, Galli, Bordogni, and the lovely Fodor sang. Further on we read: "'Young Erard took me to-day to his pianoforte factory, to try the new invention of his uncle Sebastian. This quicker action of the hammer seems to me so important that I prophesy a new era in the manufacture of pianofortes. I still complain of some heaviness in the touch, and therefore prefer to play upon Pape's and Petzold's instruments; I admired the Erards, but am not thoroughly satisfied, and urged him to make new improvements." The last evening of the year Moscheles spent with a small circle of friends at the house of August Leo.*

* August Leo, a well-known German amateur at Paris, related to Mrs. Moscheles.

## CHAPTER V.

**1822.**

Malzel's Metronome—New Work by Beethoven—Mlle. Mock, (Madame Pleyel)—Concert at Rouen—London—Cramer's Concert—A New Work of Moscheles—Broadwood's Pianos—F. Cramer—London Rehearsals—Bochsa, the Harp-player—Monster Programme—Fashionable Soirees—Concert for the Poor Irish—Excursion to Brighton—At Home in England.

IN the beginning of this year Mälzel came before the public with his Metronome, on the invention of which he had worked for years. Finding, however, endless difficulties in introducing it, he was obliged to provide himself with the bare necessaries of subsistence by the exhibition of his trumpeter automaton, and his dolls squeaking out "papa and mamma." The appearance of a new work by Beethoven was always an event for Moscheles, and the beginning of this year was made memorable by the publication of the two new sonatas (op. 109 and 110). Moscheles studied them with the greatest zeal, was quite absorbed in their beauties, and played them before his art brethren, and in particular to his friend August Leo, whom he credits with a genuine understanding of music, and a graceful turn for composition. Around Leo was collected a circle of Germans whose musical centre was Moscheles, and who were unanimous in their reverential homage of Beethoven.

"A second event was the appearance of Weber's "Freyschütz." This work, too, was welcomed by that circle with enthusiasm, its beauties enjoyed in the pianoforte arrangement, and the new era which seemed to have dawned on dramatic art in Germany was discussed often and thoroughly.

Moscheles himself wished to introduce as a novelty, at the grand concert which he intended giving with Lafont, Beethoven's Choral Fantasia, but this was no easy matter.

A German musician, of the name of Lecerf, gladly promised the co-operation of a choral body under his direction. The music was rehearsed again and again; but the ejaculations in the diary at the amount of labor required in the preparation of this particular work seem endless. The next translated by Théolon was revised and altered by Moscheles himself, at the sacrifice of many a midnight hour. In spite of this, the audience which filled the salon of the opera-house to overflowing had not the faintest conception of the composer's meaning. Moscheles complains; "I know not whether the piece was too long for the Parisian public, or whether false intonation of the choruses injured the effect—enough, the performance was almost a failure. Everything that Lafont and I played as solos and duets was received enthusiastically, so also were Cinti and Nourrit, the vocalists, and Ivan Müller with his clarinet. Receipts, 8000 francs."

An unforeseen annoyance followed. An ignorant critic, contributing to the "Miroir," fell foul of Moscheles, reproaching him with having himself added the choruses, and making thereby the Fantasia dull and wearisomely long. Moscheles was therefore obliged to justify himself publicly in the papers.

On the Dimanche Gras and Shrove Tuesday we find Moscheles in the whirl and tumult of the Carnival. The endless number of carriages, the picturesque confusion and drollery of the processions and masks, the mad crowd following the Bœuf Gras—all these things delighted and amused him. In spite of all these distractions he found time on the Shrove Tuesday to continue and finish the Adagio of his E flat concerto.

Of his lady pupils at this period, the most interesting was Mademoiselle Mock (afterwards Madame Pleyel), whose great talent he took a true pleasure in cultivating. It was also flattering to him that the immortal Catalani, who this winter gave four crowded concerts at short intervals, entrusted him with the teaching of her niece.

In March Moscheles spent a fortnight at Rouen, several influential families inviting him there. They were active and zealous in showing him the interesting city and its environs, as well as everything memorable connected with the history of Jeanne d'Arc. Pape himself brought the best of his pianofortes from Paris, and the tickets for the impending concerts were soon disposed of. He writes: "Without drudgery and running about, nothing is ever done; those confounded theatrical directors take care of that. The local manager here is called Van Ofen, and refuses his singers. Of course the influential friends interposed in my favor, and finally succeeded in bringing round the troublesome manager. The concert was a great success, and a second one asked for and granted."

In fulfilment of a former promise Moscheles returned to Paris, to conduct a performance of Mozart's Requiem at Leo's, who had admirably rehearsed the choruses.

On Easter Sunday he played by request, at the "Concert Spirituel," his Potpourri with Lafont, but took as the theme of his improvisation a church choral, which seemed to him to be suited to the day.

"Again I succeeded on this occasion," we read in the diary, "in communicating to the public my own inspiration."

The Paris season ended, Moscheles joyfully accepted the invitation of his friends to return to London. "There," he says, "I found J. B. Cramer on the point of giving his yearly concert. He showed me two movements of a Sonata which he wished to play with me, and expressed a desire that I should compose a third movement as a finale; only I was not to put any of my octave passages into his part, which he pretended he could not play. I can refuse him nothing. I shall therefore be obliged to strive and write something analogous for him, the disciple of Mozart and Handel. He played to me a part of his new pianoforte quintet, dedicated to me—a genuine Cramer composition. He urged me to play to him the three allegri di bravura, 'la force, la légèreté, et le caprice,' which I dedicated to him."

The piece which Moscheles wrote in haste for this concert of Cramer's, as a finale to his friend's sonata, is the Allegro of the well known and constantly played "Hommage à Handel," which he afterwards converted into an independent piece, by composing an introduction to it, and publishing it in this form for two pianos. This novelty, on the occasion of the first performance at Cramer's concert on the 9th of May, created a furore. To hear Moscheles, of whom the newspapers said "that his execution is most wonderful, and more wonderful because he always makes the right use of his genius," playing together with "glorious John," and in addition to that, in a composition on which both had worked, was "an unrivalled treat, an unprecedented attraction." Each of them had chosen a Broadwood instrument, Cramer as usual, Moscheles only on this occasion. "The strong metal plates," observes Moscheles, "used by Broadwood in building his instruments, give a heaviness to the touch, but a fullness and vocal resonance to the tone, which are well adapted to Cramer's legato, and those fingers softly gliding from key to key; I, however, use Clementi's more supple mechanism for my repeating notes, skips, and full chords." Cramer's D minor concerto, and the new quintet led by his brother Francois, in which Lindley, the favorite violoncello player, besides Dragonetti and Moralt, took part, pleased exceedingly. F. Cramer was a good musician, a great admirer of his brother, but himself merely a clever practical artist, without any genius for composition. He was well known as a teacher and leader at the Ancient and Philharmonic Concerts, as well as at the provincial musical festivals. Moscheles played his G minor concerto, which he had lately reconstructed, first at the Philharmonic, and afterwards at his own concert, with much applause. On the last occasion he was supported by the charming Cinti, Kiesewetter, and Dizi, the excellent harp-player. Everything went well and effectively together. "We have, however," he writes, "rehearsed here quite in a different manner from what people usually do, for, generally speaking, there is no rehearsal at all, often one-half of the band runs once through the music. And what do the singers do? They sing incessantly the few things which the orchestra know, and which the public is never weary of hearing."

A few days later we read: "What are all concerts compared with that given by that charlatan Bochsa, the harp-player? I have heard only one short sample of it, but copy out for myself the programme, although even this in itself is a gigantic work. Indeed, the incredible length of the concert deserves to be marked and catalogued as a curiosity.

PART I.

1. Overture to the oratorio, the "Redemption," by Handel.
2. Air, sung by BELLAMY.
3. Air from "Joshua." Miss GOODALL.
4. Duet. "Israel in Egypt."
5. Chorus.
6. Air from "Judas Maccabæus."
7. Air from ' Semele."
8. Air from "Theodora."
9. Chorus from "Saul."
10. March from "Judas Maccabæus."
11 Air from the "Redemption."
12. Chorus from "Israel in Egypt."
13. Duet from "Figaro."
14. Alexander Variations (played by myself).

PART II.

15.–20. Six pieces from "Bajazet," a musical drama by Lord Berghersh.

21. Violin concerto by Viotti, played by MORI.
22. Recitative and chorus from the "Mosé." Rossini.

23. Quintet.
24. Duet from "Figaro," sung by CAMPORESE and CARTONI.
25. Air from "Jephthah."
26. Duet from "Tancredi," by Rossini, sung by Madame VESTRIS and BEGREZ.
27. Recitative and air from the "Creation," sung by ZOCHELLI.
28. Recitative and air from Handel's "Penseroso," sung by Miss STEPHENS.
29. Final chorus from Beethoven's "Mount of Olives."

Moscheles remarks: "This monster programme puts even Astley's Theatre in the shade, where in one evening the public is treated to a Scotch Hercules, several tight-rope dancers, two Laplanders, two dogs and a bear!"

The grand soirées to which Moscheles was invited, to play before persons of exalted rank, were not at all after his taste. "How different," he exclaims, "is music-making in these hot, overcrowded rooms, compared with our quiet reunions among musicians! Heaven be thanked, I did not fare as badly as poor Lafont, who in the middle of a piece was tapped on the shoulder by the Duke of——, with 'C'est assez, mon cher.' I am applauded when I tickle their ears."

The bright side of the matter was the substantial profit and the consciousness of professional success. "There is something interesting, too, in being invited to the house of a Chateaubriand, and meeting frequently princes, statesmen, and men of science. I was particularly pleased to make the acquaintance of Mrs. Siddons, and the distinguished actor Charles Young, in whom I recognize a highly cultivated and amiable man." The ball given for the poor Irish is mentioned as a very splendid fête. King George IV., who was present, had ordered the Grand Opera House to be magnificently decorated. The receipts were enormous, for 3000 tickets were disposed of; as much as fifteen guineas was given for a single ticket, the original cost being two. Towards the end of this season, we find Moscheles busy with a thorough revision of several of his works, especially the Alexander Variations. For the latter he wrote a new introduction, Boosey and Schulz preparing the new edition. Fresh editions, too, of the other works were made. The Rondo "Charmes de Paris" was published, Moscheles' pianoforte edition of Mehul's opera, "Valentine de Milan," engraved, and last of all the publication started of the "Bonbonnière Musicale," the first number of which Moscheles dedicated to the young daughter of Horace Vernet, who drew a charming vignette for the title-page.

Accompanied by his friends, J. B. Cramer, Sir George Smart, and Kiesewetter, Moscheles made a short excursion to Brighton. Music there was represented by the Director of the Royal Band, Kramer (not to be confounded with the brothers Cramer already mentioned). This gentleman entertained his friends with orchestral performances of the best compositions of Handel, Mozart, and Beethoven, given by the band in a superior style. Moscheles employed the Brighton evenings usefully in writing some musical canons, which he sent to Vienna. He had half promised Kiesewetter to make a tour with him in Scotland in the autumn, but abandoned the idea. He had but little sympathy with Kiesewetter's eccentric views and mode of life, so ill adapted to his weak constitution. On the other hand, Moscheles gladly joined Lafont (whom he shortly afterwards met at Boulogne), in giving three brilliant concerts, and afterwards went to Paris, in order during the quiet time in autumn to devote all his leisure hours and strength to study and composition. In winter these labors were continued, and many concerts given.

Towards the end of the year, when the London Academy of Music sent him his diploma as honorary member of the Society, he inserted the following note in his diary: "I feel more and more at home in England, for people there evidently wish to show me respect and friendship; I feel deeply grateful for this."

# CHAPTER VI.

## 1823.

Visit to Bath—Lady Pupils—Quid pro quo—Oratorio Concerts—Unflagging Industry—Musical Engraving—Conductors and Leaders—Artistic Jealousies—English Amateurs—The Charity Children at St. Paul's—Musical Prodigies—F. Hiller, Schauroth, Malibran—Sir George Smart—Visit to Germany—An Adventure—Nights in the Birnbeck-Kneipe—Rehearsals of Weber's Curyanthe at Vienna—Visit to Beethoven—Salieri in the Hospital.

MOSCHELES went to England in the middle of January, and as in the preceding year, he had moved about between Paris and Versailles Rouen, and other French towns, so now he changed from London to Bath, Bristol, etc., for he was in request in the great metropolis as well as in the provinces. Young ladies wished in a few lessons to acquire some of the qualities which they admired in Moscheles' playing ; of course they could not learn to improvise in a few finishing lessons, for this presupposed vast musical erudition, besides his inborn talent of treating a musical subject brilliantly and elaborately. At all events they thought they might learn the art of his repeating notes, and the evenness of his running passages.

Anxious to detain him in Bath as long as possible, his pupils and friends prepared soirées for him in the leading houses, in addition to the engagements undertaken by managers of concerts. In Bath, he praised specially the hospitality of the Barlow family. "I am treated as a son in their hospitable home ; my room is always ready, and besides this, Miss Barlow is perhaps the cleverest pupil I have got." Further on we find remarks on a concerto in E major, which he began in this house, and worked out with the greatest diligence.

We also find some comical paragraphs ; among others he has chronicled a funny "quid pro quo" which occurred to him as a novice in the English language, at the table of the Barlows. "To-day I was asked at dessert which fruit of those on the table I would prefer. 'Some sneers,' I replied, ingenuously. The company first of all were surprised, and then burst into laughter, when they guessed the process by which I had arrived at the expression. I who at that time had to construct my English laboriously out of dialogue books and dictionaries, had found that 'Not to care a fig,' meant 'To sneer at a person,' so when I wanted to ask for figs, fig and sneer I thought were synonymous."

Moscheles delights in the view of the Bristol Channel, and adds: "What can be finer than the first view of the Welsh mountains from Clifton? an enchanting panorama! The very place to write an adagio; the blue mountain chain forms such a grand background to this bright Channel!" He further remarks: "The public Assembly rooms are the places of rendezvous for the fashionable world, and the weak and ailing, who use the warm spring for bathing and drinking, find that comfort which we do not know of in German watering-places; the idlers soon meet, and while away their time pleasantly together. I am assured, too, that speculative mammas, with their superabundance of daughters, prefer this place to all others." Afterwards we find Moscheles back again in London. He tells us: "I was at a so-called Oratorio Concert; one part consisted of sacred, another of secular music. The public may have found the former part rather longer than they liked, for the people stormed and stamped because certain pieces of the 'Donna del Lago,' which had been promised in the programme, were left out." He was engaged for three of these concerts, and was satisfied with his success. "The public," he adds, "may on this occasion have been in good humor, for not only had the recently omitted numbers from the 'Donna del Lago' been dished up, but the entire opera was given." Again he writes: "To-day there was an Oratorio Concert where, among other things, besides a deal of secular music, we had the whole of Crotch's Oratorio, 'Palestine.' How, I ask, must nerves be organized which can endure so much heterogeneous music?" When Moscheles afterwards heard the 'Donna del Lago' at the Italian Opera, he found that the music contained many beauties, but beyond all question what he admired most was "the charming Ronzi de Begnis and her exquisite singing."

Moscheles' industry never flagged, in spite of a rather serious indisposition which he brought with him from Bath to London. He was one of those to whom continuous employment was a necessity and delight; when at last the inevitable hours of exhaustion came, he was able to meet them by the most natural means, that of sleep, and afterwards resumed active work again with renewed powers.

During this time his chief employment was the composition of the E major concerto; in addition to this the Scotch fantasia, the altered concerto in F major, and the Sonata for four hands were prepared for publication. He says: "I wrote a Gigue as a contribution for the musical periodical 'The Harmonicon,' published by Mr. Welsh, owner of the Argyle Rooms. He asks me to send him anything I like, and pays five guineas for such a trifle. I have twenty guineas for 'Les Charmes de Paris,' and as much for the first number of the 'Bonbonnière Musicale;' but in spite of this I have a quantity of manuscript unpublished, the mere pecuniary advantages fail to satisfy me. I want to see real progress, and nothing positively objectionable in my new productions, otherwise I will not publish them."

In leisure hours he made a new arrangement of the Egmont Overture, and used to call such a task his recreation ("Handarbeit").

Every one intimately acquainted with Moscheles knew the accuracy with which he managed the engraving of his own productions. His engravers received the most precise instructions, even as to the turning over of the pages; the head of every single note had to be exactly in its right place, every rest made perfectly clear and intelligible to the reader. "All this," he was accustomed to say, "adds to precision in playing, and consequently also to the right understanding of the piece; if any one affects the great genius by writing so indistinctly that no engraver can read it, and if his music is published full of mistakes, that fact does not make him a Beethoven; *he* may do anything, and then he has his special engraver, who understands how to read him. Let them all, however, first compose like Beethoven, and then they may write as they please."

In revising for the press, Moscheles' correctness and conscientiousness were probably unique in their way, and these qualities were not less conspicuous in his lessons. No wonder he was ill at ease with his pupil Miss H—, who had lived some sixty summers, and was, like her elder brother, unmarried. "Both are dressed strictly in the fashion of the days of their youth," he writes, "which gives to this short-set couple a comical appearance. Her high head-dress, his nankeen trousers, blue dress-coat and brass buttons are enough to convulse one with laughter. As for the old lady, she does not intend to learn anything, for how often during the forty-five or fifty minutes which I devote to her do I urge her on to play, and can scarcely get her to do it. The good lady is talkative, but at the same time hospitable; I am obliged to lunch with her each time, and while I eat, she talks, until at last I compel her to hazard her gouty little fingers on a piece of modern music. When, however, we have not worked actively together, my conscience does not allow me to pocket the guinea which she hands me every time, neatly wrapped up in paper."

Moscheles was very much astonished at the English custom of placing a famous musician at orchestral concerts in front of the band, at the piano, and on the occasion of a Philharmonic Concert we find him asking the question, "What do they mean by the term 'Conductor,' Mr. Clementi? He sits there and turns over the leaves of the score, but after all he cannot, without his marshal's staff, the baton, lead on his musical army. The leader does this, and the conductor remains a nullity. And now for the programme. The C minor symphony of Beethoven, for the first time here; and immediately after this sublime work, this food for the gods, a variation for the flute, a violin concerto, and several airs. Besides this Mozart's G minor symphony, and to conclude, an overture by Romberg—a programme which I write down now, that I may never forget it." Altogether there were strange doings in the Philharmonic Society. Kiesewetter wished no longer to play at their concerts, as he thought 5*l.* for a performance too little. Moscheles and Kalkbrenner were asked to play gratuitously. The former refused from press of business. Kalkbrenner, who was glad when he could appear at a

Philharmonic Concert, accepted the invitation of the society, played his D minor concerto in a very finished style, and received well-merited applause. "I cannot recognize their claims to my gratuitous services, while my art-brethren, on the contrary, find me always ready to support them." In turning over the pages of his diary, so as to verify this saying, we find that Moscheles played during this season not only for his friend J. B. Cramer, and for the harp-player Dizi, but also for the singers Torri and Sapio, Caradori and Borgondio, and other less well-known artists.

Altogether the artists seem to have fraternized very satisfactorily, in spite of petty jealousies and professional rivalry. However, some painful scenes did occur; thus, at a soirée given by Miss B., a pupil of Moscheles, he says: "It was an awkward business! After we had all been repeatedly heard, Kiesewetter and I played Mayseder's long sonata. Cramer's exclamation, 'Cela m'ennuie,' worked like a thunderclap on the easily excited Kiesewetter; he sprang indignantly from his chair, and we subsequently had a deal of trouble and worry to reconcile the two."

There were large numbers of English amateurs who counted it a special honor to associate with artists, and to play by their side at their private soirées. Thus, Sir W. Curtis on the violoncello, Mrs. Oom and Mrs. Fleming on the piano. Prince Leopold, and Princess Sophia, sister to King George IV., were always attentive listeners to the performers. Still Moscheles complains, "I am obliged to perform and endure too much trivial music."

He describes the annual festivity of the meeting of the 6000 charity children for divine service at St. Paul's Cathedral as remarkable and edifying. "The moment when the whole host of them stand up together is an imposing one. But," he adds, "how could they all, with the powerful organ accompaniment to the Psalms, and while singing in unison, contrive to fall the fourth of a tone, and that also in unison!"

Moscheles had abundant opportunities of forming a judgment of youthful talent, for fathers and mothers brought him their budding musical prodigies, the most of whom have vanished and are long forgotten. Still he often thought in later years, with great delight, of the moment when the boy Ferdinand Hiller first played to him, and he prophesied to the father the brilliant musical future of his son; this was for a long time a delightful recollection to both. Delphine Schauroth too, when only ten years of age, astonished him, even in those days, by her brilliant execution and musical aptitude. But more than all other wonders in the way of musical children, he was charmed with the youthful, almost childish actress, Maria Garcia, afterwards Malibran, whom he saw on an amateur stage in the house of a M. Hullmandel. He writes: "The charming girl, almost a child, acted enchantingly in the 'Chauvin de Rheims,' 'Le Coin de Rue,' and 'L'Ours et le Pacha.'" At the same time he was delighted with the dramatic singing of her father, who was one of the greatest tenors of his day.

Moscheles, during his stay in Vienna, had laid the foundation of an accurate knowledge of the Italian language, for which he always had a predilection. In London he had perfected himself still more, and never failed to attend the Pistrucci evenings, where he listened with great delight to the "Improvisatore," as he enlarged, in well-sounding harmonious verses, on a chance theme suggested by the public. "It gives me food for thought in my own improvisations," he adds. "I must constantly make comparisons between the sister arts: they are all closely allied."

The London of 1823 had nothing in the shape of conveyances but two-horse hack carriages, and these were as costly as they were clumsy. Moscheles' delight, when for the first time he could use a one-horse cab, of lighter build, is recorded in the diary: "The happy change occurred exactly in one of my busiest weeks. While preparing for a concert on the 27th of June, I was forced to cross and recross London. My dear friend, Sir George Smart, has relieved me of a part of these preparations; he is always ready to accompany, to give rehearsals to singers and soloists; in a word, to spare his friend all sorts of trouble. That excellent man conducts nearly all the important musical festivals in London as well as the provinces, with the greatest care and precision. He is one of those rare beings who, in spite of all sorts of business, find time to answer their letters every day they receive them. He is always ready, too, to serve his friends, and many a foreign singer is indebted to him for a correct pronunciation in the oratorios of Haydn and Handel, and for such suggestions as enable her to carry out successfully the old traditions."

Moscheles' stay in England, so prosperous in every way, finished with the end of the London season. In August we find him already on his journey home, starting first of all for France. The first day in Paris is more pleasant than the second. "I have left at Schlesinger's a box full of valuables, which have been stolen, every one of them—namely, the snuff-box given me by the Duchess de Berry, a silver coffee-service, twelve spoons, an antique ring, a Venetian chain, and other articles of value given to me as souvenirs. We suspect a young friend of Schlesinger, who saw me pack the things, and often remained alone in the room where the box stood. We are obliged to act with great delicacy in this matter." The suspicion was confirmed, but the penitent letter which Moscheles reinceived from the young man induced him patiently to wait hopes of a restitution of his lost property. Later on we shall meet with a further development of this disagreeable affair.

He staid but ten days in Paris, previous to going to Spa, where a concert was arranged without any trouble to himself. The pianoforte question, however, was a difficult matter. Moscheles did not succeed in obtaining the very excellent piano belonging to Lady Portland, whose acquaintance he had made at a ball. "She disappoints me extremely," he writes, "declaring that I should damage her instrument. I, who am so averse to all thumping. She actually told a friend of hers present at the ball that I played with my feet!"

Some confusion may have arisen in the lady's mind from her having heard of one of Moscheles' favorite jokes—he would play with his fists, improvise pieces, introducing passages for thirds in which he would contrive to strike the under note with the closed thumb, retaining all the while the softness of his touch. Lady Portland's piano not forthcoming, a Mrs. Bayham lent him a Broadwood, which, although it had seen its best days, did not prejudice his success.

We next find him at Aix-la-Chapelle. Here J. A. Mayer, the publisher, formerly a mere acquaintance of his, was of great assistance. This gentleman, as well as the entire family, became his life-long friends, and thus the lightly knit tie of a passing acquaintance became a lasting link in the chain of Moscheles' friendship.

Moscheles had a peculiar and very marked propensity, which he retained to his latest years, for attending courts of law, and watching the progress of trials. Thus we find him, even at Aix, in the midst of a cheerful artistic life, rushing off to the court, and diligently listening to the criminal proceedings in the case of the murderers Joseph Pakhard and Josephine Herzoginrath. "His indifference shocked me," he writes. "Her sobs were heart-rending." We often come across similar notes on public trials.

At the beginning of September Moscheles returned to Germany. At first we find him in Frankfort, from whence he hurries off to Hofrath André, in Offenbach, in order to revel in Mozart manuscripts. He says, "I immediately took a note for myself of the two bars, which Mozart struck out of his overture to the 'Zauberflöte' as superfluous.

What could I, who worship every note of Mozart's, who consider him the greatest musical genius, say, when Hofrath André maintained that Mozart did not thoroughly understand declamation, since words which bear the contrary sense to that of his opera texts, might just as well be placed under his music, and be as suitable as the original words. This accusation seemed to me not worthy of defence. I remained silent. I was intensely interested in a sight of the half-finished scene of the opera 'L'Oca del Cairo.' The last numbers of this buried treasure are unfortunately only noted for the voice and bass! Who would like to end where Mozart has begun? I saw, too, an outburst of his waggish humor in a Concerto which he had written for the horn-player Leitgeb, with the following inscription, 'W. A. Mozart has taken pity on the poor Leitgeb, the ass, the ox, etc., and written for him a horn-concerto.'"

At that time Moscheles heard a new arrangement of the libretto to the opera, "Cosi fan tutte," which was given with Mozart's music unaltered, under the name of the "Fairy Mirror." This music delighted him. He heard Mozart's Requiem given by the Cäcilien-Verein, in the Cathedral, under Schelble's able direction. Here, too, he revelled in the choicest fragments of Handelian music. It gave Moscheles great delight to meet the esteemed contrapuntist, Vollweiler, as well as Aloys Schmitt, and to become acquainted with Wilhelm Speier, so well known for his Rheinlied. "*That* stamp of amateur I like," he said, "as well as an artist."

Deeply engrossed in all kinds of professional pursuits, Moscheles was still mindful of the welfare of his brother artists. Böhm aud Pixis were making a tour, and had just arrived in Frankfort. "Friend Mayer," said Moscheles, "shall get up a good concert for them in Aix." So he wrote to him, and urgently recommended them.

After his concert in Frankfort was over, Spontini's "Olympia" was just announced in Darmstadt; Moscheles, Pixis, and Böhm drove over to hear it, and they met with a strange adventure. "The wheel of our carriage was three times lost, and as there was nothing else to drive but a common cart, and we would not miss the opera at any price, we mounted this elegant vehicle, and made our solemn entry into Darmstadt at the same time with many princely and other carriages, with the inmates of which we were well acquainted. At this first hearing of 'Olympia' I found much that was grand and indicative of genius, without concealing from myself the weakness of many passages. Zelter, who delighted in opposing every modern 'eccentricity,' as he called most of the innovations, declared that he could hear plenty of such noisy music outside the opera house without going into it."

In Munich Moscheles was kindly received by the Kaula family, and delighted in meeting his brother artists in the "Birnbeck Kneipe," for beer and musical discussion. There was Winter, the composer of "Das Unterbrochene Opferfest," Molique, Andreas Romberg, Bohrer, Krebs, and others.

In consequence of the arrival of the Prince of Prussia, who was recently betrothed to a Bavarian princess, Moscheles was summoned to Nymphenburg to play before the royal party, and thoroughly enjoyed the kind reception given him by the "good King Max." He asked him, "How old are you?" "Thirty, your Majesty." "Double that number, and add seven to it, and you will have my age," said the king quickly. The Crown-Prince of Prussia, who joined in the conversation, invited Moscheles to Berlin, and the king made him promise to play again before the Court on the 4th of October. He did play on that evening, and had the satisfaction of seeing the royal party at his own concert on the 10th.

The vintage fêtes, which were celebrated in the presence of the Court, were a delightful recreation to Moscheles. There is, however, a complaining tone observable in some of his descriptions of the scenes he witnessed; he felt ill and unable to thoroughly enjoy that which was so delightful to thousands on the meadows and hills around. After attending a performance of his music to the ballet "Die Portraits," which the ballet-master Horschelt ordered to be given in his honor, he then became worse, and hurried back to dear old Vienna, in search of proper medical treatment. Vivanot, Malfatti, and Smethana did everything that friendship and their art could do. His brother came from Prague to nurse him, but in spite of their combined care, three gloomy weeks passed before he was out of danger. Then followed a period of prostration, which cramped his vital energy and spirits almost more than the illness itself. For a long time he was much depressed; he found some consolation in his Shakespeare, but seldom touched the piano; even the visits of sympathizing friends failed to rouse him from his apathy. The offer made him by Barbaja, the lessee of the Kärntnerthor Theatre, to give as many concerts as he liked and share half the profits, remained unheeded. At this period, C. M. von Weber came to Vienna, for the purpose of bringing out his "Euryanthe;" already after the rehearsals the most dissentient voices of the German and Italian factions were heard, warning notes were given of a serious battle at the first performance—nay, some ill-disposed persons had presumed to rechristen "Euryanthe" by the name of "Ennuyante." Moscheles would not on any account miss the first performance, in order to raise his voice for the German master, and against "the shallow Italian jingle" as he called it. Thus his melancholy was overcome. "The opera is not suited for uninitiated ears," said he, after he had heard it: "it is too bold in rhythm and harmony; the text so terribly far-fetched that the music must to some extent, be of the same kind; it has, however, very many beauties, and the airs 'Glöcklein im Thale' and 'Unter Blühenden Mandelbaümen,' but before all, the finale of the first act, must insure the success of the opera, even with the pit and galleries." The cast was faultless. The charming, youthful Sontag, the excellent tenor singer Haitzinger, the admirable Madame Grünbaum, and the equally good Forti, represented the leading characters. At the subsequent representations, when the house would no longer fill, the Italian faction begun to triumph. Moscheles writes: "Ludlam (the healthy art-fraternity whose acquaintance we have already made) succeeded in infusing the orthodox German spirit into the press." Besides this, the society was anxious to honor Weber, and gave him a festive evening after the first representation of "Euryanthe." Among those present were Castelli, Jeitteles, Gyrowetz, Bäuerle, Benedict, Grillparzer, and many others. Poems, written for the occasion, extolling Weber's genius, were recited, and the most jovial Ludlamslieder sung.

The success of the first concert which Moscheles gave after his return to Vienna raised his spirits once more to the old level, although he was not free from bodily suffering. Having to return some visits, he began with Beethoven, accompanied by his brother, who was burning with anxiety to see the great man. "Arrived at the house-door," says Moscheles, "I had some misgivings, knowing

Beethoven's dislike to strangers, and asked my brother to wait below while I felt my way. After short greetings, I asked Beethoven, 'May I be allowed to introduce my brother to you?' He replied, hurriedly, 'Where is he then?' 'Below,' was the answer. 'What! below?' said he, with some vehemence; then rushed down stairs, seized my astonished brother by his arm, and dragged him up into the middle of his room, exclaiming, 'Am I so barbarously rude and unapproachable?' He then showed great kindness to the stranger. Unfortunately, on account of his deafness, we could only converse by writing."

Moscheles wished also to visit poor Salieri, who, weak, old, and nigh to death, was lying in the common hospital. For this purpose he obtained the necessary permission of his unmarried daughter and the regular authorities, as hardly any one could be admitted to see him; he was not fond of visits, and made only a few special exceptions. "Our meeting," writes Moscheles, "was a sorrowful one; for already his appearance shocked me, and he spoke to me in broken sentences of his nearly impending death. At last he said, 'I can assure you as a man of honor that there is no truth in the absurd report; of course you know—Mozart—I am said to have poisoned him; but no—malice, sheer malice; tell the world, dear Moscheles, old Salieri, who is on his death-bed, has told this to you.' I was deeply moved, and when the old man in tears repeated his thanks for my visit (having already overwhelmed me with gratitude on my arrival), it was time for me to rush out of the room before I was entirely overcome with emotion. With regard to the report hinted at by the dying man, it certainly had been circulated, without my ever giving it the slightest belief. Morally speaking he had no doubt by his intrigues poisoned many an hour of Mozart's existence."

After Moscheles had made a round of visits to the artists, he went off to the pianoforte-makers, whose progress he always diligently watched, and found that Graf and Leschin had considerably improved the quality of their instruments.

In November and December, Moscheles gave a second and third concert in the Kärntnerthor Theatre, and for the last occasion Beethoven lent him with the greatest readiness his Broadwood piano. Moscheles wished, by using alternately at one and the same concert a Graf and an English piano, to bring out the good qualities of both. Beethoven was not exactly the player to treat a piano carefully; his unfortunate deafness was the cause of his pitiless thumping on the instrument, so that Graf—foreseeing the favorable issue of this contest to himself—generously labored to put the damaged English instrument into better condition for this occasion. "I tried," says Moscheles, "in my Fantasia to show the value of the broad, full, although somewhat muffled tone of the Broadwood piano; but in vain. My Vienna public remained loyal to their countryman—the clear, ringing tones of the Graf were more pleasing to their ears. Before I left the room I was obliged to yield to the urgent request of several of my hearers, in promising to repeat the whole concert the day after to-morrow." This promise was fulfilled.

He persistently refused the pressing invitations he received to give a concert in the Theatre an der Wien; he was still suffering pain, and wanted to get away from Vienna. However, he took part in a concert for the benefit of the poor, and supported his friend Mayseder on the evening of his benefit, when he played the E flat concerto.

In gratitude for the merry evenings which he had spent among the Ludlamites, Moscheles composed for them, in the midst of his preparations for departure, a jovial chorus; the society upon this elevated him to the rank of Ludlam's "Kapellmeister." At the same time the smaller but very vigorous "Schlaraffen-Verein" (Idler's Club) conferred on him honorary membership. "Thus," he says, "the close of the year found me in high spirits, but invested with the night-cap, and all the other insignia of idleness. Better thus to *end* the year than to begin the new one."

# CHAPTER VII.

## 1824.

Prague—Inauguration of the Redoutensaal—Reception by the Emperor—Series of Concerts—Respect for his Old Master—Dresden—Artistic Society—Tieck—C. M. von Weber—Performance before the Court—Leipzig—Distinguished Critics and Artists—Berlin—Relations to the Mendelssohn Family—Frau Varnhagen von Ense (Rahel)—Felix Mendelssohn—Zelter—Potsdam—Magdeburg.

ON the 1st of January, Moscheles writes in his diary: "I could not express to my dear friends and patrons, at my parting visits, my sense of obligation to them for all their kindness; but I am very sensible of all that they have done for me. Ludlam, with its jokes, was hardly in tune with my present state of feeling, but I was of course obliged to appear at the parting banquet which they gave me." No sooner had he arrived at Prague than he became dangerously ill, and was laid up for four months in his mother's house. He was therefore obliged to forfeit his engagements in England for the winter and spring. The newspapers actually announced his death, but severe as the crisis was through which he passed, he was mercifully spared to his family and friends. On this occasion, too, it is music which completes his cure. From January to April he had diverted himself solely with reading (chiefly the works of Goethe), and very seldom touched the piano. In the month of May he was asked whether he would inaugurate with his consert the Redoutensaal, in the presence of their Majesties, who had just arrived at Prague. "So I am about," he says, "to celebrate my recovery, not only with heartfelt gratitude to God and my friends, but also by a brilliant concert." The Oberstburggraf, the Stadthauptmann, and the members of the musical committee arranged everything; a new royal box was erected, the house was brilliantly illuminated, chorus and band strengthened.

On the 29th of May, Moscheles writes in his diary: "My

mother's joy at my success yesterday compensates for all the sadness of the winter." On the 2d of June he was received at a private audience by the Emperor, and greeted with these words: "You pleased me when you were merely a boy, and since that time it always gives me pleasure to hear you." In addition to his kind patronage, an unusually handsome present from the Emperor had greatly contributed to the pecuniary success of the concert, which was followed by another at the "Ständischen Theatre," and afterwards he had the pleasure of being present at the signing of his sister Fanny's marriage contract, and was able to provide handsomely for her.

On the 11th of June his brother travelled with him to Carlsbad, where he was to take the waters, but the public insisted on hearing him; he was obliged to give a concert, and at the special wish of the Duke of Cumberland, repeated it a few evenings later. Similar successes were awaiting him at Marienbad, Franzensbad, and Teplitz, and at all these places he gave concerts for the poor and assisted his artistic friends in their own undertakings. Of course, in each of the watering-places there was a concourse of artists, and Moscheles was specially delighted at his meeting with Carl Maria von Weber. He rejoices that in going to Dresden he can spare a fortnight for Prague, where he again plays to old master Dionys Weber, and listens with affectionate reverence to his remarks on his own compositions. He always maintained before him the character of a pupil, however much Dionys Weber wished to honor the master in him. "One thing strikes me as remarkable," he says, "how the good man, who first of all regarded Beethoven as half-mad and warned me against him, is obliged by degrees to change his mind; but he does this cautiously, for there are still many things which he will not approve of, and I am forced to moderate my enthusiasm considerably in order not to annoy him." These words show a sense of reverence and honor that needs no comment.

We now follow Moscheles to Dresden, where he found Carl Maria von Weber and Morlacchi, acting as Hofkapellmeisters, Rolla first violin in the admirable Court band, Herr v. Lüttichau "Intendant" of the Royal Theatre. We read of Moscheles enjoying the beautiful music in the Catholic Church, the brilliant singers Sassaroli, Tibaldi, etc. He speaks of Tieck, who delighted him with his reading of "Clavigo," of August Klengel, whose canon studies Moscheles prized as masterpieces, and with whom he spent many an enjoyable evening. Weber and his amiable wife invited him to their house at Hosterwitz (near Dresden). There, too, was Friedrich Kind, librettist of the "Freyschütz," and Weber's intention of accepting an invitation to England was earnestly discussed. "Of course," says Moscheles, "I can give him information and practical hints on measures necessary for his scheme. But I am sorry to see him in a state of debility and suffering, and dread the exertions which London will cost him." Unfortunately, these fears were destined to be realized, as we shall afterwards see in the year 1826.

Moscheles had to play again in Pilnitz before the Royal family, and again his performance was to be during the dinner hour. The redeeming feature was a jovial dinner among the artists after the performance was over, and they were much amused at receiving, in accordance with ancient custom, a thaler each for gloves, besides such valuables as the gold snuff-box with which Moscheles was presented. "The thaler," he writes, "goes well with the Vandalism of playing to royal folk at their dinner."

On the 8th of October, Moscheles and his brother went to Leipzig. Here let us briefly anticipate that important period of Moscheles' life which was spent in that city. Many years were to elapse before Moscheles, at the instigation of his friend Mendelssohn, was induced to migrate to Leipzig, where he was destined to remain and labor in the cause of art to the end of his days. It was in 1846 that Mendelssohn founded the Conservatorio of Music in Leipzig, and wished the pupils of that Institute to enjoy the benefit of his friend's experience. Alas! their joint efforts were to last but one short year. After Mendelssohn's death, Moscheles accepted as a sacred trust the duty of further developing that great Institute that owed its foundation to his departed friend.

But to return to the year 1824, and to the influence that Leipzig at that time exercised on his artistic creed. While retaining his bravura style of playing, he aspired with ever-increasing earnestness to the highest aims of musicianship, and sought to appear with the calm and self-possession of thorough mastery before judges whose criticisms he respected, and an audience whom he considered well versed in art matters.

Referring to the diary of those days, we find Moscheles at the "Birnbaum" (now called the Hotel de Pologne), and visiting the whole musical fraternity. Kapellmeister Weinlich, Schulz, the violin-player, Matthäi, Mademoiselle Veltheim, the singer—all these are favorably mentioned, and he delights in accompanying Madame Weitte, an excellent artiste. The following is an interesting notice added in after-years: "I must have seen the little Clara, afterwards the famous Clara Schumann at her father's, Mr. Wieck, and little did I think then what intense pleasure she would give me in after-years, and how her execution of my own G minor concerto in the Gewandhaus would delight me. No better reading and execution of the work can be heard; I could not myself play it more to my own satisfaction. It is just as if she had composed it herself." Later on we read in the diary: "I have done business in that famous commercial city of Leipzig. Probst bought my Op. 62 and 63 for 35 ducats, and I had 40 from Mechetti for my G minor concerto. Others, too, meet me in a very friendly way, and help me in making my concert arrangements. They introduced me to the Liedertafel, whose performances are excellent. There I met the famous critic Rochlitz, the admirable actors Devrient and Genast, etc. Bernhard Romberg, who had just come to Leipzig, agreed with me in saying that it is delightful to play before such judges." Moscheles took delight in the theatre, then under the direction of Hofrath Küstner, where he saw works by Shakespeare and Schiller acted to perfection. With regard to his own concert, he says: "It is remarkable that I gave it on the 18th of October. It appears that I, too, have won my battle; for even in the room the directors pressed me to give a second concert. I have not, however, made up my mind to this." He did so the next morning, when urged by the local paper to grant the directors' request. The times in which artists were pressed to give concerts are among the things of the past. Friedrich Schneider, the composer of an oratorio,

"Paradise Lost," showed him this new work when he visited Dessau to perform before the Court.

On the 31st of October, Moscheles and his brother arrived at Berlin. His notes on his stay here are more cursory than usual. He seems to consider all else unimportant as compared with his relations to the family of Mendelssohn. It is incidentally mentioned that he gave three brilliant concerts for the sufferers from inundation, for the blind, and for other charitable institutions, also that he played for some personal friends. We read, too, that the *haute finance*, the poets, the statesmen, were glad to welcome him. Spontini's operas, with their brilliant scenery and pageantry, the admirable singers Bader, Blum, Frau Milder-Hauptmann, and Frau Seidler-Wranitzky, even the charming actress Fraulein Bauer, are merely alluded to, and the great political event, the marriage of the King with the Princess Liegnitz is referred to in a few passing words. He writes, however, whole pages about Felix Mendelssohn's home and his family. We quote his impressions after a first visit: "This is a family the like of which I have never known. Felix, a boy of fifteen, is a phenomenon. What are all prodigies as compared with him? Gifted children, but nothing else. This Felix Mendelssohn is already a mature artist, and yet but fifteen years old! We at once settled down together for several hours, for I was obliged to play a great deal, when really I wanted to hear him and see his compositions, for Felix had to show me a Concerto in C minor, a double Concerto, and several motets; and all so full of genius, and at the same time so correct and thorough! His elder sister Fanny, also extraordinarily gifted, played by heart, and with admirable precision, Fugues and Passacailles by Bach. I think one may well call her a thorough 'Mus. Doc.' (guter Musiker). Both parents give one the impression of being people of the highest refinement. They are far from overrating their children's talents; in fact, they are anxious about Felix's future, and to know whether his gift will prove sufficient to lead to a noble and truly great career. Will he not, like so many other brilliant children, suddenly collapse? I asserted my conscientious conviction that Felix would ultimately become a great master, that I had not the slightest doubt of his genius ; but again and again I had to insist on my opinion before they believed me. These two are not specimens of the genus prodigy-parents (Wunderkinds-Eltern), such as I must frequently endure."

The pleasure, however, was mutual, and the oftener Moscheles came to dine and spend the evening at their house, the heartier was the reception he met with. The Mendelssohns had frequently begged him to give Felix some lessons, but these requests he had with characteristic modesty always answered evasively. He writes in the diary: "Felix has no need of lessons; if he wishes to take a hint as to anything that is new to him, from hearing me play, he can easily do so." Madame Mendelssohn wrote to him on the 18th of November, 1824: "Have you kindly thought over our request about the lessons? You would extremely oblige us by consenting, if such a thing can be done without disturbing your plans during your stay in this place. Don't set down these repeated inquiries as inopportune, but attribute them entirely to the wish that my child should be enabled to profit by the presence of the prince of pianists." Even after this, Moscheles seems not to have made up his mind to say "Yes," but merely to have spoken of "playing occasionally," for on the 22d of November, we find again the following note: "If I may be allowed, dear Mr. Moscheles, to renew my request that you will give lessons to my two eldest children, be good enough to let me know your terms. I should like them to begin at once, that they may profit as far as possible during the time of your stay here." This note Moscheles must have answered in the affirmative, for on the 22d of November, he writes in his diary: "This afternoon, from two to three o'clock, I gave Felix Mendelssohn his first lesson, without losing sight for a single moment of the fact that I was sitting next to a master, not a pupil. I feel proud that after so short an acquaintance with me his distinguished parents entrust me with their son, and congratulate myself on being permitted to give him some hints, which he seizes on and works out with that genius peculiar to himself." Six days later he says: "Felix Mendelssohn's lessons are repeated every second day; to me they are subjects of ever-increasing interest; he has already played with me my Allegri di

Bravura, my concertos, and other things, and how played! The slightest hint from me, and he guesses at my conception."

From this time dates Moscheles' close intimacy with the family. He delighted in the intellectual atmosphere of the house; and would listen with interest to the conversation of Felix's father, "with his sound views on art-subjects;" he attended many of their morning or evening musical entertainments, and scrupulously catalogued the programmes. "On the 23d November," he writes, "I heard a Psalm by Naumann, at the Singakademie, afterwards went to the Mendelssohns'. The brother and sister played Bach."

"Nov. 25th.—With the family of Mendelssohn-Bartholdy at the brother's house."

"Nov. 28th (Sunday).—Music in the morning at the Mendelssohns'. C minor quartet by Felix. D major Symphony, concerto by Bach, duet in D minor for two pianos by Arnold.

"Nov. 30th.—At Frau Varnhagen's with Felix. Exceedingly interesting."

Frau Varnhagen was the famous Rahel, of whose amiability and masculine understanding so much has been said and written. Her receptions were the rallying point for artists, scholars, and statesmen, for every one of whom she had a suitable word or a willing ear, and all this was done with perfect simplicity, while her good nature always prompted her to draw out the least gifted of her acquaintance. She loved music, so that a genius like Felix Mendelssohn was a heartfelt delight to her, and she invariably showed her warm appreciation of Moscheles.

"Dec. 3d, 12 o'clock.—Music at Zelter's. Fanny Mendelssohn played the D minor Concerto by S. Bach, which I saw in the original manuscript. A mass in five parts by S. Bach was performed.

"Dec. 5th.—At Geheimrath Crelle's Felix accompanied Mozart's Requiem, in commemoration of the day of his death: Zelter and others were present.

"Dec. 11th.—A birthday festival at Mendelssohns' at which we were treated to some charming private theatricals. Felix distinguished himself as an actor quite as much as Edward Devrient.

"Dec. 12th (Sunday).—Music at Mendelssohns'. Felix F minor Quartet. I played with him my duet in G for two pianofortes. Young Schilling played Hummel's Trio in G."

Zelter, the well-known teacher of Felix and his sister, never failed to attend these morning performances. Although in his outward manner rather harsh and forbidding, he was not a little proud of his pupils. He invited Moscheles to a friendly supper, upon which his guest observes: "My musical conversations with Zelter were extremely interesting to me. He is the man who corresponded so much with Goethe on Teltower Rübchen and other better things."

"December 13th.—Returned to Felix his album, in which I yesterday wrote the Impromptu op. 77. He played it admirably at sight."

On the 15th of December Moscheles reluctantly departed from Berlin, and the Mendelssohn family, to which he had become so closely attached. He and his brother travelled with Fräulein Bauer and her mother to Potsdam, where he played, according to promise, at Blum's evening concert in presence of the Court.

17th of December was a melancholy day. Moscheles and his brother had to separate. The latter was bound for Prague; Moscheles went by coach to Magdeburg. "That kind brother of mine," he exclaims, "he has spoiled me by his devotion."

By desire of the Governor, General Haack, the concert in Magdeburg, on the 20th of December had to be repeated on the 23d of the same month. After paying a flying visit to Brunswick, Moscheles spent the last day of the year at Hanover, in quiet retirement.

# CHAPTER VIII.

## 1825.

Hanover—The Duke of Cambridge—Hamburg—Marriage to Charlotte Embden—Paris—Intercourse with Distinguished Men—Reception in London—Mori's Monster Concerts—Sebastian Erard's Invention—Advantage of numbering Concert Tickets—Habits of Study—Sir Michael Costa—Sundays with the Clementis—The Collards—Holiday Excursions and Concerts—A Liverpool Rehearsal—The Christmas Waits.

THE Duke of Cambridge, a great lover of music, was at this time Regent of Hanover, and his name, with those of the Platens, Kielmansegges, and others, appeared in the list of patrons to Moscheles' two successful concerts.

Moscheles next played at Celle, and on the 16th of January reached Hamburg. The diary records the names of Clasing, Grund, Lindenau, Rudersdorf, Lehmann, and the little Louise David (afterwards Madame Dulcken), who, in spite of her tender years, played the 'Alexander Variations' admirably.

Among the great crowd of listeners in the Apollosaal at Hamburg was Charlotte Embden, Moscheles' future wife. A fair pianist herself, she was enchanted with Moscheles' wonderful playing; a short acquaintance led to an engagement, and on the first of March they were married. The day is thus marked in the husband's diary: "My 'Ehrentag' (day of honor). With the fullest sense of happiness, with purity of heart and intention, and full of gratitude to the Almighty, I entered this holy state, and pray God to bless me." We omit all the glowing passages confided to the diary by the happy bridegroom during the honeymoon. Suffice it to say that they bear witness to the love and esteem which were to lay the foundation of long years of happiness.

Moscheles gave concerts at Hamburg, Lüneburg, and Altona, for his own benefit, or for his friends, and on behalf of charitable institutions. The young couple went to Bremen and Aix-la-Chapelle, on their way to Paris, and there, at the houses of their relatives, met the painter Gérard, Benjamin Constant, Alexander Humboldt, Meyerbeer, and his brother Michael, Hummel, F. Mendelssohn and his father, and other men of note.

Moscheles writes to his father-in-law: "Charlotte has given me to-day an album, in which all the artists here assembled have written their autographs." *

On the 28th of March, Moscheles completed a contract with the Académie Royale de Musique, by which he engaged to play at the last "Concert Spirituel," in return for which he was promised the use of the Salle des Italiens, when he should next visit Paris. On the present occasion he found no time for availing himself of this privilege, but travelled rapidly to London, where he had been long expected.

On the 2d of May, 1825, Moscheles and his wife arrived in London, where he was immediately offered engagements, as also at Bath, Bristol, and other places. His pupils, too, rally round him. "My wife," he writes, "received a most cordial welcome, and friends vie with each other in showing her kindness. Can this be the insular formality which makes foreigners cry down the English as unsociable?"

In May the Philharmonic Society and the Royal Academy had their first meetings, and at the end of the month Mori gave one of his famous "monster concerts," in which Moscheles had to take a part. Mori, a clever violin-player, as well as a publisher of music, was frequently leader at the great provincial festivals, and also the originator of the "monster concerts." These were notoriously overcrowded. Angry remarks appeared in the newspapers, but inasmuch as the leading artists were always engaged by Mori, such complaints had little effect.

On the 1st of June we find this interesting note: "Pierre Erard showed and explained to me on a dumb keyboard his uncle Sebastian's now completed invention, for which

* This album was, for the space of forty-five years, enriched at every opportunity by contributions from the numerous celebrities, musical, literary, and otherwise, with whom Moscheles was brought in contact. It is now in the possession of his son Felix.

the firm has just taken out a patent. I saw the earliest experiment of this invention in Paris. It consists in the key, when only sunk half way, again rising and repeating the note. I was the first to play upon one of the newly completed instruments, and found it of priceless value for the repetition of notes. In the matter of fullness and softness of tone, there is something yet to be desired, and I had a long conversation on the subject with Erard."

His appearance at the Philharmonic, and his own benefit, are described in glowing colors by Mrs. Moscheles in her letters to her friends. From these we select one, which represents her as a novice in the mysteries of concert arrangements. "It is my business to see that the tickets are numbered. At first this seemed to me rather gratuitous trouble, but I was soon enlightened on the point. A handsomely dressed lady who came to me, asked for three tickets at half a guinea each, and pocketed them. Instead of paying, however, she said her husband was a doctor, and presented his card there and then, adding that he never knew beforehand whether he should be able to go to the concert or not. On the day after she would send back either the tickets or the money. I, as a novice, agreed to it; but my husband, when he came home, laughed, and declared I had allowed myself to be taken in. He went to the doctor in question. The doctor laughed also. 'It is certainly my card,' said he, 'but any one of my numerous patients may have taken it away from my table here, nor am I so fortunate as to possess a wife!' Thus Moscheles was right. I *had* been taken in. Then he wrote down in large figures the respective numbers, and gave them to the ticket-collector. Sure enough three ladies arrived who asked admittance, and showed the tickets in question. They were stopped, and told that they must pay or they would not be admitted. They protested they had no money with them—they would pay next morning. The ticket collector called to Moscheles, and the ladies decamped. Moral—it is a useful plan to put numbers on the concert tickets."

The season drawing to a close, Moscheles began to breathe freely, and as his pupils were leaving London, he had more time for the composition of his "Studies," which in spite of all his professional avocations were constantly uppermost in his mind. On his walk from the house of one pupil to another, he used to dot down the subjects on any letter or other scrap of paper he happened to have in his pocket. In the evening these subjects were worked out, and all fatigue and sense of ennui forgotten. His wife would try over certain passages, and practice them on. the next day during his absence from home. His latest hours of an evening were devoted to rising artists, among whom was the youthful and now famous Sir Michael Costa, who showed him his Canzonettes. In those days Moscheles already practiced in a small way that hospitality which, carried on more extensively in later years, was of such comfort to many a homeless German in London.

The Moscheles' passed their Sundays with the Clementis, at Elstree, near London. "Clementi," says Moscheles, "is one of the most vigorous old fellows of seventy that I ever saw. In the early morning we watch him from our window running about the garden bareheaded, reckless of the morning dew. He is too lively ever to think of rest. At table he laughs and talks incessantly. He has a sharp temper, too, which we set down to the hot blood of his Italian nature. He plays on the piano now but rarely, and gives out that he has a stiff hand, the result of falling out of a sledge when he was in Russia, but there is a suspicion that his unwillingness is caused by his inability to follow the great progress the Bravura style has made since his time. His wife, an amiable Englishwoman, is a great contrast to him." Clementi at that time was joint owner with the Collard brothers of a flourishing pianoforte firm. Moscheles, contrasting their pianos of those days with those of Broadwood, praised their lightness of touch, and consequently used them by preference when he played in public. Their tone, too, he found clearer, while the Broadwood, with a somewhat muffled tone and heavy ac.ion, produced a fuller sound. Moscheles called William Collard, the younger brother, "one of the most intelligent men he ever came across," and he soon became the most intimate friend and adviser of the young couple. Collard was a regular visitor at Elstree, and when the friends met, Clementi would say, "Moscheles, play me something!"

and the latter would choose one of his host's Sonatas, while Clementi, listening with a complacent smile, his hands behind his back, his short, thick-set figure swinging to and fro, would call out at intervals, "Bravo." When the last note was over, he would tap Moscheles in a friendly way upon the shoulder, and warmly congratulate him on his performance.

At last, after the season had been struggled through, the Moscheles could get away from London for a quiet holiday, and accepted an invitation from Mr. Fleming, of Stoneham Park, Southampton. The lady of the house was a pupil of Moscheles, and both she and her husband were for many years his and his wife's intimate friends.

"The house is full of company, including Lord Palmerston and some of his relatives. It is of course interesting to meet such men, and follow the Parliamentary discussion carried on at table. The principles they advocate are those of purest Toryism. It is fortunate that the art I represent stands upon neutral ground. At midnight, when we are in the drawing-room, my art is again in the ascendant; then we have music until one or two o'clock. No wonder that the first beams of morning find us sleeping."

In the next month the Moscheles went to Cheltenham for the waters. "Here," he says, "we enjoy our tête-à-tête to our heart's content; the chateau was beautiful, but the retired life, the first since our marriage, is far more to our taste." And again: "I not only give my wife pianoforte lessons, but I teach her how to copy music; and while she is practicing that art, I compose an Impromptu, for which I have a commission from the Harmonic Institution. It is to be on the march from 'Tarare,' or 'Axur,' by Salieri, which opera, concocted for the English market, is now greatly applauded in London. This march has been metamorphosed by Mr. W. Hawes into a war-song, and awakens the greatest enthusiasm when sung by Braham. He makes a great point with the passage—

"'Revenge!' he cries,
And the traitor dies."

At Cheltenham, Moscheles wrote to order three Rondos

on "Die Wiener in Berlin," besides "La Petite Babillarde," for Cramer, his B minor "Study," etc. etc.

From Cheltenham they made some pleasant excursions to Oxford and elsewhere, and then settled down at No. 77, Norton Street, London. They always regarded as the most valuable addition to their household gods a splendid piano, presented to them by Clementi, and on which was inscribed with his own hand, in front of the keyboard, the dedication: "Muzio Clementi e Socj all' ingegnosissimo J. Moscheles, ed alla sua amabilissima consorte."

The quiet domestic happiness was soon interrupted by professional business. Moscheles was invited to give concerts in Liverpool and Dublin. These offers he would have declined, as he disliked travelling alone, but at last his wife's argument prevailed, and he writes on the 4th of November, "To-day I had to endure the hard trial of parting from my wife." On reaching Liverpool, and being taken by his friends to see the Town Hall, and Nelson's Monument, by Westmacott, he exclaims: "I was struck by the grandeur of the statue; may be I was still more surprised at being repeatedly asked to give lessons during the three days of my stay in Liverpool. I visited Roscoe, and found the old man very amiable and gracious. He took the trouble to show me his new work upon West Indian plants, and to give me most interesting explanations on the subject. On the 8th of November, at noon, we had the rehearsal in the Concert Room; but what a rehearsal! Wretched is too tame an expression for it. Mori, the London artist, did all that possibly could be done, but what was to be made out of a band consisting of a double quartet and four halting wind-instruments. The director of the theatre played the entrepreneur of the concert, Mr. Wilson, the trick of keeping away the orchestral performers, so that I was obliged to play the first movement of the E flat concerto and the Alexander Variations with a bare quartet accompaniment. The brilliant and numerous audience was much pleased with my Fantasia on 'Rule Britannia,' and an Irish air; and I was enchanted with my Clementi piano. Every evening I write to my wife, and the news I get from her cheers and invigorates me for my performance. On the 9th of November I was very successful with my first concert at Chester: Phillips and I explored the interesting old city and its environs; and the next day we went on to Manchester. The better composition of the orchestra, directed by Mr. Cadmore, the general management of the concert directors, Baker and Fletcher, and the co-operation of several clever German amateurs, gave a new zest to my performance, and I was rapturously applauded. I could not, however, enjoy this fully, as I was anxious to get home." The first notice, after his return, tells us of the birth of his first-born, and then follow many expressions of anxiety, owing to the state of his wife and child. Towards the end of the year, he writes: "My mind is at ease. I can go back again to my work. I was at Erard's to-day, and saw his excellent pianos, which are built upon the new principle; but I decidedly refused his proposal to bind myself down to play solely on them, in spite of the profitable conditions he offered me. I intend for the future to be as perfectly free in this respect as heretofore." Later on he writes: "An odd incident made us laugh heartily. At Christmas time, a band of wind-instruments (the waits) plays here generally late in the evening, and they mustered in force at my door; I knew this custom of old, and as I remembered all the tortues I had endured from their falsely harmonized chorales, I ordered the servant to tell them they would certainly get no Christmas-box from me, unless they promised never to return again. Trombone, much wounded, sent back to say, 'Tell your master, if he does not like music, he will not go to heaven.'"

Moscheles, after having finished a Fantasia for Collard, remarks: "The twenty-five guineas I get for my work is the best part about it; it belongs to that class of ephemeral productions which I do not treat to the distinction of a number in the catalogue of my compositions."

On the 31st we read: "We end the year with feelings of special gratitude to God's Providence, which has permitted us to tide over great perils."

# CHAPTER IX.

## 1826.

Stormy Voyage to Ireland—Impressions of Dublin—Reception at the Castle—Return to London—Musical Activity—C. M. von Weber—Der Freyschutz at Covent Garden—Improvisation—Rehearsal of "Oberon"—Braham's Benefit—Caprice of the "Gods"—Weber's Concert—Death of Weber—Thalberg—Visit to Germany—Sontag—Felix Mendelssohn—Art and Artists in Berlin.

ON the first of January, Moscheles begins his diary thus: "To-day I can call my happiness my own; by to morrow I shall have left it. But, courage! it must be so! I am in honor bound to fulfil my engagements." He went first to Bath, thence to Liverpool, and thus describes with much minuteness the dangers and difficulties in those days inseparable from a long journey, and of which we, in our age of rail and steamer, can scarcely form an idea. "On the 4th of January, at seven A. M., I started from Liverpool, and arrived at Birmingham at eight in the evening. On the 5th I travelled without stopping day or night. At two A. M., I had a grievous *contretemps*. We were close to Bangor, and I, the only passenger, was turned out of the warm coach into the cold, raw night, and made to cross the rushing river in an open boat. It gave me the shivers, but I stood my ground, muttering my watchword, 'Courage and patience!' On the opposite shore a forlorn and solitary passenger got inside the mail-coach, which was standing in readiness. Thus we jogged on for the rest of the night—wind blowing, snow falling—until at last, at five A. M., we arrived at Holyhead."

"January 6th.—Eventful day! Severe trial! God's saving hand! In the hotel I found a respectable set of fellow-travellers, consisting of two gentlemen and one lady, ready to embark for Dublin. They were still waiting for the Chester mail, which arrived at seven o'clock. We were told that there was no steamboat to take us across the Channel; that the violent winds of the last few days had kept all the steamers on the Irish side, but that a sailing vessel would start immediately, and carry the mails across in from six to seven hours. Would we passengers cross in that vessel? We agreed, and embarked shortly after seven o'clock. It rained in torrents, and the sea was so high that we soon betook ourselves to our berths. I suffered so violently that after a few hours I was completely prostrate. The gale meanwhile increased. I counted the passing hours. It grew dark, but we did not land. The steward, on being asked when we should be released, whispered, 'Who knows? we are doing badly!'—Words too clearly verified by the lurching of the boat. Although I lay smothered in blankets and clothes, my feet were perished with cold. It cost me no slight effort to shake off my drowsiness, and groping about, to discover that the sea-water had got into my berth; the ship had become leaky. There was no longer any mystery about that, for the water came hissing into the cabin. The storm howled fiercely; it was pitch-dark. The captain could offer no other comfort than the assurance that we were not far from shore. Of course, not near enough to land. We were surrounded by rocks and sandbanks, and yet not near enough for a distress signal to be perceptible from the coast. At last, after a long battle and the most fearful shocks from the waves, which knocked our vessel about like a plaything, we were able to throw out anchors, and there we poor victims lay till daybreak. In this sad plight, however, I had not lost heart; faith in an Almighty Providence sustained me. I could think with calmness of my wife and child. They sleep peacefully, thank God, without sharing my hard fate. They will either see me again and rejoice, or bear my loss, with the help of God. I thought with painful composure of my other friends and relations. It seemed but a little step from this world to the next. At last, in the afternoon, the welcome tidings came, 'We are all right, a boat has reached our ship, and will take us up.' Whereupon, after getting together our goods and chattels, we were thrown, so to speak, with them into the reeling boat, and, after a short fight with the foaming surf, landed in Howth harbor.

There I hired a postchaise, which carried me (a seven-mile journey) to the city. The dreary, sandy plain, the country dotted over with ruins, the sorry aspect of the people, did not, I am bound to confess, impress me very favorably. At last I arrived in Dublin, drove over the beautiful Carlisle-bridge, and the Liffey, to Westmoreland Street, where I rested for a few hours in a lodging which Pigott, the music-seller, had hired for me."

On the 8th of January, Mr. Pigott took him to Christ-church, where he heard an old-fashioned anthem by Dr. Spray. He then made a round of visits, and became personally acquainted with Sir Charles and Lady Morgan. "I had often admired her as a writer," he observes, "and now find her an exceedingly amiable and sociable hostess."

"January 9th.—To-day I received, through Colonel Shaw, adjutant to the Lord-Lieutenant the Marquis of Wellesley, the intelligence that his Excellency would attend my concert, and that it would be under his special patronage. To-day he desired me to play before the Court. I drove to the Palace in a smart carriage sent for me, and found numbers of the Irish nobility assembled there, this being the first soirée given by the Marchioness of Wellesley since her recent marriage. Some good pieces, as well as a terzetto for two guitars and Physharmonica (by Schulz and his sons), were performed in dumb show,.the great folk talking loudly the whole time. The Lord-Lieutenant, addressing me in French, alluded to the very flattering recommendation I had brought him from Prince Esterhazy, and then asked me to play, and their Excellencies, as well as the whole party, were in raptures with my Fantasia on Irish melodies.

"January 11th.—Introduced to the Anacreontic Society, consisting of amateurs who perform admirably the best orchestral works. The usual supper followed. After propitiating me with a trio from 'Cosi fan tutte,' they drew me to the piano, but I did not trust the old worn-out instrument, and only played the overture to 'Figaro.' My health was proposed at supper, and I had to return thanks.

"January 13th.—First concert at Dublin, in the Rotunda. I suffered martyrdom at the rehearsal, chiefly from the wind instruments. Nor did my troubles end there, for the director of the theatre, Mr. Abbot, forbade the attendance of my singers, Messrs. Kean and Latham. It was not before four o'clock, and after the rehearsal, that I succeeded in bringing him to reason. Mrs. and Miss Ashe sang. The E flat concerto and Alexander Variations were enthusiastically received, but my Fantasia on Irish themes was the feature of the evening."

Moscheles dined with the Hibernian Catch Club, and writes: "Several glees were sung, and as a finale I improvised, whereupon the society unanimously elected me to an honorary membership."

Further on we read: "M. Allan, son-in-law of Logier, gave a public performance, where his pupils played. Pieces of my own were made to suffer. I repeat the word '*suffer.*' I feel more and more that this Logier system may produce good timeists, but what becomes of the right understanding and grasp of the composition? What of its poetry, when eight pianos are drilled into playing together with unerring precision? On the whole, I am struck by the musical taste and enthusiasm of the Irish nation." Good news from home, and a hearty reception in Ireland, amply explain the cheerful tone observable in the diary of these days.

His wife writes: "Here is a business matter for you which will make you laugh. Only think; old Nägeli, of Zurich, asks you to compose a Sonata for his periodical, but you are to avoid all repeating notes, all tenths, and all the usual signs used to indicate the expression. To conclude, he overwhelms you with compliments."

Towards the end of January Moscheles felt so exhausted with playing in public and private, incessant lesson-giving, and attention to his many and various duties, that he made short work of his preparations, and set out for London and his happy home. Here he found his wife's father, who had arrived on a visit. The debates in both Houses of Parliament, Kemble's acting, Pasta's singing, and many other attractions of the winter season—all these were delightful novelties for the new-comer—but above all, Moscheles could show with honest pride a home, the comforts and happiness of which had resulted from his own unwearied activity and the honorable position he had achieved. Although his numerous pupils necessarily occupied much of his time, he composed in the course of this season the E minor, B minor, and D minor Studies, op. 70, his "Recollections of Ireland," besides revising and correcting numbers of proof sheets, not only for himself, but also for such of his friends as were publishing compositions in England. These "Recollections of Ireland," heard for the first time in London, were warmly received at his concert. We read: "Kiesewetter played beautifully, it is true, but he, a friend, claimed a fee of ten guineas; of course I agreed, but our friendly relations must be henceforth interrupted; friends ought to assist each other gratis, that is my maxim. The great pressure of the public at the concert necessitated the use of the Royal box, and many of my patrons were obliged to leave the room for want of seats." In those days people had not become acquainted with the convenient institution of reserved seats.

The appearance of Carl Maria von Weber, who conducted the overture to "Euryanthe," and an air from the same opera, sung by Caradori, may have been the principal cause of the crowded room. The illustrious man had been staying for the last two weeks with his friend Sir George Smart, and there Moscheles often saw him, although Weber's health obliged him to keep aloof from the generality of visitors. Unfortunately, he needed that repose which he could not find in a London season. Moscheles says: "What emotion he must have felt on his first appearance yesterday, before the English public, in Covent Garden Theatre! The thundering applause with which he was greeted affected us deeply, how much more himself, the honored object of all this enthusiasm! The performance consisted of a selection from the 'Freyschütz,' conducted by himself; the overture was encored with acclamation. Braham, Miss Paton, and Phillips sang the chief numbers of the opera; they seemed inspired by Weber's presence. During the peals of applause, Weber shook hands with the singers, to express his pleasure and satisfaction; at the end of the performance the whole pit stood up on the benches, waving hats and handkerchiefs, and cheering the composer. I saw him later on in the evening, sitting in the green-room, and completely exhausted; he was too ill fully to enjoy this signal triumph in a land of strangers, but we, I mean the poet Kind, the flute-player Fürstenau, the good old harp-player Stumpff, the publisher Schulz, and myself, as being his fellow-countrymen, felt honored in our friend's reception."

On the 12th of March Moscheles, on hearing Weber improvise in Braham's house, writes: "Although it was not a remarkable exhibition of his powers, he made his performance deeply interesting by introducing some subjects from 'Freyschütz.' Unfortunately his physical weakness makes any great exertion dangerous, and yet at eleven o'clock he hurried off to a large party given by Mrs. Coutts, as he was to be handsomely paid for his services. How we grieved at his thus over-exerting himself!"

On the 13th of March Weber is a guest at Moscheles' dinner-table. "What a treat! And yet even here the sight of him moved us to intense pity! for he could not utter a word when he entered our room; the exertion of mounting the small flight of stairs had completely taken away his breath; he sank into a chair nearest the door, but soon recovered, and became one of the most delightful and genial of guests. We took him to the Philharmonic concert, the first he ever heard; the next was conducted by himself. The following was the programme:—

Overtures to 'Euryanthe' and 'Freyschütz.'
Aria by Weber, composed for Mme. Milder, sung by Madame Caradori.
Scena from 'Der Freyschütz,' sung by Sapio.

Then Schuncke, a German, played the following pasticcio, conducted by the great German composer:—

1st Movement—Concerto C minor. Ries.
2d „ Part of Beethoven's E flat major Concerto.
3d „ Hungarian Rondo by Pixis.

"On the 11th of April I was present at the dress rehearsal of 'Oberon' at Covent Garden; people attended it like a regular performance; the costumes, scenery, and the stage moon introduced with the air 'Ocean, thou mighty Monster,' were admirable. This air, which was written expressly for Miss Paton by Weber while in London, made a grand effect, and so did the scena written for Braham

(Hüon). Both singers were allowed an opportunity of displaying their fine voices, and producing certain striking effects, which told powerfully on the audience. Weber, as he sat at the conductor's desk, must have felt that it was not merely an audience, but a nation rising to applaud, and that his works would long survive him."

Poor Weber himself, in the midst of these triumphs, became weaker and weaker, yet he continued to persevere in active work, and conducted at several concerts where Moscheles played his overtures to "Freyschütz," "Oberon," etc. "On the 18th of May," says Moscheles, "we both assisted Braham in quite an original fashion: it was his annual benefit (at Covent Garden Theatre), and he, the most popular of English singers, used always on this occasion to please the 'gods' by singing sailors' songs, so we had to endure a similar state of things to-night. Madame Vestris, the popular singer, who appeared in the operetta 'The Slave,' found willing listeners among the occupants of the galleries, who ruled the house, and were delighted with such nursery ditties as 'Goosie Goosie Gander,' etc. So far so well, but Braham had calculated without his host in setting before such an audience as this good music for the second part of the concert, which he called 'Apollo's Festival,' and which, after the poor stuff that had been played and sung, began with the overture to the 'Ruler of the Spirits.' Could no one see that Weber himself was conducting? I'm sure I don't know, but the screams and hubbub in the gallery while the overture was played, without a note being heard from beginning to end, made my blood boil; in a state of high indignation, I sat down to my piano on the stage, and gave a sign to the band beneath me to begin my 'Recollections of Ireland.' At the opening bar of the introduction, the roughs in the gallery made themselves heard by whistling, hissing, shouting, and calling out 'Are you comfortable, Jack?' accompanying the question with volleys of orange peel. I heard the alternate crescendos and decrescendos; and fancied that in this chaos all the elements had been let loose, and would overpower me; but, thank heaven, they did not, for in this new and unexpected situation I resolved not to come to any sudden stoppage, but to show the better part of my audience that I was ready to fulfil my engagement, I stooped down to the leading violinist, and said, 'I shall continue to move my hands on the keyboard, as though really playing. Make your band pretend to be playing also ; after a short time I will give you a signal and we will leave off together.' No sooner said than done. On making my bow as I retired, I was overwhelmed with a hurricane of applause. The gods cheered me, being glad to get rid of me. Next came Miss Paton, with a scena for the concert room. She met with a similar fate. Three times she stopped singing, but came forward again, in answer to the calls of the well-behaved portion of the audience, who shouted 'silence.' At last the poor lady went away, burst into tears, and gave it up. Thunders of applause followed her exit, and when common ballads and songs began afresh, the gods were once more all attention and good behavior." This affair went the round of all the papers. Moscheles was highly commended for his calmness and self-possession, while the tears of poor Miss Paton were rather severely commented upon.

"I shall never forget," says Mrs. Moscheles, in one of her weekly letters, "the 20th of May, the day of Weber's concert ; for the composer, now so near his end, had made great exertions for a performance to be held in the Argyll Rooms, and yet met with so little support from the public. Lovers of music and the papers express their regret that it should be so, but say : Why hold it on the Derby-day, or allow it to clash with private concerts which monopolize the fashionable world ? It was badly timed. As to the middle classes, they can only attend the theatres, and must not be charged with the neglect of his enterprise. Be that as it may, Weber conducted the never-failing overtures to 'Oberon' and 'Euryanthe ;' his still unknown cantata, 'The Festival of Peace ;' and a new ballad, written for and sung by Miss Stephens ; Braham gave the air from 'Freyschütz' very finely ; Fürstenau, the flute-player, was heard for the first time, in some variation from 'Oberon ;' Kiesewetter played his inevitable Mayseder Variations in E major, and Moscheles took his subject for improvisation from the Cantata 'Festival of Peace,' interwoven with 'motives' from the 'Freyschütz.' Madame Caradori and Braham were the soloists in the cantata. To think of such music in an empty room." Weber's disappointment at his ill-success was so intense that he determined on forfeiting the receipts of his proposed benefit at the theatre, where "Der Freyschütz" was to be performed under his direction, and occupied himself solely with preparations for his journey homewards.

In spite of the anxiety about Weber, Moscheles' birthday was not allowed to pass without some attempt at gayety. "This time," his wife writes to relatives, "we had a tableau, quite unique in its way, but alas! matters are growing worse and worse with Weber." On the 4th of June Moscheles writes in his diary: "Sunday: When I visited the great man to-day, he talked very confidently of his return to Germany, but the frequent attacks of a dreadful convulsive cough, which left him completely prostrate, filled our minds with the utmost anxiety. When with great effort he managed to tell me that he intended starting in two days' time, that I was to prepare my letters, and he hoped to see me again to-morrow, I was deeply moved, although I never suspected that I was looking on him for the last time as a living man. I left him with his friends, Kind and Fürstenau, and exchanged a few sad words with his kind host, Sir G. Smart, who told me that on no account would Weber suffer any one to sit up with him; that every night he locked the door of his bedroom, and that only to-day he had yielded to the earnest entreaties of his friends, and promised to leave it open, adding that he had peremptorily refused to allow anybody, either friends or paid attendant, to watch beside him.

"June 5th.—Early this morning I was summoned in all haste to Sir G. Smart's. At eleven o'clock last night Fürstenau had conducted Weber to his bedroom; his friends went to his door at an early hour, but found it locked inside, contrary to Weber's promise. To do this he must have got up during the night. It was in vain to knock or call for admission; no answer came. So Sir George sent to me and other friends, and the door was broken open in our presence. The noise did not disturb the sleeper; it was his sleep of death. His head, resting on his left arm, was lying quietly on the pillow. . . . . Any attempt to describe the depth of my sorrow would be profanation. I thought Weber a composer quite *sui generis;* one who had the imperishable glory of leading back to our German music a public vacillating between Mozart, Beethoven, and Rossini. On his dressing-table lay a small washing-bill written by him. This I put in my pocket-book, where I carried it ever after. I helped Sir G. Smart and Fürstenau to seal up Weber's papers, and Sir George, feeling his great responsibility, sent for my own private seal.

"June 6th.—This morning, after the body of the great composer was placed in a leaden coffin, we opened and examined all his letters and papers, and made a list of all the property. Besides the thousand pounds which he must have earned in London, there was a further sum of a thousand pounds which he had received from the publishers, Walsh and Hawes, for the pianoforte edition of 'Oberon.' We found the manuscript of that opera, and came upon a song which he had composed for a Mr. Ward, who had paid him 25*l*. for it. The pianoforte accompaniment was unfinished. Sir George eagerly pressed me to complete it. (This was done in after-years.) I appropriated to myself a few sheets of the first sketches of 'Oberon.'"

A committee was now formed to decide upon the mode of conducting Weber's funeral. It consisted of the music publishers, Chappell and D'Almaine, W. Collard, from the firm of Clementi and Co., Preston and Power, Sir G. Smart, his brother, Mr. Smart, the composer, Sir John Stevenson, Mr. Attwood, organist of St. Paul's Cathedral, Braham, the singer, and Moscheles. It was proposed to give Mozart's Requiem in the Catholic Chapel, Moorfields, the receipts to be appropriated to raising a monument to Weber. But failing to secure the permission of the Roman Catholic Bishop, who wished his congregation to have free admission, application was made to the Dean and Chapter of St. Paul's, with a view of securing a performance of the Requiem in their Cathedral. These gentlemen would not hear of a Requiem being performed in the Cathedral, and thus, after a deal of useless discussion and writing, the body of the great man was deposited on the 21st of June in the Catholic Chapel of Moorfields. The public were admitted without payment, so that no money was collected for a monument.

"We artists," says Moscheles, "assembled for the funeral at nine o'clock in the morning, in the house of Sir G. Smart, and the procession moved on to the chapel in Moorfields. After the usual service, Mozart's Requiem was sung. Then twelve musicians (myself among the number) carried the body into the vault, while the funeral march from Handel's 'Saul' was played. Those solemn strains touched all of us most deeply."

On the 12th of June the Philharmonic Society began their concert with the "Dead March in Saul," noted in the programme "as a tribute to a departed genius." On the 17th of the same month "Oberon" was given in Covent Garden Theatre for the benefit of Weber's family, but only two-thirds of the house was filled. "This again passes my comprehension."

We read in a letter of Mrs. Moscheles: "Everything that my husband plays in public is trumpeted forth to you in the newspapers as 'matchless,' 'unrivalled,' and what not! They must soon invent some new epithet. But *I* can only tell you of the kindly use he makes of his art in a quiet way. Yesterday, for example, our good old friend, Madame G., told me, with tears in her eyes, that for the first time since her sorrow she had enjoyed a happy quarter of an hour, and that was when Moscheles played to her. He went to the house for the very purpose, and we spent the evening quite alone with the family. His sympathy is always shown by acts, not words, and yet every hour of the evening is of consequence to him."

In the course of this season we find Moscheles playing constantly for the benefit of his friends and for several charitable institutions. Being unable to spare much time for rehearsals, he often extemporized, choosing generally for his subject the motivo of some piece which had particularly pleased the audience that evening. Of his own works, "Clair de Lune," the "Rondo in D major," and the "Recollections of Ireland" were invariably welcome. The most distinguished of his pupils at that time was Thalberg, who, although still a young man, was already an artist of distinction and mark. It was a source of great satisfaction to Moscheles, who had pioneered the young pianist, to see him recognized, not merely by the public in general, but by such men as Cramer and Clementi.

Many a fashionable soirée, entailing preparation, and leaving nothing behind but a feeling of ennui, was voted an interruption in Moscheles' household, but the assemblage of celebrated men at the Rothschilds and some other houses is noted as interesting, and Prince Dietrichstein's invitation to a grand fancy dress ball in Covent Garden Theatre, from the brilliancy of the scene and the crowds that attended, quite unique in its way. Pit, stalls, and proscenium were formed into one grand room, in which the crowd promenaded. The costumes were of every conceivable variety, and many of the most gorgeous description. The spectators in full dress sat in the boxes. On the stage was a Court box, occupied by the Royal Family, and bands played in rooms adjoining, for small parties of dancers. "You will have some idea," says Mrs. Moscheles, "of the crowd at this ball, when I tell you that we left the ball-room at two o'clock, and did not get to the Prince's carriage till four."

Moscheles could not escape from the whirl of a London season until early in August, when he started for Hamburg. He marks the 7th of August, when he and his wife met their relatives, as a red letter day in his calendar. Six quiet happy weeks were enjoyed at Hamburg, and his intercourse with musical men, especially Bernhard Romberg, is often enlarged upon in the diary. The C major concerto was written during this visit. Leaving Hamburg, Moscheles, accompanied by his wife, halted first at Leipzig, where he played his newest compositions with great success, and had a pleasant meeting with his old friend Grillparzer, whose tragedy, 'Medea,' was given at the Theatre, in honor of the poet. During the next few weeks he played alternately in Leipzig and Dresden, and at the latter place speaks of an enjoyable evening at Tieck's (the translator of Shakespeare,) who recited his satirical play "Die Verkehrte Welt." After a short visit to Prague, Moscheles gave two concerts at Vienna with the same unvarying success. In private circles, too, his return was eagerly welcomed, and his wife affectionately greeted. They never failed to attend the levees of his former patroness, Frau von E., which took place daily between four and six, the interval between dinner and theatre. The old lady, painted, rouged, and reclining on her luxurious sofa, received company. Abbés, poets, savants, such as Carpani, the friend and biographer of Haydn, and others, met at these afternoon receptions, where the last new thing in politics, or Vienna gossip, was discussed by officials and statesmen. Ladies appeared in evening dress. The conversation was carried on in rather poor French, and the atmosphere generally seemed artificial and difficult to breathe. Moscheles also saw much of Czerny, the Abbé Stadler, and Schindler (l'ami de Beethoven, as he styled himself on his visiting cards). He was prevented from listening to the tempting offers of new engagements at Vienna, by a summons to attend his sister's marriage in Prague, where he gave two crowded concerts in the theatre. He notes the following: "During my improvisation, I interwove the melody in Cherubini's 'Wasserträger,' a combination which

with the Bohemian National Air:

was received with rounds of applause. I delighted in seeing my mother and wife, who sat together, enjoying my triumph." Again we find him at Dresden. "I gave another successful concert, in the presence of Royalty, and was presented by Prince Max and Princess Louise with a pin—a laurel wreath of diamonds with a sapphire for the centre."

"November 10th.—Visited poor Frau von Weber; talked a great deal about her irreparable loss, and the many sad circumstances connected with it. I promised her my best exertions to settle some business for her when I got back to London."

Next day Moscheles travelled to Berlin, and of course visited the Mendelssohns immediately after his arrival.

"November 12th.—Fanny's fourteenth birthday celebrated with music and dancing. I relieved the young composer Dorn by playing some of the dance-music, and had an earnest conversation with A. B. Marx on the subject of music."

Owing to the worry incidental to preparations for his own concert, the sociable and delightful meetings with the Mendelssohns, Beer, Bendemann, and others were sadly interfered with. His friend Blume assisted him, although he and Sontag had been forbidden by the manager of a rival theatre to sing for him.

"November 21st.—Day of the concert. Practiced a great deal on an instrument which Madame Spontini (Erard's sister) sent me, with an urgent request that I would play on it at my concert. Fräulein Sontag, who was not allowed to help me positively, did so negatively, by giving out that she was hoarse. Instead of singing in the 'Sargin,' she went with my wife to the concert, and escaped observation by hiding in the back of the box. When I thanked the famous artiste, she said with her peculiarly sweet smile, 'But, dear Moscheles, should not an old Viennese friend help to frustrate the cabals of a theatrical director?' S'Jettl is immer noch's Jettl."* In spite of her good-nature and Möser's proficiency as leader of the band, the room was only two-thirds full, probably on account of the late announcement and other unfavorable circumstances."

The meeting with Felix Mendelssohn and his family was the source of many happy hours to the Moscheles'. "How delighted I was when he and his sister Fanny played as a pianoforte duet his new overture to the 'Midsummer Night's Dream,' and how grand I thought his sonata in E major! He played me also his great overture in C, with the leading subject for trumpets, and a small caprice which he called

* "S'Jettl (familiar name for Henrietta) is still S'Jettl."

'Absurdité.' This great and still youthful genius has once more made gigantic strides, but, strange to say, these are but little recognized except by his teachers, Zelter, Louis Berger, and a select few. This prophet, too, is not honored in his own country; he must go elsewhere. I am glad that he, Marx, and some connoisseurs show much interest in my 'Studies,' by repeatedly coming to me to hear them played. Marx declares he is prepared to score one in C minor, entitled 'The Conflict of Demons,' which he thinks particularly well suited to a band." The origin of this C minor Study is curious. Moscheles had composed for his wife the "Rondo Expressif" in her favorite key of A flat major, and she practiced it with great zeal, but never satisfied herself in the running scale passage at the end, and complained to him of this. "Very well," said he; "every one who feels this difficulty like you shall have a whole study of such runs to practice, and then they will soon learn them well enough."

The Chevalier Spontini was very friendly towards Moscheles, and never classed him among the rivals and envious foes of whom he constantly complained; he consulted him privately with reference to the sum he should ask for the sale of his operas in England, and as to what means he should adopt for bringing out his works there.

At the Königstadt Theatre the charming Sontag delighted Moscheles in the "Sargin," the "Dame Blanche," and the "Italiana in Algieri." Blume showed Moscheles his new opera, "Der Bramine," in manuscript. Möser was just then studying Beethoven's ninth symphony, and Moscheles attended the orchestral rehearsals and the performance with an ever-increasing interest and admiration for that colossal work.

On the 28th of November, a second concert took place in the Grand Opera House, that was filled to overflowing. The whole Court attended. Moscheles played, among other things, the E flat major Concerto, dedicated to the King.

The last month of the year was spent at Hamburg, where he finished his "Twenty-four Studies," op. 70, and the Fantasia, "Anticipations of Scotland."

# CHAPTER X.

## 1827.

**Tour in Germany—Spohr—Elector of Hesse-Cassel—Musical Pupils—**Tyrolese Singers—Escape from a Difficulty—Liszt—Letters from Beethoven—His Melancholy Condition—Correspondence with Schindler and Rau—Beethoven's Relatives—Karl van Beethoven—Generous Assistance of the London Philharmonic Society—Death of Beethoven—Stars in London—Dinner to Clementi—Heine the Poet.

MOSCHELES inaugurated the year 1827 by giving concerts in Hanover and Göttingen, availing himself of his opportunity in the latter place of attending a few lectures of the most learned men in the University, while he was warmly welcomed by the inhabitants of the town itself and the students.

At Cassel he writes: "I am so delighted at seeing Spohr again, the consciousness that I understand this great man, the mutual interest we take in each other's performances—all this is delightful. His garden is charming even in winter." The diary gives frequent evidence of Spohr's devoting his time to Moscheles. On the 8th of January, he assists him in making his concert arrangements. On the following day we read: "To-day Hauptmann, Gerke, and others met at Spohr's, and there was no end of music. On the 10th of January with Spohr at Wilhelmshohe, and dined at his house. Next day, during the rehearsal of my concert, received (to the astonishment of every one) an order from the Electoral Prince, intimating that my concert must be changed from the Town-hall to the Theatre, since the Elector and suite wished to attend." A letter from Mrs. Moscheles supplements these remarks. "This Elector, you must know, has not chosen hitherto to attend any concert in the Town-hall because there are no boxes there, and as a rule refuses the theatre for concerts (he has done so to Hummel); you see, he honors my husband as much as it is in the power of an Elector of Hesse-Cassel to do." The success of this concert is recorded in the diary, the band under Spohr's leading called "splendid," and the singing of Wild and Heinefetter highly praised. We again quote from the diary: "When we can find a quiet hour, it is devoted to my 'Twenty-four Studies.' I write the title-page, and prefix some observations to each separately, to make the pupil correctly understand my intention, each study being meant to overcome some special difficulty. My wife makes a translation straight off into French and English, for Probst publishes the 'Studies' for Germany and Schlesinger for France. In England I have stipulated with Cramer and Beale for a share of one-fourth in the profits."

At the next halting-place—Elberfeld—Moscheles wanted to escape giving a half-promised concert, but the local music-director had already circulated a subscription list, and assured Moscheles that the public would take no refusal. "At last," he writes, "I saw that it was a point of honor, and consented. The programme will, or *should* run thus:—Symphony by Beethoven, played as well as possible by a set of fiddlers calling themselves an orchestra; my E major concerto, played by me with every possible precaution, that the band may not lag behind; Alexander Variations; air to be sung by a soprano, supposing such a one to exist; four-part songs for male voices, as a makeshift if the lady is not forthcoming; the whole to conclude with an extempore performance, after which I suppose, they will let me depart in peace. The expenses will be deducted from the receipts—all clear profits to go to oats and hay for the post-horses. Forgive all this nonsense. I only want to show you that we are in excellent spirits. . . . ."

Aix is their next station, and there Mrs. Moscheles writes: "On the very day of the Elberfeld concert half the streets were under water, so that only some of the band came to rehearsal—a fraction of a fraction! The people, however, swam to the evening performance in coaches. The room was crammed. Here, in Aix, our old friends are so taken up with us, that you must forgive me for only sending you a hasty scribble." "I, too," adds Moscheles, "will send my scribble; if only to tell you how pleased I am to think that this tour, if nothing to speak of in the pecuniary way, will give me fresh impetus as an artist. Here, where I have been so often heard, my subscription list bears witness to the eagerness with which my concert is expected, and for such honors I gladly forfeit my London lessons, but must say I delight in the thought of sending you my next letter from our dear little home in England." Shortly after his return we find him speaking in the highest terms of an Erard piano, sent to Bath expressly for him, and in the spring of this year he completes his "Fifty Preludes for the Piano," "Les Charmes de Londres," and a second rondo for the "Album des Pianistes." He wrote, too, at the instance of enterprising publishers, a number of fugitive pieces, to suit the fashion of the day. These, composed off hand, were, in his eyes, of such little value as not to be catalogued among his regular works, but they were of use to him in teaching a certain class of pupils which mustered in great force this year. "They shrink," he says, "from all serious study. Occasionally a mamma says: 'Will you give her something with a pretty tune in it, brilliant, and not too difficult?' To meet this wish I try to avoid full chords and uncommon modulations, but this makes me look upon such pieces as spurious bantlings, not as the genuine offspring of my Muse."

Allusions like these to the prevalent taste for easy flowing music, account for England's welcoming as a pleasing novelty a family consisting of four singers of the name of Rainer (three brothers and a sister), who made a pilgrimage from the Zillerthal to London. Like almost all artists fresh from the Continent, they had letters of recommendation to Moscheles. He arranged for their daily performance in the Egyptian Hall, where they sang their exquisite Tyrolese melodies, varying the entertainment with their national dances. Their freedom from affectation, the pure delivery of their characteristic songs, their dress—the genuine Tyrolese costume—all these together proved very attractive and delightful to a constantly increasing crowd of hearers. In spite of the moderate entrance-fee, the undertaking answered. More than this, these Tyrolese folk became the fashion. At the most brilliant and fashionable soirées, they relieved with their national melodies the songs of the greatest operatic singers. King George IV. was so delighted when he heard them, that he presented them with new costumes, in strict imitation of their own, of which they were very proud. These Rainers, who were constantly running in and out of Moscheles' house, either to ask his advice, or to tell him of their successes, did him quite unexpectedly a great service. There was a regular fatality attending the arrangements of his annual concert. One singer was hoarse, another was unavoidably absent, and all this at the eleventh hour. When we consider that the programme still contained the names of Caradori, Stockhausen, Galli, and de Begnis as singers, and that not only De Bériot, but also Cramer and Moscheles were to play, one would suppose that the omission of a few vocal pieces would do no harm; but your regular concert-goer is tenacious of his rights, and this made Moscheles apply to the Rainers. "I hurried off to them. 'Can you do me the favor to slip away for a little time from your soirée at Lady. . . .? Will you sing twice for me? I am in a difficulty.' 'Of course we will,' said the whole quartet, unisono. They came and sang, and the gaps in the programme were filled up capitally."

Moscheles, yielding to an importunate music-publisher in London, wrote some slight pianoforte pieces on the Tyrolese melodies; but the favored firm was sued by another, whose offer had been rejected, and the rival publishers went to law. Moscheles' publisher won his suit, and sustained no injury.

During this season the youthful Liszt was in London; although he appeared often, playing in his magnificent bravura style, his concert on the 9th of June was but thinly attended. Moscheles thus alludes to the performance. "The 'Concerto in A minor' contains *chaotic* beauties; as to his playing, it surpasses in power and mastery of difficulties everything I have ever heard."

These were busy days for Moscheles, who frequently played at two concerts on the same evening. In the midst of this cheerful and active life, the news of the mighty Beethoven's illness fell upon Moscheles like a thunderbolt. His first impressions on receiving the intelligence are thus recorded. "Shocking news from Stumpff! He tells me he has received a letter giving details of Beethoven's dangerous state. What a fearful misfortune for art, and how disgraceful that there should be a question of Beethoven's being properly supplied with the necessaries of life! Such a thing seems to me absolutely incredible. I can't bear to think of it."

In the first flush of emotion, Moscheles wrote to his old friend, Herr Lewinger, in Vienna, for accurate information about Beethoven's health and circumstances, but before the arrival of the answer so eagerly looked for (the postal communications in those days were slow, and in the winter particularly unreliable) the following letter from Beethoven to Moscheles came to hand: a letter which left no further doubt of the great man's unhappy condition.

"Vienna, 22d Feb. 1827.

"My dear Moscheles,—I am convinced you will not take it amiss if I trouble you, as well as Sir Smart, for whom I enclose a letter, with a petition. The matter shortly told is this:—Some years ago the Philharmonic Society, in London, made me the handsome offer of arranging a concert for my benefit. At that time, thank God, I was not in such a position as to be obliged to make use of their generous offer. Now, however, I am quite in a different position; for nearly three months I have been laid low by a terribly wearisome illness. I am suffering from dropsy. Schindler will give you more details in the letter which I enclose. You know of my old habit of life. You also know how and where I live. As for my writing music, I have long ceased to think of it. Unhappily, therefore, I may be so placed as to be obliged to suffer want. You have not only a wide circle of acquaintances in London, but also important influence with the Philharmonic Society. I beg you, therefore, to use this influence as far as you can, to induce the Philharmonic Society to resuscitate their generous resolution, and carry it out speedily. I enclose a letter to the same effect to Sir Smart, and have sent another already to Herr Stumpff. Please give the letter to Sir Smart, and unite with him and all my friends in London for the furtherance of my object. I am so weak, that even the dictation of this letter is a difficulty to me. Remember me to your amiable wife, and be assured that I shall always be your friend,

"BEETHOVEN.

"Answer me soon, so that I may hear if I am to hope for anything."

This letter enclosed another of the most distressing kind, written by Schindler, Beethoven's friend, who nursed him in his illness.

"Vienna, 22d Feb. 1827.

"DEAREST FRIEND,—You will see, on reading through the letter of our unfortunate friend Beethoven, that I too propose addressing a few lines to you. I have much to write to you about, but will confine my remarks solely to Beethoven; for at present his state is to me the all-important subject and one closest to my heart. His letter to you contains an expression of his requests and most ardent wishes. His letter to Sir Smart is in the same vein, as well as an earlier one in my handwriting written to Stumpff, the harp-manufacturer.

On the occasion of your last visit here, I described to you Beethoven's position with regard to money-matters, never suspecting that the moment was so near when we should see this great man drawing near his end, under circumstances so peculiarly painful. We may well say 'his end,' for, judging by his present state, recovery is out of the question. Although we keep the truth from him, he must, I think, have his presentiments. It was not before the 3d of December that he and his good-for-nothing nephew returned from the country. On his journey hither, he was obliged, from stress of weather, to pass the night in a small and wretched pot-house, where he caught so bad a chill that it brought on an immediate attack of inflammation of the lungs, and it was in this condition that he arrived here. The bad symptoms had just yielded to treatment, when dropsy of so determined and violent a character set in, that Beethoven had to be operated on on the 18th of

December. His state was such that there was no alternative. This operation was followed by a second on the 8th of January, and a third on the 20th of the same month. Scarcely was the wound allowed to heal, when the pressure increased so rapidly that I often feared the patient would be suffocated before another operation could be effected. It is only now that I find him partially relieved, and should he go on favorably, we may, I think, allow from eight to ten days to elapse before he undergoes a fourth operation.

"Now, my friend, remembering his impatience, and more than all, his quick temper, just picture to yourself Beethoven in such a fearful illness. Think of him, too, brought to this sad state by that wretched creature, his nephew, and partly, too, by his own brother; for both doctors, Malfatti and Professor Wawruch, declare that the good man's illness arises in part from the fearful anxieties of mind to which his nephew had for a long time subjected him, and that the disease had been aggravated by Beethoven's staying too long in the country during the wet season. This could not well be helped, for by order of the police the young man was obliged to quit Vienna, and it was not easy to get a commission for him in any regiment. He is now cadet to the Archduke Ludwig, and treats his uncle just as he always did, although living entirely on him, as in former days. A fortnight ago Beethoven sent him the letter to Sir Smart, to translate into English; we have had no answer at all yet, although he is at Iglau, only a few stations from here.

"Should you, my dear Moscheles, succeed jointly with Sir Smart in inducing the Philharmonic Society to comply with Beethoven's wishes, you would certainly be doing an act of the greatest kindness. The expenses of this tedious illness are unusually great; so much so that the apprehension of being impoverished, and in want, troubles Beethoven night and day, for he would die rather than be forced to accept anything from his odious brother.

"Judging by the present symptoms, dropsy will turn to consumption, for he is now worn to a skeleton, and yet his constitution will enable him to struggle for a long time against this painful death.

"It pains him still more to find that not a soul here

takes any notice of him, and certainly this lack of sympathy is most surprising. In former times, if he was slightly indisposed, people used to drive up to his door, and inquire for him. Now he is completely forgotten, as though he had never lived in Vienna. Mine is the greatest trouble, and I sincerely hope matters may speedily change in one way or another, for I lose all my time, I alone having to do everything for him, because he will not allow any one else to come near him, and it would be inhuman to forsake him in his absolutely helpless condition.

"Just now he speaks frequently about a journey to London after his recovery, and is calculating on the cheapest way we can live during our absence from home. Merciful Heaven! I fear his journey will be a further one than to England. His amusement, when he is alone, consists in reading the old Greek classics, and several of W. Scott's novels, which delight him.

"If you, my dear friend, feel certain that the Philharmonic Society will carry out the project which they started years ago, pray don't omit to let Beethoven know at once; it would put life into him. Try to persuade Sir Smart to write to him as well, so that he may receive a double assurance of the good tidings. May God be with you! Give my kindest regards to your excellent wife, with the highest esteem, Your most devoted friend,

"ANT. SCHINDLER.

"P. S.—If the Concert proposed by the Philharmonic Society for Beethoven's benefit comes off, the committee should most distinctly give Beethoven to understand that the money must be appropriated to his own wants, and not to that of his most unnatural relatives, least of all to his ungrateful nephew. This would be a most beneficial plan; if it is not carried out, Beethoven will give the money to his nephew, who will merely squander it, while he himself suffers want."

"Sick—in necessity—abandoned—a Beethoven!" exclaims Moscheles. The excitement in the house was intense. Moscheles hurried off to Smart, and their first impulse was to send the great man 20*l.*, thus enabling him to procure small comforts, and to show him that a Beethoven should never be allowed to feel want. It occurred, however, in time to Moscheles that the 20*l.* would probably be looked on by Beethoven as a kind of alms, that he might not only be offended, but probably enraged; so, abandoning the idea of sending the money, they applied without delay to the leading members of the Philharmonic Society. These gentlemen, equally shocked and as eager to help as Smart and Moscheles, reasonably asked for a short delay, so as to call together the members of their society, and to take counsel as to the ways and means of helping Beethoven. Meantime Beethoven's second letter, with an enclosure of Schindler's, arrived. They run thus:—

"Vienna, 14th March, 1827.

"MY DEAR GOOD MOSCHELES,—I have lately heard, through Herr Lewinger, that in a letter of the 10th of February, you asked for information on the subject of my illness, about which people spread such various rumors. Although I feel no kind of doubt that you duly received my first letter of the 22d of February, which will explain to you everything you want to know, still I cannot help thanking you heartily for your sympathy with my sad condition, and entreating you once more to take to heart the request made in my first letter. I anticipate with something like assurance that you, acting jointly with Sir Smart, Herr Stumpff, Mr. Neate, and others of my friends, are certain to succeed in obtaining a favorable result for me from the Philharmonic Society. Since then, happening by chance to find Sir Smart's address, I have written again to him, pressing my request very earnestly.

"On the 27th of February I was operated on for the fourth time, and now the return of certain symptoms makes it plain that soon I must expect a fifth operation. What will come of it? What will become of me, if this state of things continues? Truly my lot is a very hard one, but I bow to the decree of fate, and only pray to God constantly that, in His holy wisdom, He may so dispose of me that, however long I must suffer death in life, I may still be shielded from want. This conviction would fortify me to bear my lot, however hard and terrible it may be, with resignation to the will of the Most High. So, my dear Moscheles, once more I commend my cause to your care, and remain always with the greatest esteem,

"Your friend,

"BEETHOVEN.

"Hummel is here, and has paid me several visits already."

Schindler's letter was as follows—

"MY DEAREST FRIEND,—I add a scrap to Beethoven's letter, from which you can gather information about his present state. Thus much is certain that he is nearer death than recovery, for his whole frame is wasting away. Still matters may go on thus for many months, for his lungs even now seem made of steel.

"In the event of the Philharmonic Society granting Beethoven's request, pray contrive that the money shall be lodged with some safe person—*i.e.*, a banker—on whom Beethoven could draw by instalments. The Philharmonic Society might unreservedly explain to Beethoven that they adopt these means solely for his benefit, as they know but too well that the relatives who are around him do not act honestly by him, etc. He is sure to be startled by this announcement, but I and others in whom he confides, will make him thoroughly understand that such a line of conduct is meant in real kindness, and he will be satisfied. In any case, whatever property he leaves behind will come into the hands of the most unworthy people, and it were better it was left to the House of Correction.

"Hummel and his wife are here. He travelled as fast as he could, with the hope of finding Beethoven still alive, for it was commonly reported in Germany that he was *in extremis.* The meeting of these two men last Thursday was a truly affecting sight. I had previously warned Hummel to betray no emotion at the interview with Beethoven, but he was so overpowered at the sight that, in spite of all his struggles, he could not help bursting into tears. Old Streicher came to the rescue. The first thing that Beethoven said to Hummel was, 'Look here, my dear Hummel, here is a picture of the house where Haydn was born ; it was made a present to me to-day. I take a childish pleasure in it—to think of so great a man being born in so wretched a hovel!"

"As I looked on these two men, who never were the best of friends, they seemed to forget all the differences and quarrels of their past lives in this most affectionate conversation. They have both appointed to meet next summer in Carlsbad. Alas! alas! My heartiest remembrance to your amiable wife, and now, adieu!

"Your constant and sincere friend,

"ANT. SCHINDLER."

Meantime the Philharmonic Society had determined on and carried out a scheme that must of necessity be advantageous to poor Beethoven. It was resolved unanimously at a meeting, which Moscheles attended as a member, that Beethoven should not be kept waiting until a concert could be arranged. The season of the year was unfavorable, and a concert in a great city like London involves a delay of from four to six weeks for preparation. They desired, therefore, to hand him over at once, through Moscheles, 100*l.*; but, to spare his sensitive feelings, resolved to suggest that the money was merely in anticipation of the proceeds of a concert already in preparation. The following letter from Rau (one of Moscheles' oldest Viennese friends) proves that the money was sent and reached Vienna without delay

"Vienna, 17th March, 1827.

"DEAR FRIEND,—After a very severe attack of inflammation of the eyes, which kept me closely confined to my room for three weeks, I am, thank God, once more so far recovered that I can take up my pen, although writing is an effort. Make a guess at anything you can't read, and don't be hard on me where you find me illegible.

"Your letter, with the 100*l.* sent to Beethoven, came safely to hand. It gave me great and unexpected pleasure. The great man, whom all Europe justly delights to honor, the noble-hearted Beethoven, lies here in Vienna on his bed of sickness. He is in dire distress, and although alive, still in imminent danger, and this news we must receive from London! There it is that his high-minded friends eagerly try to sooth his affliction, alleviate his wants, and save him from despair.*

"I drove off at once to his house, that I might satisfy myself about his condition, and inform him of the help at hand. It was heart-breaking to see him clasp his hands and shed tears of joy and gratitude. You, his noble-hearted benefactors, would have been rewarded and delighted to witness a scene so deeply touching.

"I found poor Beethoven in the most wretched condition, more like a skeleton than a living being. He was in the last stage of dropsy, and it has been necessary to tap him four or five times. His medical attendant is Doctor Malfatti, so he is in excellent hands, but Malfatti gives him little hope. It is impossible to say for certain how long his present state will continue, or if recovery may yet be possible; but the recent news of the help afforded him has worked a remarkable change. The emotion of joy was so excessive as to rupture, in the course of the night, one of the punctured wounds that had cicatrized over; the water which had accumulated for fourteen days flowed away in streams. I found him on my visit next day remarkably cheerful, and feeling a wonderful sense of relief. I hurried off to Malfatti to tell him of this occurrence, which he considers a very favorable one. They intend to apply a hollow probe for some time, so as to keep this wound open, and allow the water to escape freely. May God bless these human means!

"Beethoven is satisfied with the attendance and services of his cook and housemaid. His and our friend, the well-known and worthy Schindler, dines daily with him, and manages for him in a very friendly, honest way. He also looks after Beethoven's correspondence, and controls as far

* On the margin of the original letter we find the following remark in Moscheles' handwriting:—"I have, however, several proofs of the interest and sympathy called forth in Vienna at that time by Beethoven's dangerous illness. It is clear that several of his worshippers were eager to offer him help and consolation, if they could only get at him. Access to Beethoven, or those nearest to him, owing to his life of isolation, was, however, a difficult matter."

as possible the expenditure of the household. I enclose in my letter, dear friend, Beethoven's receipt for the 1000 florins presented to him. When I proposed to him to take only 500 florins at first, and leave the remaining 500 in the safe custody of Baron von Eskeles, until he wanted them, he confessed candidly to me that the 1000 florins came to him like a perfect godsend, for he was actually in the painful condition of being forced to borrow money. This being so, I yielded to his earnest entreaty, and handed him over the whole sum of 100*l.*, or 1000 florins.

"Beethoven will tell you in his own letter how he intends to show his gratitude to the Philharmonic Society. If, in the course of events, you wish to be useful to him, and I can give you a helping hand, you may rely upon my hearty and zealous co-operation. The whole of the Eskeles family desire their kindest remembrance to you, your wife and little son, and in these I join.

"Your sincere friend,

"RAU."

It is plain, from Moscheles' observation on the margin of Rau's letter, and from notes in the diary, that he had written to many friends at Vienna asking whether it could be true that people neglected Beethoven, prostrated by sickness, and in want, and that he received, in every instance, the information that, owing to Beethoven's repelling manner, and his brother's and nephew's jealousy, friends had been kept back from visiting him. "I doubt if they could have prevented me," says Moscheles, and probably with good cause.

A very affecting letter from Beethoven himself, and one over which many tears were shed, followed that of his friend Rau. It was written on the 17th of March. Beethoven dictated it to Schindler, and signed it with his own hand.

"Vienna, 18th March, 1827.

"MY DEAR GOOD MOSCHELES,—The feelings with which I read your letter of the 1st of March, I cannot describe in words. The splendid generosity of the Philharmonic Society, which well nigh anticipated my request, has moved me to my inmost soul. I entreat you, therefore, dear Moscheles, to be my spokesman and communicate to the Philharmonic Society, my earnest, heartfelt thanks for the sympathy and assistance they have rendered me. I was compelled at once to call in the whole sum of 1000 florins, as I was just reduced to the painful necessity of being obliged to borrow money, and thus becoming further involved. With regard to the concert which the Philharmonic Society have determined to give for my benefit, let me beg of them not to abandon their generous project, but to deduct from the gross receipts of that concert, the 1000 florins now presented to me in advance. Should the Society kindly allow me the surplus, I undertake to prove my deep gratitude, either by writing for them a new symphony, the sketch of which already lies in my desk, or a new overture, or something else the Society may wish for. May Heaven only soon restore me to health, and I will prove to the noble-hearted English how highly I appreciate their sympathy with my sad fate. I shall never forget your noble conduct, and hope soon to send a special letter of thanks to Sir Smart and to Herr Stumpff. Farewell, with sentiments of true friendship, I remain, with the greatest esteem,

"Your friend,

"LUDWIG VAN BEETHOVEN.

"P. S.—My hearty greeting to your wife. I have to thank the Philharmonic Society and you for a new friend in Herr Rau. Pray give to the Philharmonic Society the symphony marked by me with the metronome tempi; these I enclose."

Marking, according to the metronome of the Tempi in Beethoven's last symphony, op. 125 :—

Allegro, ma non troppo, e un poco maestoso 88 = ♩
Molto vivace . . . . . . . . 116 = 𝅗𝅥
Presto . . . . . . . . . 116 = 𝅗𝅥
Adagio molto e cantabile . . . 60 = ♩
Andante moderato . . . . . . 63 = ♩
Finale presto . . . . . . . . 96 = 𝅗𝅥

| | |
|---|---|
| Allegro, ma non troppo . . . . | 88 = ♩ |
| Allegro assai . . . . . . | 80 = 𝅗𝅥 |
| Alla marcia . . . . . . | 84 = ♩ |
| Andante maestoso . . . . . | 72 = 𝅗𝅥 |
| Adagio divoto . . . . . . | 60 = 𝅗𝅥 |
| Allegro energico . . . . . | 84 = 𝅗𝅥 |
| Allegro, ma non tanto . . . . | 120 = 𝅗𝅥 |
| Prestissimo . . . . . . . | 132 = 𝅗𝅥 |
| Maestoso . . . . . . | 60 = ♩ |

We give a letter by Schindler, six days later in point of date, but posted at the same time as Beethoven's:—

Vienna, 24th March, 1827.

"My dear Friend,—Don't let yourself be misled by the difference of date between the two letters. I wished purposely to keep back that of Beethoven for a few days, because, on the day after it was written, we feared our great master would breathe his last. God be thanked, however, that event has not yet happened; but, my dear Moscheles, by the time you read these lines, our friend will be no longer among the living. Death is advancing with rapid strides, and there is but one wish among us all, to see him soon released from these terrible sufferings; nothing else remains to be hoped for. He has been lying all but dead, for the last eight days, and can only now and then muster sufficient strength to put a question, or to ask for what he wants. His condition is fearful, and appears by all accounts to be very similar to that which was lately endured by the Duke of York. He is in an almost constant state of insensibility, or rather stupor—his head hanging down on his chest, and his glazed eyes fixed for hours together upon the same spot. He seldom recognizes his most intimate friends, except when people tell him who is standing before him. In fact it is dreadful to look at him. This state of things, however, can only last a few days longer, for all the bodily functions have ceased since yesterday. He, and we with him, will therefore, please God, soon be released.

"People come in shoals to see him for the last time, although none are admitted except those who are bold enough to force their way into the dying man's room. The letter to you, even to the few sentences at the introduction, is, word for word, written at his dictation. I expect this will be his last letter, although to-day he contrived to whisper to me in broken accents, 'Smart, Stumpff, write;' if possible for him even yet to sign his name on the paper, it shall be done. He feels his end approaching, for yesterday he said to me and Herr von Breuning, 'Plaudite, amici, comœdia finita est!' We were fortunate enough yesterday to arrange everything respecting his last will, although there is hardly anything left but some old furniture and manuscripts. He had in hand a quintet for stringed instruments, and the tenth symphony, of which he makes mention in his letter to you. Two movements of the quintet are entirely finished, and it was intended for Diabelli. The day after the receipt of your letter he was greatly excited, and talked to me a great deal of the plan of the symphony, which was to have been on a grand scale, as being written expressly for the Philharmonic Society.

"I much wish you had made plain in your letter that Beethoven could only draw on this sum of 1000 florins by instalments, for I had agreed with Herr Rau on this matter, but Beethoven adhered to the last sentence in your letter. Well, with the receipt of the money all trouble and anxiety at once vanished, and he said quite cheerfully, 'Now we shall be able to give ourselves a better day occasionally,' for there were only 340 florins left in the drawer, and we therefore restricted ourselves for some time past, to beef and vegetables, a privation which grieved him more than anything else. The next day being a Friday, he immediately ordered his favorite dish of fish, but could merely taste them. In short, his delight with the generosity of the Philharmonic Society borders upon the childish. We were obliged to procure him a great arm-chair, which cost fifty florins; he rests on it daily for half an hour at least while his bed is being made. His obstinacy is as dreadful as ever, and this falls particularly hard upon me, for on no account will he have anybody about him but myself. I had no alternative but to give up all my lessons, and devote to him every spare moment of time I could get. Everything he eats or drinks I must taste first, to ascertain whether it might not be injurious to him. Glad as I am to do all this, it lasts too long for a poor devil like myself. I hope to heaven, however, matters will right themselves if I continue to keep in good health. Whatever remains of the 1000 florins we intend to expend on our friend Beethoven's funeral which will be performed without much ceremony in the churchyard at Döbling, a constant and favorite haunt of Beethoven's. There is the rent due on the 13th of April, that must be paid for another half-year. Then there are several small debts (the doctor's fees among them), so that the 1000 florins may just cover what is owing, without leaving much balance in hand.

"Two days after your letter we received one from the worthy Mr. Stumpff, who speaks of you in terms of the highest praise. The reading of this letter excited Beethoven rather too much, for he was fearfully reduced and weakened. We heard him to-day say repeatedly, 'May God requite them all a thousand times.'

"You can well understand that the generosity of the Philharmonic Society has created a general sensation here. The English are praised up to the skies, and the Viennese millionaires loudly abused. The *Beobachter* has an article on the subject, and so has the *Wiener Zeitung.* I enclose them.—(Interval of some hours.)—I have just left Beethoven: he is actually dying, and before this letter is beyond the precincts of the city the great light will be extinguished for ever. He is still, however, in full possession of his senses. I hasten to dispatch my letter, in order to run to his bedside. The enclosed lock of hair I have just cut from his head, and send it you. God be with you!

"Your most devoted Friend,

"ANT. SCHINDLER."

A few days later a letter from Rau brought the sad tidings of Beethoven's death.

"Vienna, March 28th, 1827.

"DEAR FRIEND,—Beethoven is no more; he expired on

the evening of the 26th of March, between five and six o'clock, after a painful struggle and terrible suffering. On the day before he died all consciousness had completely gone.

"I must say a word about the property he has left behind him. In my last letter I told you that Beethoven, according to his own statement, was absolutely without money or resources, consequently in the greatest need, and yet, when an inventory of his things was taken in my presence, we found, in an old half-mouldy box, seven Bank shares.

"Whether Beethoven purposely concealed them (for he was very mistrustful, and looked hopefully for a speedy recovery), or whether their possession had escaped his own memory, is a problem I cannot venture to solve. The thousand florins sent over by the Philharmonic Society were found still untouched: I laid claim to the money in conformity with your instructions, and was obliged to deposit it with the magistrate until further notice from the Philharmonic Society. I would not consent to the funeral expenses being paid out of this money without being authorized by the Society so to act. Should you have it in your power to dispose of any part of the money, pray let it be done in favor of the two poor servants who nursed the sufferer with endless patience and devotion. There is not a syllable about them in the will. Everything goes to the sole heir, Beethoven's nephew. As to the present which Beethoven intended sending to the Philharmonic Society, Herr Schindler will communicate with you in due time. Let me know soon, and definitely, what steps I am to take, and you may rely on me for strictly carrying out your intentions. Beethoven will be buried on the 29th of this month. An invitation has been sent to all artists, members of the different orchestras, and theatres. Twenty musicians and composers will act as torchbearers at the funeral. Grillparzer has written a very affecting address to be spoken by Anschütz at the grave. Indeed everything which can be done to render the solemnity worthy of the deceased, seems to be in preparation.

"The family of Eskeles joins me in kindest remembrances to you and yours.

"Your friend,

"Rau."

We find among Moscheles' papers several relating to Beethoven's death:

INVITATION

TO

LUDWIG VAN BEETHOVEN'S FUNERAL,

Which will take place on the 29th March, at 3 o'clock in the afternoon.

---

THE company will assemble at the lodgings of the deceased, in the Schwarz-spanier House, No. 200 on the Glacis, before the Schottenthor.

The procession starts from that point to the Trinity Church, at the Father's Minorites in the Alser Street.

---

The musical world sustained the irreparable loss of the famous composer about six o'clock in the evening, on the 26th March, 1827.

Beethoven died of dropsy, in the 56th year of his age, after receiving the Holy Sacraments.

Due notice of the day, "der Exequien," will hereafter be made known by L. VAN BEETHOVEN'S

ADMIRERS AND FRIENDS.

(The distribution of these cards is at the music establishment of Tob. Haslinger.)

---

BEY LUDWIG VAN BEETHOVEN'S LEICHENBEGANGNISS.

(*am* 29 *März* 1827).

Von J. F. CASTELLI.

Achtung allen Thränen, welche fliessen,
Wenn ein braver Mann zu Grabe ging,
Wenn die Freunde Trauerreihen schliessen,
Die der Selige mit Lieb' umfing.

Doch der Trauerzug, der heute wallet,
Strecket sich, so weit das Himmelszelt
Erd' umspannt, so weit ein Ton erschallet,
Und um diesen Todten weint die Welt.

Doch um Euch allein nur müsst Ihr klagen !—
Wer so hoch in Heiligthume stand,
Kann den Staub nicht mehr—er ihn nicht tragen,
Und der Geist sehnt sich in's Heimathland.

Darum rief die Muse ihn nach oben,
Und an ihrer Seite sitzt er dort,
Und an ihrem Throne hört er droben
Tönen seinen eigenen Accord.

Aber hier sein Angedenken weilet,
Und sein Name lebt im Ruhmes-Licht,
Wer, wie er, der Zeit ist vorgeeilet,
Den ereilt die Zeit zerstörend nicht.

---

## AT BEETHOVEN'S FUNERAL.

Ev'ry tear that is shed by the mourner is holy ;
When the dust of the mighty to earth is resigned,
When those he held dearest move sadly and slowly
To the grave of the friend in whose heart they were shrined :—

But our grief-stricken train is a wild sea that surges,
That spreads to yon starry pavilion o'erhead
And girdles the globe : for all nature sings dirges,
Where'er rings an echo, to-day o'er the dead.

But weep not for him : for yourselves sorrow only :
Though proud was his place in the hierarchy here,
This earth might not hold him ; his spirit was lonely,
And yearned for a home in a loftier sphere.

So Heaven to the minstrel its portals uncloses :
The Muse thither calls him, to sit by her side
And hear, from the throne where in bliss she reposes,
His own hallow'd harmonies float far and wide.

Yet here, in our memories homed, he abideth ;
Round his name lives a glory that ne'er may grow dim ;
Time fain would o'ertake him, but Time he derideth ;
The grisly Destroyer is distanced by him.

## AM GRABE BEETHOVEN'S.

(*den* 29 *März* 1827).

Es brach ein Quell vom hohen Felsen nieder,
  Mit reicher Strömung über Wald und Flur.
Und wo er floss, erstand das Leben wieder,
  Verjüngte sich die alternde Natur.
Ein jeder kam zur reitzgeschmückten Stelle,
  Und suchte sich Erquickung an der Welle.

Nur wenige von richtigem Gefühle,
  Empfanden seine Wunderkräfte ganz,
Die übrigen erfreuten sich am Spiele
  Der schönen Fluth und ihrem Demantglanz:
Die meisten aber fanden sein Gewässer
  Dem Andern gleich, nicht edler und nicht besser.

Der Quell versank. Nun erst erkannte Jeder
  Des Bornes Kraft, nun erst, da sie zerstob!
Und Pinsel, Klang, der Meissel und die Feder,
  Vereinten sich zum längst verdienten Lob;
Jedoch kein Lied, nicht Sehnsucht, nicht die Klage
  Erweckten ihn und brachten ihn zu Tage.

Du, der hier liegt, befreyt von Schmerz und Banden,
  Du warst der Quell, den ich zuvor genannt!
Du grosser Mensch, von Wenigen verstanden,
  Bewundert oft, doch öfter noch verkannt!
Jetzt werden Alle jubelnd Dich erheben:
  Du musstest sterben, sterben, um zu leben!

SCHLECHTA.

---

## AT BEETHOVEN'S GRAVE.

From the high rock I marked a fountain breaking;
  It poured its riches forth o'er glade and plain;
Where'er they streamed I saw new life awaking,
  The grandam world was in her prime again;
To the charm'd spot the tribes of earth came thronging,
And stoopt to that pure wave with eager longing.

Yet of these hosts few only, keener-sighted
  Than were their fellows, all its glamor knew:
The simple multitude surveyed, delighted,
  Its diamond glitter and its changing hue;
But—save unto those few that saw more clearly—
That wondrous fountain was a fountain merely.

At last its source dried up, its torrent dwindled;
And all mankind discerned its virtue then:
In minstrels' breasts and bards' a fire was kindled,
And brush and chisel vied with harp and pen:
But wild desire, and minstrelsy, and wailing
To call it back to life were unavailing.

* * * * *

Thou who sleep'st here, thy toil, thy bondage ended!
Lo! in that fountain's tale is told thine own.
Marvelled at oft, more oft misapprehended,
By the few only thou wast truly known.
All shall exalt thee, now that low thou liest;
That thou mayst live, O deathless one, thou diest

The following letters from Schindler, Rau, and others, although giving some further details about Beethoven's death, turn chiefly on the subject of the 100*l.* presented by the Philharmonic Society, a matter which gave rise to all sorts of discussion, without coming to any really satisfactory conclusion. Schindler writes:—

"Vienna, April 4th, 1827.

"My dear Friend,—I find myself induced to write to you once more, and thus to insure the safety of the letter I enclose for Sir Smart. It contains Beethoven's last expression of thanks to Smart, Stumpff, the Philharmonic Society, and to the whole English nation. Beethoven, during the last moments of his life, urged me most earnestly to carry out his wishes about this letter. Let me entreat you, therefore, to give Sir Smart the letter as soon as possible; Mr. Lewisey, of the English Embassy, has had the kindness to translate it into English.

"On the 26th of March, at a quarter to six o'clock in the evening, during a heavy thunderstorm, our immortal friend breathed his last. From the evening of the 24th until he died, he was almost constantly in a delirious state; but whenever he had a moment of relief, he remembered the kindness shown him by the Philharmonic Society, and praised the constant friendliness of the English nation.

"His sufferings are not to be described, especially from

the moment when the wound gave way, occasioning a fearful drain on the system. His deathbed was remarkable for the magnanimity and Socratic wisdom with which he prepared to meet his doom. I shall probably publish an account of his death; it would be of rare value to his biographers.

"Beethoven's funeral was, as in justice it should be, that of a great man. Some 30,000 persons crowded on the glacis, and surged through the streets where the procession was to pass. I cannot describe the scene. If you remember the fête in the Prater, on the occasion of the Congress in the year 1814, you will have some idea of it. Eight Kapellmeisters were pall-bearers, among them Eibler, Weigl, Gyrowetz, Hummel, Seyfried, etc. There were sixty-and-thirty torchbearers, among them Grillparzer, Castelli, Haslinger, Steiner, Schubert, etc.

"Yesterday Mozart's Requiem was performed as a commemorative service in the St. Augustine Church. The church, although a large one, could not contain the crowd that thronged there. Lablache sang the bass part. The leading publishers of Vienna suggested this service.

"You have Beethoven's last letter, that of the 18th of March, and Schott in Mainz has his last signature.

"With regard to his personalty, seven Bank shares, and several hundred gulden have been found, and now the Viennese talk and write about Beethoven's having had no need of aid from a foreign nation, etc., without reflecting that Beethoven, old and powerless at the age of 56, could make the same claims as if he had been a man of 70. If he had ceased working for years, as the doctors told him he must, he would certainly have been forced to sell one share after the other, and for how many years, think you, could he have lived on the proceeds of these shares, without falling into the greatest distress? In short, dear friend, I and Herr Hofrath von Breuning beg of you earnestly, in the event of such monstrous reports reaching England, to appease the manes of Beethoven, by publishing in one of the most largely circulated German newspapers, such as the *Angsburger Allgemeine Zeitung*, the letters that you have of Beethoven's upon the subject; the Philharmonic Society might do this on its own account, and thus silence these scribblers at once.

"The Philharmonic Society has the honor of having defrayed the expenses of the great man's funeral; without their help, this certainly could not have been done in a suitable manner.

"The universal cry was, 'What a shame for Austria! This mustn't go further, for everybody will contribute his share!' but with this outcry the matter ended. The Musik-Verein determined, the day after the funeral, to have a Requiem performed in Beethoven's memory, and that was all. But we people of the Kärntnerthor, intend to get up a grand concert in April, and raise a sum for a handsome monument.

"I have further to inform you that the sexton of Währing, where Beethoven lies buried, was with us yesterday, and showed us a letter in which he was offered 1000 florins if he would deposit Beethoven's head at a certain spot. This stirred the police to active inquiries. The funeral cost a trifle over 300 florins; our friend Rau will have written to you about it. Should the Philharmonic Society wish to leave the rest of the money here, allowing me, for instance, to appropriate a small sum to my own use, I should regard it as a legacy from my friend Beethoven. I don't possess the smallest trifle to remind me of him, and in this respect I fare the same as others, for his death was a surprise to him and to all of us around him.

"Do write me a few lines, and say if you have received the letters of the 22d February, the 14th and the 18th of March; and let me know, too, if Sir Smart has also had his. Beethoven's relations, when his death was imminent, behaved in the meanest way; he was still breathing when his brother came and wanted to carry off everything, even the 1000 florins sent from London, but we turned him out of doors. Such were the scenes enacted by the side of Beethoven's deathbed. Call the attention of the Philharmonic Society to the gold medal of Louis XVIII.; it weighs fifty ducats, and would be a noble reminder of that great man.—Adieu.

"A. SCHINDLER.

"Hummel plays to-morrow in the Kärntnerthor Theatre. Mr. Lewisey begs to be remembered to Mr. Neate."

Another letter was received from Schindler shortly afterwards :—

Vienna, April 11th, 1827.

"My dear Friend,—You will be shocked at the quantity and length of my letters, but read and believe if you can ! To save your honor, that of our friend Beethoven, and of the Philharmonic Society, there was nothing left to us, but to put you in possession of every detail. You heard in my last letter, that there is a great deal of talk as well as public comment on the generous conduct of the Society. But the *Allgemeine Zeitung* contains an article of the most offensive character to every one, so much so, that we have thought it our duty to answer it through Holfrath Breuning, who undertook to write the enclosed truthful account, which Pilat will send this very day to the editor of the *Allgemeine Zeitung*. Although you have never seen the original article in the *Allgemeine Zeitung*, on reading our answer you will at once guess its object and general purport. What you and Smart have further to do, is to publish in the *Allgemeine Zeitung* your letters as well, so that these wretched scribblers may be thoroughly humiliated. Rau and Pilat think our article too courteous, but neither Breuning nor I dare come out with the whole truth, although we should like to do so, and think the disclosure due to the world. Apart from the fact of my having already, as Beethoven's friend and champion, made myself many enemies, I think it would be base conduct, were I to remain silent when his memory is slandered, now that he is dead and buried, and his well-intentioned friends are publicly attacked, and their generous efforts misinterpreted.

"I wrote to you lately that the Philharmonic Society should enter the lists by publishing in its own name the letters to yourself and Smart; we are all of this opinion. The Philharmonic Society should state what is perfectly well known in London, that Beethoven, after his first concert in the Kärntnerthor Theatre, two years ago, after deducting all expenses, which came to 1000 florins, and paying the managers for the hire of the theatre, had only 300 florins of clear profit, not a single subscriber paying a farthing for his box; not even did the Court appear at the concert, although Beethoven, by my advice, gave a personal invitation to every member of the Imperial household. Every one promised to come, and not only in every instance failed to redeem that promise, but never sent Beethoven the smallest contribution, a present of some sort being the invariable rule, even at the benefits of ordinary concert-givers.

"At his second concert, given at the Redoutensaal, in the same month, the committee, who undertook the management on their own account, were obliged to pay 300 florins out of their own pockets; and I had the greatest difficulty in preventing Beethoven from making up the deficit out of the 500 florins guaranteed to him for his services on the occasion. It gave him the greatest pain to feel that the committee lost money on his account.

"When the subscription was started for his last Grand Mass, not a soul at Vienna, no, not even the Court, would subscribe, and there were other countless insults and humiliations that poor Beethoven was obliged to endure. Now is the best opportunity of making all these things known. All Vienna knew that Beethoven had been lying on a sick-bed for two or three months, and no one took the trouble to inquire into his state of health and circumstances. With such sad experiences of Vienna, could he be expected to look for help here? I declare to Heaven that had not the Philharmonic Society, by its generosity, aroused the Viennese from their inaction, Beethoven would have died and been buried like Haydn, who was followed to the grave by fifteen persons.

"As to the concert to be given by the collected forces of our theatre for raising a monument, matters stand thus: 'Norma,' which was to have been given after Easter, has been fixed for this week, so we lose our evening by this extra opera night. An afternoon concert Weigl thinks unfavorably of, and proposes its postponement until next autumn. But by that time, what little zeal there is will have completely cooled, and no one will think of doing anything more in the matter.

"I cannot help telling you about the conduct of the medical men. At the very beginning of his illness, Beethoven asked the doctors he had formerly consulted to attend him. Dr. Braunhofer excused himself on the plea of his being too far from the house. Dr. Staudenheim, after three days' solicitation, came at last, and retired after one professional visit. The consequence of this was that Beethoven had to trust himself to the care of a professor in the general hospital, whose services he obtained in a very singular way. Gehringer, the proprietor of a coffee-house in the Kohlmarkt, happened to have a sick servant whom he wished to place under the care of this practitioner. He therefore wrote to Professor Wawruch, asking him to receive the patient, and requesting him, at the same time, to visit Beethoven, who was in want of medical aid. Considerable time elapsed before I ascertained that Beethoven's amiable nephew Karl, while playing one day at billiards in this coffee-house, entrusted the proprietor with this commission. The professor knew neither Beethoven nor his constitution, treated him in his regular routine fashion, prescribing for him, during the first four weeks of his illness, seventy-two bottles of medicine, often three different sorts in one day, so that, as early as the 1st day of January, the patient was more dead than alive. At last I could not look any longer on this gross mismanagement, and went off straight to Dr. Malfatti, formerly Beethoven's friend. He required a great deal of persuasion, and when Beethoven himself implored him, most earnestly at the first consultation, to attend him professionally, Malfatti replied he could not, out of respect for the other doctor, and came at most once or twice a week to the consultation. During the last week, however, he came daily. In short, to you, I can and will say it; Beethoven might have lived ten years longer, had he not been sacrificed to the most contemptible meanness and ignorance of others. All these matters will be more fully explained at a later period.

"Hummel went back again to Weimar on the 9th. His wife and his pupil, a Mr. Hiller, from Frankfort, were with him here. The latter sends you his kind remembrances, and so does Hummel. The expenses of the funeral are now nearly settled, and amount to 330 florins.

"I might tell you a great deal more, but I must conclude. Our friend, Lewinger, sends both of you his kind remembrances. He is so kind as to send this letter by Rothschild. Rau also desires to be remembered. Write to us soon. Say everything that is kind for me to Herr Stumpff, and tell him that it was Beethoven's intention to dedicate to him one of his newest works. This shall be done, if we can only find some one work that is completed. A kind farewell from

"Your old friend,
"SCHINDLER."

After a few months Rau writes to Moscheles on this matter :—

"Vienna, June 17, 1827.

"Do not accuse me of neglect, dear friend, because I have left you so long without information respecting the state of Beethoven's affairs. I told you already that I put in a claim to the 1000 florins sent by the Philharmonic Society before he died. Herr Hofrath Breuning, the executor of the will, could and dared not take any steps in the matter, until Beethoven's creditors had been publicly summoned in the usual way. They met on the 5th of June. By the advice of Herr Baron v. Eskeles, I sent a legal friend of mine to the meeting, desiring him to renew my claim, but the 'Masse-Curator,' Dr. Bach, steadily opposed it. So in order to expedite matters, and bring them to a successful issue, I want a power of attorney from the Philharmonic Society which, duly proved at the Austrian Embassy, may confer on me full powers to demand back, by legal process, the 1000 florins, and to appoint a legal friend to settle this business. I propose Dr. Eltz as a fitting person.

"After the meeting I went off to Dr. Bach, to talk over the matter confidentially, for I could not understand the difficulties which people thrust in the way of this righteous demand. He answered me honestly and openly that it was his duty, acting on behalf of the nephew, still a minor, to dispute every counter-claim that interfered with that nephew's interests. But his opinion was that a lawsuit, and its heavy attendant expenses, would be best avoided if the Philharmonic Society would generously be induced to consider this sum as a contribution to Beethoven's monument, the remainder to be lodged in the house of Eskeles or Rothschild for remittance back to the Society. Under this supposition, Dr. Bach would do his best to further this remittance. Baron Eskeles, and many experienced jurists, gladly entertain this scheme, especially as, since Beethoven's death, one of our most important witnesses, I mean Hofrath von Breuning, has also died. This excellent man caught cold while attending the sale of Beethoven's property by auction, and died after three days. He was the single witness who could identify the 1000 florins as the same that were sent over by the Society. We shall be guided by your next letter as to our future conduct in this affair.

"The Eskeles and Wimpffens, one and all, join with me in kind regards to you and your wife.

"Your friend,

"RAU."

Vienna, Sept. 14th, 1827.

"MY DEAREST FRIEND,—By the kindness of Mr. Levisey, bearer of dispatches to the English Government, I seize the opportunity of writing and forwarding you the enclosed souvenir of our friend Beethoven. In your last letter you wished for a manuscript of some well-known composition of the great master. Here then is the last part of the scherzo of his last Symphony, and along with it one of those remarkable pocket-books in which Beethoven, while out walking, used to jot down his ideas, working them up, on his return home, from these skeleton sketches into his full score. I was so fortunate as to rescue several of them, and to me they are of the deepest interest, but they are scarcely intelligible to any but those who can trace the full flower in the germ before them. The book I send contains sketches for one of his last quartets; and should you ever hear any of these you will see by some of the passages written down at full length to which quartet they belong. I believe I cannot better prove to you my friendship than by sending you this relic, the first and only one I shall ever part with—unless a large sum of money be offered. Lewinger tells me he has already sent you Beethoven's portrait.

I only hope it is that in which he is lithographed writing, for that is the best; all the others are bad. On the sheet of paper before him are the words 'Missa Solemnis.' I wanted to send everything to you by Mr. Clementi, whose acquaintance I made in London, but I missed him before he left, and had not heard of his intended departure.

"Pixis came here from Paris, for a fortnight, and returned yesterday, travelling by way of Prague. Spontini, too, has left us. He is beating up recruits, and gave my sister an engagement. She and I may go together next spring to Berlin, as the Kärntnerthor Theatre will probably be closed again. This at all events is certain, that Barbaja's management ends next April. What will happen afterwards is an open question. People talk confidently of Madame Pasta coming here for the next winter. I should exceedingly like to hear the real truth from you. You can easily find it out for me; I should be glad, for my sister's sake, that she should see and hear such an artiste. Perhaps you would enclose a note for me in a letter to Lewinger or Rau, and give me information on this subject. I should like, too, to have an acknowledgment of the receipt of these papers, sketches, etc. Tell me how you are, and all your belongings.

"The Beethoven business proceeds very slowly; we are met by so many obstacles. In June that most amiable man, Hofrath von Breuning, died; and now the 'curator' has been laid up for the last six weeks. I am only anxious to know what is to be done with the money sent from England. The tombstone is to be placed very shortly. Piringer and others have ordered it. I have heard nothing, seen nothing of it, for everything is done secretly, probably that they may have the sole credit. At Prague, Herr Schlosser has published a most wretched biography of Beethoven. Here, too, a subscription is circulating for another 'life,' which, I hear will be compiled by Herr Gräffer, although the biographer, selected by Beethoven himself, is Hofrath Rochlitz, of Leipzig, to whom, by Beethoven's desire, Breuning and I had to deliver very important papers. The newly-appointed guardian of Beethoven's nephew has handed over Breuning's papers to Herr Gräffer. This was very bad conduct, but no harm is done, for the papers were for the most part connected with the family history, and I have the most important still in my own custody. God bless you!

"Your very sincere and obliged friend,

"ANT. SCHINDLER."

The business in which Moscheles found himself involved by the death of the great Beethoven, and the service he had rendered him, could not be brought to a satisfactory conclusion at once, as the following letter proves:—

"Vienna, Feb. 10th, 1828.

"To Herr Ignaz Moscheles, Composer of Music, and Member of the Philharmonic Society of London.

"MOST RESPECTED SIR,—After the death of Herr von Breuning, which took place in Vienna on the 4th of June 1827, I was appointed by the proper authority in that city the legal guardian of Karl von Beethoven, a minor, the nephew and heir of the composer Ludwig von Beethoven, who died—alas! prematurely for the world of art—on the 26th of March last year. I undertook this heavy responsibility solely for the purpose of trying to lead this highly-gifted youth back to the paths of virtue, from which (I say it with sorrow) he has to some extent strayed. I did it for the sake of his great uncle, who had befriended him since his childhood, although he had not always availed himself of the most discreet means to insure his welfare. I have yet another reason. The young man has expressed great confidence in me, and has conducted himself with the strictest propriety since he entered upon the military profession as a cadet in an infantry regiment.

"Judging by the legal documents before me, Beethoven's small fortune (after deducting sums for payment of some heavy debts, expenses of his illness, and funeral) consists of little more than 8000 florins in Austrian paper-money. I am on the point of negotiating the legal registration of this property, for according to the terms of the will my ward is only to enjoy a life-interest in the property, while the capital reverts to his heirs, unless otherwise appointed by will, to whom the property will be legally secured.

"In addition to several other debts legally registered and publicly announced at the general meeting of Ludwig von Beethoven's creditors, there is a further claim for 1000 florins, Austrian money, preferred by the advocate, Dr. Eltz of Vienna, as the representative and nominee of your friend Herr Rau; he is also empowered to act for the Philharmonic Society of London. This sum is said to be identified as the money sent some time since, during Beethoven's life-time, as a present in the shape of pecuniary aid, by the Philharmonic Society of London.

"As it is necessary before the legal settlement of the testator's property to prove that this claim on behalf of Dr. Eltz has been either settled or withdrawn, and as I, acting as guardian, am most anxious to arrange this business as soon as possible, I write to you, sir, as one of Beethoven's most intimate and respected friends, as the representative of that high-minded body, the Philharmonic Society of London, and as one of ourselves whom we delight to honor, although living far from us; lastly, in the name of a youth full of talent and promise, who when his uncle died lost his sole support, and is left destitute. May I beg of you, sir, to take the necessary steps that the Society may generously withdraw their claim, even assuming it to be a perfectly righteous one, through Herr Rau, and his representative Dr. Eltz; and that they empower Herr Rau to notify this withdrawal of claim to the proper authorities.

"I am deeply and solely concerned for the welfare of this most promising youth, who by the death of his uncle, Ludwig von Beethoven, who idolized him, has lost his only support. I address myself very confidently to the generous Philharmonic Society, trusting they will not ask the return of the sum given to assist Beethoven—money presented so long ago that it is impossible to say that the identical sum still exists. I would further request them, through you, not to curtail the small sum with which I am to maintain my ward, for I can hardly hope to get more than 400 florins in the shape of yearly interest. According to the accounts, more than 1000 florins have been expended in defraying the expenses of the testator's illness and funeral, besides paying other debts; so that it will be fully believed that I feel great difficulty in securing my ward from want, until he is fortunate enough to get his commission as an officer—a position which, in the absence of other support, would actually leave him still in embarrassed circumstances.

"For these reasons, sir, I shall be excused in expressing a hope that the Society, and the old friends and admirers of Beethoven, will show their honor to his memory by befriending the nephew who sorely needs their assistance. I venture to offer my services, and bind myself to invest any sum as advantageously as I can.

"I cannot bring myself to think that the Philharmonic Society would ever persist in enforcing their claim; nor, if it came to a question of law, do I doubt for a moment the Judge would give a decision in favor of the heir, but still the law expenses and the delay would seriously embarrass me. The sum left is so small, and I have got to pay law expenses, legacy duties, etc.

"Finally, I think I can explain to the Society the reason why Ludwig von Beethoven complained of poverty before his death, and asked their assistance. He considered his nephew as his son and ward, and thought it his duty to provide for his support. This feeling may confidently be asserted to have prompted him to look on the seven shares of the Austrian National Bank, not as his own property, but as that of his favorite nephew, for whose support he destined them in his will. It was a matter of religious feeling with him, and he adhered to it loyally, that the burden of maintaining his poor nephew, for whom he would have sacrificed his own life, imposed on him such a duty.

"I may safely say that the noblest sacrifice to the manes of Beethoven, and the fulfilment of his dearest wish, for which he toiled throughout all his life, would be the securing of his poor nephew from want. Were I myself blessed with a fortune, and had not duties to my own relatives, I would willingly devote it to him.

"I trust, sir, you will recognize the honesty and purity of intention with which I write to you, and will excuse me the more readily as I can assure you that I have, out of pure affection for the nephew of the great man, undertaken the duties and care of a guardian. On this point, and for references to my personal character, M. Rau will give you all the information you can wish.

"Hoping that I shall soon receive a kind and favorable reply, sent to me direct, or through M. Rau, and commending myself and the cause of my ward to your kind consideration,

"I remain, Sir, with great respect,

"Your most humble servant,

"JACOB HOTSCHEBAR.

"Imperial Hofconcipist."

Rau also wrote as follows:—

"Vienna, Feb. 10th, 1828.

"DEAR FRIEND,—I send you herewith a letter from the administrator of Beethoven's property, by which you will see that the legal proceedings are drawing to an end. I was called on to give an official explanation about the 1000 florins presented by the Philharmonic Society; but not having received further instructions from you, and being unwilling without them to make myself responsible, I asked for a delay, until I heard your wishes on the matter. The enclosed letter will put you in possession of all the facts.

"Between ourselves, if you can manage to negotiate the surrender of the 1000 florins, we shall be spared much unpleasantness, and perhaps a lawsuit. Even Dr. Eltz and Baron Eskeles think that the 1000 florins found at Beethoven's death would with great difficulty be identified, as Hofrath Breuning, who managed the inventory, is now dead. Should the money, however, be unexpectedly redemanded, a power of attorney must be sent to Dr. Eltz by the Philharmonic Society, in order that he may prove his legal claims *at the cost of the Society*. The legal process might possibly swallow up the entire sum. Pray give me a speedy and definite answer. The Eskeles, Wimpffens, Ephraims, etc., are well, and join me in kind remembrance to you and your wife.—Your friend,

"RAU."

On receipt of this note, Moscheles conferred with the

Directors of the Philharmonic Society, and induced them to abandon altogether their claim to the money, but the whole business and the comments thereon gave him a great deal of annoyance and trouble. Reports came to England from Vienna, where people were naturally ashamed of Beethoven's having had to look to London for assistance, stating that Beethoven, after all, had not been so badly off, that he had not touched the 100*l.*, and besides that he had left some Bank shares; how could Moscheles have been *bold enough* to open a subscription for him in London, or the Philharmonic Society have *ventured to force itself upon our Beethoven* with their present? Moscheles personally was profoundly indifferent to such insinuations; it was enough for him to have been called 'friend' by Beethoven himself, and to have lightened, in however humble a way, the sufferings of his latter days. Still it was due to Beethoven's memory, as well as to the Philharmonic Society, to see that the truth was properly stated, and thus to silence malignant and envious tongues. He therefore made a public statement, which went the round of the newspapers. The lock of Beethoven's hair, the sketches in his own hand, the metronome tempi of the 9th Symphony, and the sketch-book which Schindler sent him, were always kept and regarded as the most sacred relics, and are now in the possession of his son Felix.

We here insert a letter of Beethoven's which, although unconnected with the preceding correspondence, is of interest to the student of his works; it is from the collection of autographs in the possession of the late Consul-General Clauss of Leipzig.

"To Mr. Joseph von Warena, in Grätz.

"HONORED SIR,—Rode was perfectly correct in everything he said about me. My health is none of the best, and without any fault of my own, my condition in other respects is perhaps the most unfavorable I have ever experienced; that, however, and nothing in the world shall prevent me from helping as far as possible, by such small work as I can offer, your Convent ladies, who, like myself, are suffering from no fault of their own.

"Two completely new symphonies therefore are entirely at your service, an air for a bass voice with chorus, several isolated small choruses, and if you want the overture to 'Ungarns Wohlthäter" (overture to King Stephen, Hungary's benefactor), which you performed last year, this is at your service as well.

"The Overture to 'The Ruins of Athens,' although in rather a small style, is also at your disposal. Among others there is a Dervish chorus, a good signboard for a motley audience (ein gutes Aushängeschild für ein gemischtes Publikum). In my opinion you would do wisely to choose a day when you could give the oratorio of "Christ on the Mount of Olives." Since I wrote it, it has been performed everywhere. This would make up the half of a concert; for the second half you might give a new symphony, the overtures, and several choruses, and also the above-mentioned bass air with chorus. Thus the evening would not lack variety. Still you had best talk over this matter with, and be advised by, the local musical authorities. With regard to what you say respecting my remuneration at the hands of a third person, I believe I can guess to whom you allude; were I in my former position, well, I would say straightforwardly 'Beethoven never takes a farthing where humanity is to be benefited,' but just at present I am so circumstanced by my large charities (a state of things I have no reason to be ashamed of), and by other matters arising from the conduct of men destitute of honor and good faith, that I tell you plainly I shall not refuse my share, if offered to me by a person who can well afford it. The question here is not one of claims, but should the whole business about this third person come to nothing, be assured that I am even now just as ready as I was last year, without the smallest recompense, to do any good turn to my friends, the respected ladies of the Convent, and that I shall be ready to assist suffering humanity as long as I breathe.

"And now farewell; write soon, and I shall most zealously look after everything that is required. My best wishes for the Convent, with great respect,

"Your friend,

"LUDWIG VAN BEETHOVEN."

The programmes of the Philharmonic Concerts of this season bear witness to the respect paid to Beethoven's memory and that of other German composers, since their masterpieces were to be met with in every programme. Liszt and Moscheles appeared as solo performers, and the best singers were constantly heard. The programme was often composed of the masterpieces of Handel, Haydn, and Mozart. Among the vocalists we read of Madame Stockhausen, who had already become a favorite with the public; her unpretentiousness and earnestness made her a model to every young aspirant in the profession. Her voice was lovely, bell-like, and exquisitely flexible. She had created a furore in the salons of Paris with her native Swiss melodies, but devoted her best energies to serious study. When she came to London in search of engagements, a soprano was wanted for oratorios, and Sir George Smart, who at once recognized her talents, offered to study with her the English text, with a view to correct accent and pronunciation. This kind and able man offered to instruct Madame Stockhausen in the traditional method of singing in Handel's oratorios; without his aid her success in England must have remained doubtful. Sir George soon found that his gifted pupil profited by his teaching, and she became an indispensable support for the London as well as the great provincial music-festivals. Her fame steadily increased, but she continued as amiable and unpretending as before, and with all her grand performances in oratorios, condescended to charm her audiences with her light Swiss melodies.

We read in the diary, "We artists gave a dinner and musical entertainment to old Clementi. Cramer and I received him; he was greeted with rounds of applause, and ninety of us sat down with him to dinner. He was placed between Sir G. Smart and myself, and when the cloth was removed we had speeches, toasts, and music. Of course a wish was expressed and rapturously applauded, that Clementi, the father of pianoforte playing, should be heard on this occasion, and thus prove his right to the title. Clementi rose from his chair; Smart, Cramer, and I led him to the instrument. The excitement was great, the whole party eagerly listening. Clementi had not been heard for years. He extemporized on a theme from Handel, and completely carried us away by his fine playing. His eyes gleamed with youthful fire; those of many of his hearers were dimmed with tears of emotion. Amid shouts of applause, and the heartiest congratulations, he resumed his seat.

"Clementi's pianoforte playing, when he was young, was famed for the exquisite legato, pearliness of touch in rapid passages, and unerring certainty of execution. Even now the remains of these qualities were recognized and admired, but what chiefly delighted his audience was the charm and freshness of his modulations in improvisation."

On the day of the dinner given to Clementi, Moscheles writes: "I can only jot down a few words in addition to my wife's letter, before our great dinner comes off, as ten stiff fingers are waiting in the next room for me to make them flexible; they are like thirsty mill-wheels waiting for a fresh flow of water.

"Hummel wished to publish his 'New Pianoforte School' in England, and I negotiated the matter for him, although I saw the wreck of his scheme in his demand of 150*l.*, the publisher refusing to give more than 100*l.*

"During this season 'Oberon' was frequently given at Covent Garden, and also Mozart's 'Seraglio,' not, however, the pure unadulterated Mozart music, such as we Germans know, but with whole numbers cut out, and other popular English melodies substituted. A fearful desecration! The culprit who has this Pasticcio on his conscience is Kramer, of Brighton, director of the King's band. As a compensation for this musical outrage, we had some rich and often amazingly beautiful scenic effects."

Moscheles played before the Court circle assembled at the Duchess of Kent's in Kensington Palace. "The little Princess Victoria was present, and the Duchess begged me to play *at once*, so that the Princess, who was obliged to go to bed early, might hear me. She left the room after my second piece. I had to play a great deal (on a Broadwood), and accompanied the Duchess in a song of Beethoven's, besides a duet from 'Zelmira,' sung by her Royal Highness and the Princess Feodora. The Royal party took a very friendly interest in my performances, but what I think pleased them more than all was my improvisation on some of the Tyrolese Melodies, for the Duchess had twice commanded the attendance of the Rainers at the palace."

Extracts from Mrs. Moscheles' letters will show that her husband's time was socially and professionally a busy one: "Happily such a day as that of Monday last is a rare occurrence in my poor husband's life, busy as it always is. First came the inevitable nine lessons, then the dinner of the Royal Society of Musicians, where he played, and to wind up, an evening party at Sir Richard Jackson's, which lasted until two A. M."

This was the first season that Heinrich Heine appeared in London. During his residence in Hamburg, he was on intimate terms with Mrs. Moscheles' family, and since those days had become distantly related. It would have been strange if, in such a commercial centre as Hamburg, Heine's genius had been instantly recognized, and, as a fact, no one suspected it in the youth who, often absorbed in thought, was always satirical, and more than averse to the routine of "business" in a rich uncle's office, though it might prove the surest passport to the income of a millionaire. But a poet he was, and a poet he would be. Consequently all he retained of his mercantile studies was a horror of business, and a singularly beautiful handwriting.

So far from agreeable were his recollections of Hamburg that when, in 1830, Mrs. Moscheles asked him to write in her album, he treated her to a satire on her native town, which we here give in the original, and an English version of the same :—

Dass ich bequem verbluten kann,
Gebt mir ein weites edles Feld!
O lasst mich nicht ersticken hier,
In dieser engen Kramerwelt!

Sie essen gut, sie trinken gut,
Erfreu'n sich ihres Maulwurfsglücks;
Und ihre Grossmuth ist so gross,
Als wie das Loch der Armenbüchs'.

Cigarren tragen sie im Maul,
Und in der Hosentach' die Händ',
Auch die Verdauungskraft ist gut—
Wer sie nur selbst verdauen könnt!

O, dass ich grosse Laster säh',
Verbrechen blutig, colossal—
Nur diese satte Tugend nicht,
Und zahlungsfähige Moral!

Ihr Wolken droben, nehmt mich mit,
Gleichviel, nach welchem fernen Ort—
Nach Lappland oder Afrika,
Und sei's nach Pommern, immer fort!

O nehmt mich mit!—Sie hören nicht—
Die Wolken droben sind so klug!
Vorrüberreisend dieser Stadt
Ængstlich beschleun' gen sie den Flug.

H. Heine.

TRANSLATION.

I crave an ampler worthier sphere:
  I'd liefer bleed at every vein,
Than stifle mid these hucksters here
  These lying slaves of paltry gain.

They eat, they drink; they're every whit
  As happy as their type the mole,
Large are their bounties, as the slit
  Through which they drop the poor man's dole.

Cigar in mouth they go their way
  And hands in pockets, they are blest
With grand digestions—only *they*
  Are such hard morsels to digest!

The hand that's red with some dark deed,
  Some giant crime, were white as wool,
Compared with these sleek saints whose creed
  Is paying all their debts in full.

Ye clouds that sail to far off lands,
  Oh, waft me to what clime ye will,
To Lapland's snows, to Libya's sands,
  To the world's end—but onward still!

Take me, O clouds! they ne'er look down:
  But proof of a discerning mind,
One moment hang o'er Hamburg town,
  The next they've left it leagues behind.

After the publication of his "Reisebilder," he made many enemies; some persons, of whose identity with characters portrayed in that work there could be no doubt, smarted under the merciless lash of the poet, and would have retaliated on him if they could, while lookers-on at a distance chuckled with delight at the biting satire. Heine's prose was acknowledged to be that of a master. His originality of thought, striking imagery, terseness and vigorous language, contrasted wonderfully with the involved periods of some of his contemporaries. His great reputation had reached England before his arrival, and naturally his appearance in London created a sensation.

Mrs. Moscheles writes: "My old Hamburg acquaintance, the famous Heinrich Heine, is here. We delight in seeing him. He often invites himself to dinner, and I flatter myself that he feels quite at home with us. His genius and writings are a constant source of delight to me, yet I can't help feeling some slight misgiving, knowing as I do the keenness of his satire. At his very first visit we had a very curious conversation. I scarcely know how I came to muster courage, but when he told me of all the lions he wanted to see, I said, 'I can get you tickets of admission to numbers of private galleries and other sights, and shall consider it an honor to do so, but I must stipulate for one thing in return. This is that you will not mention Moscheles by name in the book you are no doubt going to write about England. He was completely taken by surprise, and I gave additional reasons. Moscheles' specialty is music; this, I know, interests you—but you have no thorough knowledge of it as an art, and consequently cannot fully enter into it. On the other hand, you can easily find in Moscheles a subject for your satirical vein, and introduce him in your work; I should not like that.' He laughed, or rather simpered, in his peculiar way, and then we shook hands over our bargain."

Again Mrs. Moscheles writes: "Heine took a walk with us in Grosvenor Square, the key of which had been lent us; he was very facetious on the number of chimney-pots, which are certainly bewildering to a gaping foreigner. Two days ago he came here, wet through, for a change of clothes. I sent him into my husband's dressing-room.

He sent back the things shortly before he left England, with the following note:—

"My dear Mr. Moscheles,—On the point of starting, I bid you heartily farewell, and take the opportunity of thanking you for the sympathy and kindness you both have shown me: I am sorry I did not find Mrs. Moscheles at home the day before yesterday. You, Mr. Moscheles, were 'engaged;' and I did not like to have you called away. I am just packing my trunk, and at last return your property, thinking it a good joke to ask for my boots, as well as the second volume of the 'Reisebilder,' left as a deposit in your dressing-room. If I possibly can I will pay you another visit, if only to assure you by word of mouth that I highly, very highly esteem and love you both.

"Your devoted,

"H. Heine.

"32, Craven Street, Strand,
July, 1827."

Carl Klingemenn, the gifted poet, and friend of Mendelssohn, who arrived in London this year, as Secretary to the Hanoverian embassy, became, after the lapse of a few weeks, a constant visitor and intimate friend of the Moscheles. His delightful verses, which Mendelssohn set to music, are well known. He was not only welcome to the Moscheles as a man of letters, but his vocal gifts and musical talent gave exceptional value to his criticism of musical compositions. In later years family ties helped to strengthen the sincere friendship which had arisen between the two families. During this season, Oury, an admirable violinist, gave Chamber Concerts; De Bériot and Cramer were shining lights, and Camillo Sivori, a boy of nine years of age, Paganini's pupil, appeared on the musical horizon. "Truly a prodigy for power, purity of tone, and execution." On one occasion, when the Hamburg relatives are invited to London, Moscheles writes:—

"We have plenty of room for you both; should you find it too narrow, there is plenty more in our hearts. Besides, you ought to see my boy clambering about me, and chattering an obligato accompaniment to my letter."

Shortly after the arrival of the guests, Moscheles rejoices at the birth of a first daughter, and a few months after, we find the whole family travelling to Scotland, Moscheles fulfilling, as he went along, professional engagements in several of the great northern towns.

# CHAPTER XI.

## 1828.

Edinburgh—Curious Architecture—Sir Walter Scott—A Delightful Visit—Highlanders and the Bagpipes—Scott's Appreciation of German Literature—Contribution to Moscheles' Album—Scotch Church Service—Visits to the Lions of Edinburgh—Spurzheim the Phrenologist—Life of a Musician in London—Mademoiselle Sontag—Peter Pixis—Fete at Vauxhall—Scott and the Prima Donna—Mademoiselle Mars.

EDINBURGH, 3d January.—Yesterday's walk through the streets was a series of surprises. As I looked at the old houses, consisting in some instances of sixteen stories, inhabited by the poorest families, renting single rooms, each with its dimly lighted window, I seemed to look at a feeble attempt at illumination. Standing on the viaduct which connects the Old and New Town, I had these old houses to my left, on the right, the handsome Princes Street, and the whole of the new quarter, now in the process of building, which is to consist of a number of crescents, squares, and streets, filled with palatial houses, built of freestone. Such buildings are to be seen elsewhere, but Princes Street is certainly unique in its way; there is a long row of houses on one side, intersected by sloping streets, from which you get a view of the Frith of Forth, while the opposite side opens to your view Edinburgh Castle on its rock, to which you ascend by a terrace garden. As I was taking my evening stroll, I saw a party of Highlanders, kilt and all, coming off guard. They marched down from the Castle and passed close by me, regaling my ears with genuine Scottish music of drum and fife.

"Our lodgings in Frederick Street, which were taken for us beforehand, were curious specimens of architecture. One peculiarity consisted in a raised ground-floor, that ran under the neighboring house, but disconnected with any staircase leading to the upper stories. The next house to that, on the contrary, had no rooms on the ground-floor, and the visitor, after mounting a staircase, found a bell, which secured his admission to the first story. House-doors and steps were quite open; many other houses were constructed on this curious principle."

The success of this winter expedition, undertaken by Moscheles for professional purposes, was seriously imperiled by an Italian Opera Company which had forestalled him, and he was obliged to put up with a third-rate orchestra, got together any how from regimental bandsmen; the Highlanders, with their bare legs and kilts, being the poor substitutes for a well-trained orchestra.

The concert room was only two-thirds full, but Moscheles, in his fantasia, the "Anticipations of Scotland," created great enthusiasm; and the newspapers, one and all, condemned the apathy shown by this poor attendance at his concert. This appeal to the good sense of the Edinburgh folk had its effect, for the two next concerts were filled to overflowing.

The Moscheles', on the occasion of this visit to Edinburgh, made the acquaintance of Sir Walter Scott, in whom the reading world had discovered "the Great Unknown," and to whose intellectual eminence thousands upon thousands looked up with feelings of the deepest gratitude and homage. The sickliness and sentimentality characteristic of the romance writers before the days of Scott, it is true, were avoided by Miss Austin, Miss Edgeworth, and some few others, who found materials for their fictions in the episodes of private life, but Scott was the first to introduce characters of real historical interest, and clothe them with flesh and blood.

The world in those days knew nothing of the stimulants supplied wholesale by Eugene Sue, Alexandre Dumas, etc., and revelled in the simplicity, picturesqueness, and wholesome truths conveyed in the fictions of the "Great Wizard of the North."

To the delight of Moscheles, Sir Walter sent an immediate answer to his letter of recommendation, saying that, being confined to his house with an attack of gout, he hoped Moscheles and his wife would come to breakfast, instead of waiting for him to visit them.

Next morning, at 10 A. M., they called at No. 6, Shandwick Place, where the illustrious man was staying for the winter, with his second, and unmarried, daughter. "He opened the door himself," says Moscheles, "and welcomed us heartily: he was suffering from gout, and walked with a stick. Before we had taken off our things we felt completely at home, and my wife's anticipated awe of the great man had entirely vanished. We sat down to breakfast forthwith, and a genuine good Scotch breakfast we had, served on handsome silver plate, by two servants in powder and livery. Scott's conversation was extremely animated and delightful: he understands German, and is thoroughly versed in our literature, and an enthusiastic worshipper of Goethe. He told us many anecdotes, but when he asked me, 'How do you like my cousin the piper?—you know, we Scotch are all cousins'—I am afraid my answer must have done violence to his sense of music, which by nature, was very limited. It was impossible for me to pretend to any enthusiasm for the bagpipes. Sir Walter had expected as much, but expatiated on the wonderful effect the national music has on the native Highlanders, arguing that a wandering piper would attract crowds in the streets of Edinburgh; also, that in battle the sound of bagpipes would inspire Scotch soldiers with a desperate valor. 'You should hear my cousin the piper play and sing "The Pibroch o' Donald Dhu," but with the Gaelic words,' said he; 'those words are the only appropriate ones to convey spirit and animation, but the melody itself carries one away.' He began to hum the tune, and beat time on the carpet with his stick, which was always by his side; 'but,' added he, 'the whole thing is wrong; I sing so badly: my cousin, who has just come in, must play the tune for us up stairs in the drawing-room.' Accordingly, we went up stairs; the cousin played me the subject; I extemporized upon it, and completely won the heart of our ever-youthful-minded and genial host. This was the prelude to my playing several Scotch airs, which I had to vary and interweave in all manner of ways. At last we parted, after a delightful visit, ever memorable to us; the amiability and sweetness of Scott's manner are never to be forgotten. Kindness, indeed, is written in every feature, and speaks in every word that falls from him. He treated my wife like a pet daughter, kissed her on the cheek when we went away, and promised he would come and see the children, and bring them a book. This he did, and his gift was the 'Tales of a Grandfather.' He had written in the title-page, 'To Adolphus and Emily Moscheles, from the Grandfather.'

"After our visit, Sir Walter was unfortunately confined to his bed with a fresh attack of gout; he got better, however, and on the occasion of my third concert, which was a matinée, to the surprise of a crowded and fashionable audience, Sir Walter stepped into the room before the music began. My wife," says Moscheles, "sat as usual in a remote corner of the room; Scott, however, found her out instantly, and sat down by her side, drawing upon her the envious eyes of many a fair beholder. His hearty bravoes and cheers, when I played, stimulated the audience to redouble their applause, which reached a climax when I gave them the Scotch airs. Between the parts he asked my wife if she knew Bürger's poem 'Der Dichter liebt den guten Wein,' and, on her answering in the affirmative, he told her how he delighted in this poem, which he had translated into English, adding, 'Would you like to have it? I shall send it you.' She begged him to recite the song in the original; this, to my wife's great delight, he willingly assented to, while all around listened eagerly. On the following day, the last before we left Edinburgh, Mrs. Moscheles received the following note:—

"My dear Mrs. Moscheles,—As you are determined to have me murder the pretty song twice, first by repeating it in bad German, and then by turning it into little better English, I send the promised version.

"My best wishes attend your journey, and with best compliments to Mr. Moscheles,

"I am truly and respectfully yours,

"Walter Scott.

"The day before we left Edinburgh we were amused to see our kind friend sitting in the Court of Justice, with a wilderness of official papers before him."

Moscheles sent Sir Walter his album, with the request

that he would contribute to its pages. Finding the following poem by Grillparzer, he translated it :—

Tonkunst dich preis' ich vor Allen
Höchstes Loos ist dir gefallen,
Aus der Schwesterkünste drei,
Du die *frei'ste*, einzig frei.

Denn das Wort, es lasst sich fangen,
Deuten lässt sich die Gestalt;
Unter Ketten, Riegeln, Stangen
Halt sie menschliche Gewalt.

Aber du sprichst höh're Sprachen,
Die kein Häscherchor versteht,
Ungreifbar durch ihre Wachen
Gehst du, wie ein Cherub geht.

Darum preis' ich dich vor Allen
In so ängstlich schwerer Zeit;
Höchstes Loos ist Dir gefallen,
Dir, und wer sich dir geweiht.

This outburst of the poet, groaning under the censorship of Austria, and gagged in every generous effort for the emancipation of his countrymen, must have touched Scott's sympathies. A few hours afterwards he sent back the album, with the following translation of Grillparzer's poem, headed with these words, "I am afraid Mr. Grillparzer's verses, and Mr. Moscheles' valuable album, are only disgraced by the following rude attempt at translation:"—

Of the nine the loveliest three
Are painting, music, poetry,
But thou art freest of the free,
Matchless muse of harmony.

Gags can stop the poet's tongue,
Chains on painters' arms are flung,
Fetter, bolts, and dungeon tower
O'er pen and pencil have their power.

But music speaks a loftier tone,
To tyrant and to spy unknown;
And free as angels walk with men,
Can pass unscathed the jailor's ken.

Then hail thee, freest of the free!
'Mid times of wrong and tyranny:
Music, the proudest lot is thine,
And those who bend at music's shrine.

This translation, evidencing Scott's accurate knowledge of the German language, Moscheles prized as one of the gems of his album.

The poet and the musician parted, Moscheles promising to find a London publisher for some pretty songs set to music by a Miss Browne, with words by her sister, Felicia Hemans. Scott, on his part, engaged to pay an early visit to the Moscheles. The music was published, and the visit paid.

Moscheles observes upon Edinburgh: "The church service, from which the organ is banished, struck me as peculiar. The Psalms are intoned by a four-part choir, in which the congregation joins. But the basses are usually in unison with the sopranos, instead of forming the support of the other voices. Dr. Thomson's sermon was very good in itself, but the nasal twang and Scotch accent coupled with the vehement gesticulation of the preacher, made it more singular than elevating. The Scotch Sunday, I must say, is wearisome to a degree. Twice or three times at church, more prayers at home, or sitting twirling one's thumbs; no music, no work, no visiting—a perfect blank. I have had to endure all this. It's a difficult matter to steal quietly off to one's own room and write letters, or clandestinely to read books of a secular kind. If I didn't do this I should not survive. The deep snow this winter only allowed us to take short walks or drives about the city; here is a description of one.

"To-day we visited Calton Hill, and had a glorious view. On one side the blue line of sea, on the other Holyrood House; above us the rock of Arthur's Seat, on which Nelson's monument stands. It is an unwieldy mass, and seems too heavy for the rock. We could hardly keep our balance here from the violence of the wind. We drove to Roslyn Castle and Salisbury Craigs, but the weather was so cold we could not enjoy ourselves. Holyrood House is very interesting; the arrangement of the rooms is the same as in the days of Mary Stuart; the bed-hangings and furniture, as well as coverlets and tapestry, worked by the unfortunate Queen, have turned yellow from age. Time has left its stamp on everything. Still, no one standing in these rooms can fail to think with sympathy of the fair—possibly guilty—but ill-fated Queen. There are to be seen Darnley's armor, boots, and gloves; the small window out of which the infant James I. was handed, because his royal mother, weak and helpless, was under arrest in this little room; and last of all, the hidden side door, near the Queen's boudoir and bedroom, which leads to an underground passage. When the Queen was surprised by her husband, while she was with her favorite Rizzio, the unfortunate musician, it is said, was repeatedly stabbed with daggers, and dragged to the door leading to an outer passage, where darks stains are seen on the floor. We looked at these incredulously, and treated them as mythical; but to vouch for their genuineness, or rather of the poet's belief in it, Mr. Ballantyne, Scott's friend, and the printer of his entire works, showed us a note which, as the testimony of the poet, is certainly of some weight. 'I have no doubt,' says he, 'of Rizzio's blood being genuine. I will look at the plan of the place; but I think I am right.'

"Another day we were shown the High Court of Justice crowded with Scotch advocates in their wigs and gowns. The din was fearful; but the judges contrived to follow the speeches of the opposing counsel, although the mere effort of listening in the midst of such a buzz seemed a mystery to me. I stood close to Mr. Murray—one of the greatest advocates in Scotland. He was in the act of speaking, but every word was drowned by the noise, and escaped me. I could see his mouth moving, and his hands raised; that was all. If the listening to the legal arguments of counsel be such a difficulty, I asked myself, what must be the task of the judges in forming an opinion, or delivering a judgment? Flights of steps behind the Court of Justice lead to a perfect labyrinth of small courts, lanes, and odd corners. Passing by these back-stairs, and through these tortuous passages, one thinks of poor Effie Deans, and for the first time begins to realize the feasibility of her seducer's escape."

Among the numerous acquaintances made by Moscheles in Edinburgh, was that of Sir John and Lady Sinclair. He also called on the great phrenologist Spurzheim, and, wishing to test his powers, gave no name, but requested him to examine his skull. Spurzheim merely uttered a few unmeaning common-places, such as a "disposition for fine art," and the like; afterwards, however, on hearing the name of

Moscheles, he explained in a learned manner, how nature had stamped him for a musician. Spurzheim gave a public lecture on the anatomy of the human brain, and Moscheles and his wife were present.

During the whole time of his stay in Edinburgh, Moscheles was obliged to give lessons, in spite of the almost prohibitory fee of two guineas an hour. "Some ladies," he says, "are bent on galloping through my compositions with me at their side, no matter how difficult the music is, or how short the time." But he was soon weary of all this. I shall be off as fast as I can," he writes, "and be proof against the numerous offers they make me; I can't be plagued with endless concerts." He was true to his word, and was soon back in London.

The "dead time of the year" is supposed to commence when the season is over; but to a busy professional man in London, all months are full of life. During February Moscheles was much occupied. April, May, and June were crowded with engagements, there was leisure in July and August for him to ask himself why he had not been crushed by the weight of private and public business which had pressed so heavily on him, why the avalanche of nine hours' lessons per diem did not sink him at once and forever, and how he managed to survive at all. He had to keep up his social position, too, to give and attend parties, to keep late hours incessantly, and play at his own and others' concerts; always remembering that his reputation—perhaps his livelihood—depended on his playing up to a standard very difficult to maintain when the artist is jaded and worn. Coming home in the small hours of the night, he would find a heap of business letters, calling for an immediate answer, before he could retire to rest. Happy the man who, after three-and twenty years of such a life, does not feel utter prostration. The real talisman against it is in a happy, cheerful home, and in a total surrender of professional business during the autumn months. Let him enjoy country air, in lieu of heated rooms and the gas of theatres; salt waves instead of deluges of lessons, and the privacy of home for the rush of society. This is well enough in theory: it is a difficult matter to reduce to practice. There are tempting invitations for a professor to make a Continental tour, and lucrative offers from the managers of provincial festivals in England. Every watering-place has its quantum of fashionables, glad to find a musical celebrity for teaching their daughters or playing at their parties. If an artist is not firm as a rock against these varied solicitations, he will carry London with him, as the snail does her house, and come back from the country to re-open the campaign: his pockets full of money, but his body and soul unrefreshed. If, on the other hand, he will exorcise for awhile the spirit of money-getting, his muse will commune with him in his solitary walks, and, so far from forsaking him, remain his steady friend.

When Moscheles returned from Scotland in February, he found a letter from his friend Peter Pixis, who wished to spend the next season in London, as Sontag's accompanist. This lady was engaged at the Italian Opera, and Pixis was to act as her secretary and entrepreneur as well. She came to London on the 3d of April, and was a constant visitor at Moscheles' house, where her beauty and fascinating gifts were a source of delight to her friends. Her simplicity was her great charm. "Sitting with her," says Moscheles, "at our homely dinner, we entirely forgot the famous prima donna whose début all London is awaiting with the greatest eagerness.

"She sang to us repeatedly in private, and with her splendid voice and gifts gave us a foretaste of that delight and fascination which was to keep her public audience spell-bound." "To-day," says Moscheles, "I was present at the dress rehearsal of the 'Barbiere,' she enchanted every one with her Rosina. When the lovely girl appeared on the balcony, she was applauded to the echo, and the magic of her voice and style captivated us in the opening air 'Una voce poco fà.' Her representations in London were a continued series of triumphs. The pressure in the pit of the Opera House was so great that gentlemen, by the time they found their seats, were minus coat-tails, and the ladies lost their head-dresses. We used to witness the rush from Mademoiselle Sontag's own box, which was always at our service." "I can't say," says Moscheles, "which of her characters I consider the most successful, for her vocalization is always enchanting; if I feel the absence of grand dramatic effect, I am more than compensated by the beauty, natural grace, and the combined charm of her voice and person. Her variations on the 'Schweizerbue' are absolutely perfect in their own way, and it never occurs to me to ask myself "How can she sing such trash?' because she sings it so perfectly."

"April 6th.—Making arrangements for my own and Sontag's first concert. That wonderful creature brought Pixis to dine with us. In the evening we had some friends who were in ecstasy at hearing the German Nightingale."

"April 8th.—At a grand dinner given in Sontag's honor, by Prince Esterhazy, Prince and Princess Polignac, Baron Bulow, Count Redern, the Marquis of Hertford, Lord and Lady Ellenborough, Lady Fitzroy Somerset, Countess St. Antonio, etc. etc., were present. Sontag sang exquisitely in the evening. Pixis and I played solos and duets."

"No success is without its alloy, for some captious newspaper scribbler volunteered to inform the world that Sontag was unfit for the position of prima donna; her success soon gave a contradiction to this libel."

On the 4th of May we read in the diary, "Busy with a musical work which brought back some painful recollections. I wrote for Willis, the publisher, an accompaniment to Weber's last composition—an English song, which he had written for Miss Stephens,* who had sung it at his last concert. Only the vocal part, and a few bars of the accompaniment, were sketched in his manuscript. I filled in what was wanting, carefully distinguishing my own writing from that of the composer, by using red ink."

On various occasions this summer, the Moscheles, Pixis, and other German friends and acquaintance of Sontag, joined her in short excursions, as to Epsom races, Chiswick, etc. The prima donna was in great request socially. The Duke of Devonshire danced with her at his own ball, where her beauty and grace made a great sensation.

The director of the Italian Opera had determined to allow his artists the privilege of engaging singers only on condition that the concert should be held in the hall adjoining the theatre; he also stipulated for a share of the re-

* The present Dowager Countess of Essex.

ceipts. Pixis consented to this arrangement, and gave a concert, where Sontag sang and Moscheles played.

"July 8th.—To-day we attended a fashionable fête at Vauxhall, given on behalf of the poor Spanish and Italian refugees. The 'Battle of Waterloo' was performed, and the Duke saw himself admirably represented. The evening concluded with a concert, in which both Pasta and Sontag sang."

"July 19th.—Velluti's shrieks in the opera were absolutely unendurable; his false intonation drove me wild. I may be severe upon him, but the wounds he inflicted were hardly to be cured by the flute-like voice of Sontag."

"On one occasion (we quote Mrs. Moscheles' letter) we had the happiness of entertaining the famous Sontag at a large party at our own house—she was enchanting as usual. Sir Walter Scott, who happened to be in London, was present. He was delighted at meeting Sontag, whose introduction to Sir Walter, on the eve of her appearing in the 'Donna del Lago,' was singularly well-timed. Lockhart, it is true, tells us in his biography that Sir Walter felt annoyed at being besieged by a crowd of flatterers and strangers, who made a pilgrimage to Abbotsford, and overwhelmed him with compliments, their knowledge of his works being based possibly on a single attendance at the 'Donna del Lago,' at the Italian Opera; but in the presence of Sontag, the great man was all ears, and eyes too, I think. When she questioned him about her costume as the Lady of the Lake, he described to her with the utmost minuteness every fold of the plaid, and was greatly pleased when I produced a genuine satin clan plaid, the present of Lady Sinclair, while in Edinburgh, the loan of which I was delighted to promise to Sontag. He showed her the particular way the brooch should be fastened at the shoulder, and would not allow any alteration. Henrietta had two worshippers that evening, the second being Clementi, who seemed as much fascinated as Scott. He got up from his chair and said 'To-night I should like to play also.' The proposition was received with acclamation." "He extemporized with all the freshness of youth," writes Moscheles, "and we listened with intense delight, for Clementi very rarely played before company. You should have seen the ecstasy of the two old men, Scott and Clementi; they shook each other by the hand, took it in turns to flirt with Sontag, without seeming jealous of one another; it was a pretty duet of joint admiration, of course the poet, musician, and songstress were the observed of all observers."

On the 24th of July Sontag finished gloriously at the Opera, with the "Amenaïde."

Moscheles composed, during the season, for Cramer and his niece, a four-hand Rondo in E flat, "La Belle Union," performed at the annual benefit concert of "Glorious John." He also wrote his G major sonata for pianoforte and flute. "I launched forth," he says, "my 'Gems à la Sontag,' and it was immediately caught hold of by my numerous pupils, and afterwards by the whole tribe of would-be pianists, attracted by my close imitation of the roulades and cadenzas of the illustrious Sontag."

That delightful concert-singer Madame Stockhausen was, in this her second London season, a recognized favorite with the English public. She had now become completely mistress of the language, and was constantly heard in Handel's oratorios. The famous Mars, old in years, young in appearance and performance, still delighted every one with her acting. "None that saw her in the part of Valérie, or in the 'Ecole des Vieillards,' can ever forget her."

"To-day a strange episode varied my daily duty of lesson-giving," writes Moscheles; "I appeared in a small court, among a wretched crowd of men and women who were sued for small debts. I myself figured as defendant, having (as it was said) refused to pay for an advertisement of my own concert. Of course the loss of time was more serious to me than paying at once the sum demanded, but I hate being cheated. I took up the matter more earnestly than the plaintiff reckoned on, but he was non-suited, as he could not even prove that he belonged to the newspaper which he pretended to represent."

Moscheles and his family passed the month of September very pleasantly at Hastings, and composed there a light piece written to order—"Strains of the Scotch Bards;" giving it some importance afterwards by a dedication to Sir Walter Scott, whose answer, upon being requested to accept it, ran thus:—

"My dear Sir,—I regret that my absence upon short journeys from home should have caused your obliging proposal to inscribe the music of 'Donald Dhu' to me to remain some time unanswered. Believe me, I feel obliged by the proposal, and will accept it with great pleasure. Tell my fair friend, Mrs. Moscheles, that I send my best compliments, and beg to retain a place in her recollection; and when you see the fine old gentleman Mr. Clementi, will you oblige me by remembering me to him?

"I am always, dear Sir,

"Your obliged humble servant,

"Walter Scott.

"Abbotsford, Melrose, October 18."

On his return to London, Moscheles began to write his long-meditated Symphony in C, which he finished about the end of November. Mathews and Yates had taken a lease of the Adelphi Theatre. "Mathews," says Moscheles, "who is an immense favorite with the English public, delighted us with his inimitable comic acting. The last piece—'London and Paris'—with the steamer crossing the Channel, was now and then rather too spicy, but we nearly died with laughing.

Moscheles plays at a concert in Brighton, but again complains of a wretched orchestra.

In London, besides private teaching, he was frequently engaged as pianoforte instructor at the Royal Academy of Music, and attended the pupils' concerts in the Hanover Square Rooms.

We read again: "Erard presented me to-day with a grand concert piano, of the value of 160 guineas. I certainly owe him my best thanks for such a present. Externally the instrument is all that can be wished for; but the tone of the higher notes is somewhat dry, and I find the touch still too heavy. My Clementi, therefore, still remains my favorite, although Erard's instruments have begun steadily to make their way. Madame de Rothschild, now that she has heard my Erard, wants to invest in one."

Moscheles kept his Christmas in the good old German fashion; for we find allusions to the Christmas tree—so suggestive of absent friends and home associations.

# CHAPTER XII.

## 1829.

Moscheles' Productions—Fugitive Pieces—Expense of Private Concerts—Domestic Sorrows—Visit of Felix Mendelssohn-Bartholdy—The Chevalier Neukomm—A Cinque-cento of Vocalists—De Bériot—"Troubadours" and "Bohemian Brothers"—Artists' Concerts—Power of the Italian Opera—Laporte—Handel's "Acis and Galatea"—Visit to Hamburg—Reminiscences of a Tour in Denmark and Sweden.

IN reading musical biographies, we often meet with elaborate dissertations on the works of composers, with an abstruse analysis of the writer's "intentions." If we look for a parallel in the history of letters, we find the commentators of Shakespeare ascribing to him intentions which do more credit to their ingenuity than to their judgment. Beethoven's works have undergone a similar ordeal. The great man wrote down simply what he thought and felt; but since his death critics, in their fancied wisdom, have interpreted his works in all manner of ways. Of course the sentiment expressed in the "Moonlight Sonata" affects most minds alike; the "Eroica" is always majestic, but such sonatas as "Les Adieux," "L'Absence et le Retour," are open to different reading, according to the feelings of the executant, and will make a different impression upon each individual listener. "And so it should be," Mendelssohn used to say; "if the composer can only move the imaginative power of his hearers, and call forth some one image, some one thought—it matters not what—he has attained his object." In accordance with this view we purposely abstain from attempting a critical analysis of Moscheles' compositions. Whatever their merits or defects, this is certain—that works which when first published made an impression, and are now listened to with delight and interest after a lapse of from thirty to forty and fifty years, must possess more than ephemeral value. Such compositions are to be found in the G minor concerto (1820), the "Twenty-four Studies" (1825 and 1826), the "Hommage à Handel," the Rondo in A, the E flat major Sonata, the Sonata Mélancolique," the "Recollections of Ireland," the three Allegri di Bravura, "La Force," "La Légèreté", "Le Caprice," and others.

From about the year 1840 Moscheles' appearances in public were less frequent than formerly. His later concertos (in C major, the fantastique, pathétique, and pastorale) did not become so popular as his earlier compositions, the proper readings of which he himself made known to the public. He used frequently to complain that people only played his G minor concerto, the other seven being noways inferior in his estimation. He would have desired that his twelve grand characteristic studies, intended for practiced artists, able to master their difficulties, should all have been played in turn, without exclusive preference being given to the "Nursery Tale." Of these twelve studies, he thought the "Dream," "Terpsichore," and others more especially adapted to the concert-room.

As to the light fugitive pieces which publishers from time to time demanded of him, he says: "They are my poor-box; with what they fetch I can support many a poor devil in Germany who writes well and is ill-paid. I have raised the price to thirty guineas apiece, so that I may not be molested too frequently with such orders."

We see the rate of remuneration current in those days, by the following account of payments made to artists for private concerts. Moscheles writes, "I had the management of Madame de Rothschild's concerts, and paid on her account the following sums:—Madame Stockhausen, 35*l.* for two evenings; M. de Bériot, 5*l.* for one; M. Mori (violin-player), 7*l.* for one; Mlle. Pisaroni, 20*l.* for one; Schütz and wife, 15*l.* for one; De Begnis, 25*l.* for two; myself 40*l.* for two; making in all 167*l.*,—a pretty little sum according to our German notions."

In January Moscheles, when playing at a concert in Bath, says: "Certainly I thought myself so much out of practice that I doubted my success; the public, however, thought otherwise."

In the early spring of this year, Moscheles is deeply

moved by domestic sorrow and anxiety. His eldest boy died on the 23d of March, and the only remaining child was in delicate health all winter. "The poor mother," he says in his diary, "knows nothing but anxiety, sorrow, and sleepless nights. One of our darlings is in his grave; with God's help she will be spared her one remaining treasure. As a man I have a load of sorrow to bear, as an artist I belong to the public." Moscheles was spared the fresh sorrow that at one time seemed so imminent. Change of air and scene worked so beneficially on the child's health, that as early as June the parents were free from all anxiety, and able to enjoy the society of artistic friends who visited London in this year, and were carried off by Moscheles to spend their Sundays with him in the country. During this season Malibran reappeared, Pisaroni also was engaged at the Italian Opera, and Sontag earned fresh laurels; but by far the most delightful and interesting visit of all was that of a young friend from Berlin—no other than Felix Mendelssohn-Bartholdy, at that time a youth of nineteen years of age. "Felix's father," says Moscheles, "had asked me in a letter if I thought, and believed, and counselled that his son should visit London, bringing some of his compositions with him, among them the Midsummer Night's Dream Overture. Well, I thought and believed that the young man was a genius, so I counselled that he should come to us at Easter, and I promised with all my heart to introduce him to the great London world."

Further on we read—"I took for him a lodging in 203, Portland Street, and I have enjoyed the purest happiness in his friendly and musical intercourse. As a friend, he is of untold value; cheerful, yet full of sympathy with us in our recent loss, and our anxiety for the frail treasure still left to us; he is always ready to exchange the attractions of London for our rural solitude, where his society acts like healing balm on our wounded spirits. He seems to have set himself the task of compensating us for our sufferings. How delightful it is, when he brings some of his new compositions, and after playing them, waits with childlike modesty for an expression of my opinion. Any other would long since have become aware that in him I recognize my own master, and that I am in raptures where he is expecting to be sharply criticised. Do what I will to give him a correct view and appreciation of our relative positions he always insists on subordinating himself to me as his teacher. The brilliant reception given to the public performance of his Midsummer Night's Dream Overture did not dazzle him. 'I must do better in everything,' was his motto; and to my praises he merely answered: 'Do *you* like it? Well, I am glad of that.' He showed me the manuscript of his sacred cantata on a chorale in A minor; an unpublished chorus in sixteen parts, 'Hora est;' and a stringed quartet in A minor. He was always fond of bending his genius to the composition of little pieces—vocal or instrumental—as presents to his friends." In Moscheles' album, for instance, he wrote a charming piece, entitled "Perpetuum Mobile" (in C major); and another day brought the pretty Miss C— an English ballad, written expressly for her, etc. etc.

At the same time with Mendelssohn there appeared in England the Chevalier Neukomm, Haydn's pupil, a noble-minded and highly cultivated man, and the most loyal of friends; but, unfortunately, without artistic genius; he was merely a solid, well-intentioned, and correct composer, "with a pitiful lack of Attic salt," says Moscheles. His oratorios, the "Ten Commandments" and "Christ," were performed, and he had written some effective things, such as the "Midnight Review," for the favorite singers Braham and Phillips. At first these pieces roused the audience to enthusiasm; but in the long run they failed to obtain for the composer the lasting recognition of an English public, which is, generally speaking, faithful in its devotion to artists.

Mendelssohn and Neukomm, who often met in the quiet home of Moscheles, became very friendly; their mutual appreciation, however, being confined to the social virtues of one another; for Neukomm, a tame musician, found, by force of contrast, his friend Mendelssohn too impetuous, noisy, and lavish in the use of wind-instruments, too exaggerated in his Tempi, too restless in his playing; whereas Mendelssohn would turn on his heel, exclaiming in a fit of youthful impatience, "If only that excellent man Neukomm would write better music! He speaks so ably, his language and letters are so choice, and yet his music—how commonplace!"

Fétis, and his lectures upon music, were equally distasteful to Mendelssohn. "What is the good of talking so much about it?" he says; "it is better to write well; that is the chief matter. What is the good of this embodiment of 'la musique mise à la portée de tout le monde,' lectured on in French to an English audience, who certainly understand only half of the technical expressions; and perhaps do not realize for the lecturer one-half of the receipts he expects?" Fétis at this time joined Moscheles in sketching the plan for the "Méthode des Méthodes," in the joint publication of which, Fétis's skill as a linguist was of the greatest service to Moscheles, as he translated into excellent French his friend's musical treatise on the study and higher branches of pianoforte playing.

In the world of vocalists there was an "absolute cinquecento," to quote Moscheles' own words, "for besides Malibran, Sontag, and Pisaroni, we have Madame Stockhausen, Camporese, Velluti, Donzelli, and other singers. In addition to these, a German opera company, under Schütz, he and his wife are excellent singers." Sontag, always kind and charitable, gave a "concert monstre" on the 13th of July, for the benefit of the sufferers by the inundation in Silesia, and every one lent a helping hand. Mendelssohn's "Overture to a Midsummer Night's Dream" was given for the second time, and more vehemently applauded than before. His double Concerto, too, in E major (manuscript), which Moscheles played with him, was a great success. The receipts amounted to 500*l.*

The favorite violinist of this season, beyond all question, was De Bériot—then at the very zenith of his power. His latest composition, the B minor Concerto, written after his marriage to the unrivalled Malibran, and possibly with her aid, was more interesting than his former bravura pieces. With regard to pianoforte players, the most important of the new-comers was Madame Dulcken, the highly-gifted and distinguished sister of Concert-meister Ferdinand David. She left Hamburg to settle in London, and was welcomed by all genuine artists and connoisseurs.

The "one-shilling" performances were represented by

the so-called "troubadours" and "Bohemian brothers," the former French, the latter village musicians from Bohemia. These performers, common-place as they were, reaped a plentiful harvest for their employers, Messrs. Bochsa and Logan.

"We artists fare worse," says Moscheles, in noticing these exhibitions; "we look to something more than mere gain, regarding our concerts as the means of producing our newest works before large musical audiences, and subjecting them, year after year, to the ordeal of criticism at the hands of competent judges. The speculation of Laporte, the Opera Director, places a great stumbling-block in our way."

The state of things was this. Those artists who had annual concerts were anxious to let their patrons hear the best dramatic singers, and accordingly often engaged them with a view of enhancing the attractions of their programme.

Laporte, who had become in 1828 the lessee of Her Majesty's Theatre, was peremptory in his dealings with concert-givers, his dictum being: "Hire my opera concert-hall, or you must do without my singers," and the high price he put upon this arrangement made the acceptance a very difficult matter. The pill of course was sugared over with many honeyed French conversational terms and phrases, but Bochsa, the "manager's manager," knew how to translate them into good English, while negotiating with Moscheles behind the scenes during the opera performance—the only time one was tolerably sure of meeting with these gentlemen. Moscheles had several novelties ready for his concert, a Symphony, a Fantasia, "Strains of the Scotch Bards," which, from being dedicated to Sir Walter Scott, was sure to excite great interest; "and yet," he says, "I was obliged, like the rest of us, to have Italian singers, and to experience all the endless worry of negotiating their costly services; I hired Laporte's concert-room at great expense—not only this, I had to offer the owner of the Argyll Rooms, which I had already engaged, a forfeit of 10*l.* This he contemptuously refused, and threatened me with a lawsuit; I always had a wholesome dread of lawsuits, and so I consulted a legal friend, who at last persuaded the man to accept the 10*l*." Laporte knew his advantages only too well; he was master of the position, virtually monopolizing the services of Malibran and Sontag, the idols of the public. Indeed, the power of the Italian Opera was such that none of the national theatres could compete with it.

We read on the 22d of June:—"One of the choicest entertainments this season was the dramatized representation of Handel's 'Acis and Galatea,' performed at Bochsa's concert; the music allotted to the chief characters was admirably sung by Miss Paton and Braham; Zuccheli, with a gigantic eye in the middle of his forehead, was a very good Polyphemus. In spite of his Italian name, he is an Englishman by birth, and, loyal to his Handelian traditions, gave every word and note of that master's music in the classical and orthodox manner. What else had we? Next in order after Handel's music, the Grave-scene from 'Romeo and Giulietta,' exquisitely sung in Italian, by Sontag and Malibran, and for a finale, that German trifle the 'Pastoral Symphony;' but that I missed, for an overdose of music is not good for the health."

On the 31st of July, when the Moscheles were free to embark from England for Hamburg, he exclaims: "Who so happy as we?—we leave the chronic miseries of concerts and the whole season behind us, and join our friends and relations, among whom, if sorrow for our recent loss be reawakened, we shall find comfort and sympathy." Moscheles during this holiday planned several sketches for his later compositions.

Pressing offers were made to Moscheles to give concerts, but he refused them as being foreign to the purpose of his visit to Hamburg. The German theatre, however, now that he and his wife had become half Anglicized, offered much that was novel and attractive; and they were enchanted with Auber's "Stumme von Portici," the cast including Cornet and the younger Fräulein Schröder, the sister of Devrient.

Moscheles travelled alone to Copenhagen; and we insert some passages from letters written to his wife during his two months' absence.

"Schleswig, Sept. 27, 1829. The entire road hither is extremely like the Lüneburger heath. At times the carriage was all but upset, but I should only have landed on the sand. I have wandered through Schleswig, which in length and narrowness is only to be compared to miles of German sausages. Ahlefeld, the Kammerherr, was very friendly, but to give a concert here, and realize from sixty to seventy thalers, would be a ridiculous waste of time. So the horses are put to, and I shall drive on to Flensburg."

On the 29th of September he crosses the Little Belt, but, no steamer being ready, is forced to pass a long dull day (30th) at Nyborg. On the 2d of October he passes the Great Belt, and after a night's journey reaches Copenhagen. After describing his delight with the beauties of the place and its art treasures, he observes : "I heard for the first time Weyse, the musical theorist, and a perfect idol here, play an extempore fugue upon the organ in the Frauen Kirche. When it was over, I went home with him, and read several of his interesting works. I also made the acquaintance of Kuhlau, the clever composer. Both these artists amuse themselves by constructing musical canons in the shape of riddles, and by finding their solution. At a party given by Mr. W., I met not only these two men, but also the poet Oehlenschläger, and all the connoisseurs and art critics of the place. Kuhlau and others played, and then came my solo. When urged to improvise, I begged to hear Weyse, who could not be prevailed upon, so to the piano I went, and found myself, as it were, fenced in by a wall of listeners, who were silent as death, while I was collecting my thoughts ; I would try to be learned as Kuhlau and Weyse, interesting in harmony, plaintive and sentimental, and I would wind up with a storm of bravura passages. I must have succeeded, for the burst of applause was unisono, and the astonishment on the faces of all was such as neither you nor I have ever witnessed. Old Professor Schall fell on my neck and kissed me ('for shame!' the English would say). Kuhlau and Weyse besieged me till I gasped for breath. For shame ! I say to myself, to be blowing my own trumpet in this way ; but for whom am I writing ? This success promises well for my concert ; but another fortnight must elapse before that can come off ; a second or a third is out of the question. I might have to wait till 1830. It can't be done !

"I had to play before the Court; and here I give you the programme and all particulars. . . . . When my solo and duet with Guillou were finished, and I was asked to improvise, the old Queen came up, and making a thousand excuses, hoping she would not be in the way, etc., sat by my side at the piano, where she was soon joined by the King. I let myself go like a race-horse—fire, passion, even coquettishness—I tried everything to act on the royal nerves. First of all, I Rossinified a little, for I knew that the Rossini fever rages at the Court here. Then I was a Dane, and worked up some national melodies. The shouts of applause made me desperately confident, and I wound up with the Danish 'God save the King' ('Kong Christian'). When I had finished—I leave you to imagine the rest, only it certainly was a novelty to see a King running about among the musical veterans present, to express his astonishment and hear them confirm it."

The next letter is from Helsingborg, on the way to Gothenburg, where Moscheles, instead of waiting at Copenhagen, wishes to give a concert. "The passage from Copenhagen to Elsinore took six and a half hours, and three-quarters of an hour in the afternoon to cross the Sound. Here I was advised to hire a carriage, and a compound of coachman and servant, styled a 'Husar,' for the journey to Gothenburg. 'Glücklicher Prinz,' I can call myself as usual, for I have the most lovely weather."

From Gothenburg he writes: "The day before yesterday, after despatching my few lines from Helsingborg, I had a very successful although fatiguing journey. My hired carriage, as they called it, was nothing more than a small seat, attached to a four-wheel car. My box and portmanteau I had between my legs. I was knocked and thumped about most unmercifully. I could not make out a word my talkative Husar said, but I could converse all the more freely with lovely nature, glorious in every climate and under every zone; here on the shores of the Cattegat displaying an endless variety of romantic rocky scenery, interspersed with noble forests. Generally speaking, the roads were good; a notice sent on twelve hours before insured us fresh relays of horses, but, alas! we got the start at Kungsbacka, and found out to our dismay that we had in consequence two hours to wait. The comforts of the hostelry consisted of a sort of measly-looking buscuit, and a tallow candle, at which I lighted my cigar, then on we went again in the dark and rainy night. A halt at eleven o'clock, but not at Gothenburg, merely to fetch an extra horse, as we had a stiff mountain pass before us. At one o'clock, however, the welcome light greeted us from the lantern at the Gothenburg Custom House, more welcome than the police search I had to submit to on alighting. After tremendous knocking at 'Blone's Hus,' we aroused a servant girl from her slumbers, but although my bed had been ordered beforehand, all I could get was a room on the topmost story, where my head touched the ceiling. To my question whether I could not have an empty room on the first story, I was answered by a Swedish shrug of the shoulders, which was Greek to me. I had a fire lit in my garret, allowed the dense smoke to fill it, wrapped myself up in my furs, and went to bed. My bad temper vanished at the thought of you. Th. Hell's poem 'Macht der Frauen' (Woman's Power), which I lighted on accidentally, expressed sympathetically my own thoughts. This morning I got the identical rooms I saw last night, they had been bespoken for me. My concert is advertised and arranged for the 27th, three days hence, and immediately afterwards I go back to Copenhagen. I am incessantly occupied with calculations about the Danish and Swedish postal arrangements, to see that our correspondence may not be interrupted. In a foreign town like this, I always mount the ramparts, from which I can command a view over the town: how awfully grand these precipices and torn fragments of rock around the harbor, and actually in it! The winding river 'Gôta-Elf' reminded me of our Elbe, and I was no longer alone. . . . The city has spacious streets and squares, one of which really reminds one of the Linden. The weather is clear and beautiful."

He goes on to tell of two great families, who in all musical matters are the despots of the place, and of course rivals. "One has a Clementi piano, and the other a Graf. Which shall I choose for my concert? That is 'the burning question,' and I answer it by playing on both. Before the concert I attended a real Swedish dinner. The host, a regular character, a fit subject for Hogarth, did the honors at his large dinner party in the queerest fashion, as you will see. First, I must tell you that, before the company sat down, schnaps and herring were relished by gentlemen, standing at a side table, only three glasses being allowed for twenty-five people. We had veal, pike and soup to begin with, then roast goose, plum-pudding, and splendid fruit for dessert. My 'original' is a stumpy man, over sixty years of age, with sparkling eyes peering out from under his greyish-brown wig, his upper teeth gone, four under teeth remaining as a sort of palisade to his enormous, pendent, moist under-lip. He starts every topic of conversation, entirely regardless of all the notabilities present, while his wife must have signed a silence-clause in her marriage contract. Herr S. was so full of the great event of seeing Professor Moscheles in Gothenburg, and beneath his own roof, that he continued to shower down praises on the Professor in the most ridiculous style. He too has travelled in foreign parts, there to learn (or unlearn) manners—his wanderings are á la Wilhelm Meister, he is as sentimental as Sterne; he has been in England, and feels bound to toast 'the Professor.' I give you a slight sample, as faithfully as I can, of his rigmarole nonsensical speech: 'Gentlemen, would it be bold, may I with some confidence use my privilege as master of the house, and make a speech? Heaven defend that I enjoy the honor and the chance—you, my honored friends, who know me as a plain honest man to speak—the chance, do I say? What is chance? Gothenburg enjoys the honor, etc.' Here followed the most silly compliments to myself, and then again, 'Heaven defend, without trenching too near on the modesty of this man—all admiration set apart—will, no doubt, make a lasting impression. Long may he live, the master of music in the kingdom of the beautiful.' You can imagine my state of mind on hearing such a farrago of nonsense; I had to bite my tongue to prevent myself from laughing. The Governor, the Rath, the Commandant of the place, and the other guests, did not seem at all surprised; they must know him. When he had finished his speech, a part song was performed by one amateur, 'the refrain,' suggested by the occasion, always being the words: 'Es lebe der Meister.' There was a jingling of glasses as I rose from my chair to return thanks, but hardly had I said that it was no accident that brought me there, but a wish on my part to be heard by the art-loving public in Gothenburg, when Herr S. cut me short by modestly interrupting me with : 'Heaven defend that the Professor thinks that I think that accident (for everything in the world is accident) has given us, not him, the happiness of seeing a man in our walls whose modesty—Heaven defend—I should offend.' More trash followed. Then the ladies left us, and the gentlemen remained sitting round an enormus bowl of cold bishop. Our host's silly tongue never stopped wagging. Songs were sung, they did not much edify me ; as far as I could I remained a passive spectator. After leaving the spacious dining-hall, we passed through several elegant salons, to a room where the Clementi piano stood, and I was obliged to extemporize. This I did in a way to humor the particular kind of audience; and you may easily guess the result. Schwartz, the pianoforte teacher, and Birnroth, organist of the Cathedral, proposed that I should play on the organ. This I did the following afternoon, in the presence of the same company. I dashed into it, and worked away at the pedals as though I had Vestris's feet.

"My concert was attended by every one with any real or fancied taste or ear for music, so that I had a brilliant and crowded audience. You will see the programme in the newspaper. In obedience to a challenge from the company, I improvised on Swedish airs, which were given to me in writing. I think I must have been pretty successful, for they cheered me lustily, and flocked round me on all sides. All invitations after the concert I firmly refused, for I want to get back as fast as I can. . . . To-night, in spite of all my hurry, I must remain in Helsingborg, where I am writing to you. I have sent you a short extract from my last letter by another and shorter route than usual, that I may insure your hearing from me."

Moscheles would not go to Stockholm, although he had half promised to play there ; travelling alone was not at all to his taste. From Copenhagen he afterwards writes: "I can't think of a second concert here, as it would cost a whole fortnight of my time ; consequently there is a great rush to secure seats at my one public performance.

"I have seen the favorite Liederspiel 'Elverhoy' (founded on an old Danish fable, with characteristic songs and choruses) and most tastefully arranged by Kuhlau. The overture, which is a compendium of all the music that follows, pleased me exceedingly. I have again paid a two hours' visit to Weyse, for I think him the most interesting person here; he entertained me with learned dissertations on art, considered technically and æsthetically. His fugues are good, his enigma canons really masterly. To-morrow he comes to me, and we shall frequently exchange visits."

On the 10th of November he writes from Copenhagen: "Yesterday was a memorable day in my calendar. I was literally besieged from eight o'clock in the morning until six in the evening. People scrambled to get the most expensive boxes, and almost went on their knees for single tickets; many had to pocket their money again, for no more tickets were to be had, and I advertised to-day that no money would be taken at the doors. Everything has been sold at double prices; the result is a net profit of 1500 thalers. Notwithstanding I should lose too much time were I to give a second concert, as Guillou and Milder are fighting for the only possible nights. They both gave their first concerts at the usual prices and had a good attendance. What can I say about my reception? Nothing; you can guess what it was like. Well, the applause grew louder and louder. In spite of my own disloyalty towards the Alexander Variations, I was obliged to play them, as you will see by the programme herein enclosed; and the Improvisation—well, on that subject I cannot write. Guillou, who was going to give his second concert at the usual prices, offered me to join him, and we would have double prices. It only made three days difference to me, so I accepted the offer. Well, these three days, we can bear like the rest, can't we? The concert is announced in G.'s name, with my assistance."

Later on he writes: "The same scene enacted at my last concert has now repeated itself, and that too directly the first announcement appeared. Everything again sold off at double prices; 641 thalers came to my share. Besides this, I shall turn snuff-taker, for His Majesty honored me with the present of a gold enamelled box. Prince

Christian sent me a diamond ring: Frau —— a gold watch-chain; I had besides all sorts of complimentary messages from the Court."

The month of December was spent in Hamburg, and at the close of the year we find Moscheles in Paris.

## CHAPTER XIII.

### 1830—1831.

An Accident—Hummel—Madame Malibran—Music in England—Failure of Beethoven's Ninth Symphony—Erard's Pianos—Henry Litolff—Neukomm—Philharmonic Concerts—First Railway Journey—Operatic Celebrities—Field's Return to London—Paganini—Prodigies from the Continent—Visits of Intimate Friends—The Reform Agitation—A Musical Festival—Celebration of Christmas.

AFTER the first six weeks, spent happily in Paris, the family returned to London. There Moscheles met with an accident. He was thrown from his carriage, but, however serious the accident at first appeared, fears of any permanent injury happily proved groundless. Scarcely was his wife relieved from anxiety on his account, when her serious illness (after the birth of a second daughter) weighed heavily on his mind for nearly three months. No wonder that in the diary there is a comparative scantiness of musical incident, when measured by the richer harvest of former years.

"Hummel is here, he intends giving a concert, and happily I can distribute many of his tickets among my pupils. I wish I could have talked him over, and prevented his appending so curious a notice to his advertisement; it was to this effect; 'People were not to suppose he would play at the Philharmonic Concert; only in case a very profitable engagement were offered him, could he be heard anywhere except at his own concert.' He hoped by this announcement to undeceive the frequenters of the Philharmonic who might reckon on hearing him there, without going to his own concert. A few days later, at Malibran's matinée, he made a mistake, in improvising on 'God save the King,' for while George IV. was still lying dead and unburied, people hardly thought of William IV. For this he was taken to task by the public and the press, and, generally speaking, he added nothing to the well-deserved laurels he had gathered in Vienna. It was noticeable that he began to dislike trouble and exertion, for he possessed no longer the elasticity requisite for plunging successfully into the whirl and maze of London life; besides that, England, proud of Cramer, discovered that his legato was equal to Hummel's, and preferred native to foreign talent. Hummel, annoyed possibly at seeing this view adopted by many of the newspapers, refused when asked by Cramer to play a duet with him at his concert, and this refusal created an unpleasant feeling against him. At that time Malibran's genius and sad fate attracted the liveliest sympathy. Married in very early years to a husband who had been forced upon her, but liberated afterwards by special favor of the Pope, she had clung to De Bériot with true devotion, and now appeared in London as his wife; but, in this marriage also, hers was the unselfish, self-sacrificing, part; for out of affection for her husband she not only sang in the opera, but, after the fatigues of performance at the theatre, appeared at private or public concerts, "and," says Moscheles, "she always sings exquisitely, and with true inspiration; she is never the mere vocalist, but a musical genius. If obliged to repeat a cavatina, as is generally the case, she improvises new passages more beautiful and original than the first, unsurpassable as they seemed. Her very smile captivates the orchestra and conductor, and she kindles with a spark of her own spirit the most inanimate of orchestral players. Of this fire she has such a quantity in reserve, that she can scatter it about without harm to herself. Some of her lightnings she has darted upon De Bériot's smooth, finished, but occasionally lukewarm performance, and I plainly enough see Madame in Monsieur's 'B minor Concerto.'"

In a season so beset with domestic anxieties, Moscheles could think of no serious original compositions, but was obliged in pursuance of a contract to finish some of his light fashionable pieces, such as the "Gems à la Malibran;" a light pot-pourri of her most popular songs, written in the closest possible imitation of her original 'fioriture,' which Moscheles had committed to memory. On the eve of his own concert already advertised, and with a view of bringing out some novelty, he put together within a few days his "Recollections of Denmark," the echo of his travels in that country; and these national melodies lost none of their effect by the composer's treatment.

We find constant complaints this year about the condition of music. "It is a mistake to give at every Philharmonic Concert two symphonies and two overtures, besides two grand instrumental and four vocal pieces. I never can enjoy more than half." Another time we read: "Beethoven's Ninth Symphony failed! What am I to think of this? Must the fault be laid at the director's door? Are the orchestral players or the public to blame? I do not know; but things shall not remain so." And as a fact they did not remain so, for when the Directors, after this and another abortive attempt in the year 1824, determined never to produce the work again, persuading themselves into the belief that the deaf composer had written some senseless trash because he never heard it, the German press beat the alarm so furiously and lashed so mercilessly the depreciators of this colossal work, that the production and proper appreciation of it in England was made a point of honor. It took several years to convey to the English public the correct perception and appreciation of this Symphony, and later on we shall see that the Philharmonic Society turned to Moscheles for directing the study and rehearsals of the work, and making it accessible to the public. This once done, the Symphony maintained its place in the programmes of the Society.

Looking further on in the diary, we find the following notice:—"What musical follies are daily perpetrated, for one shilling a head, in the Egyptian Hall! Michael Boai, a German, who hits his chin with his fists, producing thereby sounds in which a tune is discernible and variations thereon, and an Englishman who pretends he can produce two tones at once by humming like a clarionet and muttering a bass tone simultaneously. What rubbish all this! Equally ineffective is a band of Russian horn-music, each member having a reed-pipe capable of producing but one note, which, in the performance of pieces, he brought in with unerring precision."

Important in the history of pianoforte-playing is the fact that Erard's pianos became very popular, having attained this year a great excellence. "The touch in particular is vastly improved, I begin to revel in these instruments."

When the season was over the family went to Ryde, in the Isle of Wight, the Revolution in Paris interfering with their intended visit to that city. "Charles X. set aside for Louis Philippe, and now an exile with his family at Castle Lulworth. What a change!" At Ryde, where Moscheles revelled in his Erard piano, he composed the "Recollections of England," which he dedicated to Queen Adelaide, and the C minor Trio, dedicated to Cherubini. In the latter half of the autumn Moscheles moved to 3, Chester Place, Regent's Park, where he lived for more than sixteen years, before he finally quitted England and settled in Leipzig. At one of the first parties given in his new house, the new Trio was played, with Lindley and Cramer, before many enthusiastic friends, and Moscheles' home henceforth became a place where artists were always welcome. With so kind a host—himself free from envy and jealousy—they could forget all rivalry and meet on neutral ground. In January of 1831, Moscheles made a short professional tour to the provinces (York, Leeds, Derby), where he labored to improve much that was defective in the condition of music.

We have seen how Moscheles, starting as a bravura player, gradually took broader views of his art both as a composer and player. His powers steadily matured, and this year we find in his compositions and execution a depth of feeling and expression in advance of former years; witness the adagio of his Concerto in C major, written about this time, and the new Trio, upon hearing which Hummel said that no modern pianoforte player but Moscheles could write such an adagio. It should, however, be stated here that this progress, although mainly originating with Moscheles himself, was greatly favored by the improvements made in Erard's pianos; their organ-like tone and full resonant sounds gave Moscheles such pleasure that no doubt he had every incentive to bring into relief these great excellences, and display them in his adagios. "A very violoncello," he used to say, praising the tone, which he could prolong without using the pedals; to the excessive use of these he had a rooted aversion. "A good player," he used to say, "must only rarely use the assistance of either pedal, otherwise he misuses it." Frequently he would listen to an excellent pianoforte player, praise him in many respects, adding, "I wish he had not his feet so perpetually upon the pedals. All effects now it seems must be produced by the feet—what is the good of people having hands? it is just as if a good rider wanted forever to use spurs."

Among his pupils of those days was Henry Litolff, then a boy of ten years of age, who was introduced to him by his friend Collard, as a poor, clever, but rather neglected child. Moscheles immediately recognized his talent. His father—an Alsatian, who with difficulty supported his large family by playing dance-music—was too poor to have a piano for his son Henry, who practiced in Collard's warehouse, and was so well prepared at every lesson that he delighted and surprised Moscheles with the playing of his Studies and Concertos.

The leading musical star on the dreary horizon of this winter's season in London was Neukomm. He had written for the impending Philharmonic Concerts a new Symphony in E flat major, which, according to Moscheles, was "lacking in Attic salt," and yet in the course of this year he was destined to achieve great popularity, which he owed to some extent to some spirited verses by Barry Cornwall. "David's Lament for Absalom," declaimed in deep tragic tones by Braham, and "The Sea," by Phillips, given with all the spirit due to a national song, were frequently items in the programme, but so powerful an impression was made by the "Midnight Review," that Moscheles was obliged to write a Fantasia upon it. This production, regarded by its author as a step-child, was called by his pupils "charming" and "delightful," and was played by many a fair lady. About this time Neukomm's more serious works were given, and his oratorio the "Ten Commandments" put into rehearsal for the musical festival at Derby in September, after having been given with the greatest applause by the Classical Harmonic Society in London. A performance of the work on a small scale was arranged at Moscheles' house, with Madame Stockhausen and Clara Novello for the solo singers. Moscheles, who appreciated the high musical cultivation and artistic aims of his friend, says of him: "I am sorry he writes such an inordinate quantity of music, and carries out the principle which he advocates: that one must be writing daily. What becomes then of inspiration, which alone shields one from vulgarity?" Neukomm's society was highly prized in Moscheles' household, where he went by the name of the "Encyclopædia;" for whoever wanted information on any subject was sure to get it from him.

In criticising the Philharmonic Concerts of this year Moscheles finds fault with the "conductor still sitting at the piano, and turning over the leaves of his score; without a bâton of course he has no influence over the band, which is under the sole command of the first violin—a process leading to constant unsteadiness in the performance of large orchestral works. In the programmes the most heterogeneous things are often huddled together, orchestral works alternating with chamber music; then again, we have the first part of Spohr's 'Last Judgment' and a miscellaneous second part by other composers. That doesn't suit a German ear; what would Spohr say to it?"

In February Moscheles, on a professional tour in the north of England, speaks of his first railway journey. "On the 18th I went by rail from Manchester to Liverpool; the fare was five shillings. At 1.30 I mounted one of the omnibuses, which carried all passengers gratis to the great building called the 'station.' Eight to ten carriages, each about as long as an omnibus, are joined closely to one another; each carriage contains twelve places with seats like comfortable arm-chairs; at a given signal every traveller takes his place, which is marked with the number of his ticket, and the railway guards lock the carriages. Then, and not before, the engine is attached to the foremost carriage; the motion, although one seems to fly, is hardly perceptible, and the traveller is amazed when he looks out of the window and observes at what incredible speed the train approaches the distant object and suddenly whirls by it. Words cannot describe the impression made on me by this steam excursion on the first railway made in England, and the transports I felt with an invention that seemed to me little short of magic. The famous engineer, Sir John Stephenson, has realized his project amid untold struggles and difficulties."

Coming back to London, he reports of his visit to the theatre. "A new opera by Pacini—'Pompeii;' the beautiful scenery is the only part I cared for, the horrors of the night of the city's destruction being represented in a masterly way."

Then again: "Saw Kean as Richard the Third; he makes one shiver in one's shoes, but rants too much—perhaps because he is too old, and yet determined to make his points."

He is enthusiastic on the subject of Pasta and her magnificent acting. "The voice, at first veiled, comes out triumphantly at a later stage, like the sun breaking through the mist.

"Lablache, with the grandest of all voices—the 'voce sul labbro'—his drollery, especially in the 'Barbiere,' and his deaf old man in the Matrimonio Segreto, can never be surpassed. Rubini, too, is exquisite; the ballet of 'Kenilworth,' representing the whole of Scott's romance, is beautifully put upon the stage. Taglioni, in every ballet in which she appears, is as ladylike as she is graceful, a danseuse quite unique and enslaving every one."

Moscheles says of Field, who after a twenty-five years' absence appeared once more in London: "His legato playing delights me, but his compositions are not at all to my taste; nothing can afford a more glaring contrast than a Field's 'Nocturne' and a Field's manners, which are often of the cynical order. There was such a commotion yesterday among the ladies, when at a party he drew from his pocket a miniature portrait of his wife, and loudly proclaimed the fact that she had been his pupil, and that he had only married her because she never paid for her lessons, and he knew she never would. He also bragged of going to sleep while giving lessons to the ladies of St. Petersburg, adding that they would often rouse him with the question, 'What does one pay twenty roubles an hour for, if you go to sleep?' He played to us a good deal in the evening;

the delicacy and elegance, as well as the beauty of his touch, are admirable, but he lacks spirit and accent, as well as light and shade, and has no depth of feeling."

At evening parties Moscheles had to endure a great deal of amateur music, and often played as a matter of self-protection, where otherwise he would have declined. On the other hand he never wearied of making music with his brother artists. At his annual concert, which was densely crowded, he introduced the "Recollections of Denmark," with their original northern melodies, and, for the first time on such an occasion, used an Erard in preference to a Clementi piano.

Paganini made his appearance in London, and public attention was concentrated on him. All sorts of scandalous stories about him had already circulated in England, as well as upon the Continent. He was supposed to have murdered his own wife, and during the years of his imprisonment to have taught himself upon the single G string which remained to his violin those "tours de force" with which he astonished foreigners first, and the English afterwards. Then his avarice was supposed to border on the fabulous, and his appearance reminded one of an apparition from the realm of ghosts.

Mr. Embden (Mrs. Moscheles' father), a great lover of music, had, previous to Paganini's visit to England, rendered him substantial service by securing him an engagement of a most lucrative kind, which but for such timely aid, he would never have succeeded in obtaining. "On his first visit to us, his gratitude found vent in such exaggerated expressions as are known only to an Italian vocabulary; we were the children of his 'onoratissimo, etc.,' and he took down from the mantelpiece a miniature portrait of his benefactor, covered it with kisses, and addressed it with the most high-flown epithets. Meantime, we had leisure to study those olive-tinted, sharply-defined features, the glowing eyes, the scanty but long black hair, and the thin, gaunt figure, upon which the clothes hung loosely, the deep sunken cheeks, and those long bony fingers. Our study and his deluge of compliments both well over, we began to discuss Paganini's plans, the first of which, that of playing at double prices in the Italian Opera House, had come to nothing, owing, it is said, to the opposition of the Duke of Devonshire. Suffice it to say that only two boxes were sold, and the concert had to be given up. This induced him to play in the Opera House at the usual prices." We read later on: "My assistance is of use to him here, and I am paid with quite as many honeyed epithets as my father-in-law received. This face of mine is as much kissed as my father-in-law's painted one. Paganini often comes to us. We receive him well, although I suspect he is rather too sweet to be genuine."

The impression made by Paganini at his first concert was overwhelming. "The crowd in the Opera House was wild with excitement. He had to play nearly everything twice over, and was not only greeted with vehement clapping of hands, but every lady leaned forward out of her box to wave her handkerchief at him; people in the pit stood up on the benches, shouting 'Hurrah! Bravo!' Neither Sontag nor Pasta made such an impression here, much less any other artist."

Moscheles complains in his diary of his utter inability to find language capable of conveying a description of Paganini's wonderful performance. "Had that long-drawn, soul-searching tone lost for a single second its balance, it would have lapsed into a discordant cat's-mew; but it never did so, and Paganini's tone was always his own, and unique of its kind. The thin strings of his instrument, on which alone it was possible to conjure forth those myriads of notes and trills and cadenzas, would have been fatal in the hands of any other violin player, but with him they were indispensable adjuncts, and lastly, his compositions were so ultra original, so completely in harmony with the weird and strange figure of the man, that, if wanting in depth and earnestness, the deficiency never betrayed itself during the author's dazzling display of power."

The fever of enthusiasm continued, and to enable Paganini to understand the rapturous phrases in the newspapers, Mrs. Moscheles translated them into Italian for him; these encomiums, high-flown as they were, were outdone by Paganini's own letters of gratitude. Paganini is frequently at friends' houses, where he plays both violin and tenor alternately in his own quartets. Mori commissions Moscheles to write for him a piece, "Gems à la Paganini," but takes the precaution of first securing Paganini's consent. A day and a half suffice to complete this composition, and then Mori and Moscheles go together to the wily Italian. Moscheles plays to him his "Musical Portrait," a piece written in close imitation of Paganini's roulades and cadenzas. Paganini falls on his neck and smothers him with compliments. "This wonderful imitation, this manner, this accurate rendering of his cadenzas, he found 'stupendous.'" At that moment of course there was but one Moscheles. What was Hummel in comparison? Hummel and others had also written Fantasias "à la Paganini," but they had displeased him; he had protested against them. This arrangement was the only right one, a real honor to him, etc. etc. He went on in this strain: but we shall see further on what amount of sincerity and truth lay beneath it.

Of course Moscheles heard him frequently, in order to study his manner and style more accurately. After the sixth concert he makes the following admission: "My mind is peculiarly vacillating about this artist. First of all, nothing could exceed my surprise and admiration; his constant and venturesome flights, his newly discovered source of flageolet tones, his gift of fusing and beautifying subjects of the most heterogeneous kind; all these phases of genius so completely bewildered my musical perceptions, that for several days afterwards my head seemed on fire and my brain reeled. I never wearied of the intense expression, soft and melting like that of an Italian singer, which he could draw from his violin, and dazzled as I was, I could not quarrel with him for adopting the 'maniera del gatto,' a term of opprobrium, showing how averse the Italians are to this style, which I dislike so intensely that I should only like to hear it once in every leap year. Suffice it to say, my admiration of this phenomenon, equally endowed by nature and art, was boundless. Now, however, after hearing him frequently, all this is changed; in every one of his compositions I discover *the same* effects, which betrays a poverty of invention; I also find both his style and manner of playing monotonous. His concertos are beautiful, and have even their grand moments; but they remind me of a brilliant firework on a summer's eve, one flash succeeding the other—

effective, admirable—but always the same. His 'Sonate Militaire,' and other pieces have a southern glow about them, but this hero of the violin cannot dispense with the roll of the drum; and completely as he may annihilate his less showy colleagues, I long for a little of Spohr's earnestness, Baillot's power, and even Mayseder's piquancy. It may possibly be that the man, who grows more and more 'antipatico' to me every day, prejudices my judgment of the artist. He is so disgracefully mean. I can't vouch for the truth of the story, that he gave his servant a gallery ticket on the condition of his serving him gratuitously for one day, but this at all events is certain, that Lablache offered him 100*l.* to play at his benefit, but Paganini refused, and the great singer had to allow him one-third of the receipts of his concert. When the Opera concerts, thirteen in number, ceased to command full attendances, he began a series in the London Tavern, in the City. This was thought unworthy of a great artist; but it was all one to him, for he makes money there."

The letter which supplies these extracts was written in July. A few weeks later, immediately after the publication of the second and the third book of the "Gems," Paganini made a legal protest, declaring the work a musical piracy. Of course this was a question concerning the publisher. Moscheles however went to Paganini and asked him: "Why, didn't you give me your permission?" Answer: "Yes, for the first book, but not for the second and the third." The conversation led to nothing; Paganini went to Scotland, and the lawsuit continued. On his return Paganini visited Moscheles, and, after a great deal of circumlocution, offered him the free sale of the three books of "Gems," if he would consent to make a pianoforte accompaniment for twelve small violin pieces of his own. Moscheles gave a rather unwilling consent; refusing, however, Paganini's further demand that he should put his name to the title-page. This point Paganini gave up, and then a discussion ensued about the law costs. At last Mori was glad to be moderately victimized, Paganini having at first talked about no less than 500*l.* damages, and Moscheles rejoiced "at being quit of an episode so little worthy of an artist, and having done with those dreadful lawyers."

This business over, Moscheles applied with fresh zest to his peaceful studies, but the following note proves how often they were interrupted. "All the would-be prodigies from the Continent visit me, and I have had such heaps of them lately, that I could almost fill an orchestra with the new arrivals."

On the other hand, he had the pleasure this year of seeing many intimate friends; Paul Mendelssohn (Felix's brother), Professor Fritz Rosen, and Klingemann. To these must be added the names of Professor Grahl, a portrait-painter, and a young phrenologist of the name of Holm, who was indebted to Neukomm for an introduction to Moscheles.

That fearful scourge, the Asiatic cholera, made Moscheles deeply anxious about his friends and relatives abroad, and we find him writing to them: "True, when thinking of you we have many an anxious hour, but my art, as well as my trust in God's mercy, must help us to tide over our anxiety." Fortunately none of his friends at Hamburg or Vienna were attacked.

The great political reform at that time agitating England is frequently alluded to in Moscheles's letters. It was after the rejection of the Reform Bill and the dissolution of Parliament that he happened to go to a ball in Camberwell. "The most interesting part of it was the driving there and back. You know, from the newspapers, that many people illuminated in honor of the dissolution. Many, however, refused to do so, and fared badly, for the mob smashed their windows. The whole way to Camberwell, seven English miles in length, nearly every house was illuminated, and many transparencies bore the most ludicrous inscriptions. 'The Bill! the whole Bill! and nothing but the Bill!' A patriotic butcher flaunted the following sentiment: 'The enemies of Reform, to be sent to the dominions of Don Miguel.' 'William the Restorer!' and 'William the Patriot King!' were to be read a hundred times over, but the owners of some houses obstinately refused to illuminate. The principal streets were besieged by an enormous crowd which stopped all traffic in the thoroughfares." At this period Moscheles seems to have been ubiquitous. He was present at the opening of the new London Bridge, and saw a splendid pageant upon the Thames. King and Queen, with Lord Mayor and, Aldermen in their mediæval dresses, servants and retinue, made up a picture of costume that took the spectator back to the days of the Tudors.

After a few quiet days at Richmond, Moscheles went to Derby, to attend a musical festival, where Neukomm's oratorio, "The Prophecy of Babylon," and his most popular songs were performed. "The mixture of sacred and secular music was rather too much for me, but I was compensated by hearing Handel's 'Messiah.' Among the singers were Madame Stockhausen, Miss Masson, and Phillips—always first-rate."

"Derby.—The Committee is hardly satisfied with the pecuniary results of the Festival, two hundred tickets at a guinea each, two hundred at twelve shillings, and two hundred at seven shillings, being all that were sold."

On Christmas Eve the Moscheles, after the good old German fashion, have their gorgeous Christmas tree, and Barry Cornwall and Neukomm add to the children's merriment—the former writing a poem, the latter setting it to music, with an obligato accompaniment of "Mirlitons." Judging by the encores, which were no less than five, the piece, with its chorus of sighs and the children's laughter, must have been a grand success.

# CHAPTER XIV.

## 1832.

Moscheles as an Orchestral Writer—Death of Clementi—German Opera in London—The Italian Opera—"Robert Le Diable"—Centenary of Haydn's Birth—The Elder Mathews—Pianists and Prime Donne—Literary and Artistic Friends—Mendelssohn's "Lieder Ohne Worte"—Art Congress—Anecdote of Schröder—Moscheles' Birthday—Paganini—Visit to Berlin—Intercourse with the Mendelssohns—Leipizg and Weimar—Souvenir of Goethe—At the Pavilion, Brighton—Beethoven's "Messe Solennelle."

WRITING about the Philharmonic Society, Moscheles says: "I had the honor of being made a Director, and I was elected, they tell me, without a single black ball; there are seven of us, however, six of whom agree in their views; they are the conservatives, while I alone advocate musical reform. Several matters are uncongenial to me—but I am out-voted. Grand orchestral works and quartet music are played at one and the same concert, third-rate singers are engaged; the antiquated Trio by Corelli is to be heard year after year, played by those old campaigners—F. Cramer, Lindley, and Dragonetti, radiant with complacent smiles and triumphant airs. Lindley, with his inevitable Cadenza, seems to lead up to a happy close, but it is only to return to his everlasting arpeggios and flageolet tones. It reminds me of the fly which will come back to the sugar on the plate. And yet this has its charms for a certain class of subscribers. No wonder they don't venture on Beethoven's last quartets.

Moscheles gave his new Symphony, and played his new C major Concerto. "I don't set much store," he says, "upon the praise bestowed on my new things, for this audience applauds even common-place music." The Symphony was repeated several times, but Moscheles (who was always a severe critic of his own playing and compositions) soon discovered his inferiority as an orchestral writer to many of his contemporaries, and acknowledged that his beloved Mendelssohn had already far outstripped him. The instrumentation of Moscheles' G minor Concerto, which to this very day is so effective, warranted people in expecting that the composer, who was very young at the time, would further distinguish himself as an orchestral writer, and the ballet "Les Deux Portraits," composed in his earliest days at Vienna, had won for him the favorable suffrage of competent art judges; but Moscheles, although he made some attempts later on in life, saw clearly that the piano was always his peculiar and legitimate field—that in composing for that instrument he could benefit and delight others. He therefore confined himself chiefly to pianoforte compositions, and not unfrequently introduced into these great orchestral effects. In the early part of this year Clementi died, at the age of eighty-four years, and was followed to his grave in Westminster Abbey by many of his brother-artists. The Philharmonic Society, wishing to honor his memory, gave a performance of Mozart's "Requiem," but that noble work was utterly out of place in the midst of all sorts of secular music. Cinti on the same evening created a "furore" with the cavatina from the "Barbiere," while no one seemed to understand Mendelssohn's "Hebrides Overture," which was coldly received. Here was a commemorative festival, which did no honor to Clementi nor to those who survived him!

The melodrama "Rob Roy"—founded on Walter Scott's romance—was successful, and at a time when the poet, alas! lay dangerously ill in a London hotel. Braham, in spite of his advanced years, was still admirable in "Fra Diavolo;" and the inimitable Mars as great as ever in the part of Valérie.

The German opera, with Schröder-Devrient, Haizinger, Hauser, etc., had a long run of unbroken successes. Schröder's Fidelio, always grand, need only be alluded to in these pages, which frequently record her triumphs. The charming artiste used to sing in Moscheles' house, to the delight of her host and hostess, and when they thanked her she would reply, "It's a pleasure, children, to sing to you; here I can do as I like, but oh! the horror of a stiff English soirée, where the ladies stare at me, and quiz my behavior."

The new director of the Italian Opera was Monk Mason. He had bought the score of "Robert le Diable" for England, but the pianoforte edition had only just been published when the English theatrical managers laid violent hands upon it, having it scored by English composers and sung by English singers. "I attended," says Moscheles, "one such mongrel representation, and found in that piece of patchwork, 'The Demon,' Meyerbeer's best intentions utterly destroyed; fine scenery and ignorant listeners could alone save this performance from complete failure. Drury Lane, in rivalry with Covent Garden, wanted to produce another version, and having better singers, partially succeeded; still there was no Meyerbeer in it."

On the 31st of March, the centenary of Haydn's birth was celebrated by a banquet, which is alluded to in the diary. "Ninety-two of us musical men attended the dinner; the ladies occupied the gallery. Barry Cornwall wrote a song in praise of the great musician, and Neukomm introduced into his commemorative ode a number of his old master's most beautiful airs. Field, Bohrer, and I played; we had choruses out of the 'Creation,' and the music was worthy of the occasion, but the endless toasts spoilt everything. Not only did we drink to the memory of the 'immortal Haydn,' but all musical celebrities, living and dead, absent and present, were toasted; the consequence was that some of the executants' fingers were rather heavy when it came to the second part of the music. We Germans on this occasion had clearly the best of it."

We again find allusions to formal and distasteful musical soirées; but on the other hand Moscheles speaks with delight of Mathews, the famous comedian, who at a private party improvised scenes illustrating the recent opening of the new London Bridge. "His changes of voice and exquisite drollery belonged to a high order of wit."

On the 14th of April we read: "Yesterday, the Reform Bill was passed, and to-day, at a dinner party, we heard interesting discussions on this subject; but, alas! a great musical soirée followed, attended by the whole Tory party, the Duke of Wellington at the head. One cannot play one's best in the presence of these great men, who concentrate all their attention upon an Italian prima donna; it doesn't matter whether I or any other artist plays the piano, they don't care about it; their applause on these occasions, I regard as an expression of delight that they have got rid of me. My wife and I sacrifice as short a time as possible to such soirées, and hurry home again, as soon as good manners will allow us."

In the quiet of his own home, Moscheles found his real element of happiness, brightened as it was by the faces of many dear and distinguished friends. More than one is still among us to remember that home where social intercourse and the cultivation of art for its own sake were so happily blended, and will recall to mind the image of Moscheles as he would alternately play, listen, or converse, or as he would sit correcting proof sheets, not only of his own works, but of those of friends who frequently delegated such duties to him.

Chorley, the well-known art-critic of the *Athenæum* who now settled in London, soon became intimate with the Moscheles' and was for many years their highly-esteemed, generous, and often indispensable friend. The respected authoress, Mrs. Bowdich Lee, whom Cuvier complimented as a first-rate naturalist, was not only a constant visitor at Chester Place, and a keen enthusiast for good music, but she took pleasure in instructing and amusing the children. We read in the diary of Meyerbeer's arrival, and of many interesting meetings with that amiable and gifted artist, who, as an old friend, soon felt himself at home under Moscheles' roof, but the crowning joy of all was the arrival of Mendelssohn, who, to the delight of Moscheles, appeared in London on the 23d of April. "We had been long expecting him, but a slight attack of cholera detained him in Paris. He now swam back to us islanders laden with his precious cargo of new compositions; now the glorious days return again."

To illustrate the great intimacy existing between Mendelssohn and Moscheles, we need only let the diary, the record, as it is, of an almost daily meeting of the two friends, speak for itself:—

On the 24th of April, the day after his arrival, Mendelssohn, after dinner, played to Moscheles for the first time his so-called "Instrumental Lieder für Clavier," now the famous "Lieder ohne Worte,"* and his "Capriccio in B minor;" "all his music breathes spirit and life; the Lieder are full of deep feeling and tenderness, and his 'Capriccio' is suited to the concert room. He was particularly pleased with the Adagio in my new C major Concerto."

"April 25th.—Mendelssohn, Klingemann, Meyerbeer, and Madame Schröder-Devrient dined with us. Felix and I played his Symphony; he made me repeat my Concerto, and Schröder delighted us with her singing."

"April 28th.—Rehearsal of the Philharmonic Concert, where a regular Art Congress assembled, including Mendelssohn, Lablache, Field, and J. B. Cramer; in the evening we joined Meyerbeer in his box at the Opera, and saw 'Il Barbiere' with Cinti and Lablache; it was a first-rate performance."

"April 30th.—To-day Mendelssohn played us his Cantata 'Die Erste Walpurgisnacht,' which I had heard and admired in former days in Berlin. Now that he has completely re-written it, I admire it still more. He also played me that charming Liederspiel, 'The Son and Stranger,' written for the silver wedding of his parents, and lastly his overture to the 'Hebrides.' My wife's invitation for this evening he answered in the following way, 'I thank Mr. Moscheles exceedingly for wishing to see something of my new compositions, and if he promises to tell me when he has had too much of me, I will bring a whole cab-load of manuscripts to your house, and play every one of you to sleep.'"

"May 1st (Sunday).—Mendelssohn and Klingemann came to the children's one o'clock dinner. The former gave me the score of his overture to the 'Hebrides,' which

* In the original MS. in my possession, the title-page, in Mendelssohn's handwriting shows that he first named these "Six Songs for the Pianoforte alone," which he corrected to "Melodies for the Pianoforte," composed by Felix Mendelssohn-Bartholdy. London: published (for the author) by Novello, 67, Frith Street, Soho. Bonn, by N. Simrock. Paris, by Maurice Schlesinger.—F. MOSCHELES.

he had finished in Rome on the 16th of December, 1830, but afterwards altered for publication. I often thought the first sketch of his compositions so beautiful and complete in form that I could not think any alteration advisable, and during our stroll in the Park we discussed this point again to-day. Mendelssohn, however, firmly adhered to his principle of revision."

Madame Moscheles writes:—"Our interesting guests at dinner were the Haizingers; he the admirable tenor singer of whom the German opera company here may well be proud, she pretty and agreeable as ever; we had too our great Schröder, and our still greater Mendelssohn. The conversation of course was animated, and the two ladies were in such spirits that they not only told anecdotes, but accompanied them with dramatic gestures. Schröder, when telling us 'how he drew his sword,' flourished her knife in a threatening manner towards Haizinger, and Mendelssohn whispered to me, 'I wonder what John (the footman) thinks of such un-English vivacity? To see the brandishing of knives, and not to know what it is all about! Only think!' . . . . .We had the most beautiful music in the evening, one artist surpassing the other."

"May 7th.—To-day with Mendelssohn at a dinner party, where he would not play, and Field was a poor substitute."

"May 8th.—A charming, homely evening with Mendelssohn and Klingemann; we cut a thousand jokes, while planning our programme for our evening party on the 10th of May."

"May 9th.—In Meyerbeer's box to see the first German representation in the Italian Opera-house. 'Der Freischütz,' was given, with Madame Méric, Maschinka, Schneider, Haizinger, and Hauser the chief singers, Chelard conductor, Everything went well; the public called for the singers repeatedly, and cheered them enthusiastically."

"May 10th.—Our grand soirée; we had a happy union of German and English music."

Between the 11th and 16th of May, the friends met every evening.

"May 18th.—First representation of 'Fidelio' for the début of Schröder-Devrient: she and Haizinger inimitable, and the public so enthusiastic during the whole evening that the 'Overture,' the 'Canon,' the 'Prisoners' Chorus,' and the whole 'Finale' were encored."

The following comic episode will perhaps be new to some of our readers:—"In that deeply tragic scene where Madame Schröder (Fidelio) has to give Haizinger (Florestan) a piece of bread which she has kept hidden for three days for him in the folds of her dress, he does not respond to the offer; she in rather strong language whispers to him, with a coarse epithet: 'Why don't you take it? Do you want it buttered?' All this time, the audience, ignorant of the by-play, was intent solely on the pathetic situation."

"May 20th.—Mendelssohn breakfasted with me, and we began the day with music, and afterwards strolled into the Park. In the evening Haizinger came, and I tried with him a new variation which he is to sing at my concert, in the 'Abschied des Troubadours.'"

"May 21st.—With Mendelssohn, at John Cramer's concert."

"May 24th.—Second representation of 'Fidelio,' if possible, finer than the first. But is it credible that the Directors made Lee, the able violoncello-player from Hamburg, play some variations after the opera was finished, and had an act of 'Otello' to wind up with? We could not stay out such a tasteless exhibition."

"May 25th.—After giving my inevitable nine lessons I was permitted to enjoy Mendelssohn's society at dinner. In the evening he played his charming 'Capriccio in B minor,' at Mori's concert."

"May 28th.—Rehearsed for my concert 'Mozart's Concerto for Two Pianos,' with Mendelssohn at Erard's. Felix dined with us, and in the evening we went together to the Philharmonic Concert: he won a genuine triumph by the performance of his new 'G minor Concerto.' Invention, form, instrumentation, and playing: everything gave me perfect satisfaction. The piece sparkles with genius."

"May 29th.—My wife had prepared a pleasant surprise for me. Mendelssohn and the German artists came to dine with us on the eve of my birthday. Madame Haizinger recited a Prologue by Klingemann, explaining that to-morrow being a busy day, they had anticipated the celebration. A packet was then handed to me, containing a sheet of paper on which Mendelssohn had transcribed a regular catalogue of the themes of my works, illustrating them with humorous drawings in the margin. I was, however, allowed no time to study the interesting present, for a four-part song broke in upon us; then Schrödes, the Haizingers, and Hause, sang a Canon by Mendelssohn, upon four lines of a stanza written for the occasion by Klingemann; the music founded on the motive of my 'C major Concerto.' It was a charming fête for me, as an artist and a man."

"May 30th.—Mendelssohn, Klingemann, and our mutual friend, Dr. Fritz Rosen, Professor of Sanscrit in the University of London, at dinner."

In the month of June we find Mendelssohn playing with Moscheles at his own concert, besides giving a masterly performance of fugues in St. Paul's Cathedral, and playing at the Philharmonic Concerts, where he is obliged to repeat, amid salvos of applause, the whole of his "G minor Concerto." "The quiet evenings," observes Moscheles, "when we chat and make music together, are incomparably delightful. To-day we went carefully through his pianoforte duet arrangement of the 'Midsummer Night's Dream;' this is just about to appear in print. The dinner party to-day at Sir George Smart's—the first since his marriage with the charming Miss Hope—was very agreeable; the music was worthy of the occasion."

Further on Moscheles writes: "Mendelssohn and I admire Horsley's glee 'Cold is Cadwallo's Tongue.' The death of the Celtic hero could not have been bewailed in more tragic tones than in this glee. . . . . Again we agree about Paganini; he has just returned to London and played in public, but no longer exercised the old charm over us. That eternal mawkishness becomes at last too much of a good thing."

On the 22d of June Mendelssohn comes to take leave. "We were in high spirits, talked in riddles; but when the parting moment came, it was a melancholy business."

As late as the 24th of June we still find Moscheles busy. "I slept for once up to eight o'clock. This morning I listened, as I was dressing, to little Litolff, who had come for his promised lesson. Then a hasty breakfast, but while

I was sipping my first cup of coffee, in came the Ladies B., who staid so long that I had to make up my mind to give Litolff his lesson in their presence. Next in turn was a Viennese pianist, who brought a Rondo, the chief feature of which was a 'Crescendo à la Rossini.' Close on his heels came the two Eichhorn boys, who had to wait while I saw the doctor. No sooner had he gone than I had the exquisite treat of hearing the boys play, and as a finale :—enter a musical friend, with an insatiable appetite for my performances."

The month of July, allowing for business "poco a poco decrescendo," differs very slightly from its predecessor, but the hour of release is at hand, and on the 14th of August Moscheles gets away for his quiet holiday-time with his relatives in Hamburg. His ideas of happiness consisted, as we know, in composing and playing; and this he did privately with the best artists of the town, publicly for charitable objects.

On the 4th of October the family went to Berlin to meet Moscheles' mother, who for the first time enjoyed the happiness of seeing her grandchildren.

Of course the great centre of attraction was Felix Mendelssohn, and the house of his parents. The father was Moscheles' confidential adviser in matters of business, and as to music, Moscheles says: "I practice daily on Felix's magnificent Erard, and he is going to lend it to me for the concert; we often extemporize together, each of us trying to dart quick as lightning on the suggestions inplied by each other's harmonies, and to construct others upon them. Then Felix, whenever I introduce any motive out of his own works, breaks in and cuts me short by playing a subject from one of my compositions, on which I retort, and then he, and so on *ad infinitum*. It's a sort of musical blindman's buff, where the blindfolded now and then run against each other's heads."

On the 11th of October Moscheles was present at a delightful performance of the "Walpurgis Night," given at the house of Felix's parents; the solos were performed by Mantius, the Devrients and Frau Thürschmidt. Beethoven's Polonaise and Moscheles' Sonata in E flat were played by him and Felix, and Mantius and Devrient sang from the

Liederspiel, "The Son and the Stranger." It was a charming evening. A similar party is alluded to on the 14th of October.

"Neukomm's arrival in Berlin was generally welcome. Felix and I heard his oratorio, the 'Ten Commandments' in the Academy, as well as the 'Crociato,' given for the first time on the birthday of the Crown Prince. Unfortunately the Crociato himself was quite hoarse, but Frau Kraus Wranitzky was excellent as Palmyra—the men nothing to speak of; choruses and scenery splendid." The Moscheles admired in the Exhibition just opened, 'Die Trauernden Juden,' a picture by Edward Bendemann, a youth of twenty-one years of age, whose great reputation dated from the production of this work.

Moscheles says again: "I enjoyed the privilege, but only once during my short stay in Berlin, of hearing Schleiermacher preach."

On the 17th of this month Moscheles' crowded concert was given at the Opera House. He says: "My third of the receipts amounts to 301 thalers net. Graf Redern, Intendant of the Royal Opera, met me in a very friendly manner, and the public so heartily applauded my C major Concerto, the Danish Fantasia, and an improvisation upon 'Che farò,' 'Voi che sapete,' and 'Namenlose Freude,' that I was in great delight, especially as my mother and my wife were both present at my triumph. Felix supped with us at 'Jagor's.' He was in high spirits."

On the following day, the last that Moscheles spent in Berlin, there was a matinée at Mendelssohn's. Felix played, with the violinist Ries, Beethoven's C minor Sonata, and Moscheles his Trio, the scherzo of which he was obliged to repeat. At dinner the whole family begged him to play once more at the Opera House, and Felix jumped up from table to ask Redern if a concert could be arranged by Sunday. The answer was that it could not be done before Wednesday, and this confirmed Moscheles in his resolve to leave Berlin immediately, but not before he got from Felix a promise, with reference to an expected event, that he would come to London and be sponsor to a child, which, if a boy, was to bear the name of Felix.

On arriving at Leipzig, Moscheles found two hundred

subscribers' names down for his concert; the instrument to be used was lent by Wieck, "whose dear little clever daughter played to me."

The arrival at Weimar, and a visit to Hummel, are next recorded, and Moscheles, speaking of a déjeuner at Frau von Goethe's, says: "There was plenty of titled people who made a great deal of me and my playing, but my wife and I thought sorrowfully of Goethe, the great genius of the place, who had died some months since. We were in his house, but were not even allowed to see his own rooms, as everything in them was still disarranged. Frau von Goethe gave us, as souvenirs, a few fac-similes of the great man's handwriting, the last medal that was struck of him, and a lock of his hair. The ladies of the court were of opinion that the Grand Duchess would keep Sunday disengaged for my concert; she was very gracious and well-disposed towards me. There was an obstacle however, for the Grand Duke had to receive two foreign ambassadors on that day; I played once before the Court, was treated with marked kindness, and presented with a diamond ring."

"October 26th.—Dined at Hummel's. We extemporized on the pianoforte, and delighted our audience. Hummel, however, I felt, was no Felix. We were soon in our travelling dress, and drove on to Erfurt."

On arriving at Frankfort, he writes: "Hofrath André, in Offenbach, showed me an unfinished Opera, by Mozart, 'Bettulia Liberata.' The printed Libretto shows that the composer, Gassman, wrote the music to it in 1786. André undertook to complete Mozart's work, and showed me the score of his overture. I played it, and think it has merit."

On the 7th of November Moscheles gives a successful concert at Frankfort, and after fulfilling an engagement at Cologne, hurries back to London. Once at Chester Place, he records in his diary his delight at finding himself home again, and the success of this winter campaign, adding: "To-day, the first after my return, I gave a lesson to a pupil who had been waiting many anxious weeks." On the 30th: "True to my habit of composing something new on my wife's birthday, I began, this year, not as hitherto, a mere trifle, but a Septet, which I am commissioned to write for the Philharmonic Society. It is to be their exclusive property for two years, after which I may publish it."

As he worked at the Septet steadily every evening, a royal command to play before the Court at Brighton was an unwelcome interruption, but being assured by a friend that he would play immediately after his arrival, he started on the evening of the 11th of December.

"All alone in the Brighton coach with Goethe's 'Götz' as my companion. Arrived at two o'clock, gave my letter, but didn't meet a soul. Great crowds in the street on account of the impending elections. The two candidates paraded the streets with bands of music and the shouts of their partisans. Theatre deserted, empty and cold, the farce of 'Harvest Home' was a dreary ballet, but Mr. and Mrs. Keeley in 'Master's Rival' were excellent."

"December 12th.—Matters did not go as smoothly as I had been led to anticipate, and from the difficulty I had in procuring a personal interview with Sir Andrew Barnard, for the purpose of talking over the necessary arrangements for my appearance at the Pavilion this evening, I feared that there was truth in the report that he was prejudiced against German art, and reserved his courtesies for the Italians. When at last he did condescend to admit me to his presence, he apologized for having kept me waiting, and, after a few polite phrases, asked me if I would try the Erard in the Pavilion. I found the instrument stiff and unmanageable from having stood so long in a cold room, but I was obliged to get my hand in somehow, and had not a single moment to spare for rehearsal with the King's band. We met in the evening in the fantastically decorated and beautifully lighted music-room attached to the Pavilion. The scene was a brilliant one. King William IV., Queen Adelaide, and their suite, sat at the farthest corner of the room. The guests were a long way from the piano, and I was not presented. I played my new 'Fantasia upon English National Songs,' which was dedicated to the Queen. During my performance the King alone approached me and seemed to be listening; he bowed condescendingly when I rose, but did not say a syllable; the company talked loudly. Sir Andrew asked me to play on the organ, and later in the evening had to accompany eight imperfectly trained performers, in some selections from Haydn's 'Creation.' Only the Princess Augusta and the Marchioness of Cornwallis took any interest in my 'Alexander Variations' and extempore playing, and that in spite of the general buzz of conversation. Some numbers of 'Robert le Diable' were given by the band, and the performance finished with 'God save the King.' The Court withdrew after Sir Andrew had handed to the Queen a copy of my 'English Fantasia,' an honor I myself had solicited, but been refused. Sir Andrew dismissed me as before with a few polite courtly phrases about the satisfaction felt by their Majesties, but none of the company exchanged a word with me." No wonder that Moscheles left Brighton in a bad humor, and was only too glad to get home again after this cold reception, if only to forget the unpleasant impressions he brought away with him. Mr. Grimal, a great musical enthusiast, brought him Beethoven's Mass in D (op. 123); a work hitherto unknown and unheard in London, requesting him to conduct it at the house of Mr. Alsager, the contributor of the city article to the *Times*, and a complete fanatic in his Beethoven worship. In his large music-room Beethoven's works were given with full orchestral accompaniments. On the 23d of December, Moscheles first acted there as conductor of a most efficient band, although consisting partly of amateurs, and subsequently his services as conductor were repeatedly called for. "I had," writes Moscheles, "become by dint of study, completely absorbed in that colossal work (the Messe Solennelle). Occasionally isolated phrases seemed unequal to the elevation of church music, but these compared with the work in its entirety, are as the details of a broadly conceived picture. The enthusiasm of my English friends also fired my zeal to give an interpretation worthy of the great work. Miss Novello and Miss H. Cawse did their best. The 'Benedictus,' with the heavenly violin solo (Mori), enchanted us all."

After Christmas, Moscheles finished his sketch of the Adagio of the Septet, devoted a few days to copying the parts and arranging the music for the orchestra, and then had the satisfaction of successfully rehearsing his music on the 31st of December before some musical friends.

# CHAPTER XV.

## 1833.

Concerts in the North of England—Birth of a Son—Congratulatory Letter from Felix Mendelssohn—John Parry—Herz—Handel's Messiah—Pasta—Madame Malibran—Chopin's "Studies"—Mendelssohn in London—Illness of Mendelssohn's Father—Coleridge—Moore—Lockhart—Seaside Music—Lessons given during the year.

THE Septet, begun in the old year and finished in the new, became a special favorite with Moscheles, and with Mendelssohn too, who asked in his child-like modest way, "Will you allow me to arrange it as a duet for the piano?" And later on, when engaged on the work, "Do you like it?—I am certain you would have done it better yourself." We used to smile at such speeches as these, and call them his "culpable modesty" (frevelhafte Bescheidenheit), but were for all that quite satisfied that the great artist, underrating his own value, was thoroughly sincere in what he said.

The following extracts from letters to his wife, refer to concerts in the north of England:

"York, February 4th, 11.30 A. M.—The concert is over. I may say, without self-assertion, that I was the only one applauded at all this evening; we had but one solo-singer, a few glees, some miserable overtures, in which the flute was the sole support of the harmonies. O, misery! Anyone less thick-skinned than I am, would have died straight off, but I could listen without as much as a fainting fit. I assure you I was obliged to nerve myself, as I should have to do if I were attending an execution. I was not only enthusiastically received, but forced to improvise twice. The singer, Mr. W., wanted to have 'The Midnight Review,' accompanied by the orchestra, and at the rehearsal I took all possible pains to make the thing go, but there was no more life or spirit to be got out of the band than from stones or pebbles. I advised him to give up the band, and offered my services to save a catastrophe, by accompanying the cantata myself. At six in the morning I start in the mail-coach for Sheffield, and as I have to pack up, I must finish."

"Sheffield, February 5th, 11 o'clock.—The concert is over. To-day was a busy one, and while writing to you I feel like a stage-coach horse just arrived, and steaming after his work is over. I was up at 5, started at 6, here by 3.30. Immediately went off to rehearsal; then dinner and concert. They wanted the 'Fall of Paris' again, but I only played the finale twice, and escaped a threatened encore of my extempore playing by bowing my acknowledgments."

On the very day of his return to London, his son was born. Great was the joy in the house of Moscheles who writes: "I sat up half the night writing the happy news to relations, and the expectant godfather, Felix Mendelssohn, expressing to the latter a hope that he would come, and hold the child in his own hands at the font."

The following letter, with the annexed pen and ink sketch, came by return of post, in answer to Moscheles' letter :—

"DEAR MOSCHELES,—Here they are, wind instruments and fiddles, for the son and heir must not be kept waiting till I come; he must have a cradle-song, with drums and trumpets and Janissary music; the fiddles alone are not near joyous enough. May every happiness and joy and blessing attend the little stranger; may he be prosperous; may he do well whatever he does; and may it fare well with him in this world! So he is to be called Felix, is he? How nice and kind of you to let him become my grandchild in formâ, and the first present his godfather makes him is the above entire orchestra; it is to accompany him all through life: the trumpets when he wants to become famous, the flutes when he falls in love, the cymbals * when he gets a beard; the pi-

* The German word "Becken" has the double meaning of cymbals and basin.

*Facsimile of the Sketch referred to in Mendelssohn's Letter of Feb. 27, 1833.*

anoforte explains itself, and should people ever play him false, as they will do to the best of us, there stand the kettle-drums, and the big drums in the background. Dear me! forgive this rubbish, but I am ever so happy when I think of your happiness, and of the time when I shall have my full share of it. By the end of April at the latest I intend to be in London, and then we will give the boy a regular name and introduction to the big world. It will be grand!

"To your Septet I look forward with no small pleasure. Klingemann has written out eleven notes of it for me, and those I like ever so much; I can quite imagine what a

bright lively Finale they would make. He has also described and analyzed for me the Andante in B flat major, but after all it will be better to hear it. Don't expect too much from the compositions I shall bring with me. You are sure to find frequent traces of a moodiness which I can only shake off slowly and by dint of an effort. I often feel as if I had never composed at all, and had to begin and learn everything over again; now, however, I have got into better trim, and my last things will sound better.

"Nice it was too, that your letter really found me, as you said it should, alone and in the quiet of my own room, composing to my heart's content, and now I only wish my letter may find you some quiet evening at home, with your dear ones well and happy around you. We will see whether I am as lucky at wishing as you were. I am in a hurry, and must end. I had but half an hour to write to you in, and that beautiful bit of art has taken up all my time; besides, I have nothing further to say but this: I wish you joy, now and hereafter, and may we soon meet again. My friends here send their kindest remembrances and congratulations, and are well; all but my father, who suffers constantly from his eyes, and is in consequence much depressed. This re-acts upon us, and we pray that there may soon be a change for the better. My sister and I just now do a great deal of music; every Sunday morning we have stringed accompaniments, and I have just received from the bookbinder a big grass-green volume of 'Moscheles,' for next time we are going to play your Trio. Farewell, farewell, and remain happy.

"Yours,

"FELIX MENDELSSOHN-BARTHOLDY."

"Berlin, 27th Feb. 1833.

"DEAR MRS. MOSCHELES,—To-day, although I can write but a few lines, I must send you my best congratulations, and tell you how I can enter heart and soul into your happiness. How delightful it is, but I shall soon make the personal acquaintance of the new arrival, and how delightful that he is to be called after me; mind you wait, please, till I am there, so that I may really avail myself of the old invitation to the christening; I will come with all possible haste, and be in London as early as I can. I'm glad it's a boy; he must become a musician, and what we all would fain do, and cannot, may it be his destiny to achieve, or if not, it matters little, for a good man he will become, and that's the great point. To be sure, I see it plainly, that the two grown-up sisters, Misses Emily and Serena, will tyrannize over him; by the time he is fourteen he will have to suffer from many a side-glance at his too long arms, and his too short coat, and his bad voice; but by-and-by he will become a man, and protect them in their turn, and do them all manner of services, and he will have to go through the boredom of many a soirée as their chaperon. I am sure you are a little, perhaps very, angry with me as being so lazy a correspondent, but only pardon me, and I promise to amend, more particularly so when I am once in London, and can myself carry and improvise my answers and questions; but I will improve even before that.

"My sisters send you heaps of good wishes and congratulations; so do my parents, and we all heartily rejoice in the event of the first-born son. I must now begin the last movement of my Symphony, which, lying as it does on the tips of my fingers, spoils my style and robs me of my time. Pardon these hurried lines; you know how they are meant.

"Your devoted
"FELIX MENDELSSOHN."

The question of shifting the place of their meetings gave rise this winter to violent discussions among the members of the Philharmonic Society. In the Argyll Rooms there were boxes for the more fashionable members among the subscribers, in the Hanover Square Rooms there was but one large box (called the Royal Box from being reserved for the Court); the proposal to have stalls was hotly contested, but not carried. The orchestra was differently arranged in the new room, the basses being separated and placed more in the background than hitherto, and on trying the overture to the "Zauberflöte" the new arrangement proved effective. The programmes included among the works of the great masters—Mendelssohn's Symphony in A major, performed with great applause on the 13th of May, and on the same evening Mendelssohn played Mozart's Concerto in D in a masterly style. Hummel also was heard in his new Concerto in F major, and Moscheles in his new Septet written for the Society, accompanied by Dragonetti, Lindley, Mori, and others.

At the conclusion of this season's concerts, there was a first performance of Mendelssohn's Overture to "Ruy Blas;" the unrivalled Malibran appeared again, and Moscheles was re-elected a Director of the Philharmonic.

Moscheles found an opportunity of introducing at Mr. Alsager's meetings Beethoven's Sonatas, op. 109 and 111, and remarks: "I found some of my hearers listening with deep devotion, while at my own house artists seem comparatively indifferent; some certainly are moved, while others are scared by the extravagances of the master, and do not recover their equanimity until I favor them with the more intelligible D minor Sonata."

At a concert given by the Royal Society of Musicians "there was an amusing performance, for old Parry, dressed in the costume of a Welsh bard, carrying his harp, sang his national melodies. He is a favorite with us musicians, who gave him a complimentary dinner and a present of silver plate, in recognition of his many years' services as one of our guild, and in token of his efforts on behalf of poor musicians. His gratitude and emotion were very touching."

The influenza, which first appeared in a virulent form in London this spring, attacked Moscheles and his household severely. We read: "We are now in the middle of April; my annual concert is announced for the 1st of May, and the indispensable novelty (with which alone I can meet my public with a good conscience) has still to be composed. How can I tell whether my fingers will be fit for action, and whether I should not act wisely in giving up this concert?"

Mendelssohn came to London; his visit seems to have acted on Moscheles like a panacea, and the joy of seeing Felix once again to have contributed to his recovery, for a few days later, Moscheles, resolving to venture on his concert, the two friends determined to write and play together a piece for two pianos. They agreed on the necessity of a brilliant piece, but were at a loss to select one out of a number of popular subjects. Several were proposed; at last the Gypsy March out of Weber's "Preciosa" was chosen.

"I will make a variation in minor, which shall growl below in the bass," exclaimed Felix; "will you do a brilliant one in major in the treble?" And so it was settled that the Introduction as well as the first and second variations should fall to the lot of Mendelssohn, the third and fourth, with the connecting Tutti, to that of Moscheles. "We wished to share in the Finale; so he began with the Allegro movement, which I broke in upon with a 'più lento.'"

In two days the music was written, and they went from the Philharmonic at a late hour to Erard's, to have their first rehearsal. "We found two pianos ready, and our hasty patchwork delighted my wife, our solitary listener. If this midnight pianoforte rehearsal was a hurried affair, the orchestral one on the morning of the 30th of April was still more so; we had only half a band, in consequence of the long rehearsal at the Opera, and only a few over-tired players arrived, and hastily ran through the new piece. In spite of all these obstacles the Concert on the 1st of May was a real success. Not a soul observed that the duet had been merely sketched, and that each of us was allowed to improvise in his own solo, until at certain passages agreed on we met again in due harmony. The scheme which seemed so very hazardous, ended triumphantly, and was received with applause.

Mendelssohn, having undertaken the conductorship of the Düsseldorf musical festival, was for a short time withdrawn from his friends in London, but soon returned, and this time accompanied by his excellent father. The two friends were rejoiced to meet again, and, at the christening of little Felix, Mendelssohn presented his godchild with an album, which, in spite of the repeated calls on his time in London, he had inaugurated with two sketches and a piece of music. "One of these drawings is a view of our own house, and the other a charming view in the Regent's Park. The composition is the 'cradle song,' with Klingemann's words, now so well known as 'Slumber and Dream.' There probably never was a happier christening fête than that of to-day. Our friends Neukomm and Barry Cornwall celebrated it with music and poetry."

We find several notes which illustrate the constant intercourse between Moscheles and Mendelssohn. On one occasion the latter answers an invitation thus: "Alas! we cannot! To-day we have a dinner party of our own. I have just ordered salmon and lobster sauce for five people, so I must 'present my regrets.' Seriously speaking, Rosen, Henzler, and Klingemann have promised to spend the evening with us, and therefore, alas! we cannot come to you. My father hopes to see you this morning to thank you." Here is a note of Mendelssohn to Mrs. Moscheles: "Dear Mrs. Moscheles,—It is two o'clock, I am just back from the country and have received your note. At ten o'clock I ought to have been in Grosvenor Place. I should like to have done what you wanted; but you must own that the fates won't allow either of my appearing to be, or really being fashionable. Lately you were kind enough to say to me that we might all three come to dine to-day (for Dr.

Franck has actually arrived), but now I should like to know if you mean this in earnest, or if you do *not*, or if we may come. Please send by bearer a verbal decision!"

The answer was of course in the affirmative. On the 6th of May Moscheles complains: "How deadly slow and monotonous was H. in his Fantasia this evening at our house; Mendelssohn yawned an obligato accompaniment. When we were once more alone, Felix and I had some glorious extempore playing together."

H. Herz, the brilliant player, suddenly appeared on the musical horizon. His rapidity of finger, his marked accent, as well as his light, melodious, and easily intelligible music produced a great effect. We read in the diary, "H. Herz completely drowned me with his furious bass, in the duet on subjects out of Auber's 'Philtre,' which I played, as a favor, with him at his own concert." This duet, however, ultimately became a favorite.

Very comical was the contrast when J. B. Cramer consented to play, as a pianofore duet, with Herz at his concert, the brilliant 'Polonaise' of Beethoven. Moscheles compares Herz to a "young frisky colt," and Cramer to a "well-fed, cream-colored state-horse, harnessed on great occasions to the royal carriage." Cramer and Hummel played in this same Concert Mozart's Fantasia in F minor, and that was far more effective.

The concerts now follow closely on one another; in that given by young Schulz, Moscheles took part, as one of six pianoforte players of the "Zauberflöte" overture. At Mori's he played with Mendelssohn the new piece on the "Preciosa" march.

On the 10th of July all the musicians gave a grand concert for the benefit of a poor artist's family; and Mendelssohn and Moscheles were two of the players in a piece written by Czerny for four pianos.

On the 12th of July, Mr. Hope, owner of the famous picture-gallery, lends his house for a concert given for the benefit of the Hospital for Sick Children. "The music, to which I contributed my mite, was performed in the room of the masters of the Italian school; if inclined to migrate, one could enjoy a stroll in a room full of Dutch pictures, but as Malibran and Paganini were among the performers, every one was satisfied to stop and listen." On one occasion, when Paganini ventured upon Beethoven's "Kreutzer Sonata," Moscheles called it "a desecration."

Incidentally, we read of a performance of Handel's "Messiah." "I swallowed my dinner hastily, so as not to miss a note of this masterpiece, but, after listening with close attention for some time, I was mortified at finding that the small amount of vigor left to me after the rough-and-tumble of the season, was not enough to enable me to take in and digest such a colossal work. Such considerations always lead me back again to the thought of enjoying hereafter in Germany the fruits of my independence, won by my active exertions in England. What a melancholy evening last Thursday, when I heard Pasta's 'Romeo;' she sang terribly out of tune. This great artiste, long past her prime, has lost her voice, and actually consents to barter her reputation for a heap of guineas; it shocks me."

The first performance of "Euryanthe," on the 29th of June, in Covent Garden Theatre, and the admirable singing of Schröder and Haitzinger, were some compensation for Pasta's shortcomings.

At Drury Lane the sparkling, and in the vocal and histrionic way unique Malibran made a "furore" in the "Devil's Bridge" and "Sonnambula" set to English words. She was thoroughly realistic, and in her dress and movements despised everything conventional. Thus, in the sleep-walking scene, unlike other great representatives of the part, whose muslin négligé would have suited any lady, she adopted the bonâ-fide night-cap of the peasant girl, and the loose garment of a sleeper; her "tricot" stockings were so transparent as to veil her feet but imperfectly. Her acting in this opera was exquisitely touching, her outburst of sorrow so natural that she enlisted the sympathy of her audience from beginning to end of the piece.

Moscheles' studies of Chopin's music led him to make the following observation: "I gladly pass some of my leisure hours of an evening in cultivating an acquaintance with Chopin's Studies and his other compositions. I am charmed with their originality, and the national coloring of his subjects. My thoughts, however, and through them my fingers, stumble at certain hard, inartistic, and to me incon ceivable modulations. On the whole I find his music often too sweet, not manly enough, and hardly the work of a profound musician."

Again we find Mendelssohn mentioned in a letter: "What endless music we have made together! I made him play over and over again his own things, which I followed in the score. He would on these occasions imitate some one wind-instrument, or take up a point in a chorus with his clear tenor voice. Whenever he has arranged one of his overtures as a pianoforte duet, we try it over together, until we find it perfectly suitable for the piano."

They often play to one another Beethoven's Sonatas, which not unfrequently diverge into joint improvisations of the maddest kind, and musical caricatures. On one occasion the nursery song, "Polly put the kettle on," is chosen for a subject on purpose to please the two little girls, with whom Felix liked to laugh and play; in a jovial mood he would often take them to the Zoological Gardens, and amuse them with all kinds of jokes. Among the many kind friends who visited at Chester Place, the children had the discrimination to fix on Mendelssohn as prime favorite. He and Moscheles were mutually attracted to one another as much by kindred tastes and sympathies as by music. Moscheles admired his friend's genius, and watched, without a particle of envy, the steadily increasing fame of the young composer, his former pupil; Mendelssohn, on the other hand, was all devotion, all gratitude for the rich treasure of experience which the older master had stored up in his pianoforte works. They loved and esteemed each other, these feelings were reciprocated mutually in the two families, and the strength of this friendship was proved when the days of sorrow came.

Mendelssohn, hearing of the death of his old master Zelter, goes off in haste at an early hour in the morning to Moscheles, announcing himself in such words as: "I cannot work, I should like to spend the day here." On one occasion, Mrs. Moscheles being too unwell to accompany her husband away from home, Felix goes to spend the evening with her, and she records his conversation in letters to her father. If Felix came to her complaining of weariness, she used to make him sit down quietly on the sofa in a dark corner; there he would rest for a few minutes while the children would stop their game and keep perfect silence. Then, after taking some slight refreshment, he would rouse himself and discuss with his usual animation some severe musical rehearsal, a morning concert, or a political meeting, where he was constantly to be found. She could venture to lecture him on his yesterday's visit, to tell him that he had fidgeted and been fretful and impatient, in fact thoroughly unamiable, whereupon he would say, "Yes, but why does *that* person come just at that particular moment when I should have so enjoyed making music with Moscheles." Whenever about to leave England, he asks her to write. She is to tell him of this, that, and the other, for Moscheles has so little time; she promises this, adding, "But don't answer; you are a celebrated man, you have something better to do,"—a thing he would never allow. In his letters he frequently sends Serena messages about the carnation, his and her favorite flower. In the midst of the worries incidental to a musical festival, or on the journeys which Moscheles and he take together, he would add some words or pen-and-ink sketches to the letters of his friend, and when abroad send a first copy of his later published "Lieder," neatly written in the letter, immediately after they were composed, to Mrs. Moscheles. "A little song has just come into my head;" or, "Here is a song; unfortunately it does not suit your voice (referring to the tenor song 'Leucht' heller als die Sonne'); I send it, however. Moscheles, perhaps, will hum it.' . . . Pages such as these are carefully preserved among the family treasures.

During this visit to London, the elder Mendelssohn was laid up for weeks by a tedious illness, and the family were very anxious about him. His weakened sight made constant reading impossible, so his friends, Mrs. Moscheles in particular, spent all their spare time with him. She writes to her father, "I read him the *Times* aloud, as I did to you, and he gives me very sound views about the education of children. I hope they will benefit my own, but whatever amount of time I am in his company, the hours fly rapidly, his conversation is so agreeable." On one occasion during this illness, Felix sends the following note to Mrs. Moscheles:—

"My father begs to say that he cannot accept the offer of your carriage to-day; the Miss Alexanders have sent him theirs; but, that if you can make him a present of your time, you will oblige him by walking over with it to his house. This is expressed in very bad style; but anyhow it's not your Platt-Deutsch, but rather my Berlinese—no offence—yours,

"FELIX MENDELSSOHN-BARTHOLDY.

"P. S.—Yesterday the doctors were very hopeful. Brodie does not want to come again. Second postscript (the chief point): How are you?"

Felix did not recover his good spirits and capacity for work until his father had been completely restored to health, and the departure of their two friends on the 4th of August was a melancholy event to the Moscheles family.

Among a number of commonplace and tedious soirées mentioned in the diary, Moscheles makes an exception in favor of one at the Lockharts. "His wife, Sir Walter Scott's eldest daughter, has all her father's amiability. We saw there for the first time Thomas Moore, the poet, a little lively sparkling Irishman, who, on the strength of his passion for music, immediately made acquaintance with me. He sang his own poems, adapted to certain Irish melodies, harmonized and accompanied by himself on the guitar. 'Le genre est petit,' thought I, but the novelty made it interesting to us. The poet Coleridge was there too, still bright and cheerful, although looking an old man. Of authoresses we had the Ladies Stepney and Charlotte Bury. After Moore had given us his Irish melodies, I was obliged to go to the piano, and share with the poet the exaggerated compliments paid us by the company."

In August Moscheles and his family went to Hastings. "What a pity," writes Moscheles, "that a bevy of lady-lodgers in the house spoil, by their strumming, all my musical enjoyment, not to mention my musical thoughts. They play on the piano and guitar, 'La ci darem,' as a presto, and Reissiger's Waltz as a sentimental Andante." To bear this for any length of time was intolerable; and, finding no suitable lodgings in Hastings, the Moscheles withdrew to St. Leonard's.

On returning to London, we read of visits to both Houses of Parliament, an interesting debate in the Commons, when O'Connel spoke, and of a four hours' discussion on "Captain Napier's victory on behalf of Don Pedro."

On the 11th of November Moscheles writes: "Yesterday at the performance of 'Hamlet,' at Drury Lane, I was forcibly reminded by a celebrated passage of what I am always preaching to my pupils, 'Self command in the midst of a difficult performance, and a quiet mastery over oneself.' The great poet makes Hamlet say, 'Do not saw the air too much with your hand thus, but use all gently, for in the very torrent, tempest, and, I may say, whirlwind of your passion, you must acquire and beget a temperance that may give it smoothness." With regard to the first performance of Auber's "Bal-masqué," we read: "The music is often deafening, but often piquant, the ball wonderfully brilliant."

Moscheles' chief employment this winter was composing during his evenings at home the B major Concerto (fantastique). Besides this he wrote the Impromptu in E flat major and the more common-place Divertimento, "Operatic Reminiscences." His well-known good nature was put to the test by frequent interruptions of these labors. "A friend," he says, "brings me his 'Swiss Divertimento' for revision. I deal with it as Kotzebue makes his amanuensis do, who only leaves the words, 'My dear friend,' standing at the top of the page, and adds the rest. Adding the rest cost me two quiet evenings. A third I was forced to sacrifice to the Hungarian Baron Rathen, who wanted to play over to me from beginning to end his 'musical love-scene interrupted by a storm.' On his English card he calls himself 'Teacher of the Organ, Piano, and Doro-Bass (thorough-bass)."

On the 31st of December, Moscheles writes in his Diary, "On reckoning I find I have given this year 1457 lessons, of which 1328 were paid, and 129 gratis. Of the latter class, those I gave to Litolff, who is making rapid strides, were the most interesting."

## CHAPTER XVI.

### 1834.

Stars of the Italian Opera—Grisi, Rubini, and Tamburini—De Vrugt—Vieuxtemps—Lady violin-players—Festival in Westminster Abbey—Distribution of the Chorus—Comparison of the two Festivals in 1784–1834—Solo-Singers—Tenor and Sopranos—" Israel in Egypt "—The " Messiah"—Demeanor of the Audience—Festival at Birmingham—Overture to " Joan of Arc"—Byron's " Manfred " at Covent-Garden.

MOSCHELES writes at the beginning of the year, " We are in January, and already the chief topic of conversation is the grand music festival to be given next June in Westminster Abbey. It is *the* musical event of the year."

Before that takes place we should record the sensation created by the stars of the Italian Opera, Grisi, Rubini, and Tamburini. Grisi, although inferior as an actress to Pasta, as a musician to Malibran, and lacking the charm and loveliness of Sontag, still captivated her listeners by her youth, beauty, and the freshness and glory of her voice. Rubini maintained his long-recognized position as a master of his art, and Tamburini, with his classical profile and fine mellow voice, contributed his full share to the triumph of this world-renowned trio. Ivanhoff, an Italianized Russian, attracted the public by his great flexibility of voice, but displeased my German ear by using his head voice too frequently, particularly when singing Schubert's " Serenade." His sickly sentimental style became so wearisome, that some wag circulated a joke about him, declaring his real name was, " I've enough."

Moscheles played his new Concerto Pathétique at the Philharmonic, and directed on the same occasion Mendelssohn's still unknown overture to " Melusine ; " both novelties were received coldly. Mrs. Moscheles writes an account of the concert to Mendelssohn, whose characteristic answer we commend to our readers: "So the people at the Philharmonic did not like my 'Melusine?' Heigh-ho! The news won't kill me. I certainly was sorry when I got your letter, and I played off my overture right through, to see if I too dislike it now; but it does give me pleasure, so there's not much harm done, or would you have me believe that you would receive me in a less friendly way at my next visit? That would be a pity, that would distress me very much. But I hope not, and perhaps it may please somewhere else, or if not I will write something else, and that may please better. But after all, my chief delight is in the fact that such a thing exists in writing; and if besides that, such kind words are bestowed on it as you and Moscheles send me, it *has* been well received, and I can quietly go on working. I utterly fail to understand what you tell me in your letter, of the cold reception given to Moscheles' new Concerto. I should have thought it as clear as noonday that that must please them, and still more so when he plays it to them. But when will it be published? I am longing to attack it."

We find Moscheles less inclined than ever to come to terms with the Manager of the Italian Opera. He writes: "Now I will see if I am not able to be quit of an extortionate impressario, and to fill my room without the assistance of his Italian singers. If I don't succeed, so much the more shame for me, and I must hang up 'my harp and music on the willow-tree.'" He did succeed, however, some artists supported him, among them a new tenor just arrived from Holland, De Vrugt, who soon made himself a name; he engaged Madame Stockhausen—the room was full, and the audience enthusiastic. At the beginning of the season, a host of artists put in an appearance; among them Vieuxtemps, a wonderful boy, who attracted great attention by his fine violin-playing. There were two lady violin-players as well, Filiepowitz and Paravicini, who were much talked about. Mrs. Anderson, the favorite English pianist, had been selected by the Duchess of Kent to teach the Princess Victoria. Her concert this year, patronized and attended by these Royal ladies, was one of the most brilliant of this season.

With regard to the festival in Westminster Abbey, it is

owing to Moscheles' scrupulous care in arranging and preserving the accounts written at the time, that we are enabled, after a lapse of eight-and-thirty years, to give an accurate and faithful description of all that took place. "Handel," observes a writer of the day, "introduced the oratorio into England: no wonder the festival named after him should be held in Westminster Abbey, where he lies buried." According to the paper we quote from, the proceeds of a series of Festivals between the years 1784 and 1791 amounted in all to 50,000*l.*, and were entirely devoted to charitable purposes. It mentions, too, the legacy left by Handel to the "Society of Decayed Musicians and their Families," and eulogizes King William IV. and Queen Adelaide, who, after a lapse of fifty years, zealously promoted this new festival, devoted to the same charitable objects, and for which the sympathies and aid of the English nobility were called forth by the generous support of the Royal patrons.

With regard to the festival itself, Moscheles writes to his relatives: "The festival took place in the nave, which was covered over with stout deal boards; at one end of the Abbey was seen the Royal box, with its heavy red satin curtains, rich ornaments, and luxurious velvet carpets and cushions, and adorned with the Royal Arms artistically carved. The Directors of the festival sat immediately under the Royal box, with a canopy above them. The public, on this occasion, as in 1784, occupied seats arranged in the style of an amphitheatre, and reaching as high as the capitals of the pillars. 2700 persons found accommodation; the best seats cost two, and the others one guinea each. These seats, covered with red cloth and gold ornaments, contrasted tastefully with the white and gold lyres on red draperies, which were hung upon the walls. The orchestra, on this, as on the former occasion, was erected opposite the Royal box, and in the following fashion. In front were the solo singers, then the small chorus, 40 strong; close to this chorus, at a piano, sat Sir George Smart, the director of the music; behind him, the band, ranged in tiers; the cellos on either side, the violins in the centre, then the wind-instruments; above all, the magnificent organ, built by Gray for the occasion, and adorned with a richly carved Gothic façade; by a clever arrangement the player was made to face the Director instead of the organ. The distribution of the vocalists forming the grand chorus greatly prejudiced the effect of the music with numbers who were packed closely in the side aisles and niches of the Abbey; in fact, the choral music to a part of the audience sounded as though it were smothered by the orchestra; in other parts of the Abbey the effect was reversed, and the performance as a whole could only be enjoyed in a small part of the vast building."

We give a list of the executants as represented on the occasion of the two Music Festivals in 1784 and 1834 (the list of the first is copied from Dr. Burney's Musical History):—

| INSTRUMENTAL. | 1834. | 1784. |
|---|---|---|
| Violins | 80 | 95 |
| Tenors | 32 | 26 |
| Violoncellos | 18 | 21 |
| Double Basses | 18 | 15 |
| Flutes | 10 | 6 |
| Oboes | 12 | 26 |
| Clarinets | 8 | |
| Bassoons | 12 | 27 |
| Horns | 10 | 12 |
| Trumpets | 8 | 12 |
| Trombones | 8 | 6 |
| Ophicleides | 2 | |
| Serpents | 2 | |
| Kettle-drums | 3 | 4 |
| | 223 | 250 |

| VOCAL. | 1834. | 1784. |
|---|---|---|
| Sopranos | 113 | 11 |
| Sopranos (boys) | 32 | 47 |
| Altos | 74 | 48 |
| Tenors | 70 | 83 |
| Basses | 103 | 84 |
| Solo-Singers | 5 | 2 |
| The above Instruments | 223 | 250 |
| Total | 620 | 525 |

We quote from the diary: "On the 20th of June at twelve o'clock in the forenoon, Sir George Smart for the first time raised his baton, and Handel's Coronation Anthem, performed by such a host, in such a place, was so grand that none present are likely to forget it; the newspapers talked of several ladies weeping, and some actually fainting. I was deeply moved by these sounds, and must confess I never heard such an effect produced before. We had the whole of the 'Creation,' and a part of 'Samson.' The solo singers were old Bellamy, who had sung in 1784, E. Seguin, a young pupil of the Royal Academy of Music, and the admirable Phillips; the tenors were represented by Hobbs and the inimitable Braham; Miss Stevens and Madame Caradori Allan, both excellent, sang the soprano parts. The chorus and orchestra were first rate, and the first day might deserve to be called a perfect success."

The second day was opened by another Coronation Anthem by Handel; and the "Hallelujah" electrified the audience. Then with a view of producing certain effects in preference to giving any one work in its entirety, a selection had been made of sacred pieces, in which singers, as well as wind-instrument players, could have an opportunity of display.

Everybody was to have his or her chance, Rubini, Zucchelli, with Lindley's violoncello, and Braham, with Harper's trumpet-obligato. Phillips had a song with a bassoon accompaniment, Miss Stevens and Grisi also had parts assigned them in this selection. Then followed the finest perhaps of all Handel's oratorios, "Israel in Egypt," which was splendidly performed. The newspapers were rapturous on the subject. With reference to the closing numbers of that Oratorio, the *Athenæum* said, "One feels so elevated by this music that we seem to live in those great days when the Lord went before His people in the cloud or pillar of fire. But once let the celestial strains end, and we wake again to the pale reality of our shadow-like everyday existence." "My own impression," adds Moscheles, "far exceeded all that I ever dreamt of realizing, and I believe my feelings were in unison with nearly all of those who were present." On the 3d day, unfortunately, a medley of airs, choruses, and ensembles was again given; a programme with abrupt transitions from ancient to modern compositions. For the 4th day the Queen, following the precedent of Queen Charlotte, had commanded the "Messiah." To a German musician it seems but natural that the chief interest should be concentrated on this majestic work. The tickets for admission to the performance, as well as for the rehearsals, were soon bought up, and the public, unable to procure any at the regular prices, was forced to pay exorbitantly. Every nook and corner of the Abbey was occupied, and a truly devotional spirit seemed to prevail. The *Times*, which during the previous days had never resented the want of taste shown in giving disjointed works, found room in its columns, when the festival was over, for imparting as a piece of advice: "The effect of such performances would be enhanced, if the oratorios were given, not piecemeal, but in their entirety, just as the composer intended they should be given." Moscheles writes on this subject:—"The advice on this point came certainly too late—of course to a German musician, much of the arrangement of these programmes was an offence, and yet the general effect was so grand that it would be thankless to point out the obvious anomalies. The veneration with which the English traditionally regard their noble abbey, found expression in the dignified attitude and frame of mind observable in the audience, which crowded within the sacred walls, and the thrill of awe which penetrated these large masses spoke more eloquently than any cheers or clapping of hands. The King and Queen, who attended daily, were regarded as the patrons of a great and beneficent work, that was fittingly supported by the whole nation. Such are my feelings—you may call them fanciful if you please, but they were suggested to me by the bearing and demeanor of the crowd that was present."

Moscheles had only just returned from the seaside, where he had gone for fresh air and change, when he found himself once more obliged to prepare for a grand musical festival at Birmingham; there he performed his "Alexander Variations" and the "Recollections of Ireland." The powerful tones of the Erard were heard all over the colossal and crowded hall, which was not intended for solo instruments; and the *Spectator* went so far as to say that a large crowd outside enjoyed the performance. The proceeds of the whole festival realized 14,000*l.*

"16th October.—I was hard at work with my overture to 'Joan of Arc,'" Moscheles writes, "when the fearful news reached me that the House of Lords was on fire. The fact was only too soon confirmed by flames appearing on the horizon." . . . . When the overture was finished and arranged as a pianoforte duet, he substituted for the brilliant and noisy finale a soft pathetic strain, which he thought more suitable to Johanna's death. On this subject we read in a letter of Moscheles: "In this overture I have aimed at elevation, harmony, and unity of ideas. Assuming I have the proper audience, the work might please ; but whoever looks for trivial, easy, Italian sing-song, will find nothing in it ; nor will those be pleased who think a minute working out of individual parts, or the introduction of unexpected harmonies, too learned. They just give the keenest relish to those initiated in the secrets of counterpoint. I hold that the treatment of a melody, and clearness as well as unity and an interesting fusion of the leading subjects, are the most important ingredients in a composition, and shall always strive to attain these objects. . . . . Mendelssohn's Octet, in which you complain of an absence of melody, has a tendency to the elaborate (künstlich), and yet the frequent hearing of that admirable work, and that, too, in a spirit of careful analysis, is well worth the trouble, if it leads to the proper appreciation of an originality which never degenerates into anything extravagant. . . . . There is not much sympathy here with Spohr's 'Weihe der Töne.' Haslinger offered through me to the Philharmonic Society the copyright of the work for two or three years, but the Society refused."

"This winter Byron's 'Manfred,' with choruses set by Bishop, was given as a novelty in Covent Garden Theatre. There was an immense outlay in scenery and decorations, the music was not much more enjoyable than that of the 'Bravo,' by Marliani; a mélange made up of the well-worn phrases of Rossini, Pacini, and Mercadante. The beauty of the *mise-en-scène* would have done equally well, apart from the ear-torture."

"My wife," writes Moscheles, "who reads aloud to me while I correct my work, happened at this time to select 'Uhland's Poems.' This suggested to me vocal settings of 'Der Schmidt,' 'Das Reh,' and 'Das Gärtnerslied.'"

Towards the end of the year he was busy with preparations for a private performance of the "Israel in Egypt." Some chorister boys from the Westminster Abbey Choir, and some well-trained amateurs, were asked to join. The chief supporters, however, were Madame Caradori-Alan, Röckel and Taylor. This performance was a worthy finale for the year 1834.

# CHAPTER XVII.

## 1835.

"Trial Night" of the Philharmonic Society—An Unmannerly Nobleman—Litolff's Compositions—Berlioz' "Symphonie Fantastique"—Musical Pains and Pleasures—Julius Benedict—Cramer's Retirement—Visit to Germany—Leipzig—Intercourse with Musical Artists—Felix Mendelssohn—Letters to Madame Moscheles—Concert—Berlin—A Family Fete—Musical Absurdities—A Painful Affair—Death of Mendelssohn's Father—Holland and Belgium.

AT the beginning of this year, the Philharmonic Society held its first "Trial Night" for new compositions, when Spohr's "Weihe der Töne" was conducted by Sir George Smart. "This able conductor," says Moscheles, "succeeded at this first rehearsal in carrying the band through the whole of the work correctly, although of course without that delicacy, light, and shade requisite for so intricate a work, the Andante of which, with its 3-8 and 9-16 time, constituted in itself a considerable difficulty. I followed the performance with the score, and was delighted with the solidity of the entire work, as well as the beauty of its details; still, the too great predominance of Spohrish color and form to some extent quenched my enthusiasm. Nothing but genius and wealth of invention can kindle me into rapture."

When Moscheles conducted, there was a successful performance of his overture to "Joan of Arc," and the youthful Sterndale Bennett, a pupil of Cipriani Potter, played a pianoforte concerto of his own composition; Moscheles thought highly of the performer, his playing, and the concerto as well.

Moscheles' services as a public performer and teacher were in constant requisition at this time in Bath, Manchester, and other places. In the midst of all his numerous engagements, he never neglected his habit of writing daily to his wife, but his letters at this period, being for the most part of a domestic character, are omitted.

When once back in London, business engagements accumulate, and Moscheles might exclaim with Figaro in the "Barbiere di Siviglia," "Tutti mi chiedono, tutti mi vogliono." To one treated, as we have seen, with marked courtesy by all with whom he came in contact, the following episode must have been eminently distasteful. "I had," he says, "during the last season given lessons to two young ladies, the daughters of Lord —. The treatment I experienced in this household, where even the servants were disrespectful, was only to be met by the independent airs I was forced to assume, to assert my rights as a gentleman. Although not offered a chair, I sat down in presence of the lady, and insisted on walking up the principal staircase, although I was shown the back one. After waiting in vain for nearly nine months for 35*l.* due to me, a steward appeared at my house, and, finding only my wife at home, produced my account, on which the noble lord had written—'Pay this man 15*l.* on account.' My wife remonstrated, whereupon the steward answered in a sympathizing tone, 'Well, Ma'am, I advise you to take it while you can get it.' It then occurred to her that, the family being reported somewhat impecunious, she had better accept the man's advice. Soon afterwards my lady sent to beg I would again resume my lessons with her daughters. I refused. Then came an exceedingly polite question from my lord, asking the reasons of my refusal, and would I state them verbally? etc. I did so. Lord and Lady —— overloaded me with civility, and I agreed once more to give four lessons a week. Such people should be taught manners as well as music."

Moscheles says of himself in a letter: "I am always longing to compose, but how am I to find time? To be sure I have published two little Lieder; one a setting of Byron's 'There be none of Beauty's daughters,' and 'Im Herbste,' by Uhland. Owing to interruptions, I have not succeeded in finishing my 'Concerto Pathétique;' besides these, I should like to write a new Introduction to my 'Hommage à Handel,' which I composed in the year 1822." This intention he carried out at this period, and the work in its entirety has frequently been performed in public.

Later on we read: "To-day Klingemann brought us two organ fugues, arranged as duets by Mendelssohn. My wife and I attacked them instantly; they are admirable, like everything else that he presents to the musical world."

Just at this time Litolff published many of his early and very promising compositions, and at the same time Chopin's graceful "Scherzo" and "Grand Studies" appeared. "I am a sincere admirer of his originality," says Moscheles; "he has given pianoforte-players all that is newest and most attractive. Personally, I dislike his artificial and forced modulation. My fingers struggle and tumble over such passages; practice them as I will, I never can do them smoothly." With regard to Berlioz' "Symphonie Fantastique," which the publishers sent him in a pianoforte edition, he observes: "I can hardly form an opinion of the work before I know the score, but I cannot reconcile myself to the eternal unisons, octave passages, and tremolandos. I do not find a healthy sequence of harmonic progressions. His 'Dies Iræ' and the 'Witches' Sabbath' seem to me indicative of a diseased fancy; and the development of figures heaped one on another often ends in a tight Gordian knot—who will cut it asunder? The young man, however, has warmth and poetic feeling, and certain isolated passages remind me in their grandeur of an ancient Torso."

Moscheles is amused and displeased alternately with his strange experiences during the London season. "If called on to reckon up our musical pains as well as pleasures, I must compare the swarm of foreign musicians who obscure the horizon, to the locusts which darkened the Egyptian sky. One of our visitors carries the German simplicity to such an extent as to speak no other language but his own; yet he travels hither on purpose to be recognized by the English. In language and conduct he is an exact counterpart of Dominie Sampson, and insists on bringing with him each time his pupil—a tiresome young Dutchman. Yesterday they both met with that strange fellow H—, with his odd medley of French and German; the party were joined by a regular John Bull, who speaks and composes only in his own language. The result of these compounds is a strange medley of discords. At dinner, the German takes kindly to everything on the table ; but the Frenchman turns up his nose at every little grain of pepper, and the Englishman, before he touches anything, covers the rim of his plate with mustard, cayenne, and spices, so that it looks like a painter's palette. Having to do the part of interpreters, we didn't get much dinner, and it was all we could do to smother our laughter ; for at last, in despair of communicating with one another, the German and the Englishman talked Latin, but were out in their reckoning—for each one pronounced it in a different way, and confusion became worse confounded."

In this year Julius Benedict first became a member of the great musical guild in London, and asserted his position at once as an excellent musician and pianoforte player. His long residence in Italy made him peculiarly fitted as an accompanist to the Italian singers; and in Moscheles' house he was heartily welcomed as a distinguished compatriot.

J. B. Cramer, wishing in his old age to retire to Munich, gave a farewell concert, and was invited by his friends to a musical banquet. "We pianoforte players," says Moscheles, "had selected Cramer's compositions for our performance ; he himself played with much grace and delicacy Mozart's Concerto in D. Lastly, when called on to extemporize, I selected themes out of his works ; this delighted and affected him also." Cramer did not long remain in Munich, but chose to end his days in strict retirement in England.

In July, Moscheles writes: "The season is closing, and soon I shall have no ladies' fingers to doctor. I cannot undertake to doctor the ears of my pupils." He travels to Hamburg, leaves his family there, and goes to Leipzig, where Mendelssohn has just entered on his duties as conductor of the Gewandhaus Concerts. He writes from Leipzig :—

"My Dear Wife.—You may fancy how I enjoy this meeting with my mother and sister. Kistner, who is very zealous in my interests, accompanied me to Mendelssohn, who is comfortably and agreeably settled outside the town, in Reichel's Garden. He received me with his usual simplicity and heartiness, making eager, nay, affectionate inquiries for you. I don't think him looking handsomer or more blooming (being as he is between youth and manhood), but he was more full of wit, liveliness, and cleverness than ever. He played me three new 'Lieder ohne Worte,' which are worthy successors to those already written. I have played him nothing of my own as yet. My mother looks remarkably well. People on all sides call her a handsome old lady, and she really seems to me much younger than she is. I visited the Wiecks, and Clara played to me a good deal; among other things a manuscript sonata by Schumann—very labored, difficult, and somewhat intricate, although interesting music. Her playing was admirable, and void of all affectation. After dinner, I returned to my mother's, and then adjourned with Felix to Hauser's for a cup of coffee. We amused ourselves by serious and desultory playing upon his Streicher piano, which I shall probably bespeak for my concert, although Felix has offered me his own. Felix took me afterwards to Dr. Härtel's new country-house, close to the rampart. In the evening I was again at the Wiecks, to meet Schumann, who is a retiring but interesting young man. Again I made Clara play to me, and again she distinguished herself. I gave them a taste of my extempore playing."

On the 2d of October he writes: "8 A. M.—I expect Felix; meanwhile I will begin the day as I like best, by asking after you and the children. Is Emily composing? Serena learning an epic poem by heart? Felix storming a fortress somewhere? On all these points I hope information is on the road to me. Nine o'clock—Felix is here, and I am going with him to his lodgings, to hear him play over his new oratorio." "And now"—Mendelssohn adds—"let me slip in with all haste between the envelope and wafer, my hearty greetings and thanks. I hope one of these days to write more fully; at present we are in all the hurry and confusion of Moscheles' first day, and all my morning will be occupied in hearing a deal of his new music. You may fancy how eagerly I look forward to *that!* But you really spoil me by sending me such a wonderfully pretty present. We must be off; good-bye for to day. My love to your little ones, among whom Emily can't any longer be reckoned."

On the following day, Moscheles says: "Kistner

accompanied me on a visit to that dear venerable old man, Hofrath Rochlitz, who received me most kindly, and was very communicative. After expressing his gratification with my present visit, my playing, and my compositions, he recapitulated the various impressions which I made on him since my first appearance with the Alexander March in the year 1815, and said many flattering things about my development in art. He was to me quite as interesting as his 'Essays for Musical Amateurs,' the reading of which we used to enjoy. Towards evening I spent an hour with my mother, amusing her with stories about our London life. I then went to Felix, who asked me to drink tea with him every evening; he is very comfortably settled—it reminded me of my own bachelor days. His Erard stands in the middle of the room, and in his book-case—a perfect storehouse of musical scores—I saw a splendidly-bound edition of Handel. On the table his silver inkstand, presented by the Philharmonic Society, on the walls two charming engravings, one of Titian's daughter; and the other a portrait of Schätzel (a celebrated singer), on the piano a delightful litter of scores and new music, still cleanliness and neatness prevailing everywhere. We drank tea and chatted until the advocate Schrey (one of the concert-directors) joined us. He is a musical enthusiast, with a fine tenor voice, and sang a couple of delightful new Lieder by Felix, which I hope to copy and bring to you. I played my 'Concerto Fantastique' and the 'Pathètique,' about which many kind things were said, and lastly the Rondo which Felix dedicated to me. We played together my Overture and his Octet; everything went smoothly, as you may fancy. We went on till eleven o'clock, and Felix lent me his cloak, that I should not catch cold after the number of 'hot notes.' He is a glorious fellow. By-the-by, Felix cheerfully consented to play my last duet with me at my concert, but the Committee must be duly apprized of the fact. Yesterday, when he called upon my mother, she wanted him to play, but he had a fit of his well-known modesty, and declined. I must now tell you what befell me to-day. . . . . I went with Felix to the rehearsal; his admirable conducting, speeches, and observations—in fact, his general behavior to the orchestra—fills his subordinates with affection and respect. His overture to the 'Calm Sea and Prosperous Voyage' (of which one can get no idea from the pianoforte arrangement), as well as Beethoven's B flat Symphony, went beautifully. The rehearsal lasted until 12.30; then I went to my mother, and thence with Felix to the table d'hôte. We were invited to Wieck's to meet Schumann and others; Clara Wieck played in Beethoven's great Trio superbly. I went to the theatre to hear Auber's 'Cheval de Bronze;' but oh, misery! bad music, singers, and subject! What a pity to lose my evening, and be forced to pay dearly for my curiosity!"

"Eleven at night.—Late as it is, I must tell you that I made my concert arrangements with Kistner, and then went to Felix, with whom I tried over, from the proof-sheets, my 'Hommage à Handel,' but in a curious manner. He has but one piano—his own Erard—but he remembered to have heard some one practicing occasionally in the next room, occupied by an elderly lady. Before his door, leading to her room, stood a wooden press, too big to be moved without great trouble. Felix went to the lady, and asked her leave to play in her room while I played in his; the lady gladly consented; we opened the doors, but the press remained immovable. The instruments happened to be in tune together, and the whole thing went capitally; Kistner, and an organist of the name of Reichard, were present, and were so delighted that we determined to play this piece at my concert. Among the new things which Felix played again to me are two pianoforte Capriccios and a Fugue in quick-time in F minor—all admirable in their way. We dined at Hauser's (the bass singer at the theatre and Felix's intimate friend), and after dinner played all sorts of music, grave and gay, upon his Streicher, which he lends me for my concert. Felix played me a Concerto by J. S. Bach, out of Hauser's fine collection; Hauser then sang a very funny song by the old composer Hiller, in which the word 'nose' plays a conspicuous part. I intend to copy it and bring it to you. (Hauser wished to do this himself, and sent the song to Mrs. Moscheles, who still has it.) I took my mother and sister to the subscription concert, and remained the whole evening with them. Felix was very well received. His 'Meeresstille' was delightful, and received with great applause. The rest I will tell you by word of mouth. After the concert I took my ladies home, met Felix and Hauser at supper in the hotel, afterwards accompanied and walked home with them in the bright moonlight, and now I bid you good night."

"October 5, 11.30 P. M.—I am just entering my room, which I have not seen since early this morning: only fancy, I could not have a piano in it, there is such a dearth of good instruments in Leipzig. Your letter came early to hand. Felix and I are so glad you have been playing his Octet. He tells me how grieved he is at not having as yet been able to thank you in writing. In fact he speaks of his gratitude as he would write it. . . . Table d'hôte, with Schumann, the tenor, Wild, and others."

"October 6.—I went on with my letter at noon, when all business in Leipzig, save that of knife and fork, is at a stand-still. I wanted, just now, to go through my part of Bach's triple concerto, but found all the pianoforte warehouses shut. I had no time to go to Felix before dinner at one o'clock; I am sure to do justice to it, for I am in unusually good health here. To-day I visited my mother, and amused her with my album. I have come across a little volume called 'Bettina's Diary,' which precedes her correspondence with Goethe. If you are curious in the matter, you can easily get a copy."

"Five in the afternoon.—I am just come from Wieck's, where Clara played admirably in one of Schubert's trios. Bach's Concerto for three pianos, performed by her, Felix, and myself, was very interesting; I am having it copied for London. You ought to have seen poor Felix accompanying a very inferior singer, and watched him as he sat on the stool of penitence, with thirty listeners around him. His eyes sparkled like those of a baited tiger, and you could have lit a candle at his cheeks, they burned so. I am just going to mark my newly-printed concert tickets. I miss your helping hand, but as I write each separate ticket, I can think quietly of you, which is a delightful feeling. To-day Felix told me the Directors wished me to play next Sunday in the second subscription concert. He advised me to make them give me room and lights, gratis, for my concert, instead of the customary five or six louis d'or, and I find he is right. One thought troubles me about my return home. The coach only goes on Monday mornings early at five, and on Tuesday evenings at nine. The first is too near to the Concert, the second too late for my impatience."

"October 9.—I am writing to you just after I have received your letter. . . . My one absorbing thought is *when* I shall talk to you. On Sunday I play at the subscription concert my G minor Concerto, and I hope I shall find some time for writing before the coach leaves. My concert will be a brilliant one this evening; there is a great rush for tickets; seven hundred and fifty are already disposed of, and probably as many will have to be sent back from the doors. My mother and sister send best love."

"October 10.—I wish I could give the post wings to tell you the news of my unusually brilliant concert at Leipzig. The crowd was immense. My mother felt quite young again. My overture was admirably played. The Concertos 'Pathétique' and 'Fantastique' received with immense applause. My duet with Felix created a regular 'furore.' They wanted to encore it, but we resisted, the heat was so great. My Fantasia, too, was very well received. The gross receipts were 497 thalers, expenses 70 thalers, so there is a surplus of 427. By playing at the subscription concert I shall defray the other expenses. Besides the G minor Concerto, which went very well at the rehearsal to-day, my overture was repeated, as well as our duet, which we played by request. Felix is so good to me, so amiable and unpretending; he told me that, before I came, he had been thinking, and hoping, and wondering whether I would like to play a duet with him, and how he intended to have written to me on the subject. He is idolized here, and lives on the most friendly terms with many musicians and notabilities, although he is intimate with but few, and reserved towards many. He is particularly attentive to my mother. You are right; my intercourse with him quickens my energies, independent of the pleasure I have in his society."

"Sunday.—We had to attend a dinner, which was anything but pleasant, and when we went away together, Felix fired off a volley of indignation. I spent one part of the evening with my mother, and the other tête-à tête with Felix. We drank tea, and after a cosy chat he played me several of his glorious fugues, and 'Lieder ohne Worte' (manuscript). To-morrow, early, my mother leaves us. My time will hang heavy when she goes, but I must act like a man."

"Afternoon.—I have just come from a very pleasant dinner at Kistner's. Hauser, Dr Schleinitz, Weise, Fink, and others were there, and I write you a few lines before I dress for the concert. Felix had just heard that his youngest sister had arrived; his parents write, asking me to take her on to Berlin, and stay with them; Felix begs me to do this, but I don't know if I can spare the time. Before dinner Felix and I went to my mother's house, where he played a great deal to her. Adieu! Au revoir!"

The next letter is dated from Berlin: "14th October. I received your letter, with which I was delighted, on Monday, at Leipzig. After my mother's departure it came like soothing balsam."

"Monday.—Now that you had encouraged me so heartily, I felt inclined to allow myself the trip to Berlin. You set all my doubts at rest. Felix and I accompanied his sister hither. Monday night we were up till twelve o'clock at a party given by Härtel, where I played solos and duets with Felix; then I packed my things from one to two, and by six A. M. we were seated in the carriage. We had plenty of cheerful and delightful talk—you were a constant topic. Felix, whose sister is a very nice, amiable creature, had sent a letter to his parents, giving them notice of our intended arrival, but the letter miscarried, for, when we came after midnight, not a soul was stirring. The servants had to prepare our beds as best they could. There was nothing to eat, and we were all ravenous, so a big slice of my cake, brought by my mother from Prague, did excellent service. The meeting of the aged parents and their children next morning was a family fête, and gave me, a mere spectator, feelings of indescribable delight. This was enhanced by the fact of my being received and welcomed as affectionately as if I were a son. I see I shall be besieged on all sides, to abandon my purpose of starting off again this evening, and that it will end in my leaving Berlin twenty four hours later. My nights, which have been broken into, my happy time here, and your words of encouragement, will, I suppose, make me fix on to-morrow."

Felix adds:—

"If you want to be angry at Moscheles' staying away from you a few days longer, you must be wroth with the whole of No. 3, Leipziger Strasse; they are all guilty. He wanted to go away, although he only came yesterday (or rather to-day) at half-past one in the morning; but we humbly memorialized him and would have called in the police to detain him; besides, you will have him again in Hamburg, and Holland, and London, whereas we must separate to-morrow, and shall not exchange words for a long time to come. In short, I entreated him, as fervently as I could, and hope you will put yourself in my position, for then I am sure you would have done just the same thing; when you meet, Moscheles will bring you all my and our greetings. The post is just going, so farewell, and don't be angry with

"Your sincere friend,

"F. MENDELSSOHN-BARTHOLDY."

In addition to this, Felix's father had dictated to him the following lines. "I must add my best remembrances, and in telling you of my delight in the unexpected visit of our excellent friend brought here by Felix, express my regret at the shortness of his stay. Pray accept my thanks for prevailing on him to give up this real pleasure. I hope you will thank me too for having induced Moscheles, after travelling all night, not to start off again this evening in a 'Beiwagen,' whereas to-morrow evening he will have a place in the 'Postwagen.' Farewell, and remember me kindly, etc., etc."

During this short visit Moscheles was an eye-witness of Felix's child-like sunny cheerfulness and perfect happiness in the bosom of his family. In a letter which Moscheles wrote to his wife late one evening, he says: "We have had a regular day of it. First of all I played with Felix Mozart's 'Duet in D,' for two pianofortes; and my 'Hommage à Handel.' We then allowed ourselves all manner of extravagances, extemporized jointly and alternately on two pianos—an intellectual sort of tournament. I played Felix's 'Rondo Brillant in E flat,' and my 'Concerto Fantastique,' he supplying a substitute for an orchestral accompaniment on a second piano. We played by turns his 'Lieder ohne

Worte,' and then perpetrated all sorts of musical absurdities. Fanny Hensel pleased me immensely by the playing of her own compositions; Felix and I had a good hunt in his collection of old music. Suffice it to say, I shall never forget the hours I passed here, and I unwillingly part from my delightful hosts, but I must pay a visit here and there before I leave."

During this short stay in Berlin, curiously enough, the theft practiced on Moscheles in the year 1823, and mentioned in page 54 of this volume, was once more brought under Moscheles' notice. He knew well enough who had defrauded him, but the young man's confession and repeated promises to restore the property, induced Moscheles to abandon all idea of going to law. On the eve of Moscheles' departure from Berlin, the young man writes that he has met and recognized him in the streets, invokes on him all kinds of blessings for his forbearance, and, after informing him how he has hitherto subsisted as a literary man, ends by saying that he is unable at present to compensate Moscheles for his loss, offering however to give him a written acknowledgment of the debt. Moscheles declines this as an unnecessary formality, but on being told, by Felix's father, that the young man belongs to a respectable family in Berlin, requests the elder Mendelssohn to act on his behalf, and obtain, through some other member of the family, a restitution of the property. Several letters during the next few days pass on the subject, when on the 29th of October he hears of the young man's sudden death. Mr. Mendelssohn then offers to proceed in the matter, and writes:—

"The whole history, told in your simple language, is certainly a wonderful one, and illustrating, as it does, your discretion, kindness, and forethought, reminds me of Schiller's golden words, 'Und die Tugend, sie ist kein leerer Schall!' (And virtue is no hollow sound.) Unhappily the poor young man had no opportunity of redeeming himself; after making so many false steps, one would have hoped he had just begun to improve—that again reminds me of the golden rule of the Rabbis: 'Bessere dich eine Stunde vor deinem Tod (Try to improve an hour before your death).' Further, it shows how talent and the best education are mere delusions, which lead their possessor to certain destrnction, if the true inner light, character, and conscience do not sustain him in the right path. It shows, moreover, that all sin avenges itself in this world. "Well, 'Requiescat in pace.'

"Always yours,

"A. MENDELSSOHN BARTHOLDY."

The sequel of this episode was as melancholy as it was unexpected. Felix's honored father, Moscheles' faithful friend, died on the 19th of November in the same year, and the blow so prostrated Moscheles as to make him utterly indifferent to take any further action. To institute legal proceedings was utterly distasteful to him. He remained a considerable loser; the family of the young man, although reputed wealthy, having never thought it worth the trouble to clear the memory of their relative.

After a short stay at Hamburg with his relatives, the last two months of the year were devoted by Moscheles to the pains and pleasures of concert-giving in Belgium and Holland. Writing from Amsterdam, he observes: "I can't complain of the phlegmatic Dutch. In the year 1820 I enjoyed the hospitality of my friends the Konigswarters, and there wrote my Concerto in G minor, which was received as warmly as my subsequent compositions are now. I must play everywhere, and the pecuniary results are very gratifying." "But," adds Mrs. Moscheles, "in spite of all the musical honors heaped on my husband, we find some odd customs here. At the Subscription Concert, the first part is scarcely finished when all the gentlemen vanish. Where are they? My olfactory nerves soon answer the question, as the tobacco fumes issue from the adjoining room. The ladies meanwhile drink chocolate and lemonade, and I, in my solitude, found time for studying the bareness of the four whitewashed walls of the concert room." Moscheles, here as elsewhere, complains of the bad orchestra. "The Directors take every imaginable pains. I myself seldom sit at the piano, when I rehearse a concerto, but run about between the leading violin and double drum, up and down, whispering the note into the ear of every player; after all my trouble, the music will not 'go.' I often omit a difficult Adagio, and in Rotterdam, where I had a very poor instrument to play upon, extemporized on Mozart's air, 'I can do nought but pity you,' and applied the words to myself. In spite of a violent attempt to encore me, I would not a second time face a struggle with the refractory keys of the pianoforte."

The troubles of concert-giving in the Belgian towns are largely compensated for by visits to the galleries, churches and museums. Once returned to England, Moscheles can look back upon Holland as a store-house of happy memories for future years.

# CHAPTER XVIII.

## 1836.

Letters from Members of the Mendelssohn Family—Braham at St. James' Theatre—Malibran—Thalberg—De Beriot—John Parry—The Duke of Brunswick's Bouquet—Death of Malibran—Ole Bull—Holiday Occupations—Felix Mendelssohn's Betrothal—The Oratorio of St Paul at Liverpool—Thalberg's Compositions—Schumann—Account with Cramer and Co.—Twelve Characteristic Studies.

WE read the following passages in a letter written by Moscheles in January. "As yet not a word from our friend Felix Mendelssohn; he has not recovered from the shock of his father's death, or he would certainly have written. What I do hear of him is anything but consolatory, they say he cannot work, from feeling an indescribable void in the loss of one whom he regarded as the chief mainstay of his life; but such a state of things cannot last. I can well understand his grief when my mind goes back to the autumn days I spent with him in his old home. His father, old, weak, and almost blind, was a man gifted with such activity of mind and clearness of judgment that I could not only understand the deep reverence my friend felt for him, but also share it with him. The following letters from other members of the Mendelssohn family testify to their sorrow. The first is from Mendelssohn's widow:—

"Berlin, 12th January, 1836.

"I know you have a deep sympathy with me, dear Mrs. Moscheles, prostrate as I am under this terrible and utterly unexpected blow, and I know that you will find some alleviation of your own sorrow in my honestly assuring you that the two days your excellent husband spent with us in October were among the brightest and most cheerful that gilded *his* declining days; nay, they left a remembrance which to the last gave him the deepest joy. Everything then seemed in harmony with his wishes, and events appeared to shape themselves as he would have thought best for his own happiness. He was deeply sensible and grateful for such blessings, and what a noble, gentle, beneficent spirit his was, day after day ripening, aspiring to higher aims! How thoughtful his observations the very last night he was with us, as he sat listening to our reading the 'Profession de Foi du Vicaire Savoyard,' out of Rousseau's 'Emile.' How sweet, how cheerful our interview, before that last sleep, the sleep of death! I had never thought death possible in that painless, ethereal form. I could not realize the dread face. Without any foreshadowing of my sorrow, I found myself bereaved and in deepest misery. My children, one and all, behave like angels, and I were ungrateful indeed, if in my hour of agony, I were blind to the many blessings still left to me. Felix's struggle with the sorrow brought on him made me at first very troubled and anxious; when we are with him tears seem to give him relief and courage for the battle of life before him. It is a good thing we should have him just now living near us; he has twice visited us since the event. Pray accept, my dear friend, my warmest thanks for all the kindness you showed to my dear one when he was in London; he always spoke of it with emotion and gratitude, at last, when the state of his eyes prevented him from working, he would repeatedly say: 'I don't feel in the least dull, I have seen in the course of my life much that is beautiful and interesting!' And his visits to London, and your friendship, he reckoned among his highest enjoyments. He never forgot any of his numerous friends, pray assure them all how deeply sensible I am of their kindness.

"L. MENDELSSOHN-BARTHOLDY."

We give an extract from a letter of Fanny Hensel, to the Moscheles; she was Mendelssohn's elder sister in point of years, but like a twin-sister in her tastes and susceptibility for art. After acknowledging, in language similar to that in her mother's letter, the care and attention paid to her father while he was in London, she continues: "Do you remember, dear Mrs. Moscheles, how Felix one autumn evening you spent with us played the exquisite Adagio in F sharp major from one of Haydn's quartets? My father had a special love for Haydn's music, the movement was new to him, and so powerfully affected him that he wept as he listened, confessing afterwards that it impressed him as being so deeply sorrowful. Felix was much struck by this view, for although 'mesto' was marked, we had all been impressed rather the other way. My father's judgment in musical matters was often wonderfully acute, and singularly correct for one uninitiated in the technicalities of the art. For you, dear Mrs. Moscheles, he had the greatest esteem and affection. My anxiety about Felix is at an end, he has collected all his energies, and deep though his sorrow be, it is natural, and not of that distressing kind that deepened our sorrow and made us doubly solicitous on his account. The coming season and travelling will, I trust, completely restore him to that state of mind that he must recover, if he wishes to live up to his father's standard, as he never failed to do while they were together. Such intense sympathy as theirs is very rarely found in the world. I now bid you both heartily farewell.

"FANNY HENSEL."

Moscheles' sympathy and thoughts were far away with his afflicted friends, but the duties incidental to his position in England were paramount considerations, and he found it impossible to withdraw from the busy vortex of London. Adverting to theatrical matters he says: "Braham has taken a lease of a small house, the St. James's Theatre, and had it decorated very tastefully in the Louis XIV. style. He has an excellent company, headed by Jenny Vertpré, and other well-known celebrities of the French stage; they attract the best society of London by their exquisite rendering of dramas which have already become popular in Paris." At a later period French operas were given, with the lovely Cinti and famous tenor Nourrit, who shone particularly in two pieces, "La Reine de Seize Ans" and "La Jeunesse de Charles II." Once at this theatre Moscheles joined Malibran and other stars in a concert, which began after the opera and lasted till midnight. Balfe produces with great success his first opera, "The Siege of Rochelle." "The music light, after the manner of the composer himself, but cheerful and pleasing like the author;" after this he writes for Malibran "The Maid of Artois." That versatile artist, equally at home in the English, Italian, French, and Spanish languages, was engaged as an English prima donna at Drury Lane Theatre. "Did Balfe intend her to do battle with those incredibly difficult passages at the beginning, or were they improvised by her on the spur of the moment? I can't say; somehow or other the enchantress conjured them forth. I don't like her so well in Fidelio, and prefer our own unrivalled Schröder-Devrient in the part. Malibran's forte lies in passionate acting, which contrasts too violently with the enduring womanly love of Fidelio, and why she brings two pistols into the prison, neither I nor any one else can understand."

Malibran's protracted stay in London led to a close intimacy with the Moscheles, at whose house she was a constant visitor. She was married to De Bériot. Her sparkling genius, sunny cheerfulness, and never-failing spirit and humor contrasted forcibly with his apathy, not to say coldness, more especially as the two artists were constantly seen and judged together. Other singers may captivate by their art, and gifted and amiable women by their manners and conversation, but Malibran had magic power to lead us captives, body and soul. In Moscheles' house she had every one at her feet, the children looked on her as their own property, she alone knew the right way to play with the doll's house, and none other but Malibran had a certain black silk bag of irresistible attraction to the little ones. The contents of this bag were not, however, the commonplace things—toys or sugar-plums—but a paint-box, paper, and brushes. She would come into the room, and the minute afterwards she would be down on the carpet with the children, letting them pull out everything, and then the picture-making began, and she would throw her whole energies into the work, and share the children's intense delight.

We quote from the diary of the 12th of June: "Sunday.—I began my day with setting Goethe's 'Meeresstille und Glückliche Fahrt' as a song for Malibran. We had great fun the other day, when she and De Bériot joined our early dinner. The conversation turned upon Gnecco's comic duet, which Malibran sang so frequently and charmingly with Lablache. Man and wife ridicule and abuse one another, caricaturing alternately each other's defects—when she came to the passage: 'La tua bocca è fatta apposta pel servizio della posta;' 'just like my mouth,' said Malibran, 'as broad as you please, and I'll just put this orange in, to prove it.' One must have known De Bériot to appreciate his amazement and agony at seeing his wife open her mouth wide, and discover two beautiful rows of teeth, behind which the orange disappears. Then she roared with laughter at her successful performance.

"She came at three o'clock; with her were Thalberg, Benedict, and Klingemann. We dined early, and immediately afterwards Malibran sat down to the piano, and 'sang for the children,' as she used to call it, the Rataplan and some of her father's Spanish songs; for want of a guitar accompaniment she used, while playing, every now and then to mark the rhythm on the board at the back of the keys. After singing with exquisite grace and charm a number of French and Italian romances of her own composition, she was relieved at the piano by Thalberg, who performed all manner of tricks on the instrument, snapping his fingers as an obligato to Viennese songs and waltzes. I played afterwards with reversed hands, and with my fists, and none laughed louder than Malibran. At five o'clock, we drove to the Zoological Gardens, and pushed our way for an hour with the fashionables. When we had had enough of man and beast, we took one more turn in the Park, and directly we got home Malibran sat down to the piano and sang for an hour. At last, however, she called out to Thalberg: 'Venez jouer quelque chose, j'ai besoin de me reposer,' her repose consisting in finishing a most charming landscape, in water-colors (an art in which she was self-taught). Thalberg played by heart, and in a most masterly way, several of his 'Studies,' and fragments of a newly written Rondo, then my 'Studies,' 'Allegri di Bravura,' and 'G minor Concerto.' We had supper afterwards; there again it was Malibran who kept us all going. She gave us the richest imitations of Sir George Smart, the singers Knyvett, Braham, Phillips, and Vaughan, who had sung with her at a concert given by the Duchess of C.; taking off the fat Duchess herself, as she condescendingly patronized 'her' artists, and winding up with the cracked voice and nasal tones of Lady —, who inflicted 'Home, sweet Home' on the company. Suddenly her comic vein came to a full stop; then she gave in the thorough German style the scena from Freyschütz, with German words, and a whole series of German songs by Mendelssohn, Schubert, Weber, and my humble self; lastly, she took a turn with 'Don Juan,' being familiar not only with the music of Zerlina, her own part, but knowing by heart every note in the opera, which she could play and sing from beginning to end. She went on playing and singing alternately until eleven o'clock, fresh to the last in voice and spirits. When she left us, we were all rapturous about her music, languages, painting; but what we liked best was her artlessness and amiability."

Moscheles composed for her a song with Klingemann's words, "Steigt der Mond auf." ("The moon rises.") She made him play to her constantly, knew several of his "Studies" by heart, and told us that her father made her practice them.

Moscheles, speaking in one of his letters of a concert at his own house, adds, "Malibran and De Bériot appeared at eleven o'clock, after our eighty guests had satisfied their musical appetite with English vocal music, solos by Lipinsky and Servais, and my own 'Concert Fantastique.' She looked weary, and, when she sang, one scarcely recognized Malibran, she was so voiceless. We only heard subsequently that she had been thrown from her horse when riding in the park. Although suffering no injury, she had not yet recovered from the violent shock. She was soon herself, however, and sang two 'Freyschütz' scenas in German, a comic English duet with John Parry, three Spanish, Italian, and French songs, winding up with the duet, 'Cadence du Diable,' for herself and De Bériot, in which she prefaces his daring and marvellous violin passages with the words, 'Voyez comme le diable prélude." The proper name of the piece is 'Le Songe de Tartini,' and the supposition being that the master has, in a dream, seen the devil, and heard him play the piece right through, every latitude is allowed for whims and eccentricities. When my wife showed some anxiety lest she should over-exert herself, she replied, 'Ma chère, je chanterais pour vous jusqu'à extinction de voix.' It was interesting to watch her raptures in listening to a duet composed and played by Benedict and De Bériot; certain passages in the work seemed to me possibly to have emanated from her pen. I was called on at the end of the evening to improvise; and that the comic element might be properly represented, young John Parry amused us with his masterly parody of the scena in the Wolf's Glen in the 'Freyschütz.' With a sheet of music rolled up, with one end in his mouth and the other resting on the music desk, he produced the deepest horn or trombone notes; his hands worked the keys, and his feet a tea-tray. There was the 'Wilde Jagd' complete. Thalberg had a bad finger, and couldn't play; but he and De Bériot staid with us until three in the morning, gossiping and commenting on the events of the evening." On the 11th of May Moscheles is assisted by De Bériot at his concert given in the Italian Opera House. "I had an 'embarras de richesses;' besides the great star Malibran, there were Lablache, Grisi, and Clara Novello. I played a concerto of Bach's that had never been heard in England, and my own 'C minor Concerto.' It was a tremendous success for all concerned. After a performance of the 'Maid of Artois,' in which Malibran performed marvellously, we went to see her in her dressing-room. There she sat, surrounded by wreaths and an enormous bouquet in her hand. She talked and laughed with us, adding: 'Si vous vouliez me débarrasser de cette machine, c'est cet abominable Duc de Brunswick qui vient de me l'apporter,' and so saying, threw a colossal bouquet at me, which I caught. What must 'the abominable Duke' have thought, when, a few moments later, he saw me mount *my* carriage and carry off *his* bouquet? For so it happened at the entrance-door of Drury Lane Theatre." The exertions of the famous artiste were incessant; for, independent of her three operatic performances per week, she was repeatedly engaged for morning and evening concerts, and accepted all sorts of invitations to fashionable breakfasts, fêtes champêtres, and private parties. To attend three parties on the same evening was a matter of constant occurrence. "On the 16th of July," writes Moscheles, "before the De

Bériots started on their journey, we spent an hour with Malibran, by appointment; we found her at the piano, and Costa standing by her. She sang us a comic song that she had just composed: A sick man weary of life invokes death; but when death, personified by a doctor, knocks at the door, he dismisses him with scorn. She had set this subject so cleverly, and sang the music so humorously, that we could scarcely refrain from laughing; and yet we couldn't endure to lose a single note. After this, she wrote in my album a charming French romance; this she sang to us, and presented my wife with one of her original water-color landscapes. At last we parted; they went to Brussels for a few days, and returned to Manchester for the music festival, where she sang so bewitchingly, on the 20th of September, that the audience boisterously called for an encore. Malibran, already in a very dangerous state, and one requiring absolute rest and cessation from work, summoned all her remaining energies; after repeating her song, and her inimitable shake on the high C, she fainted away and became unconscious. She was taken to the hotel; the doctor bled her, and she awoke to apparent consciousness; but alas! this only lasted till the 23d of September, when she died." . . . . "Expressions of sorrow are inadequate, for such a loss as this penetrates the whole world of art, and plunges into grief the more confined circle of her friends. I felt impelled to clothe my sorrow in sound, and composed a fantasia on Malibran's death."

Thalberg, who in the year 1826 had parted from Moscheles as a pupil, now returned as a master. "I find his introduction of harp effects on the piano quite original," writes Moscheles. "His theme, which lies in the middle part, is brought out clearly in relief with an accompaniment of complicated arpeggios which remind me of a harp. The audience is amazed. He himself remains immovably calm; his whole bearing, as he sits at the piano, is soldier-like; his lips are tightly compressed, and his coat buttoned closely. He told me he acquired this attitude of self-control by smoking a Turkish pipe while practicing his pianoforte exercises; the length of the tube was so calculated as to keep him erect and motionless." We quote from a letter:—

"At 10 in the evening of the 2d of May, we heard a knock at our door, and Ole Bull, the Norwegian violinist, stepped in; this was his first visit to us. In less than five minutes he had poured forth a torrent of talk, giving us his exalted opinion of himself, and rattling on in such an impetuous, eccentric fashion that we were completely dumbfoundered. Is this the genuine *feu sacré?* The description he gave of his own life (it has appeared in print) is so full of adventure that it threw Paganini completely into the shade, and we asked ourselves, when he was gone, whether his talent as a violin-player would do as much. His playing, no less than his demeanor, at his own concert, created a sensation. I shouldn't like to mention Spohr's name in connection with his, nor that of other musicians, his inferiors in execution, for they will permanently be recognized as first-rate artists, when the impetuous Norwegian, pitted against them, is forced to succumb in the art arena. I must add," says Mrs. Moscheles, "that Ole Bull, shortly before he announced his concert, stepped in to see us at our dinner hour, when Moscheles had just come home after a weary day's lesson-giving. I can't say he was a welcome guest, much less did we relish his request that Moscheles would play for him. Moscheles tried to get off, and for a time withstood manfully his tormentor, but consented at last. Such incidents are time-killers." "To-day," she says in another letter, "I will enumerate for you some of the strange contrasts we are subjected to. The other day we had a small party on purpose for the Lockharts, when my husband's respected friend and colleague, the famous Schnyder von Wartensee, turns up unexpectedly, and, as if he were not enough, in comes Sanklow, the Polish Jew, in his robes; he is not attractive to the olfactory nerves, and while Moscheles is playing his trio with Lipinsky and Servais, he is all impatience for the last bar, that he may have his turn, and give us the benefit of his straw and wood fiddle, with its petty shakes and passages. He is not up to the mark of Gusikow, his compatriot and predecessor, on the poverty-stricken instrument. And how would you have liked a grand performance of Handel's oratorio, 'Solomon,' in Exeter Hall, and immediately afterwards the dance-music of a ball-room, where we were obliged, in spite of the unpleasant contrast, to look in for an hour or so, or we should have been thought rude? In London, no fête, ball, or evening party is thought successful unless 'one has everybody,' therefore, that we might have 'everybody,' our friends the H.'s, who, as you know, are a good deal mixed up with Indian affairs, brought to our house, a few evenings since, his Excellency Prince Jam-hod-deen, the tawny son of Tippoo Saïb. On this evening, however, we had only a few select listeners, bent on enjoying with us the Kreutzer sonata with Lipinsky, and the Bach concerto, with quartet accompaniments. How the tawny prince must have longed for his tam-tam! We find the parties at Lady —'s very agreeable. She is a zealous pupil and admirer of Moscheles, engages the entire troupe of Italians at an immense cost, and fills her three splendid reception-rooms with the rank, fashion, and beauty of the day. When invited on such nights, we are given to understand that there is no design to make my husband play to a set of people who would only talk during an instrumental performance."

H. Herz introduced his seven-octave piano in the concert market, but the tone was declared to be thin, and his invention met with but faint praise. Broadwood, on the other hand, made his first essay with his bichord (semi-grand) piano, and proved the possibility of gaining a powerful tone through the medium of only two strings. These instruments attained most deservedly a large circulation, and Moscheles always delighted to play on them.

Moscheles, writing from Ramsgate, talks with delight of shaking from his finger tips the dust of lesson-giving, and adds :—

"If my wife asks me the reason of my not utilizing my spare time for composing, I can only answer that my conscience will not allow me. After the harum-scarum of a London season, the mind and fingers become paralyzed, and the former can only be healed by the latter, which means that I must play a great deal of the best music before I can allow myself to indulge in an idea of my own, or commit it to paper, otherwise it would be mere shallow hackneyed stuff. After escaping illness, the exhausted patient should take strengthening medicine, before he again resumes his professional calling." During the close of his visit to the seaside he writes a Greek war-song for Phillips, who, on receipt of it, replies, "I shall sing it at the Philharmonic, and everywhere else, and will answer for its success." Besides this he composes music for Uhland's beautiful poem, "Schäfers Sontagslied," and is so delighted with his holiday time that he gives it in one of his letters the epithet of "heavenly."

The happy news of Mendelssohn's being engaged to be married surprises him on his return to London. Four years before, on the 3d of September, 1832, Mendelssohn had written to Mrs. Moscheles: "Klingemann still remains a knight of the order of bachelors, and so do I; thirty years hence we shall both want to get married, but then no girl will care to take us. When you burn the letter, cut this prophecy out, and preserve it carefully, in thirty years it will be seen whether it was worthy of credit." On the 6th of October, Mrs. Moscheles receives the following letter, in a different strain, from Mendelssohn's mother.

"Berlin, October 6th, 1836.

"Dearest Mrs. Moscheles,—You have probably already heard by report, which travels now-a-days so much more rapidly than people or railways and steamers, that Felix is engaged to be married. I cannot, however, deny myself the pleasure of personally communicating to you and your husband, Felix's excellent friend, the news which is a matter of such happiness to us all. You, an affectionate mother, can imagine how strange it seems to me, not to know either his bride elect, or any one of her numerous relations; nor can I recollect ever to have heard the name of the family. As a penalty for excessive liveliness, quite out of place, considering what an old lady I am, I shall be forced to wait a long time before I can see the fair unknown, who is already so precious to me. You know, however, how disinterested are a mother's feelings, and will form a correct estimate of the joy we all feel, for Felix himself seems so completely happy. There is, however, a bitter drop to this cup of joy, and the thought is constantly arising in my mind, had his dear father but lived to share our happiness! He desired such a blessing for Felix so earnestly, and yet scarcely ventured to hope for it. That sad event (his father's death) supplied Felix perhaps with the strongest incentive for taking such a resolve. When he paid us his last Christmas visit, he was so inexpressibly wretched, so thoroughly heart-broken, so absorbed in silent suffering, so vacillating and purposeless even in his art schemes, that his sisters persuaded him he must turn over a new leaf, and give his mind a fresh start.

"His acquaintance with a young lady in Frankfort soon enabled him to shake off the thraldom of low spirits, and he is now happily betrothed to his Cecile; Madame Jeanrenaud, her mother, was a Miss Souchay, and is related to the Beneckes and Schunck.

"Malibran's death has shocked and grieved me exceedingly; Felix always reckoned her talents as among the greatest in our times. What a loss! As you may imagine, a mother's egotism too puts in its word, for she was to have sung in 'St. Paul,' at Liverpool, on the third of this month. You, and your dear husband, and our London friends will excuse him if he has not written for a long time; I too am not favored with many letters just at present. Rebecca, who on returning from Eger, is paying a fortnight's visit to her brother, writes, as a justification, that he is in the midst of whirl and bustle, without a quiet moment to himself. Pray excuse him, and heap kindness on kindness by announcing his engagement, in his and my name, to our London friends.

"Your ever faithful and devoted,

"L. MENDELSSOHN-BARTHOLDY."

The happiness of Mendelssohn's friends on hearing of his engagement with Cecile Jeanrenaud was perfectly intelligible, for it soon became plain that he had found a mind in harmony with his own, a woman who understood him and knew how to value him as he deserved. At the same time he was to enjoy a great musical triumph in England, although he was not present to witness it; for the oratorio of "St. Paul" was given for the first time in Liverpool, and received with the greatest enthusiasm. Moscheles, who had undertaken the correction of the work for England, writes in his diary: "To my great delight, I am constantly busy with the magnificent 'St. Paul,' and often become completely absorbed in the work. Its chief qualities are, in my judgment, majesty, a noble simplicity, deep feeling, and an antique form. In this work he has given the most brilliant proofs of a mastery already generally recognized." In the quiet time of his autumn holiday Moscheles had begun to work at the "Characteristic Studies," and to send occasional contributions to musical periodicals. The song, "Whatever sweets we hope to find," the Terzet, "An Argument," etc., belong to these fugitive pieces.

"The proper ground for finger gymnastics," he writes in his diary, "is to be found in Thalberg's latest compositions; for 'mind' (Geist) give me Schumann. The Romanticism in his works is a thing so completely new, his genius so great, that to weigh correctly the peculiar qualities and weaknesses of this new school I must go deeper and deeper into the study of his works. He sends me his sonata 'Florestan and Eusebius,' which has just been published, accompanied by the flattering remark that I am the only person who can review the work properly, and would I do it for the 'Neue Zeitschrift der Musik,' in Leipzig."

This was done conscientiously and earnestly, and Schumann inserted the review in his "Gesammelte Schriften:" he also dedicated to Moscheles his "Concerto without Orchestra," which the latter zealously studied. He objected to the title as contradictory, and disagreed with Schumann's method of translating the musical signs—such as piano, forte etc.—into German, as not being generally feasible, and whenever he discovered in one and the same piece both German and Italian terms employed, he found fault with the practice.

Taking a retrospective glance at his dealings with his publishers, Moscheles again complains that only his arrangements of operas and pieces of a similar calibre prove remunerative, whereas his larger and important works command inadequate terms, and the sum paid for the elaborate and conscientiously prepared edition of Beethoven's pianoforte works is actually no compensation for the time expended upon it. After some discussion Moscheles obtained better terms for his larger compositions, and agreed, in addition to his already prepared arrangement of Balfe's operas, to edit a pianoforte version of Donizetti's "Belisario." He cannot suppress a sigh in his diary with reference to the latter. His chief work, however, was upon the twelve great characteristic "Studies." "They are not intended for pupils," he writes; "there are difficulties in them which only a master can overcome. Thalberg, Liszt, all such players will find their work cut out for them." "Juno," "The Dream," "The Bacchanal," were finished when the lovely "Nursery Tale," was begun, a harbinger of the coming event—the birth of a third daughter—a circumstance which occurred soon afterwards under very happy auspices.

# CHAPTER XIX.

## 1837.

Recitals for Pianoforte Music—Production of Beethoven's Ninth Symphony—An Old Harpsichord—Revival of Old Masters—British Concerts—Popularity of Italian Music and Musicians—Thalberg's Second Season in London—Foreign Guests—Assaut de Pianos—Chopin—Remarks on Pianoforte Makers—Schröder-Devrient—Operatic Affairs—The Antient Concerts—The Beethoven Monument in Bonn—Holidays in Hamburg—Return to London.

IN the course of the preceding winter many delightful evenings had been devoted to stringed quartets, which were repeated in the present year. Hitherto there had been no recitals for pianoforte music, and these were introduced by Moscheles. Many of his colleagues called this a venturous undertaking. Moscheles, however, held to his purpose, taking the precaution to interweave a little vocal music with the instrumental, so as to relieve the monotony which people warned him against. He was like the farmer in the fable, however, who was advised by some to ride himself, by others to put his son on the saddle. The newspapers were loud in their praises of the new scheme, but censured the introduction of vocal music, adding that it was an interruption, and the one blot in an otherwise perfect entertainment. On three successive occasions Moscheles played some music of Scarlatti and his contemporaries on a harpsichord, built in the year 1771, and still in possession of Messrs. Broadwood. Externally the instrument was shaped like an old Viennese piano. When the cover was lifted, one saw a contrivance somewhat in the shape of a Venetian blind, which, like the shutter covering the swell part of the organ, was acted upon by the pedals—by using this, greater sonority was given to the tone, which otherwise, was rather thin, and less agreeable. Moscheles gave much attention to the invention, and turned it to good account. The upper and lower keyboards of the instrument were evidently intended for the rendering of such passages of Scarlatti and other masters as on modern pianos require constant crossing of the hands; and one row of keys being connected with two, and the other with three strings, certain shades are produced in the quality of the sound.

Bach's D minor concerto, with quartet accompaniment, was now heard for the first time, and all agreed that a real feeling for music was fostered and promoted by an acquaintance with such masters; the papers expressed a hope that the crowded audience in Moscheles' three concerts would induce him to repeat them next winter, and introduce in his programmes even older composers than Sebastian Bach. A novelty in England was to be seen in the "British Concerts," the introduction of which was well timed, for the fashionable world was so prejudiced in favor of the light and often shallow Italian music, that young native talent felt piqued, and ready to measure itself with the vapid productions of Italian rivals, in the event of a series of performances being given, in which none but English artists and English music should be heard. "Exclusiveness," remarks Moscheles, "is a constant hindrance to art-progress; in this case, there was such a frequent want of originality in the composition, and such inadequacy of performance, that the fashionable world remained loyal to their favorite Italians, and only third-rate people took any pride or delight in "native talent." One of the great successes of the season, however, in which all classes joined, was obtained by Litolff, who brought out the first concerto he had composed. "Here, anyhow, is originality," says Moscheles, "although rather unpolished, and his powers as an executant are undeniable; the storm of applause and enthusiasm was on this occasion perfectly justified."

The diary, as well as the letters of this winter, show how earnestly Moscheles, as a joint-director of the Philharmonic Concerts, again labored to bring out Beethoven's Ninth Symphony, which, in the year 1824, had been pronounced impossible, and failed in consequence. Great as were the obstacles thrown in his way by his colleagues, they at last resolved to hand over to him the leadership in this purely venturous scheme; as for success, not a soul dreamt of such a thing. Now began a series of weeks of labor. Instead of one orchestral rehearsal, Moscheles was allowed two, but that was all, and, consequently, he seized the opportunity of rehearsing every difficulty with each individual player. Every singer and instrumentalist knew his part; owing to Moscheles' accompaniment and explanations, each man had some knowledge of the colossal work before the time of the first orchestral rehearsal; the second he used for the acquirement of light, shade, and expression, and although much was wanting, and two solo-singers not perfectly up to their work, still the performance was brilliantly successful. Moscheles writes in high spirits to his relatives, and says, "You can imagine my excitement before and during the concert on the 17th of April. I don't speak of my work and labors, for by this accompanying article, out of the *Atlas*, you will see how they have been rewarded. I don't know who the critic is, but I send you this article, because it deals with the chief points of the performance shortly and concisely; all the newspapers are fairly in raptures with this colossal music, and unanimously insist on its remaining a fixture in the 'Répertoire,' and being performed, on a grander scale, either in Exeter Hall or at the Birmingham Festival. Suffice it to say that wealthy England has enriched herself by one additional treasure, and how I rejoiced that I have been permitted to disinter it!" The weightiest part of the article lying before us consists in the remark that conductors who have not a thoroughly deep knowledge of the work itself, would labor in vain to make it understood, and that the performers themselves, if not penetrated with a sense of its beauties, would impose on the audience an intolerable ennui. Moscheles' peculiar capabilities and efforts are enumerated, and a due meed of praise is awarded both to singers and orchestral players.

In his second season in London, Thalberg enjoyed extraordinary success. His Fantasia on "God save the King" acquired a sort of political significance, as it was produced during the last days of King William IV.'s fatal illness—at Moscheles' own concert, on the 31st of May. Thalberg played, with him and Benedict, Bach's triple concerto—it was a regular triumph, and more enjoyed by the audience than Scarlatti's "Cats' Fugue," performed by Moscheles on the harpsichord; the "Characteristic Studies," the "Concert Pathétique," both novelties, were very well received.

In a letter from Moscheles to his relatives, the following passage occurs: "You might well suppose I was tired after the concert, but how could I be so? An exquisite performance was in readiness for me when I returned home—this was in honor of my birthday—nothing more or less than the 'Abt und Kaiser' dramatized, in which Felix appeared mounted on a horse—I beg his pardon, a rocking-horse.... Everything else analogous, and to a father's eyes unsurpassable."

In a letter from Mrs. Moscheles, written in the month of May, we read:—

"Certainly 'Dame Music' is more than ever the guardian patroness of this house, and you will believe this when you hear of all that passes in it. Czerny from Vienna, Jaques Rosenhain, the brothers Ganz and Franchomme, Mühlenfeld from Rotterdam, Gerke from St. Petersburg, Concertmeister Möser from Berlin, with his wife and talented son, all are our welcome foreign guests. Thalberg and Benedict often join our circle as habitués. Every one wishes to exchange music with Moscheles—*i. e.*, the pianoforte players produce their new compositions, listen to his, and the instrumentalists have their solos accompanied, or take part with him in Sonatas and Trios. Besides this, Ries has the score of a new oratorio, 'Saul and David,' Neukomm an incredible amount of sacred and secular music; all this Moscheles reads through with them at the piano, and often says to me, "Thank Heaven I have such good eyes, for Neukomm's delicately written small scores are a veritable eye-dust( *Augenpulver*), and I can prophecy no future life for the music itself. We are forced, alas! this year to do without our 'ace of trumps,' Felix Mendelssohn; instead of him, however, we have a third series of 'Lieder ohne Worte,' and a new series of 'Lieder' dedicated to Miss Julia Jeanrenaud, and we revel in both. Only think, I had lately to fight a pitched battle with, and, to save his interests as an artist, against —. He and his family can't speak a single word of English, and his son being about to give a concert, I had offered myself as translator of the advertisements, programmes, etc. But the worthy concert-giver brings me a regular German essay, reminding me more of a 'Café-chantant' than a Concert-room, and I decline the task of a faithful translation, being determined to omit all the laudatory epithets lavished on his son, a boy of ten. It was long before he consented, but out of regard for his position as an artist I remained firm. I must now tell you a good thing. At an evening party lately at our house, when half-a-dozen pianoforte-players were present, an awkward pause ensued; no one wished to be the first to play, every one, when asked, declared this one or the other must begin. My husband of course could have filled up the time by his own playing, but the great thing we wanted was to make the foreign artists and English amateurs acquainted with one another. What was to be done? In my difficulty, I proposed to write down on paper all the names of the gentlemen, and throw them into a hat, if they would promise to play in the order in which they were drawn. This was agreed to, and we had a regular "Assaut de Pianos.' Luckily the presence of Mrs. Shaw, with her fine alto voice, and Miss Masson, as well as Balfe, with his tenor, enabled us to give our friends some vocal music as well. Chopin, who spent a few days in London, was the only one of the foreign artists who did not go out, and wished no one to visit him, for the effort of talking told on his consumptive frame. He heard a few concerts and disappeared."

"I wrote to you lately about pianoforte-players" (we are quoting from another letter), "to-day, therefore, you shall have a chapter on pianoforte-makers; I shall call them only birds of passage this season, for 'birds of prey' would certainly be too strong an expression. And yet I see P.'s vinegar face, whenever at our house or at concerts he hears Moscheles upon an Erard or Clementi, and can fancy him muttering to himself, as he hears the Erard: 'Anch' io sono pittore,' or the Clementi: 'We are far ahead of that,' or the Broadwood, upon which Moscheles occasionally plays: "How can one prefer those to a P.?' G. too, who came here with Czerny, wanted to hear every instrument, to visit all the pianoforte-makers, and finds the touch of this instrument too heavy, the tone of another too muffled, and will allow his pianos alone to be brilliant.

We have, too, an inventor of a method for the art of tuning pianofortes; last year it was a Crefeldman, this year a Parisian, Monsieur le Père, but in spite of his assurances that it is so easy a matter to tune a piano half a tone higher or lower 'que vous le feriez faire par votre domestique, ou votre femme-de-chambre,' the thing didn't turn out practical. I could name many more, but it would weary you. Every one consults his own interests, but all agree in asking my poor husband for verbal introductions and written certificates to contain nothing but praise. 'And one can't help having a conscience,' he very correctly observes. 'One would not like to pay such equivocal compliments as the great M. has done occasionally; those who are commended are enchanted, but the recipient, if he is wide awake, knows how to interpret such stereotyped overwrought phraseology."

Schröder-Devrient appeared again; her Fidelio was incomparable as ever, her Norma, however, not up to Pasta's mark. The German Opera was obliged to close for want of support. "Love in the City," an opera by W., was given once in the English Opera House and then withdrawn. Puzzi, the fashionable horn-player, brought to London an opera buffa company, in which Ronconi, who afterwards became so famous, appeared; he, however, was the only star.

The Royal Opera House in the Haymarket had the great vocalists we have already mentioned; but the "Puritani," and such operas, were given so repeatedly that an amusing article appeared in the *Atlas*, headed "On Operatic Affairs." Director and company were treated as evildoers, and subjected to a severe cross-examination. For instance, questions are asked of Grisi: "How often this year has she sung 'Son vergin vezzosa '(her cavatina out of 'Puritani')? Has she sung it morning, afternoon, and evening, waking and sleeping?" And on her answering in the affirmative, the cross-examiner proceeds: "Does she like that music?"—"Not particularly." "Why does she sing it then?"—"Because she has for three years electrified the public; and the effect is as strong to-day as three years ago." "But isn't it better to please than to astonish?"—"Oh yes; but the public is only able to gape with astonishment because it lacks intelligence." Then comes Lablache's turn, and he is made to say: "John Bull loves him for his powerful voice. John Bull cares for nothing but loud bellowing and roaring, and such old hackneyed things as have been thoroughly drummed into his ears—that's enough to kill every good singer." Rubini, on the other hand, admits that he "enjoys singing the same things over and over again; that the composer may give him one note, but receives fifty in return; that Bellini, Donizetti, and Mercadante have become immortal by means of 'the broderie' lavished on their music by him and his colleague David, men whose singing can melt hearts of stone." "And what of Mozart?" is next asked. "Rubini knows him, and is obliged to sing his music occasionally. 'But, to make a hit, give me other operas.'"

The bitter truth underlying the humorous form of this article may thus be summed up: Mozart when sung by Italians, really lacked warmth; performers and audience were equally indifferent, and not once in the evening do the glorious voices show to advantage.

In the year 1776 the "Antient Concerts" had been organized by the Earl of Sandwich, and during Moscheles' residence in England, from 1820 to 1836, they alternated with the fortnightly Philharmonic Concerts, each Society giving yearly a series of eight. The intention was to bring out the very oldest music, English, Italian, German, and French; to use for this purpose old instruments which had slumbered for years in cabinets of antiquities, and thus to mark the progress of modern days by showing the improvements on old inventions. A 'viol di gamba,' 'viol d'amore,' etc., were heard among other instruments. During these concerts the music was sometimes interrupted by the loud observations of the Duke of —. "In spite of his fondness for music," says Moscheles, "he puts no restraint on himself; the subscribers are quite aware of the inevitable drawback; if a stranger happens to say, 'What noise is that?' he is simply told, 'Oh, it's only the Duke,' and that's enough. His abrupt sentences burst in like beats on a drum that is out of time with the orchestra.' This year Moscheles introduced as a novelty at the "Antient Concerts," Bach's "D minor Concerto," which could not fail to be received with great enthusiasm. Lord B., one of the directors of these "Antient Concerts," summond the artists to a consultation and meeting, with reference to the Beethoven monument in Bonn. He wished England to raise a splendid subscription, to be realized from a grand performance of Beethoven's compositions. The noble lord, however, was opposed by every one. It was said in one newspaper, "that the Germans never contributed a shilling to the monuments of illustrious Englishmen." In another Lord B. was reproved for never troubling himself about German music, and only caring really for the shallowest works of the Italian masters. At one of the meetings, Moscheles gave his decided vote against Lord B.'s proposition. "For," he said, "we are already in July, and besides, owing to the King's death, many a concert has been a failure." His opinion, however, although backed by all the other artists, was not allowed to prevail, and a concert was given on the 20th of July to empty benches. Happily, some subscriptions raised by Beethoven's admirers defrayed the costs of the concert; but the exaggerated promises made by Lord B. to the Bonn Committee evaporated in a letter of apology to Baron Schlegel.

The nine weeks' holidays were again spent very happily among Moscheles' Hamburg relatives at Flottbeck, one of the prettiest spots on the banks of the Elbe. Two "Studies" were composed there, and Moscheles' during his walks in the park, thought out the preface and characteristic marks and directions affixed to the twelve grand "Studies" which were published in the course of the winter. Moscheles sent the E flat fugue which is in these Studies to Schumann, with whom he frequently corresponded. It was a matter of regret to the Moscheles that Mendelssohn was in London during their absence, and afterwards in Birmingham, where he conducted at the Festival his oratorio of "St Paul," with what success is well known.

Returning in autumn to the half-deserted streets of London, Moscheles found Neukomm, Benedict, and Thalberg still there; these artists, as well as his friend Klingemann, were constant visitors; the house, as in all former years, was a musical centre, one evening every week being devoted to chamber music. Moscheles' chief occupation was reading pieces of ancient and modern music; for in the early part of the year, 1838, he intended giving a series of historical concerts, and among so many art-treasures much had to be examined before he made the final selection.

# CHAPTER XX.

## 1838.

Historical Concerts—The Trial Nights at the Philharmonic Concerts—Musical Pupils and Publishers—Influx of Foreign Artists—Johann Strauss's Music—Alfred De Vigny—Lady-Morgan—Great Event of the Season—A Month at Hastings—Beethoven—Chamber Music—Flattering Offer from Weimar.

"MY fingers are in proper order," he writes on the 1st of January in his diary, "and the programmes for my coming concerts are already made. I have burrowed again and again into the ash-covered treasures of the musical Pompeii, and brought many grand things to light. Beethoven is great—whom should I call greater?—but as the public is forever listening to his music, alternating with modern pieces written merely for display, I intend to introduce, first of all, those composers who gave the impetus to Beethoven's eagle flight. To have a proper appreciation of the art of our own day, we should not forget its past history; although I have begun with the old masters, I intend to lead my audience gradually up to our own time, and then they can compare and draw their own conclusions." After the second performance, he says: "The success of these concerts certainly proves that the public is capable of receiving true impressions of the really beautiful, that to rivet their attention, one has no need to worship at the shrine of fashion; my audiences rejoiced with me over these old specimens, whole and entire, such as I gave them; as dessert, Lindley and I indulged them in Beethoven's variations on a theme by Handel." The newspapers were loud in their praises of the undertaking, and improve the occasion to hurl anathemas at the Italian 'swindle,' and point to Moscheles as the representative of a higher order of musical devolopment; they all eulogize warmly his new characteristic "Studies," some of which he played on these occasions. "Why did he not play all the twelve?" they say; "people wish to hear them all, and repeatedly; Moscheles should not carry his modesty too far," etc. Mrs. Moscheles writes: "The Duke of Cambridge quite took the lead at these concerts, he often asked for an encore, and the audience backed him in spite of the lengthy programmes. He is so kind to my husband, and after every concert asks him: 'Pray when is the next? I must make a memorandum not to forget.' This winter there are classical quartet concerts, wind-instrument concerts, British concerts—in short, music without end. In February Moscheles, as one of the conductors of the Philharmonic Concerts, had to be present at the two "trial nights," of new compositions; these he called "very unsatisfactory." "Some German and some English symphonies and overtures have no vitality; an orchestral Fantasia, with a printed explanatory programme, containing 'Conspiracy, Revolution, and Deliverance,' is fit for a melo-drama in a suburban theatre; one symphony and a couple of overtures are better, but nothing much to speak of; not one of them found a place in the programme of the eight concerts given this year, for the Directors rather than risking a fiasco preferred adhering to the classical masters."

The Philharmonic Society opened this year's series of concerts with a funeral march in honor of their member, Ferdinand Ries, who had lately died. There were several novelties in the way of pianoforte compositions. Mrs. Anderson played Mendelssohn's Concerto in D minor, which was greeted, and justly, with great enthusiasm. Madame Dulcken was well received in Hummel's posthumous Concerto in F major, Moscheles played his own "Sonate Pathétique," a work which, in spite of the general sympathy of the public and the press, provoked one angry article, in which the writer took him to task for again conducting a performance of the Ninth Symphony, and parodied a short address which Moscheles made to the band on that occasion. The circumstance is only worth recording, inasmuch as it brought into relief the calmness and equanimity of Moscheles' character, whenever he became the victim of such petty annoyances. The hostile pages, let us add, had a short life, and the Ninth Symphony rewarded the Directors with fresh expressions of thanks and recognition on the part of the public; he found an ample reward in the accomplishment of so great a task, contrasting as it did with the yoke of lessons, and the exacting caprice of fashion, which necessitated those inevitable piano arrangements for the use of his pupils. Occasionally, when some importunate publisher would press on him some sensational title, we find remarks in the diary like the following: "The man positively drives me wild. He insists on dictating to me laws about title pages, making alterations without asking my leave. I don't allow this, he has no right to do so."

Frequently, too, does he complain of the multifarious duties, many so "unartistic," of the professional man in London; he regrets also that he has so little time for epistolary intercourse with his musical friends. Mrs. Moscheles writes in May: "My husband says it is far better you should accustom yourselves to my letters, even when dealing with musical matters, for we hear music together. He tells me exactly what he thinks of everything, so that, although it is second-hand, you have a minute and ungarbled account, and more in detail. He cannot write, so long as, independent of his own business, he must be the 'Deus ex machinâ' who is to conjure up honor and appreciation for foreign artists. And how are they to get ways and means when their artistic means and ways are so slender? As in the case of H.'s son. Heaven keep our boy from becoming such a nullity, and trading on his father's name! The poor fellow gave a concert, and he excited nought but compassion. Once more we have numbers of strangers here, Madame Oury, *née* Belleville, with her husband, the violinist; Kapellmeister Bott, from Oldenburg, an excellent musician, and his daughter, a pianiste; besides these, two Poles, one a pianoforte, the other a violin player, the latter decked in a superlatively white waistcoat, watch-chain, and with other mighty pretensions besides; two worthy Hanoverians, the flute-player Heinemeyer, and Hausmann the cellist; Müller, the double bass player, whose variations on the lovely 'Alexis' are an infliction; Braum, the hautboy player, and a whole family of trumpeters, the Distins; just imagine, a father and four sons, all trumpeting together; rather too much of a good thing. These artists are all more or less excellent, and from their repeated visits to our island will appropriate much of its gold dust; but as the competition is immense, the speedy success they expect for their undertakings is an impossibility, and we often find ourselves in the unpleasant position of helping less than they expect. Every one comes in and goes out of the house without any ceremony, so I call it the artists' kaleidoscope, which brings us daily new combinations, sometimes in glaring and obtrusive, at others in soft and sympathetic tones. Of course Thalberg is again high up in the world of pianists. Herz, Rosenhain, and Döhler have also their public, and belong to the brilliant stars of my kaleidoscope; when on a sudden is discovered Johann Strauss, then it is no longer a kaleidoscope, but Oberon's horn; where he fiddles, all dance—dance they must. In the concerts which he gives with his small orchestra, people dance as they sit; at Almack's, the most fashionable of all the subscription balls, aristocratical little feet hop to his tunes, and we too the other night at a party had the good fortune to dance to his fiddling, and, old married folk as we are, felt ourselves young again. He himself dances 'corps et âme,' while he plays, not with his feet, but with his fiddle, which is continually going up and down, while the whole man marks the accent of every bar; he is a good-tempered Viennese, not of the refined type of a drawing-room man, but amusing and always cheerful; one has had quite enough of the melancholy specimens. We are always delighted to make the acquaintance of a literary celebrity, as for instance Alfred de Vigny, the arch-enemy of George Sand. . . .

"Sir Charles and Lady Morgan had been very kind to my husband when he was in Ireland. He had told me already a great deal about them, and lately introduced me to the famous authoress. I am quite aware that it is to her sincere respect for my husband's talent that I am indebted for her kindness and friendliness shown towards myself. Her eyes still sparkle with fire in spite of her sixty years. She must have been very beautiful, and her liveliness is of the genuine Irish sort."

Barnett wrote a new opera, "The Mountain Sylph," and was still a popular composer. Benedict produced "The Gipsy's Warning," Lord Burghersh, "Il Torneo," and "Lucia di Lammermoor" was still in the ascendant, the people never tiring of Rubini's "Fra Poco." The warbling of the lovely Cinti enchanted the public, and Fanny Elsler, the essence of all grace, made a furore. The great event of the season, however, was the Coronation of Queen Victoria. Sir George Smart put Moscheles into a surplice, and placed him as a bass singer in Westminster Abbey, that he might witness the splendid ceremony, for tickets were not to be had for love or money. We quote from the diary: "What an imposing sight, the gorgeously decorated temple, crowded with splendidly dressed women, and what an impression was created by the sight of the youthful Queen in her robes, surrounded by all the grandees in her kingdom! Everything was imposing, but most of all Handel's chorus "Zadock the Priest," and his 'Hallelujah,' which moved one almost to tears; it was a deeply interesting moment when the venerable Archbishop of York placed the Crown upon that virgin brow. We were rather roughly recalled from our poetical dream to the work-a-day world by W. K.'s Coronation Anthem—new and yet old-fashioned—composed expressly for this part of the ceremony; the materials were borrowed; it was as a composition grammatically correct, but utterly uninteresting." Mrs. Moscheles copies this extract from the diary for her relatives, and adds, "Before Moscheles drove to the Abbey, he took me, my daughter, and niece to Lady A.'s. We were invited to be there not later than nine in the morning, so as to avoid the crush, and there we were well taken care of. The house, as you know, is in Piccadilly, almost opposite Constitution Hill. The A.'s had had a set of benches erected in the shape of an amphitheatre, reaching from the drawing-room door down to the street. The seats were covered with scarlet cloth, and from our point of vantage we could see on the left the whole length of Piccadilly, along which the Coronation Procession passed, coming and going, and to the right, into the Park beyond. There was a numerous and fashionable company assembled, so that the time passed quickly, and Lady A. had provided an excellent cold collation for her friends; I needn't tell you how choice it was. Shortly after nine o'clock the streets began to fill with a surging crowd, all London was out in the streets, mothers with babies in their arms, fathers holding up their little ones to get a view, boys climbing on lamps and rail-ings; such a medley and crowd as you can scarcely realize. I may further add that the gold State-coach, drawn by eight cream-colored horses, is a splendid specimen of mediæval furniture; that the young girl of eighteen, England's Queen, looked very pretty, and that the Mistress of the Robes, the Duchess of Sutherland, who sat opposite her, is a really noble and majestic beauty."

August and the first half of September were a pleasant holiday time, spent partly with some dear friends in Sussex. Moscheles writes: I have found a good organ in the church here, and the other day, at a funeral, I played the people out of church with Handel's 'Dead March.' I am puzzled to know what the farmers, rustics, and gravediggers think of my playing." After a month spent in Hastings, he writes in the middle of September: "Our bright holidays are at an end, and 'sweet home' sounds once more comfortable; to-day, however, the sky has caught a cold, and the rain pours in such torrents that it almost invites men to drown themselves; to escape the invitation I shall hold fast like Haydn, 'an meinem Spinettl' (by my piano). I play all the new works of the four modern heroes, Thalberg, Chopin, Henselt, and Liszt, and find that their chief effects lie in passages requiring a large grasp and stretch of finger, such as the peculiar build of their hands enables them to execute; I grasp less, but then I am not of a grasping school. With all my admiration for Beethoven I cannot forget Mozart, Cramer, and Hummel. Have they not written much that is noble, with which I have been familiar from early years? Just now the new manner finds more favor, and I endeavor to pursue the middle course between the two schools, by never shrinking from any difficulty, never despising the new effects, and withal retaining the best elements of the old traditions. . . . The 'Pastoral Concerto' I am writing just at present, has the shorter modern forms of three connected movements, and is more light and lively than my last concertos; I don't want to repeat myself in my own manner. My lessons, about which you ask me, are just enough this autumn to pay my tradesmen's bills." We quote a passage from another letter: "I recommend you a small pamphlet by Ries and Wegeler upon Beethoven, it has just been published at Coblentz by Bädeker; and gives one an insight into the wonderful life and works of Beethoven. I consider every part of it authentic. What a pity it is that his last letters are not complete, for they end with those written to Ries, after which his correspondence with me began. I must call your attention to the fiftieth page, where Beethoven says he has dedicated his last symphony with choruses to the King of Prussia, and has sent him the manuscript. For all that, at each of the three performances of the Ninth Symphony, which I have conducted this year, I have had a score before me corrected by Beethoven's own hand, and the title also in his handwriting runs thus: 'Ninth Symphony, composed for the Philharmonic Society in London, by Beethoven.'"

In another letter he writes: "We intend having Chamber Music every Saturday, and Emily will help us; our chief pillar of strength will be that painstaking cellist Hausmann. On the very first evening Emily played the first and second movement of Mozart's 'Quintet in E flat, major;' she has studied it thoroughly in the three days, and certainly is very gifted by nature." Moscheles himself plays Beethoven's grand Sonata op. 102, and says: "I am not quite on good terms with that very learned fugue; in my judgment Beethoven's 'genius' ranks higher than his learning." Later on he plays Schubert's new Trios in E and B flat, "with their admirable construction and beautiful thoughts, only occasionally a trifle too diffuse." On one occasion we read in the diary: "Yesterday, our Saturday soirée introduced us to some less interesting Ensembles, but for all that, we must go through all the novelties, invariably, however, interspersing them with classical works." There were also two delightful Mendelssohn Saturdays, one for the whole of "St. Paul," the other for pianoforte music. Moscheles writes: "I tried my Pastoral Concerto; it pleased my friends, but occasionally doubts arise in my mind as to whether my mode of composing on fixed principles does not spoil that easy flow and freshness which in my early youth was so attractive, and yet I am glad to show the musical world my greater earnestness and deeper aims, however short my present success may be of what I might wish."

In the course of this winter Moscheles wrote his Study in A, 6-8 time, and the song "Liebesfrühling." Progress was made with the edition of Beethoven's works, and proof-sheets corrected of Mendelssohn's "Andante and Presto in B Major and B Minor," and of Liszt's new "Studies." We read: "I declined the honor of being a director of the Philharmonic for next season: for what can I do among seven? I, a passionate musical reformer, stand always alone; it ends always with my being made responsible for what I consider the mistakes of others." Hummel was dead, and Moscheles had the flattering offer made him to fill his place at Weimar. He hesitated for a moment, but preferred the freedom of his position in London to the restraints of a court and theatre, although he was very devoted to the Grand-Ducal family, and convinced of their kind feelings towards him.

# CHAPTER XXI.

## 1839.

Ferdinand David—Successful Concert—Composers and Publishers—Bernhard Romberg—Musical Novelties—Prince Louis Napoleon—A New School of Playing—Paris—Chopin—Musical Entertainments—Impressions of Artists—Aimé Martin—Cremieux—Rachel—Plays, Operas, Actors, and Singers—Performance before the Court of St. Cloud—Chamber Music—Musical Education—Mendelssohn—Adams the Organist.

THE Moscheles passed a very cheerful time in January with their friends the Flemings at their country seat in Hampshire. The winter was spent as usual; and as early as March he writes: "I am already very busy, and must swim with the tide."

The visit of Ferdinand David from Leipzig was a great delight to the Moscheles. This worthy pupil of Spohr played his master's music in a grand and noble style, his own bravuras with faultless power of execution, and his quartet playing at Mori's and Blagrove's soirées delighted every one with any genuine artistic taste; before he came, such a perfect *ensemble* had never been realized. David and Moscheles appeared together at the second Philharmonic Concert, David with a Concerto of his own, and Moscheles with his new "Pastoral Concerto." On this his first appearance, David gained the high position which he always retained, and the reception given to Moscheles' new concerto was most favorable. From that time the two artists frequently played together "At the house of Sir W. Curtis, the great amateur violoncello player; at Madame Dulcken's concert given in Sir William's drawing-room; at ——, where, before the echo of our 'Kreutzer Sonata' had died away we heard the lively strains of a quadrille; and finally in our own house, in the presence of, and with, other artists; it is there after all we enjoy music most."

Mrs. Moscheles writes: "To-day I must tell you that Moscheles intends giving his concert jointly with David, who was quite ready merely to assist as a friend; but Moscheles preferred to share the undertaking with him, for by that act he would prove to the public in what high esteem he held his brother-artist. In him he has found a powerful colleague of the German school, and one he is proud to introduce to the English public." In a subsequent letter she says: "This letter is a concert dispatch. It is over, and gloriously over. The room was excellently filled without the aid of Italian singers; the Russian Grand Duke took two tickets; Prince Napoleon was in the stalls." Moscheles played his new composition, the "Pastoral Concerto," dedicated to Mendelssohn; it was received with great applause.

"German and French artists," writes Moscheles, "the latter with faultless gloves, meet at our house with English friends, music forming a bridge of communication between the different nationalities. If I could but link together composers and publishers! Just now, for instance, I am annoyed at being unable to bring about the publication of Bernhard Romberg's 'Violoncello School.' The fashionable wares of his rivals are now the order of the day, and yet the work of this excellent man is of great value to the students of that difficult instrument. Talking of difficulties, Thalberg again astonished me at his concert; he is a perfect Jupiter in power and bravura, and in his new 'Studies' he has achieved the labors of Hercules. Mendelssohn, with whom I correspond upon the subject of all musical novelties in our days, shares my opinion. He and I are greatly delighted with Bennett's overture to the 'Naïades,' and the public greets it with enthusiasm."

This overture is so highly appreciated in Germany that to this day it retains its place in the programmes of the Gewandhaus and other concerts.

Mrs. Moscheles says in a letter: "We frequently meet Prince Louis Napoleon at large evening parties, and are naturally interested in seeing the lion of the season. He talked in a very friendly way to Moscheles of years gone by, when his mother, the Queen Hortense, took such delight in his playing, adding that he would never forget the impression he had received as a boy. He was very polite and agreeable to me, but I was not struck particularly with anything he said; generally speaking, on such occasions as these he remains in some quiet corner of the room, as though he preferred looking-on to talking." We find another meeting recorded: "Our friend Löwenstern has brought back from his travels all sorts of remarkable things, and when by invitation I took the children to visit his new museum, we met Prince Louis Napoleon there; not a soul was there besides. Again he admired in silence, examined the beautiful armor with the airs of a connoisseur, and was, as on the former occasion, very obliging; we had no opportunity of a regular conversation."

During this summer the subject of Moscheles' ceasing to play in public was often discussed. Hitherto he had basked in the sunshine of admiration, and the success of his performances was beyond dispute. "How delightful it would be to retire in the full tide of popular favor, in full consciousness of powers; to leave the field open to others, and thus to escape being made the butt of such remarks as: 'So-and-so plays still very beautifully, although he is no longer what he was ten years ago; he has lost his vigor, his improvisation is no longer what it used to be,' etc. It is the old story of a beauty famous in her day, but now faded, who ought to give place to her more youthful rivals. I think of Clementi, who has bequeathed to Art and her disciples an imperishable treasure, and who gave up playing while his juniors in the profession flourished by the adoption of his method, only slightly modifying it and using it as the basis of a new school. The leading features of this school are the cultivation of amazing powers of execution, overwrought sentimentality, and the production of piquant effects by the most rapid changes from the soft to the loud pedal, or by rhythms and modulations, which, if not to be completely repudiated, are only allowable on the rarest occasions. It is quite natural that I should not ally myself to this modern faction; a great deal they do, I would not; their power I could not imitate, although in my own school of playing I feel in full vigor without any trace of age or want of nerve. In my school such a prodigal display of mechanical power was a thing unknown. For the future, should the world take less interest in my performances as an executant, my desire will be the more ardent to cultivate music in accordance with my own taste and convictions. As to how and what I shall compose, this too is veiled in the future. Hitherto I have introduced my works to the public by the medium of my own pianoforte playing; will the musical world when I retire continue to take interest in them? 'Nous verrons.'"

In the course of the summer his father-in-law suggests his doubling the price of his lessons, in order to diminish their number, but he replies: "I can't make up my mind to such a step, for people might well accuse me of selfishness, and that too in a country to which I am very mainly indebted for my present position."

The family enjoyed their stay at Boulogne before going to Paris for two months, and forgetting for awhile public concerts and professional duties, made themselves acquainted with the environs of Paris, and explored the Louvre, Luxembourg, and other galleries. Such things of course delighted him, but we find Moscheles always glad to turn to musicians for his real interest, and one of his letters shows us he was about to gratify his long-harbored wish of making Chopin's acquaintance. "We are living here in the fullest enjoyment of our freedom and independence, and at Leo's, where I love to make music, I first met his friend Chopin, who had just returned from the country. His appearance is completely identified with his music—they are both delicate and sentimental (schwärmerisch). He played to me in compliance with my request, and I now for the first time understand his music, and all the raptures of the lady world become intelligible. The *ad libitum* playing, which in the hands of other interpreters of his music degenerates into a constant uncertainty of rhythm, is with him an element of exquisite originality; the hard inartistic modulations, so like those of a *dilettante*—which I never can manage when playing Chopin's music—cease to shock me, for he glides over them almost imperceptibly with his elfish fingers. His soft playing being a mere breath, he requires no powerful forte to produce the desired contrasts; the consequence is that one never misses the orchestral effects that the German school demands of a pianoforte-player, but is carried away as by some singer who troubles himself very little about the accompaniment, and follows his own impulses. Enough ; he is perfectly unique in the world of pianoforte-players. He professes a great attachment for my music, and at all events knows it perfectly. He played me some of his Studies, and his latest work, 'Preludes ;' I played in return several things of my own." Who would have believed that Chopin, with all his sentimentality, had also a comic vein? And yet among repeated notices about the playing and listening to music in artist and amateur circles, we read the following : "Chopin was lively, cheerful, nay, extremely funny in his imitations of Pixis, Liszt, and a hump-backed pianoforte connoisseur." Again: "To-day he was quite a different Chopin from the Chopin last week. I visited him by appointment with Charlotte and Emily, who are his enthusiastic admirers ; they were profoundly impressed with the Prelude in A flat major in 6-8 time, with the perpetually recurring A flat resembling the pedal bass of an organ. Chopin's excellent pupil Gutmann played his manuscript Scherzo in C sharp minor, Chopin himself his manuscript Sonata in B flat minor, with the Funeral March." On another occasion Moscheles plays his own Trio and Mendelssohn's D minor Concerto, which to his annoyance is "not understood." Beethoven, Weber, his own "Studies," his Irish Fantasia, and Mozart's Fugue in F minor, with Cramer (who is living at the time in Paris), and Moscheles' Sonata in E flat major, for four hands, are never-failing items in the programmes of these musical entertainments. Stephen Heller is called in the diary "an interesting and pleasant young artist," Bertini's "Studies" "admirable for practice, but diffuse in form." "Thalberg is here, and after crowded concerts receives as much blame as praise ; but when one of the wise reviewers goes so far as to compare him with Van Amburgh the lion-tamer, one can only laugh." Moscheles says in one of his letters : "I have now come to the end of my round of visits to artists, and have received very varied impressions. Berlioz, whose acquaintance I was anxious to make, was very cold and unsympathizing. His exquisitely-penned score of 'Romeo and Juliet' lay upon the table ; I turned over some of the pages, but found the work so complicated, and the noise (at my very first glance) so overwhelming, that I cannot venture as yet to give any judgment on the music. One thing, however, is certain—that there must be new effects in it. At the house of Auber, who received me in the most friendly way, I was greatly interested by seeing the square piano on which he has composed his operas. He made me play on his Erard as well, and Zimmermann, the professor of the Conservatoire, happening to come in, between them they kept me at the piano some time. Cherubini, usually not the most courteous of men, was very friendly; we had a good hour's earnest conversation on art matters. He said that, with the exception of his Directorship at the Conservatoire, he had nothing more to do with music; he couldn't write another note, he wasn't strong enough to hear and enjoy musical impressions. I think I might have assured him without flattery that he belongs to the few who even in their lifetime have already earned immortality. Heine I found the genius I have ever known him to be. As for my poor Lafont, I saw him lying in his coffin while the funeral service was being held in the church of St. Roch; the music was Cherubini's, but without organ accompaniment, to my taste an indispensable adjunct.

"We were delighted to make the acquaintance of Aimé Martin, the writer; his work 'Sur l'Education du Genre Humain par les Mères de Famille,' had been long known to us, and we found the author's conversation as entertaining and instructive as the book itself. Crémieux is charming also, but in another style. As an advocate he speaks with ease and fluency; as a man he is highly intellectual, fond of art and artists. He calls the great Rachel his adopted daughter, although her parents are still alive; poor thing, she is just recovering from a severe illness, and consequently we unfortunate people cannot get a glimpse of her. A bachelor party at Meyerbeer's yesterday was very interesting. Halévy, Duponchel, Duprez, Habeneck, and Küstner, the Intendant of the Munich theatres, were there. Habeneck and I entertained each other at dinner by talking about the Conservatoire and the Philharmonic, as two ministers of different States discuss their politics. He wanted me to send him something of my own for his orchestra. I promised him my overture to the 'Joan of Arc.' He offered to come to-morrow and hear me play. Meyerbeer acted as my friend on all occasions ; he said aloud at dinner that I was the only one who could play Beethoven perfectly."

Of course the Moscheles, during their stay at Paris, were in the way of every theatrical novelty, and actors and artists are constantly discussed in letters. "Arnold's comic acting," says Mrs. Moscheles, "is very amusing ; but the piece, 'Passé Minuit,' is too realistic to my taste. The new opera, 'La Jacquerie,' is said to be nicknamed by Auber 'An Opera in D,' from the fact of that key being so prominently used throughout the work." "Guido and Ginèvre," by Halévy, Moscheles calls "excellent well-written music ;" but he cannot feel any enthusiasm for it. After seeing "Robert le Diable," a great part of which Moscheles admired and praised, Mrs. Moscheles writes : "Can you understand how people can set such horrors to music ? The one writes about the plague ; the other worse. I am no saint ; but organ-playing and church music are out of place in a theatre. And when the graves open, and the dead nuns rise, I can't help shuddering." "And I ditto," adds Moscheles, "when deafened by such a mass of horns, bassoons, and ophicleides that they drown the rest of the orchestra, and make a buzzing in my ears, much as I honor and respect Meyerbeer's great talent. The chorus was much too weak to struggle against these orchestral masses. The scenery, even including that of the nuns, fell short of my expectations. Mario and Dorus Gras were admirable ; the rest only second-rate. Halévy's 'Sheriff' is a clever piece of mosaic, but not so neatly joined." Again : "Doesn't one see and hear every mortal thing in Paris ? We, for instance, heard the 'Huguenots' for the first time ; it is a great, nay, Meyerbeer's greatest work, and it produced a powerful effect upon me. Rossini's 'Barber of Seville,' with Pauline Garcia, Rubini, and Tamburini, is also not to be despised ; for the extraordinary vocal powers of these three artists cannot fail to excite wonder. Duprez is an admirable Tell. Bouffé at the Gymnase, Déjazet at the Palais Royal, and Sanson and Mars at the Theatre Français, give us enjoyments we would fain share with you ! To-day I got a note from Count Perthuis, Adjutant to King Louis Philippe. The Count has often heard Chopin and myself play my 'E flat major Sonata.' I expect he has talked a good deal about it at Court, 'for,' he writes, 'the Royal Family wish to have the great treat I lately enjoyed.'" Accordingly Chopin and Moscheles were both commanded to go to St. Cloud. Moscheles writes on the 30th of October: "On the day when Kalkbrenner called I said, 'To-day I shall play on a piano of yours at St. Cloud.' He jumped up from his chair and declared that not a moment was to be lost; he must see if the instrument was in the best order. He also told me that the Duchess of Orleans, having taken lessons from him in playing and composition, knew perfectly well how to appreciate good music. At nine o'clock Chopin and I were called for by P. and his charming wife. We all four went off in a pelting storm of rain, and felt more comfortable when we entered the warm and brilliantly lighted palace. We passed through some splendid apartments, to a 'salon carré,' where only the Royal Family was assembled; the Queen at a round table, with an elegant work-basket before her (I wonder whether she was knitting a purse for me?). Next to her was Madame Adélaïde, the Duchess of Orleans, and the ladies of the Court. They one and all treated us kindly, as if we were old acquaintances. The Queen as well as Madame Adélaïde, declared that they still remembered with gratitude the delight I gave them at the Tuileries. The King came up to me to say the same thing, adding, he supposed an interval of between fifteen and sixteen years had elapsed since that time. I said he was quite correct, but thought all the while of the poor Count d'Artois, who had then been present. The Queen then asked if the instrument—a Pleyel—was placed as we liked it; was the lighting what we wanted? if the chairs were the right height, etc.; and was as anxious for our comfort as a Citizen Queen might well be. First of all Chopin played a 'mélange of Nocturnos and Etudes,' and was extolled and admired as an old Court favorite. I followed with some old and new 'Studies,' and was honored with similar applause. We then sat down together at the instrument, he again playing the bass, a thing he always insists on. The small audience now listened intently to my 'E flat major Sonata,' which was interrupted by such exclamations as 'divin! délicieux!' After the Andante the Queen whispered to one of her suite: 'Ne serait-il pas indiscret de le leur redemander?' which was tantamount to a command; so we played it again with increased *abandon*, and in the Finale gave ourselves up to a 'musical delirium.'

"Chopin's enthusiasm throughout the whole performance of the piece must, I think, have kindled that of his hearers, who overwhelmed us both with compliments equally divided. Chopin played another solo as charmingly as before, and met with the same reception. I then improvised on some of Mozart's sweetest airs, and finally dashed away at the 'Zauberflöte' overture. Better than all the words of praise which flow so glibly from the lips of princes, was the king's close attention during the entire evening. Chopin and I revelled like brothers in the triumph achieved by the individual talent of each, there was no tinge of jealousy on either side. At last, after being allowed to enjoy some refreshments, we left the palace at 11.30, this time only under a shower of compliments, for the rain had ceased, and we had a clear night." Naturally after this time Chopin and Moscheles were called upon almost daily in musical circles to repeat the Sonata, which came at last to be called and only known by the name of "La Sonate." Shortly after this Moscheles is asked privately whether the *légion d'honneur* or any other mark of royal favor, would be valued as a reward for his playing at St. Cloud. He prefers something else to the order so lavishly bestowed, and receives a valuable dressing-case, on which are engraved the words "Donné par le Roi Louis-Philippe."

When the Moscheles return to London, chamber music on Saturdays is again revived; he works on the "Méthode des Méthodes," to be published with Fétis, and writes the "Lieder:" "Mit Gott" and "Liebeslauschen."

In answer to a question, whether constant piano-forte studies under a teacher are beneficial, after a certain pitch of excellence has been attained by cultivation, he says: "Any one who has heard and studied a great deal that is good, ought to need no teacher to spur him on. The student should always bear in mind the greatest models and emulate them, playing a great deal with accompaniment; he should become more and more familiar with masterpieces, and enter earnestly into a sense of their beauties: thus the gradual development the pupil attains, will place him above the common run of amateurs." This year there was an improvement at the Philharmonic, for the directors determined at a meeting to put a stop to the mischief of admitting a large audience to rehearsals. "We had however a violent debate," says Moscheles, "before we carried our point."

With regard to Handel's "Solomon," he writes: "That glorious work could not be spoiled by the organ being below pitch, painful as it was. Clara Novello, Phillips, and the other singers were admirable." "Mendelssohn," writes Mrs. Moscheles, "has not merely written a letter, but copied into it a new, and of course exquisite Lied, set to old German words: 'Es ist in dem Wald gesungen.' Nobody like him for kindness and real friendship. At present the song is sung constantly in the 'room,' not in the 'wood;' and each time it seems prettier than the last. Last week we heard the two new organs built by Gray, one for Belfast, the other for Exeter Hall, and Moscheles admires exceedingly the finished execution and extempore playing of Adams the organist, who tried them. On the last night of the old year we had charades, etc., the musical friends taking the chief parts: Thalberg, grave and solemn at the piano, is up to any fun away from it. Benedict, the hard-worked, enters into the mirth of the masqueraders; last, not least, Moscheles enlivens the scene with his gymnastics on the piano."

## CHAPTER XXII.

### 1840.

Letter to a Friend—Sir Gardner Wilkinson—Appointed Pianist to Prince Albert—Literary and Artistic Acquaintances—Liszt—Political Questions—Mendelssohn at Birmingham—Visit to Germany—Correspondence—Intercourse with Artists at Leipzig—Chorley—Prague—Moscheles' Mother—Reception at Concerts—Dionys Weber—Auf Wiedersehen—A Hit at Thiers—Works on Music—Letter from Mendelssohn.

THE first letter now before us is to Frau von Lewinger, one of the oldest of Moscheles' friends:—

"London, 8th January, 1840.

"DEAREST FRAU VON LEWINGER,—You must allow your old friend Moscheles to have a little chat with you, and question you to find out what you are about, and if you still love him. I fear that, judging by my scanty letters, I must have sunk considerably in the scale of your good opinion, and I can only hope to find the old indulgence. . . . The gifted Thalberg is brilliantly successful, and is now on his way to Scotland. It interests me to watch the younger artists making their career, as I now begin to play the part of a quiet looker-on, and to follow my art-vocations with an ever-increasing devotion, but still in greater privacy than before. Accordingly I hold a weekly meeting of friends and artists at my own house, where none but the most select music is performed. My eldest daughter, now twelve years old, contributes her mite, and develops a solid power of execution on the pianoforte. I delight in giving my children a thorough education, without having the ambition of seeing them pass for prodigies. Besides that, I don't wish them to make music their profession." . . . . "Thalberg intends to go to America. The clashing here with Liszt is, I suppose, too much for him."

At this time Moscheles received his appointment as pianist to Prince Albert, but it was little more than nominal, for, much as he would have liked to have had close artistic relations with that music-loving Prince, he was never called on to examine any of the Prince's compositions. As we have already mentioned, pianoforte-playing in public became more distasteful to him, but, in spite of his resolution, he did not like to refuse the often repeated invitation of the directors to play at the Philharmonic, where he again enjoyed a triumph. Among Moscheles' literary acquaintance at this period were Sir Gardner Wilkinson, Mr. Grote, the famous historian, Mrs. Austin, Mrs. Jameson, and others; of musical celebrities, we read the names of Döhler, Litolff, Liszt—the latter never looked on as a rival, but as a friend of the family. How sincerely Moscheles appreciated Liszt, will be seen from the following letter:—

"At one of the Philharmonic Concerts, he played three of my 'Studies' quite admirably. Faultless in the way of execution, but by his powers he has completely metamorphosed these pieces; they have become more his Studies than mine. With all that they please me, and I shouldn't like to hear them played in any other way by him. The Paganini Studies, too, were uncommonly interesting to me. He does anything he chooses, and does it admirably, and those hands raised aloft in the air come down but seldom, wonderfully seldom, upon a wrong key." "His conversation is always brilliant," adds Mrs. Moscheles; "it is occasionally dashed with satire, or spiced with humor." "The other day he brought me his portrait, with his 'hommages respectueux' written underneath, and, what was the best 'hommage' of all, he sat down to the piano and played me the 'Erl-King,' the 'Ave Maria,' and a charming Hungarian piece. He now intends making an excursion to Baden-Baden, after that a tour of the English provinces with Cramer (at 500*l.* a month), and then to go to St. Petersburg for recreation."

Moscheles writes: "We have now to tell you of a Russian episode in our mad harum-scarum life in the height of the season. It is merely this; that Lwoff, recommended to me by Mendelssohn, is distinguished as a violin-player, and is a downright good musician. I delight in making music with him before other enthusiastic Russian amateurs now in London. Yesterday, I am sorry to say, a letter came from Mendelssohn to Charlotte, in which he represents himself as tired and weak, adding that possibly he will be obliged by his doctor's advice to give up the Birmingham Music Festival. This question will not be settled until he returns from Schwerin; so we still hope, in spite of his letter, which is a Job's comforter."

During the summer holidays Moscheles, by request of Mr. Murray the publisher, put together his recollections of Beethoven.

Anxiety on Mendelssohn's account is at last relieved by a letter from Felix himself, announcing his intended arrival in September. Before he came there was a private rehearsal of his "Lobgesang" at the Hanover Square Rooms. Moscheles writes on the subject thus: "I am greatly charmed with his composition, and as Knyvett, the conductor, and F. Cramer knew of my thorough knowledge of the work, they asked me to sit close to the organist, in the centre of the orchestra, that they might consult me about the Tempi. I was like a general sitting in his tent and issuing orders for operations on the field of battle; at the same time, I carefully guarded against any appearance of wishing to usurp the duty of the regularly appointed conductor. In spite of this, the *Morning Post* says that the rehearsal was conducted by me and Knyvett."

We see by the following letter that Moscheles interested himself in the political questions of the day: "Let me begin with Prince Louis Napoleon. I pity him, for I know him personally as a polite, well-educated young man. Certainly one would not have predicated of him that he ever meditated the scheme that has now proved abortive. Dark clouds are still lowering on the political horizon, although in my judgment they do not immediately threaten. I have been trying zealously to make out the cause of discord between the opposing states; between ourselves, I think Mohammed Ali unfairly treated. I don't believe that the Allies will allow England to be involved in a war with them merely on the ground of France being excluded from the treaty. Let the worst come, the Continent will not be so shut out from England as to prevent Prince Albert's pianist from travelling unmolested to and fro between the two countries; consequently we are always thinking of our trip to Boulogne. To-day we are impatiently expecting Mendelssohn; on Saturday he is to have a rehearsal in Birmingham."

On the 20th of September Moscheles and his friend, who had safely arrived, go to Birmingham together; Mrs. Moscheles, who is to follow next day, receives the following letter from her husband:—

"Take fresh courage when you read these lines, and fly to Birmingham as fast as we did. My conversation with Mendelssohn was lively as it was interesting; you often were the subject, and our thoughts were constantly of you. I put up at once at the comfortable Stork Hotel, and dined with Mendelssohn and Ayrton at the house of Mr. Moore—one of the Festival committee—where Mendelssohn is staying. I wrote in his bedroom, from whence we were called away to dinner, and now, instead of taking my siesta, I resume my pen, to tell you that the choral rehearsal is to be this evening. Before it begins I am to go with Mendelssohn to the Music Hall, where he is going to play on the organ. I will receive you at the station." Mendelssohn writes:—

"I must be allowed to smuggle in my greetings, and say how delightful and kind and affectionate he was to me during our journey hither; how the hours flew by as if they were minutes, and how I am forever thinking what one could do in return for such real kindness. Such a return, however, I cannot find, not even in writing; but all the more in my heart. To our happy meeting to-morrow! My best love to the children.

"Ever yours,

"FELIX MENDELSSOHN-BARTHOLDY."

At the same time Mrs. Moscheles writes:—

"Our dear Mendelssohn—I can call him by no other name—arrived at 4 P. M. on the 8th. At seven o'clock he was with us; the same hearty, cheerful, delightful old friend as ever. In a word he is a model man. At dinner, and the whole evening, we talked over memories of bygone happy hours; then he drew Moscheles to the piano and made him play all his favorite 'Studies;' and as each is a favorite, and kindled him to fresh enthusiasm, it was not before midnight that he paid any heed to my third summons to be off to bed and rest. On Saturday he was again with us between four and five o'clock, and Moscheles being called away to a pupil, he and I were left for an hour alone together. He played with Emily his overture to the 'Fingal's Cave,' and was greatly pleased with her performance, and with her own little compositions. Chorley and Klingemann came to dinner, and in the evening little Felix enjoyed such a game of romps with his famous godpapa that the whole house trembled. Who would have thought that the same man who romped about with a tiny boy could extemporize as he does? For the two M.'s improvise together on themes for each other's works; when I call this 'glorious,' 'fine,' 'remarkable,' etc., the epithets all fall short of true description. I hadn't heard them play together for seven years, and my impression was, it was worth the trouble of waiting seven years for. On Sunday at nine o'clock Mendelssohn was again with us; he and Moscheles started, and the children and I accompanied him and papa to the railway station, for Birmingham, and I followed next day. Early on Tuesday morning we strolled down to the Music Hall, and Mendelssohn sat by us until he got up to play the organ. He played a fugue of Bach's in a most masterly way; besides this we had 'Israel in Egypt,' and the inevitable 'Miscellaneous Selection.' We did not go to the evening concert, but sat at home chatting with Mendelssohn, who had much to tell us about his wife. The portrait he showed us makes her very pretty, and according to him she must be an angel."

On the 23d of September Moscheles writes: "Mendelssohn's appearance here has given me fresh enjoyment of life. After my own family, he ranks next in my affections. I see him in various characters, as a brother, son, lover; but chiefly as a fiery musical enthusiast, who appears but dimly conscious to what a height he has already attained. He knows so well how to adapt himself to this commonplace world, although his genius soars so high above it. While Birmingham prided herself on bringing out his newest work, he still found time to make a pen-and-ink drawing of Birmingham for our children. We have a view of the town with its chimneys, warehouses, Town Hall, and the railway carriage in which he and I sat—the perspective is throughout remarkably good, and there are some witty explanations added. In the evening I walked home with him; our chat was so delightful that he insisted on walking back with me two good English miles, but I would only allow him to go part of the way. The night was coldish; he had only just recovered from an illness, and with so much work before him, I knew he wanted rest. Yesterday at an early hour the Town Hall again looked very imposing. The second part of the performance was devoted to Mendelssohn; he was heartily received with ringing cheers, but seemed all anxiety to make his bow to the public, and get the thing over. Of course this was sheer modesty. His conducting of the band in this performance of the 'Lobgesang' effected a marvellous unity and precision, and one of the chorales of this glorious work told so powerfully that the whole audience rose involuntarily from their seats—a custom usually confined in England to the performance of the Hallelujah Chorus. At three o'clock in the afternoon, when the hall was emptied, Mendelssohn, fresh as ever, played for three-quarters of an hour upon the organ before a select circle, as though his day were but just beginning. The same evening we heard, first of all, in the theatre, one act of the 'Gazza Ladra,' with Caradori and Lablache, then Mendelssohn's 'G Minor Concerto,' played by himself with wonderful fire and delicacy, and last of all, Lablache, who had joined the party, gave his irresistible comic scene from the 'Prova d'un Opera Seria.' What a musical maw the English must have, to be able to digest such a quantity in one day!

"To-day at an early hour we leave Birmingham. Charlotte has started the idea of my accompanying Mendelssohn to Germany to see my mother, who is in ill health. Mendelssohn will remain in London until I have installed my own family in some country place."

Before leaving they ask Chorley to join them in their journey, and as a parting gift to Mrs. Moscheles, Mendelssohn fills a whole sheet of her album with pen-and-ink sketches. Chorley illustrates these with doggerel verses. Moscheles adds some parting words, and at midnight the Dover mail-coach rolls away with the three travellers. Unfortunately there is a fourth seat occupied by a stranger, happily asleep. One of the friends remarks, "What shall we do with him when he wakes up?" "Kill him, that's the only way," says another. At that moment the sleeper stirs. Of course the speakers are alarmed, fearing they have been overheard; but Moscheles, with that admirable presence of mind peculiar to him, breaks in with the following words in English, 'And afterwards she said she never would have that man for a husband," a sentence which from that moment became a proverb among the party. Mendelssohn, like the people in Homer, "laughs through tears," and the fit becomes contagious. What must the man, still asleep, have thought of his companions?

When the three friends, after a roughish eight hours' passage to Ostend, are sitting in Moscheles' warm bedroom, it is his first business to write to his wife. Chorley supplements the letter with a few words; Mendelssohn again makes a pen-and-ink sketch, a steamer rolling about in a stormy sea, and underneath the words:—

"Heiss mich nicht reden, heiss mich schweigen."—SCHILLER.

"Es giebt Augenblicke im Menschenleben."—GOETHE.

"Here the ship gave a lurch, and he grew sea-sick."—BYRON.

"But," says Mendelssohn, "all three of us are sitting very comfortably around the fire in Moscheles' room, and think of you."

They proceed in Mendelssohn's carriage with post-horses, and Moscheles writes from Liége:—

"Sunday Evening, 4th October, 1840.
"Hotel du Pavillon Anglais.

"We had an excellent journey with sunny weather to help us, and I had much confidential talk with Mendelssohn. We have communicated to one another many details of our courtship days, as to the where and how we came to pop the question, ending by declaring that we were thoroughly satisfied with our choices. He reckons on my staying eight days with them in Leipzig."

"Same Evening, Eight o'clock.

"We wanted to sleep at Aix, but are obliged to stay here, as the axle of the carriage is broken. He is inconsolable, particularly on our account, although we tried to put him in spirits. He was expecting letters here from his wife, and as I had unfortunately none to expect from mine, I ran to the door to fetch his letters, making believe it was for myself. The letter I brought him restored him his natural good humor. At dinner, Chorley proposed, in champagne, the healths of the Frau Professorin and Frau Doctorin; and then Mendelssohn and I read in the Café of the abdication of the King of Holland, Napier's taking of Beyrout (I fear it's a bad business for Mehemet Ali, now seventy-one years old), and Louis Napoleon's defence by Berryer, and here I begin to nod."

"Aix-la-Chapelle, Monday, 5th October, 1840.
"Eleven at Night.

"Not having chatted with you all day, let me do so before I go to bed. This is my third letter. While waiting for Mendelssohn's carriage, we found time to see some churches. The journey was a satisfactory one, and here we have had no end of friendly meetings, first with the Mayers, whose geniality delighted Mendelssohn as well as myself; then Ole Bull and Eicke, the singer, joined us: afterwards in came a long gaunt figure of the Don Quixote kind, and embraced me—it was Schindler. He greeted Mendelssohn, who returned the salutation, although, as I saw, with some mental reserve. I purposely did not introduce him to Chorley, and only gave him a secret hint that he had the biographer before him. To Schindler I said that the Englishman was our common friend. Ole Bull bored Mendelssohn to death on the subject of G. Schelling, who had attacked him fiercely in print. Schindler emphatically annihilated music and musicians of the present day.

Mayer fondly recalled old days, and there sat Chorley looking on, biting his handkerchief, and getting materials for the *Athenæum*."

The travellers go by way of Cologne and Frankfort to Leipzig; there Moscheles writes to his wife: "We arrived late last night, and I have a great deal to tell you. Felix, in the room next to me, is teaching his little boy to sing. I have been very heartily received in his house, his wife is very charming, very unassuming, and child-like, but not in my judgment a perfect beauty, because she is a blonde. Her mouth and nose are like Sontag's, her way of speaking is pleasing and simple, her German is 'Frankforty,' therefore not pure; she said naïvely at dinner: 'I speak too slowly for my Felix, and he so quickly that I don't always understand him.' She is so simple in her ways that she often got up to hand us something. I told her I hoped you and she would become intimate, and she echoed the wish; meanwhile you are often the subject of our conversation.

"At this morning's rehearsal I was received with open arms by the Concert Directors as well as David, Schumann, and his wife. They, as well as Mendelssohn, keep on saying 'Do stay and play;' but I am undecided. I intend, however, to be as fresh and lively as Mendelssohn, who jumps about with his children. Dear children, I can only kiss you in imagination, but when I return, I shall have a pretty story to tell you. Dear Clara! Adieu!

"The Mendelssohns send affectionate messages."

"Leipzig, Monday, 12th October, 1840.
"Eleven o'clock at Night.

"A little about myself. Yesterday afternoon I was a long time alone with Mendelssohn, who played me some numbers which had been intended for 'St. Paul,' but which were never performed or printed. They are admirable, only treated in a more dramatic way, and therefore perhaps more adapted for isolated pieces in the concert-room than to be heard in connection with the oratorio itself. He played me also some charming MS. 'Lieder ohne Worte.' At 2.30 we dined at David's, where we met Cécile's sister, Madame Schunck, and her husband; she is a bright, clever woman. Madame David too was a new and very agreeable acquaintance; her manners are very refined. David played us after dinner his new violin 'Concerto in D major,' which is certain to create a general sensation; Mendelssohn accompanied, then I had to extemporize, and I hope tolerably well. At 6.30 we went to the Gewandhaus, which was already filled to overflowing. I was in the orchestra with Mendelssohn who was received with acclamations, well warranted by the performance of the Euryanthe Overture and Beethoven's B. flat Symphony. His influence over the band gave it the fire, tenderness, and requisite 'nuances.' I was in ecstasies. Fancy the concert over at eight o'clock! It rained heavily, and no cabs to be had at Leipzig! When once home we found the warm room and tea most comfortable; then Mendelssohn sang me some of his recently published songs, which I shall bring with me, and said: 'Cécile, you must venture on singing a little Leid to Moscheles, and let him accompany you.' She made the same excuses that certain people always do, and then sang the old German Leid

and two others; her voice is small, but her intonation correct.

"Monday.—I called on Schumann and Rochlitz; Madame Schumann played me a fugue of Bach's. I staid a long time at Hofrath Rochlitz's. The directors came, wanting me to play a week hence, but I refused.

"Tuesday, Midnight.—the Mendelssohns gave an evening party, when David's quartet playing was admirable. I played my 'E major Concerto' and 'Studies.' To end up, Felix called for my repertoire of tricks on the piano, and we extemporized together as a finale, a production quite as good as our last effort in London. Now G-o-o-d Night."

On the 11th of October Chorley gives Mrs. Moscheles a long account of all the doings at Leipzig, and Mendelssohn adds: "Dear Mrs. Moscheles, a thousand, thousand thanks for the plan of your own and no one else's devising, and to which we are now indebted for such delightful, such glorious days. Would that you were present! for your absence is a radical fault, only too obvious to every one of us here; I wish I had insisted on carrying off your wardrobe myself; we are so happy and cheerful here altogether; still I fancy I often see how Moscheles longs for quite another part of the world. How gloriously he played again yesterday, enchanting us all. 'Had you been present,' that is the old song with the old burden. Cécile wants to write to you herself. A thousand loves to the children, and yourself.

"From yours,
"Felix Mendelssohn-Bartholdy."

Moscheles adds a postscript: "For the last two days we have had the most glorious summer weather, but the vintage, they tell me, will be very bad. Mendelssohn's Carl, as usual, is in my room while I dress myself; he is an excellent, lively, clever boy, and helps to compensate me for my absent pair of juveniles, Felix and Clara. His ear for music is the most subtle I have ever observed in a child. He sings the following Prussian Posthorn signal as a duet with his father:

"Leipzig, 18th October, 1840.
"(A day worthy to be remembered.)

"Chorley, being unwell, had to stay in his hotel, and

Mendelssohn in his kindness sent him an Erard piano, upon which he played for him Schubert's 'Grand Symphony' and my 'Grand Sonata.' Mendelssohn and I had again some glorious hours at the piano. Yesterday we were together at Schumanns', who gave a party in their own house. Madame Schumann played my 'Trio' and Mendelssohn's in a consummate way; David accompanied, and as a finale I was made to play some 'Studies.' Fräulein List sang some 'Leider' in a pretty, cultivated style. On Friday a gigantic dinner at Kistner's . . . . In the evening with Schleinitz at Mendelssohn's; we passed most of our time at the piano, and rummaging among old and new manuscripts.

"The Directors have been to me repeatedly, to persuade me to play on the 22d; Mendelssohn did the same; I remained firm. 'Possibly,' said I, 'I may be here again for the concert on the 29th, and shall write about it from Prague.' I will not plague you with a volley of questions, for I know that you write to me of everything that is agree-

*Mrs. Moscheles*
*is invited to a Musical Party on Monday the 19th inst. at 6 o'clock precisely, in the Concert-room of the Gewandhaus by*
*Felix Mendelssohn-Bartholdy,*

to hear there his "42nd Psalm," with orchestra and full Chorus, as well as the overture to the "Hebrides" and that to "Joan of Arc." The veteran pianoforte-player (as Fink calls him in the *Musik-Zeitung*) Moscheles, will play his G minor Concerto and Bach's Triple Concerto with Madame Schumann and Dr. F. Mendelssohn; some Characteristic Studies will also be heard.

*This card you will be asked to show on entering the door of the Concert-room.*

[If the card be not produced, Prof. Moscheles is to be sent back to London, in order to meet with that applause which here can only be incomplete.]

Please answer by return of post.

able to you—don't spare me should you have to write to me of anything disagreeable; I will bear it manfully . . . . . Yesterday evening, at a party given by David, Mendelssohn's Octet was admirably played, and I tried my Septet." The preceding card of invitation accompanied the letter.

Moscheles writes from Prague:—

"Prague, 21st October, 1840, 10 A. M.
"(One hour after arrival.)

"Hurrah! I have seen all,—my mother better than I expected." . . . . "And now a few words about Leipzig. At the Fête in the Gewandhaus, given me by Mendelssohn, there were about three hundred connoisseurs invited, who surrounded the three Härtel pianos, the room was brilliantly lighted, there was a full orchestra and chorus, a hundred and forty strong. It was so pretty to watch Mendelssohn and his lovely wife, before the music began, doing the honors for the various guests, and taking care that every one had refreshments offered them. Here is the programme:—

FIRST PART.

The two 'Leonora Overtures,' gloriously performed.
Mendelssohn's '42d Psalm.' A noble work. The Solos excellently given by Madame Frege.
'Hommage à Handel.' Played with fraternal enthusiasm by Felix and myself.

SECOND PART.

'Overture to the Hebrides.'
My 'G minor Concerto.'

"The orchestra, conducted by Felix, played splendidly; there was not a slip. I played 'con amore,' Chorley declares, better than ever I did before. Applause deafening. S. Bach's 'Triple Concerto' with Madame Schumann, Felix, and me—judge how it went. To wind up I played some 'Studies.'

"The day I started, kind Madame Mendelssohn wanted

us to dine at 12.30; but what with leaving cards, and preparing for my journey, I had often to get up from table, and finally to leave my pudding unfinished; a help of it however was handed me into the railway carriage; Felix and Chorley escorted me to the station. Truly the hospitality of the Mendelssohns knows no bounds.

"At Dresden, I visited Schröder-Devrient, who inquired kindly for you and the children."

"Prague, 24th October. Evening.

.... "To my intense delight, my dear mother, who had been kept in doors for several weeks past, walked out with me; she had to lean on my arm, but was sufficiently bright in the evening to play the part of hostess to a family party, which she had actually ventured on giving. Since that day she has got much better, and one evening when the youngsters wanted to dance, and I had to play Strauss' Waltzes, who should attempt to dance but my juvenile mother? It was a pleasure never to be forgotten. I could laugh and cry over it."

On the 31st of October he writes: "I have just played for the benefit of the Charitable Institutions of the town, but decline all other concerts. I was recalled five times—all other particulars when we meet.

"To-day I have many congratulatory visitors after my success of yesterday; among them Dionys Weber, who is loud in my praise. He organized for my special sake an orchestral performance by his pupils at the Conservatoire, and took me to the library, where, in accordance with his suggestion, the authorities have put up a marble bust of Mozart, of whose works they have a collection."

The next letter is from Hof in Bavaria: "The dreaded event of my departure from Prague had been so well and skilfully managed that my mother did not break down as hopelessly as I feared she would. By various innocent devices, I kept her mind intent on anything but the approaching hour of separation. I made her help me to pack my things, and diverted her thoughts all the while by all manner of jokes; she couldn't help laughing, and I could scarcely suppress my tears. To blurt out 'Auf Wiedersehen,' to kiss away the tears that would come, and to rush down stairs—all this was the work of a moment! . . . . My people are the worst off, I have you to look forward to."

"Würzburg, 5th November.

"My fellow-travellers, a brewer, a commercial clerk and an exciseman, were such dull people that Walter Scott could not have drawn them out."

"Frankfort, Friday Morning, 4 A. M.

. . . . "I wonder if the last political squib about Paris has travelled as far as England. In Magdeburg, where there is an illumination in honor of the King of Prussia, some one showed a transparency, on one side of which was an eagle in full flight, on the other a cock crowing, and under it these words, 'Honor the eagle, and don't mind the chattering of the little Thiers' (Thiers being the German equivalent of 'animal')."

Writing to Hamburg from London, where his family and numerous pupils so impatiently awaited his arrival, Moscheles says: "I am so glad you are in the presence of that rare art-phenomenon, Liszt; he is a connecting link in the chain of art-development, and his extraordinary powers are sure to be appreciated among you. I have always stood well with him. . . . . You ask about myself. Well I have a great many irons in the fire. A series of German Lieder is to be brought out by Kistner; the 'Méthode des Méthodes,' by myself and Fétis, must be published in a fortnight from hence. I have therefore to correct, not only these proof-sheets, but also those of the Beethoven Biography, which are pressingly demanded by the publishers."

In the midst of all these occupations, Moscheles and his wife are gladdened by the following letter from Mendelssohn:—

"DEAR MRS. MOSCHELES,—I am now thinking of Moscheles once more at home with you, 'comfortable at the fireside' (that can't be said in German), and I must now write and tell you how much, how often, and with what heartfelt gratitude, I recall the time just gone by. After we parted from you at the London Post Office, we had some delightful days, which M. and Chorley have described to you at length in their letters; but the quiet peaceful time since Moscheles started in the railway, and Chorley in the mail-coach, is no theme for description; in fact happiness cannot be defined, and certainly, I ought neither to have nor to express any wish, seeing that I happen just now to be hard at work, with my wife and children in good health and spirits around me. We were all of us, however, very grieved to receive a letter from Moscheles, in which he announces definitely that he is not coming. During his few days with us, he had become just like a member of the family, so that we all felt his departure. My wife, too, he seems to like—at least, if it be true that such sympathies are usually reciprocal, for that she liked him I knew the first day. When will my old prophecy at last be realized, that you too are to love my Cécile, and become confidential and feel at home with her? I'm afraid this can't be next spring, and it is still a question whether Germany has made so favorable an impression upon Moscheles that he would like to renew it. Still I do hope that he has thoroughly felt, what we all had very close at heart, what each one of us would gladly have shown and expressed (were not demonstrativeness and outspokenness the weak side of us Germans), what he can find nowhere stronger than among us here—I mean the most intense respect and affection for him personally, and his art as well, and the sincerest gratitude for the intellectual feasts he has given us. These are daily the subjects of our conversation, even little Carl lets no day pass without asking: 'Papa, how does Uncle Moscheles play?' And then I try, as well as I can, to imitate his fist playing in 'E flat major 6-8 time,' but it's a miserable failure. Now comes a song.* . . . . I will now hand over the pen to my wife, merely adding my best greetings for Emily, Serena, Felix, and Clara; be sure and remind the dear children of me occasionally. The letter is partly for Moscheles. I needn't say how delighted I was with his success at Prague; may he too

* This is the Shepherd's Winter Song: "O Winter, schlimmer Winter."

sometimes think of us as a friend, and not keep us too long waiting for the news of his happy arrival home. Farewell, dear Mrs. Moscheles.

"Always your devoted

"FELIX MENDELSSOHN-BARTHOLDY."

# CHAPTER XXIII.

## 1841.

The Philharmonic Society—Moscheles as Conductor—Generosity of Liszt—The Kemble Family—Madame Viardot—German and Italian Artists—Mendelssohn's " Leider ohne Worte "—Mendelssohn and Spohr—Rachel—Thorough Bass—Pianoforte Practice—Some weeks in Boulogne—Musical Publications.

DURING this winter the peace of the musical world was much disturbed by the proceedings of the Philharmonic Society, where injudicious counsels, and a too rigid conservatism on the part of the Directors, had resulted in a poor subscription list and inadequate performances. Most of the performances, notably that of the "Lobgesang," were found fault with. In deference to public opinion, which called loudly for novelties, Berlioz's overture to the "Francs Juges" was given, but most unfavorably received. "Was the composition, or was the bad performance to be held responsible for that chaos? I can't settle that question after one hearing."

Again we read: "Strangely enough, the 'Melusine' was coldly received, the music was not understood, and failed to kindle any enthusiasm, perhaps for the want of a brilliant finale. Suffice it to say that the jealous and thick-headed are already glad to talk about failure, while we are up in arms against them."

There was a loud call for the Ninth Symphony, and Moscheles, who this year had not been re-elected as one of the Directors, was now requested to conduct it.

He writes in his diary: "A truce to selfishness. If I can make this gigantic work accessible to the public, it is my duty to do so." How successfully he performed this duty, we may gather from the following passages in the *Times* of the 4th of May: "Artists and amateurs now are glad to own that Beethoven's Ninth Symphony is as much remarkable for majesty and grandeur as for simplicity. For this recognition we are in a great measure indebted to Moscheles, who conducted the work with great care and conscientiousness. As a conductor he surpasses almost all our musicians, for whenever he swings his bâton he leads the orchestra, whereas others are led by it. Nothing would so much tend to elevate the character of these concerts as the permanent appointment of Moscheles as a conductor; he is one who inspires the orchestra with a respect due to him, and would always lead it onwards to new successes."

At the eighth concert the attention of the audience was entirely centred upon Liszt. "When he came forward to play in Hummel's Septet, one was prepared to be staggered, but only heard" (we quote the diary) "the well-known piece which he plays with the most perfect execution, storming occasionally like a Titan, but still, in the main, free from extravagance; for the distinguishing mark of Liszt's mind and genius is that he knows perfectly the locality, the audience, and the style of music he brings before that audience, and uses his powers, which are equal to everything, merely as a means of eliciting the most varied kinds of effects."

After this season Liszt made a tour with Lavenu in the provinces; this scheme proving unsuccessful, the generous pianist released the entrepreneur from his pecuniary obligation. Liszt and Moscheles were heard several times together in the "Preciosa" variations, on which Moscheles remarks: "it seemed to me that we were sitting together on Pegasus." When Moscheles showed him his F sharp and D minor "Studies," which he had written for Mechetti's Beethoven album, Liszt, in spite of their intricacies and difficulties, played them admirably at sight. He was a constant visitor at Moscheles' house, often dropping in unexpectedly, and many an evening was spent under the double fascination of his splendid playing and brilliant conversation. "The other day he told us: 'I have played a duet with Cramer; I was the poisoned mushroom, and I had at my side my antidote of milk.'"

The Kemble family was a favorite topic with Moscheles. "What an interesting and gifted family the Kembles!

Charles Kemble, for so many years one of the chief glories of the English stage, has two daughters—the eldest, Mrs. Butler (illustrious in her maiden days as Fanny Kemble), and the youngest Adelaide, gifted with a glorious voice, which she uses with equal success in Italian bravuras, German Lieder, or old classical music. She is so thoroughly versed in languages that when she sings you can fancy you are listening to an Italian, French, or German; she is gifted with an extraordinary musical memory. Kemble and Mrs. Butler read to the family circle scenes from Shakespeare's plays; no wonder such intellectual reunions attract the most select and cultivated audiences. The other day Kemble, after reading some scenes from 'As You Like It,' ended by way of a joke with the words, 'Come, let us sing, cousin;' whereupon Madame Viardot and Miss Kemble set the example, and we other musicians followed.

"Miss Kemble's version of the 'Erl-King' at her own concert, accompanied by Liszt, was really thrilling. In the following winter her 'Norma' and other characters won for her the reputation of being the first singer and actress of the day. A worthy scion of the Kembles!"

The gifted Viardot is thus referred to: "Viardot is a musician to the core; she not only knows and understands the classical masters, but overcomes all the technical difficulties of modern 'fioriture.' One can justly apply to her the French expression, 'Elle crée son rôle.' I seem to realize and understand a character after seeing Viardot in it—not before; she is a linguist and composer as well; in a word she is one of the greatest phenomena of our time." Persiani performs incredible difficulties, but, says Moscheles: "Her high, thin voice is like a violin with very thin strings; I can't say I care much for her 'Beatrice di Tenda.' Madame Dorus Gras, in the matter of organ and flexibility of voice, is in reality a second Persiani; Meerti an excellent and sympathetic concert-singer, and so simple and amiable. Our Germans, Frau Stöckl-Heinefetter, Staudigl, and Haizinger, were perfect in 'Jessonda' and the 'Zauberflöte.'"

"Staudigl often sings in our house," writes Mrs. Moscheles; "his sound German style is the healthiest antidote I know of for the mawkish sentimentality of the Italians."

Although separated from one another, Mendelssohn and Moscheles were constantly in communication. Moscheles, referring to Mendelssohn in one his letters, observes: "It is refreshing to my mind and heart that I have to revise the proofs of the fourth book of 'Lieder ohne Worte;' I play them and the 'Variations Sérieuses' over and over again—each time I enjoy their beauties afresh." When Moscheles in return sends his friends copies of his new MS. Studies in F major and D minor, he remarks: "Felix will play them at sight quite as well as Liszt."

Not only was there a constant interchange of compositions, but also of home news. Mrs. Moscheles had alluded in one of her letters to a newspaper article, in which some busybody had indulged in ill-natured comparisons between Mendelssohn and Spohr. To this Mendelssohn replies: "The only thing that vexes me in your charming letter is that you have taken any interest in the strange comparisons and the 'cock-fights' which have been started in England between Spohr and me. These things are unaccountable, and I heartily deplore them; in truth, not the slightest idea of such a competition or comparison has ever entered my mind. You will smile, or be angry with me for answering so seriously such a ridiculous matter; but something serious lies at the bottom of it all, and this competition, suggested Heaven knows by whom, does good to neither of us, but injures both—let alone the fact that I never can or should like to be pitted as an opponent to a master of Spohr's standing. Even from boyhood I have had far too deep a respect for his character and person (this has not bated a jot with my riper judgment) to choose to enter the lists with him now. Pardon, as I said, this dreary tone in answer to so amiable a letter, but it all occurs to me involuntarily, whenever I think of the cross-grained T. and his behavior generally."

"Moscheles writes: "A Mr. B., one of my most zealous pupils, came to me to-day with the request that Spohr, Mendelssohn, and I would each write for him a psalm with orchestral accompaniments, and he offers to pay 20*l.* for each. Mendelssohn chose the 13th, I the 93d Psalm, and Mr. B. wishes them to be published with the utmost care.

"We saw Rachel in 'Les Horaces.' How noble, how

grand is her declamation, appearance, and movement; she inspired me with awe, and in writing about her genius, I feel the insignificance of my praise. What I most admired in her was her power of rising gradually to a climax, an element in any art production, and yet so seldom met with. As she stands leaning against a pillar, motionless as a statue, one has time to admire her classical profile, and the no less classically arranged folds of her drapery; during the story of the battle she becomes a living being, her features betraying every shade of emotion, and, when at last she speaks, her tones peal forth like a solemn measured hymn; as she proceeds she seems to gather inspiration, the measured 'Tempo' becomes a 'Vivace,' then a 'Presto,' and then a 'Tempo rubato.' But throughout this scene the voice retains its full power, articulation, and clearness; not a syllable is lost, and it is only when she stops that one is sensible of having followed her breathlessly."

Moscheles writes from Boulogne: "Here we are. I breathe freely, and can say with pride I am a free man. There is a noise below in the harbor, tri-colors and flags are waving in every direction to celebrate the anniversary of Louis Napoleon's abortive attempts to land; but all honor to the first Napoleon, whose birthday, on the 15th of August, is to be kept with great festivities."

How earnestly Moscheles interested himself in his children's music we gather from the following letter: . . . . "While writing this, I hear Emily playing my 'Nursery Tale' and 'Reconciliation,' and am happy to say that she gathers my intentions from the slightest hint, and can be left to practice without fear of her adopting a fault. As to my little Serena, she has learned her scale in C as a surprise to me, and I, to try her as a timist, have accompanied her in the bass in different rhythms; as this does not put her out I augur well of her taste for music. Thus I take great delight in my children's education, my own, I fear, being past praying for. They must play before company; one can't get them too, early over that dilettante shyness which borders so closely on affectation; one must teach them not to think of their own petty selves, but of the greatness of the work of art they are to interpret." . . . . "You ask me if your daughters ought to learn thorough bass? I say yes. Of course no practical application can be made of the study unless it be pursued for a number of years, yet even when followed in a dilettante way, it helps to the better understanding of good compositions and the rules of their structure; being the grammar of the art of sound, it is an indispensable aid to the deeper comprehension of music. The reading of a figured bass is necessary, as a step to the reading of scores. Choose for your teacher a good theorist or organist."

Writing to a friend in Vienna, he observes: "In reply to your question about your children's technical studies, let me advise you to bestow particular attention to the working of the fourth and fifth fingers, which are naturally the weakest, and ought to acquire the firmness of the others. The 'hand-guide' (Hand-leiter) I consider quite unnecessary. The pupil must from the first be made to hold the arms and hands in a natural manner, neither raising the elbows or wrists too high, nor allowing them to drop too, low. A careful teacher will attend to this, and of course the children must work up to good models; time and expression should be cultivated also, a little later, however. Variations and fantasias upon operatic airs are less fitted for the cultivation of individuality of style, because in such music the ear depends too much on well-known forms; original works by good masters are more useful. But if all that is practiced with the 'hand-guide' (as Kalkbrenner recommends, and still daily uses), all feeling must be dormant, while the hand moves with admirable accuracy and stiffness. What would have become of us older pianoforte-players, and of Thalberg and Liszt, if they had used the hand-guide!' Would art have stood higher?"

During these weeks at Boulogne Moscheles wrote his "Tarantella" (dedicated to his daughter Emily), the "Serenade" (for the two works and arrangements Chappell gave the sum of 80*l.*), besides these, the "Romanesca," two very difficult "Studies," a small Barcarole in D flat major, "to remind me that I am at the sea-side." He also arranged Beethoven's Septet as a pianoforte duet.

# CHAPTER XXIV.

## 1842.

The Bunsen Family—Performance before the King of Prussia—A Trying Time—Correspondence with Madame Moscheles—Rossini's "Stabat Mater"—Conversation with Neukomm—Family Trials—Rehearsal of Spohr's Symphony—Anton Rubinstein—Dedication of a Work to Prince Albert—Presentation to the Prince—Great Fire at Hamburg—Concert in Aid of the Sufferers—Jullien's Concerts.

AT the beginning of this year Moscheles alludes to his acquaintance with Bunsen, at that time the representative of Prussia in England, and the recognized centre of all that was distinguished in politics, science, and art. At the end of January Moscheles, at a party given by the Bunsens, plays before the King of Prussia on an Erard piano. "I chose it by command of the King; it is to be sent to Berlin, and I was glad the King approved of it. Neukomm played on the 'orgue expressif." Alexander von Humboldt, and other famous compatriots in attendance on his Majesty, took a very friendly interest in my performances."

February was a month of severe trial for Moscheles and his family, for the scarlet-fever broke out in the house. Remembering Dickens's words: "They sat together and talked of their illness," we shrink from inflicting a dreary story on our readers. Suffice it to say that Moscheles was obliged to leave the house, to avoid spreading infection among his numerous pupils. Between his lodgings and the sick-room innumerable letters passed, and from these we extract a few passages. "I trust to Providence and your strength of mind; if your strength to bear our separation increases, I will fancy myself on a journey, returning home, the road a rugged one, the diligence dragging lazily along, and occasionally stuck fast in the mud, the arrival home delayed, until finally the conductor calls out, 'You are now at the last stage,' and the custom-house officer, 'You can pass.'" . . . . Sometimes he forgets his office as consoler, and strikes another key: "A cell in Newgate couldn't be so repulsive to me as a lodging separated from you." A more favorable bulletin suggests the remark: "This was sent to me at the 'Singverein,' and in the joy of my heart I immediately ordered a 'Gloria' to be sung. Tell Felix I shall empty a whole cask of wine to his health. Since we parted, Rossini's 'Stabat Mater,' which we were so anxious to hear, has become known to me, and Benedict and I are now studying it with our class. It is, as you may imagine, a model of 'singableness' (if I may say so), but it is not sufficiently church-music to my taste; his solitary fugue is clumsy. The criticisms on the work are very various, some agree with me, but the majority delight in the captivating Italian phrases, which I admire too, but which I cannot think are in the right place. Now, I hope the time is not so far distant when you will again take part in the class, and become acquainted with this work. . . . Pray, let us settle as to the exact time when I can see you at the window; certainly it is a plague of Tantalus, but whenever I look out for you, and you are not there, I feel as if I had missed a correct Tempo."

He often tries to amuse his wife by telling stories of his friends and acquaintance. "I heard B. M. play a piece of his own composition, but it was a paraphrase of Thalberg and Döhler, consequently dilution twice diluted." . . . . "How my ears suffered at a soirée, where Rode's Variations and Weber's 'Concertstück' were played in amateurish fashion. At last I determined on scaring away all these unpleasant sounds by playing myself." Speaking of a very small and overluxurious house, he says: "It seems to me like a child who has put on his grandfather's court dress. . . . . At a dinner the lady of the house gives her orders, the husband his, the sons issue fresh ones, and two poor inexperienced maid-servants run about like sheep which find themselves separated from their flock, and are driven together by dogs." . . . . "I had a curious conversation with Neukomm, and played him my Psalm (93); he said repeatedly, 'Fine! Good, good!' and declared that the second number, a chorus full of melody, was his favorite. I asked for criticism, and he showed me some harmonic progressions, which he declared were too bold. I thought how useful they would be to his classically correct but often monotonous compositions, but merely said: 'The unapproachable Beethoven has ventured still further.' He added: 'There you follow a bad example.' To this assertion I would only give modest evasive answers, and young Bunsen came in most opportunely to interrupt us." . . . . "Last Saturday we sang some of Neukomm's music, a vocal piece in sixteen parts, for which Bunsen had written a commentary. Neukomm has in this music harmonized and arranged Chorales, a 'Miserere,' by Palestrina, and the Liturgy of Passion Week (with pianoforte and organ accompaniment). I sang my bass part only a trifle weaker than Lablache."

His gratitude for the preservation of his son and the recovery of his wife, his deep sorrow on receiving the news of his mother's death, and his resignation to the Divine will—all these feelings find expression in the following lines: "This blow has almost stunned me. Never was a son loved more affectionately. Never has a son more heartily responded to such love than I did. This gap must remain unfilled. But God has wonderfully preserved to me wife and children. To Him be thanks!"

During this saddest of winters, Moscheles had, by express wish of the composer, to study and rehearse Spohr's Symphony for doublė orchestra, which was to be performed at the Philharmonic Concert.

"The work," says Moscheles, "has all the great qualities which one knows and loves in Spohr: beautiful treatment of the subjects, admirable modulation and instrumentation, but there is a want of novelty in the leading ideas, and I should like more episodes and contrasts; so much unity leads to monotony. It may satisfy the harmonist, but there is too much sameness throughout. The orchestra played zealously and 'con amore,' but the work was only moderately applauded."

This season was memorable for the deluge of foreign artists. Among them was the youthful Anton Rubinstein. "This Russian boy," says Moscheles, "has fingers light as feathers, and with them the strength of a man." Native artists, too, were on the alert. Blagrove gave quartet evenings, Bennett published his Sestet in F sharp minor; and the Royal Academy of Music performed Spohr's "Last Judgment." About this time Bunsen secured for Moscheles the permission to dedicate his great "Pianoforte School" to Prince Albert, and on the day fixed by the Prince for receiving the presentation copy, Moscheles finds himself in Buckingham Palace, where he writes to his wife as follows:—

"Ante-chamber, Buckingham Palace.—It is now a quarter-past one, and I have been sitting all alone here since twelve o'clock, giving audience to my thoughts without keeping them waiting as long as the Prince does me, or I do my pupils. On one side I am warmed by the sunbeams as they pour through the large window, and on the other by a large fire—isn't that bliss? But freedom! golden freedom! would you were mine once more, and that I was sitting at home instead of looking at these bleak walls! Luckily I found writing materials, and can thus prove to you in black and white, that on all occasions I think of you . . . Two o'clock.—At last Dr. Schenck appeared in my prison, and told me, with an air of great embarrassment, that owing to the forgetfulness of one of the pages, the Prince, who happened to be busy when I arrived, had not been reminded that I was in waiting. He said the Prince would certainly reprove the page for his neglect . . . . . Five o'clock.—I am back again to what I, poor exile, call my home, and must give you the sequel of my Court adventures. The Prince walked in after Dr. Schenck, made his excuse, and said he was vexed I had lost so much of my time. He was so amiable that my impatience vanished. I handed to him the 'Pianoforte School,' and he turned over several of the pages, saying he thought he would have to work at the easiest of the 'Studies;' to this I naturally answered, that he had only to command me, whenever he might want to hear me play him the difficult ones. He answered me kindly, but a page entering the room with 'Her Majesty the Queen is ready,' the Prince took a hasty farewell of me and Dr. Schenck; I too hurried off to my lessons."

In May Moscheles received the news of the great fire at Hamburg. When all anxiety about the safety of his relations was over, and it became evident that the misery of the thousands left without a roof to shelter them required immediate assistance, he conceived the plan of giving a grand concert for the benefit of the sufferers. The selection of a day and place, and the means of reducing the expenses of preparation, were matters for anxious deliberation. The ball for the Spitalfield Weavers, the number of impending concerts, the Director of the Italian Opera, with his enormous demands, were serious obstacles, but Lablache most kindly came to the rescue, promising his own assistance, and that of all his compatriots. German and English artists also joined, but the Hamburg Committee tried to hamper Moscheles with doubts as to the success of the scheme, and hinted at the advisability of another well-known pianist sharing the enterprise; this he steadily refused. The admission tickets had a rapid sale, and at the eleventh hour Mendelssohn appeared in England and eagerly joined. When all the tickets were disposed of, the orchestra was converted into stalls; the boxes let at high prices; some of the Royal Family attended, and for the accommodation of crowds unable to get admission, tables and chairs were ranged like seats in an amphitheatre, at the entrance door. Moscheles wrote for the occasion a Study in F major, 2–4 time, always after this called the 'Hamburg Study.'

We give the sum total of receipts and expenditure:

| | | £ | s. | d. |
|---|---|---|---|---|
| Lumley, director of the thèatre | | 50 | 0 | 0 |
| Refreshments for the Artists | | 2 | 10 | 9 |
| Extra seats | | 2 | 3 | 6 |
| Police | | 1 | 8 | 6 |
| Porters and Billposters | | 4 | 7 | 0 |
| Paper-hangers—Joiners | | 8 | 8 | 0 |
| Advertisements | | 23 | 0 | 0 |
| | | £91 | 17 | 9 |
| Gross Receipts | £735 2 3 | | | |
| Surplus | | £643 | 4 | 6 |

"Of this sum I asked the Senate," says Moscheles, "to allow me 1000 marks for distribution among families selected by myself. The Town afterwards presented me with a medal made of the molten bronze of the Church bells; it bore the inscription 'Hamburg thanks.'"

Mendelssohn's hopes that his Cécile would not belie the anticipations raised by his letters were abundantly realized. Mrs. Moscheles writes: "At last my ardent wish is fulfilled; I have learnt to know the charming and beautiful Cécile. Mendelssohn was quite right in anticipating that we should learn to understand and love each other, I for my part had not to learn this, for to see her was to feel at once attracted towards her. We spent some delightful days with them at her aunt's; in fine weather we had running matches in the garden, when Mendelssohn's feet proved to be as active as on the organ pedal. We performed charades too, Felix acting as stage-manager, and Moscheles doing the orchestra. But when the time came for serious music, then were the two M.'s in their real element; then did they give us their very best, winding up as usual with a grand improvisation à quatre mains. Then followed such remarks as these: 'How insane of you to bring in my madcap Scherzo while I was just fairly launched in your A flat major Study, which I wanted to do ever so sentimentally;' or, 'Isn't it a wonder it went at all? Upon my word, we have been too reckless to-day!'"

"One must congratulate the excitable and effervescent Mendelssohn that he has met with a wife so gentle, so exquisitely feminine; they are perfectly matched." Moscheles says; "He played me his Choruses from 'Antigone,' singing or humming the voice parts; even with this hearing I see plainly that the work is grand and noble. The Bacchus Chorus is in the true genuine spirit. His new A minor Symphony is a gem; the subscribers to the Philharmonic are quite ready to acknowledge it as such, how much more then we artists!"

The Handel Society, of which Moscheles was a member, was founded for the purpose of publishing an improved edition of Handel's works, and the scheme necessarily involved a number of meetings and consultations. "The children were differently occupied," Mrs. Moscheles writes; "we have a novelty more interesting to them than Christmas trees—I mean Jullien's new Promenade Concerts. Drury Lane Theatre is converted into a large room, in which the 'one shilling' public freely circulates, regardless of the music; the boxes are filled by the 'haute volée.'

Jullien directs a good orchestra, sometimes with a bâton, sometimes playing a 'flauto piccolo,' which with its shrill tones marks the rhythm. After each piece he throws himself back as if he were exhausted, on a red velvet arm chair; his dress-coat discovers half a mile of white waistcoat; his dance tunes, strongly spiced with drum, bassoon, and trumpet, are attractive to all, but specially to the schoolboy, who would not think it Christmas if he did not go to Jullien's concerts."

Moscheles, while enjoying with his children this kind of entertainment, was contemplating for them a musical pastime of a very different description. "Since I accompanied my little girl in the C major scale, I have had an idea running in my head of making a 'harmonized work on scales.' This is to make the dry mechanical practice of the different scales pleasant to the pupil, and form her taste by hearing a melody; it will also make her a good timist. Such a work might possibly become useful to the world of pianoforte-players; the sooner the purely mechanical part of study is put into the background, the higher will be the cultivation of the artistic element." The idea of writing this new work was soon realized.

We quote from the diary:—"I advise the pupil to practice the scales with both hands, and that too 'con amore;' the master, who has the responsibility of listening to his pupil while he practices his scales, should not weary over his work, as too often happens; both should be agreeably employed, the master in reading his own part and paying attention to that of his pupil, the latter in hearing a rhythmical piece, a melody, and accustoming himself to count, instead of having to run up and down the bare scales. "You wouldn't believe," says Moscheles, "with what enthusiasm the children rush at every newly finished piece of the work on scales; Emily naturally acts as Professor; they must play it all even before the ink is dry, and 'La Danse des Fées' is their favorite."

## CHAPTER XXV.

### 1843.

Operatic Arrangements—John Parry—Mrs. Shaw and Clara Novello at Exeter Hall—Hallé the Pianist—Inauguration of the Leipzig Conservatoire—Alexander Dreyschock—Sivori and Ernst—Spohr in London—Concert by Hullah's Pupils—Anecdote of Fontenelle—Music and Drawing—Heinrich Lehmann—Playing to the Blind in Paris—visit to Halévy in Prison.

MOSCHELES has, early in the year, to make two books of operatic arrangements—this time on "Don Pasquale"—for Cramer; he next revises three numbers of "Fidelio," published after Beethoven's death. "We had," Mrs. Moscheles writes, "a long musical evening in Exeter Hall—too much for the German taste; I give you the programme in extenso:—Anthem, by Dr. Crotch, Beethoven's Mass in C, and the 'Lobgesang.' How did we possibly manage after this to go to Mrs. Sartoris? how could Moscheles play, and successfully too? how could we laugh even at John Parry's performances? Without him no party is thought complete; I have already told you how he sings a trio all by himself; every one laughs, as soon as he sits down to the piano, over which he has perfect mastery; in his 'parlando' songs, which are for the most part in verse, he generally satirizes some folly of the day. He may truly be called the musical Molière of our time." Again: "We have had a performance of Beethoven's oratorio 'The Mount of Olives,' at Exeter Hall. . . . . There was a strange scene the other evening, when the 'Messiah' was given. Those excellent artists, Clara Novello and Mrs. Shaw, stirred the audience to great enthusiasm; it literally rained encores. Mrs. Shaw seemed willing to comply with the wishes of the audience, Miss Novello the reverse; she withstood all the shouts, clapping of hands, and other noisy demonstrations, and Phillips' song, 'Why do the heathen rage?' seemed well suited to the occasion, and was only half listened to by an audience shouting 'Miss Novello!' 'encore!' It was no good, she declined to repeat her song, and left the orchestra. At last the music was allowed to proceed without interruption, and when it came to the heavenly air 'I know that my Redeemer liveth,' Miss Novello stepped forward again, this time accompanied by a member of the committee, who was about to speak, but some one shouted out 'bad temper,' and the Witch's Sabbath began afresh, so that the poor lady sang the greater part of her sublime song amid the alternate hisses, applause, and screams of the audience. At last, however, her fine singing prevailed, and the turmoil was at an end."

At this time Moscheles, in a letter to his father-in-law, says, in reference to Berlioz's great symphony, which had just been heard in Hamburg, "I only know this work from the pianoforte copy, and am therefore not competent to form a judgment upon it, but I shall be with difficulty won over to it, because I feel very strongly Berlioz's want of melody, rhythm, phrasing, and contrapuntal proportions. I have heard his overtures 'Francs Juges' and 'Benvenuto Cellini' performed with full orchestra, but his effective instrumentation could not compensate, in my judgment, for the loss of the qualities I have referred to, especially in passages where he attempts to be melodious and poetical, but lapses into prose. Generally speaking, I am too glad to prove to the world and my friends that I am not ultra-conservative, and know how to value the modern composers. Just now I play Chopin a great deal, nay, I try to master his music, although it is not quite my 'genre.'"

Moscheles writes: "Hallé, the pianist, has lately arrived from Paris. He is very fond of playing Chopin's music, and brings with him, no doubt, the correct tradition of the Notturnos and Mazurkas. He is applauded also for his playing of other compositions." . . . .

"Just at present the Tableaux mania is our specialty, and we are assisted by such distinguished people as Landseer, Horsley, and Westmacott. Mrs. Sartoris as the 'Sibylle' was quite classical. Her musical parties are very choice." . . . . "I expected great things from the Handel Society, but we lose much precious time in discussion, and the preliminary conferences are not as pleasantly conducted as I should like. At last, however, matters look more business-like, for we have agreed that three Coronation Anthems are to be published as the first number of the new edition, and that later on I am to undertake the 'Allegro' and 'Penseroso.' . . . I am once more to conduct the Ninth Symphony for the Philharmonic Society."

Moscheles thus records an event of great importance in the annals of modern music: "The Leipzig Conservatoire was inaugurated on the 10th of April when pupils were admitted for the first time. With Mendelssohn at the head, one may expect great things of the young Institution; Felix is always trying to persuade me to join him and become one of the staff of teachers. It would be a noble vocation to work in conjunction with him, to shake off the yokes of lesson-giving and dilettantism in order to educate young artists."

Alexander Dreyschock, lately arrived in London, is thus alluded to: "He is still young in the art, but his powers as an executant are marvellous; he has an exquisitely delicate touch, and performs astonishing 'tours de force' with his left hand; but alas! his playing is restricted to twelve pieces, which he has toiled at incessantly. He has no style, and cannot read music, as our little girl discovered. You shall hear the story: he was trying over with me some 'Scale pieces,' and played the 'Pupil's part,' but was so often at fault with the time, that Clara ran up to her mamma, calling out (luckily in English, which Dreyschock probably did not understand), 'Mamma, hasn't Mr. D. learned the scales?' You may imagine my horror at the 'enfant terrible.'"

Sivori gave four crowded concerts, earning golden laurels, especially in his "Carnaval de Venise." Ernst also appeared, charming every one with his grand tone and fine German reading of the great masters. At a concert given for the benefit of the newly opened German hospital, Ernst first displayed his great and versatile powers before an English audience, selecting such music as Spohr's "Gesang Scene," the "Carnaval de Venise," and variations from "Otello."

The arrival of Spohr, the king of violinists, created a considerable sensation in London, where his great artistic gifts met with a very wide spread recognition. The musical societies in London vied with each other in welcoming the great musician. His "Macbeth," his "Weihe der Töne," and the oratorio "The Fall of Babylon," were performed under his own direction. "We artists, making up a party of ninety, gave him a grand dinner at Greenwich; I was placed next to him to interpret the proceedings and numerous speeches; I also accompanied him in three of his manuscript duets. In my improvisation at a later period of the evening I endeavored to be completely 'Spohrish,' and worked up themes out of his Symphony, 'The Consecration of Sound.'" A grand party in his honor was given by the Moscheles, and another by Mr. Alsager. The music was Spohr throughout, and Moscheles played his Quintet. He says: "You know our friend is not demonstrative, but after the first movement he came to the piano to shake hands with me. Hallé turned over the leaves, while all the native and foreign pianists in London formed the audience. Spohr's 'Nonet' was a great treat! so finely played too by the author, now a man of fifty-nine years of age!"

Hullah's pupils gave a grand performance at Exeter Hall, when Moscheles' four-part song "Daybreak" was well given by the admirably-trained choir, and encored.

Moscheles says: "They tell me that some newspaper has sharply criticized my song; I can't help being reminded of an anecdote of Fontenelle, who all his life long was the King of humor, and worshipped by the million as an elegant and refined writer. There was a little room in his house, that was always kept locked, no one ever entered it but himself. When it was opened after his death, it was found crammed full to the ceiling with all kinds of newspapers and periodicals, containing attacks upon him, and this laconic comment upon them: 'I have never read a line of these. I have never answered them.' I too am ready to endorse Fontenelle's views."

In August Moscheles writes from Boulogne: "Our good ship *Harlequin*, when crossing the Channel, certainly bounded like his namesake, but that's all forgotten now.

We have been very kindly received here. . . . . In watching my children at their studies, I discover that they are as fond of drawing as of music. In my young days I was just like them, only my profession tied me exclusively to music, by which I was to earn my bread, so that pencils and paint-boxes were soon laid aside."

The family leave Boulogne for Paris, and we read: "Our cousin Heinrich Lehmann has become a famous painter. His frescoes in the church of St. Mary, his ornamentation of the Chapelle des Aveugles, are very fine." This artist has executed many important works in churches and public buildings; the most deservedly celebrated of these were destroyed at the burning of the Hotel de Ville, during the days of the Commune. His brother Rudolf lived many years in Rome, where he produced his well-known pictures of Italian life. "When we went to see the frescoes," says Moscheles, "I was asked to play something for the poor blind people in the hospital. They stood round me, and their enthusiasm deeply affected me; not only did they thank me, but kissed my hands with an earnestness that brought tears into my eyes. We have passed many happy hours in Paris with Meyerbeer, Ernst, Hallé etc."

On the 3d of October we read: "I was extremely amused with my visit to Halévy, who, having been guilty of some breach of duty as a 'garde national,' was locked up for eight and forty hours. Many famous painters before him must have endured the same fate in the same place, for artistic sketches and eccentric caricatures were drawn and painted on the walls. We chatted as easily in 'Aux Haricots' (the nickname of the prison) as we should have done in his own house; all the more as his young wife was present." Balzac's drama, 'Pamela Rigault,' and a representation by Madame Georges, who was famous even in the days of the Empire, are marked as specially interesting, but on returning home to London, Moscheles' first exclamation is, "What a delight my Erard and my Collard give me! They are not even out of tune; my new 'Study' in C sharp minor, 6-8 time, sounded well."

This winter Mr. Hullah gave at his own house an excellent performance of Mendelssohn's "Athalie," which

Moscheles accompanied on the piano; Balfe produced his opera the "Bohemian Girl." "Jullien still thrives; he has actually taken to Beethoven's Symphonies, and by way of contrast we are favored with Roch Albert's Tone-picture the 'Destruction of Pompeii,' with storms, crashes, prayers, Bacchante dances, oracles, utter darkness, and then a blaze of fireworks; great and small effects, for great and small children! . . . . Jullien is witty too, or he pretends to have discovered an echo on some Irish lake which repeats the final notes the wrong way round, as for instance:

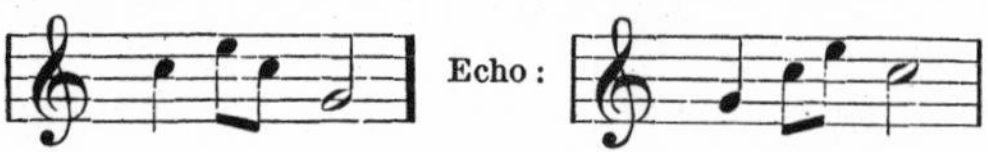


Other similar effects are produced, one and all equally bewildering to a musician."

Moscheles ends the year with the following commentary on a reporter who from an opponent had become an admirer, "I am always the fortunate Prince, my detractors cannot do me any harm, so they are obliged at last to become my friends."

## CHAPTER XXVI.

1844.

New Year in Austria and England—Joachim—Teaching the Theory of Music—Mendelssohn in London—Golden Hours—Moscheles Visited by Nesselrode—Visit to Germany—Concert at Frankfort—Chairs for the Concert—Auerbach—Kaulbach—The Artist's Studio—King Louis—Musical Life and Doings in Vienna—Ernst Pauer—An Imposing Scene in Vienna—Court Concert—Leipzig.

THE following is the entry for the 1st of January: "I was struck with the contrast between the modes of celebrating this day in Austria and England. There it is a regular holiday, here a day of business. To do at Rome as the Romans do, I worked at the Pianoforte edition of the 'Allegro and Penseroso' for the Handel Society. A proposition was made to Mendelssohn to undertake the editing of the 'Messiah,' but he felt scruples on account of Mozart's additional accompaniments, and therefore the 'Israel in Egypt' was offered to him instead."

The arrival of one who since those days has become world-renowned, is thus briefly recorded: "Joachim, a boy of thirteen years of age, has come to London, bringing with him a letter of recommendation from Mendelssohn ; his talent, however, is his best introduction. We organized a small party expressly for him ; I listened with delight to him and Emily playing in Mendelssohn's lovely 'D minor trio ;' after that I was fairly taken by surprise by Joachim's manly and brilliant rendering of David's 'Variations' and De Bériot's 'Rondo.' Mendelssohn is right, here we have talent of the true stamp."

. . . . "At Drury Lane Theatre, I heard Benedict's opera 'The Brides of Venice ;' there are fine orchestral effects and the vocal parts are well treated, and worthy of special commendation. The music was well received, and the composer called for. . . . Incredible, and yet true. At

Caradori's morning concert I accompanied some twenty-two vocal pieces, in which the concert-giver and a host of vocalists took part; the legion of instrumentalists was headed by Joachim, who played Ernst's 'Otello' Fantasia in the most masterly way. Of the newest pianist importation, Leopold von Meyer, I can only say he thundered forth a Fantasia of his own upon 'Lucrezia Borgia,' with immense force and execution; but where was the soul?"

Mrs. Moscheles writes: "Fancy what we went through the evening after Caradori's concert: first of all Sivori's concert, then the quarter party given by Macfarren and Davison, the chief feature of which was Ernst leading Beethoven's posthumous quartet in C sharp minor, and lastly, Mrs. Sartoris's musical soirée, which we were unable to enjoy—we had had too much of a good thing."

The one incomparable delight of this season was the presence of Mendelssohn, who conducted five of the Philharmonic Concerts, and a full rehearsal of the Schubert and Gade Symphonies, which were heard for the first time in England. "When Mendelssohn appeared in the orchestra," Moscheles writes, "he was received, as he deserves, with raptures and enthusiasm. With him for a permanent conductor the Philharmonic Concerts must improve. The mediocre performances were often a source of annoyance and regret to me, and the one remedy, the appointment of a permanent conductor, was unwisely from time to time postponed; now I feel quite relieved. Once more, to my great delight, I heard Mendelssohn's 'A minor Symphony;' with its fine piquant and original instrumentation. His 'Midsummer Night's Dream' music, given at the fifth, was repeated at the sixth concert, when the Court was present; last of all we had the 'Walpurgis Night,' all the more delightful to me as I had studied its beauties in the pianoforte score. The 'Suite of Bach' is a most interesting novelty—this too, we owe to my dear friend. He played himself Beethoven's 'G major Concerto,' improvising splendid cadenzas, and introduced his young friend Joachim in the same great master's Violin Concerto—both performances were triumphant. Of course Felix was the bright star of my birthday party on the 30th of May. He brought a most welcome contribution to my album. It was a sequel to the illustrated catalogue of my works, the first page of which he had filled in 1832; the present continuation is as witty and clever as its predecessors. At the bottom of the page he had written the words, 'God willing, to be continued.' It was decreed otherwise."

After a performance of the oratorio "St. Paul," we find an allusion to a conversation on the subject of the publication of Mendelssohn's works, and Moscheles endeavored to impress Felix with the necessity of dealing fairly by himself, instead of undervaluing writings the sterling worth of which was everywhere acknowledged. Mrs. Moscheles writes: "Mendelssohn is the amiable friend we have ever known him. He gave out that after conducting the last Philharmonic Concert, on the 8th of July, he should leave England, but he arranged with us to meet our common friends at our house, and at Klingemann's, on the 9th. You may imagine how delighted 'nos intimes' were, and what glorious instrumental music we had; Mrs. Sartoris, too, was in splendid voice. Our guests were so grateful and happy, not happier than the hostess herself, for those were golden hours indeed!"

In the record of this year we find the names, more or less famous, of politicians, authors, and artists, who became acquainted with or brought letters of introduction to Moscheles. One visitor was the son of the illustrious C. M. von Weber; he came to London charged with the sad duty of superintending the removal of his father's remains from Moorfields' Chapel to their final resting-place in Dresden. We read, too, of the painters Magnus and Jacob, of Berlin, Mrs. Jameson, the accomplished authoress, and the distinguished Nesselrode, who expressed a wish to hear Moscheles, and honored him with a visit. He was attended by Baron Brunow, the Russian Ambassador. Mrs. Moscheles writes: "The great man was very amiable, and called on Moscheles to play several of his own compositions; Emily also was made to play, and Nesselrode not only paid elaborate compliments to father and daughter, but expressed an earnest hope that he would meet us in Russia." The invitation was endorsed by Michael Vielhoursky, called by Moscheles "one of the first amateurs in St. Petersburg." The project of going to Russia, which had almost been determined on, was abandoned in consequence of the death of the Grand-Duchess Alexandra. Mrs. Moscheles writes: "I really think a man like Nesselrode can't sneeze, without the fact being noticed in the newspapers; his visit to Chester Place is not only recorded but prettily embellished by a highly imaginative reporter, in the *Morning Post.* I suppose a blank had to be filled up with some gossip."

The journey to St. Petersburg being abandoned, Moscheles realized the project of taking his wife and daughter with him on a visit to "dear old Vienna." Halting awhile at several German towns for the sake of "Auld Lang Syne," and exploring the beauties of "Father Rhine," they reach Frankfort, and, to their great delight, find that the Mendelssohns are at Soden, "only half an hour from us." "There is a regular congress of pianists here, and in spite of that people insist on my giving a concert." Mendelssohn insisting too, a concert was arranged for the 25th of September, and the two friends played the "Hommage à Handel" to a crowded audience.

An amusing incident is described in a letter from Moscheles' daughter:—"The room, long before the concert began, was crammed full, but still people came; there was a small empty room adjoining. 'What will the Frankforters say when they find no seats?" said Mendelssohn to Rosenhain. 'Let us be off together and hire chairs, without bothering Moscheles just before the concert." Our good friend Rosenhain jumped at the proposal, but it was no such easy matter to get chairs, for it was the time of the fair, and there were none to spare in the crowded hotels. At last they found four dozen in a small pothouse. 'These must be sent immediately,' says Mendelssohn. 'But who is to pay?' inquires the landlord. 'A great artist—Moscheles—who is giving a concert, and the room is so full that more chairs are wanted; your money's safe.' 'Those artist gentlemen,' says the canny landlord, 'often give concerts, pocket the money and bolt—I must have something down.' Our two friends empty their pockets, which happened to be poorly filled. The landlord, however, is satisfied; they then mount a 'Droschke' Mendelssohn shoves two of the chairs inside, and two more in front of the driver, and then calls out, 'Now off with you as fast as you can drive to the Mühlens'schen Saal.' When they get there the other chairs are sent after them, and all the audience are seated, although Madame Mendelssohn, mamma and I had to make shift with two between us. What pleased Mendelssohn far more than the history of the chairs, was my father's addition of the deep bass C in his A flat 'Study.'. 'You surprised me with that, he said 'it has a splendid effect, which ought not to be forgotten; I will write it in Mrs. Moscheles' album at once.' He did so, drawing at the same time a picture of the Droschke, Rosenhain, and himself, and the chairs and all, but only half a horse. 'I can't draw that by heart he said."

"Darmstadt, Heidelberg, Carlsruhe, are all visited in turn, and at the latter place the Grand-Duchess (a Wasa), a truly amiable and gifted princess, delighted in playing pianoforte duets with me and Emily. Here, too, we made Berthold Auerbach's acquaintance, and were struck with the originality of the extracts he read to us from his works." At Stuttgart the public insist upon a second concert. "At Augsburg," Moscheles writes, "I went to the theatre to engage some vocalists. They were just rehearsing 'La Clemenza di Tito;' to me too, the 'Tito' was 'clemente.' Vitellia smiled condescendingly, Sesto, in her costume (more becoming at a distance), claimed acquaintance as an old Viennese friend, while the chorus director embraced me, and Hummel's son offered me his services as accompanist.'"

From Munich Mrs. Moscheles writes: "Here the feet of Fanny Elsler are in opposition to Moscheles' hands. It is impossible to secure band or public, as she is forever dancing. When Moscheles talks of leaving without giving a concert, his friends, with Kapellmeister Lachner at their head, are up in arms, so he has made up his mind to stay till the 9th of November."

During the interim we have frequent notices of visits to Kaulbach's studio. "He comes repeatedly in the dusk of evening to my hotel when I am practicing, and sits by my side a rapt listener." Mrs. Moscheles describes a comical adventure that took place in Kaulbach's studio: "The artist's atelier consists of several rooms. In one, the largest, he is just now painting his great picture of 'The Destruction of Jerusalem.' It is nearly finished, and we so delight in watching the great artist putting the final touches to this masterpiece. In an adjoining room stands the piano; there Moscheles was playing away to his heart's content, when suddenly King Louis, who is quite at home in any artist's studio, and more especially in Kaulbach's, walks in. With ready wit, he says, 'Ah! came to see one artist and find two!—and the ladies!' The ladies were duly introduced to him, and had to stand the fire of his abrupt but friendly conversation.

"Moscheles has to play and be complimented, and when H. M. has left, Kaulbach tells us how the King was much displeased at his working for 'the Prussian,' and had severely taken him to task for it. (The picture is one of the series executed in Berlin.)" Asher, a pupil of Kaulbach's, makes a hasty sketch of this scene for Emily's album. Count Pocci presents us with some of his inimitably beautiful pen-and-ink sketches; and Kaulbach gives Mrs. Moscheles one of his original and masterly drawings for Schiller's "Robbers." This is so elaborately finished that it requires a practiced eye to tell it from an engraving.

The Munich Concert is described as a most brilliant one. The Court attended; the King between the parts made (as usual) the round of the room. The young ladies are not a little in awe of His Majesty, for he will come up to them and ask, "How old?" They have to shout their answer, as he is very deaf, upon which he will retort, "What! no husband yet!"

Moscheles is impatient to reach Vienna. He writes to Frau von Lieben:

"My heart beats, dear friend, when I think of the prospect before me, that of once more seeing my old Viennese life reflected as in a mirror. With God's help, you and I will revel in the memories of happy days and old associations.

"Until then, as ever, your old friend,

"I. MOSCHELES."

From Vienna Mrs. Moscheles writes: "Moscheles, when

visiting old friends and brother-artists, is received with open arms, and Emily and I share this kind reception. This journey, never intended as a professional tour, has become one, we scarcely know how; but we rejoice in the fact, for the hearty reception he has met with, being in no way inferior to that experienced in former days, has refreshed him in body and mind."

His busy life in Vienna leaves him little time to devote to his diary. We give a summary of his short entries: "I heard Haydn's 'Seasons,'—'Hasselt-Barth excellent.' Instead of Beethoven, Donizetti is now the sun of the music world. That sun does not warm me, nor does it light me forward on my path. . . . . There was an evening party at Court yesterday, where the Improvisator, Professor Wolff, of Jena, was the attraction. There was music as well; Klatke, on the Jew's-harp, and Moreau on the guitar. . . . Frau von Cibbini still lives, a remnant of the good old times, and the Baroness Erdmann, *née* Erdödy. I was not to be put off, and insisted on hearing Beethoven's C sharp Minor Sonata, which she played splendidly as of old. She is an interesting relic of the great days of real pianoforte playing. . . . . To-day I had a delightful reminder of my youth, in Frau von Beer's highly successful trial and performance with me of my Rondo in A for four hands, which I wrote for her when she was Fräulein Sihny. . . . . Aloys Fuchs visited me for the purpose of showing me Handel's MS. Cantate con Stromenti, 'Hero and Leander,' written in Rome for Cardinal Ottoboni in the year 1709. It came into Fuchs' possession in the year 1834. It begins thus:

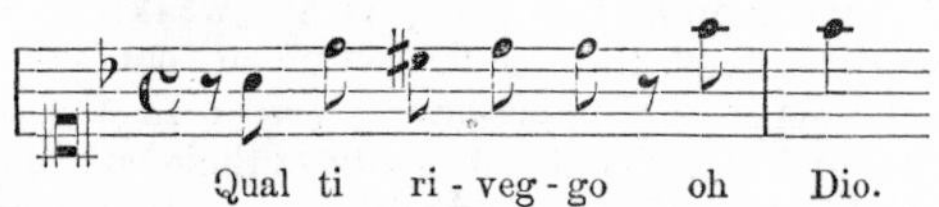


"Jaell brought me his marvellous boy Alfred: he is only ten years old, and played my 'Nursery Tale' wonderfully well. Heard Nicolai's opera 'Die Heimkehr der Verbannten,' good in a dramatic point of view, but too much Italianized. At Saphir's concert Heindl opened with his flute variation—Furore. I played my 'Serenade,' without applause, 'Nursery Tale,' ditto, 'Hungarian March,' vehemently encored. Saphir wound up with a speech full of humor and wit, giving us to understand that his best points were cut out by the public censor—he only hoped he might live to recover his capital so cruelly withheld."

"After some passing remarks on new and unimportant operas, we find severe strictures on the constant usage of the Tyrolese or Italian cadence, while great eulogy is bestowed on a performance of "Don Juan" with Hasselt and Draxler. Young Strauss's playing of dance-music is allowed to equal that of his father. "At the 'Concordia,' I find again many of the old Ludlamists, among them the celebrated poets Castelli and Grillparzer, with several others of note. Fischhof, the great collector of manuscript music, brought me, to my great delight, 'Bach's MS. Concertos,' which we tried over. He promises to let me have some of his treasures for production in London."

At his three concerts in Vienna, Moscheles played the old favorite pieces, and many of his new compositions as well; among the latter was the "Hommage à Handel." "This time the applause pleased me more than ever, for it was shared by my young and highly gifted friend Ernst Pauer." Mrs. Moscheles writes: "People laugh when we talk of a three weeks' stay here. 'A Moscheles,' they say, 'who has not been in Vienna for eighteen years, could just as well pass a winter here as Liszt.' It rains concerts; to-morrow, for instance, there are five.

"I must tell you of a splendid fête we attended lately, where the youthful Archdukes, who looked charming in blue and white satin, were made 'Knights of the Golden Fleece." Ferdinand, the poor, puny, weakly Emperor, when about to invest the youths with the accolade, could only lift the massive old-fashioned sword with the help of his Kollowrat. The Imperial family in their box, the Hungarian 'Noble Guard,' covered with jewels, the picturesque turbans and mantles of the knights of the order, made the whole scene a very imposing one."

After much deliberation, it had been decided that Moscheles should prolong his stay in Vienna, and that his wife and daughter should precede him to Hamburg. Moscheles writes: "I chained myself to my piano, in order to scare away my melancholy and sense of loneliness. You are now driving out into the cold night; I am just home from the Court concert, and will sit up with you, in order to give you particulars about it. . . . Suffice it to say the Imperial family were kind as ever; they inquired for you both, and reminded me of the concert at Prague after my illness. I really came to grief with my extempore performance, for, on asking their Majesties for a theme, they chose something out of Donizetti's 'Linda di Chamouni.' Of course I was forced to confess my ignorance of that 'most glorious of all operas,' so they proposed to me 'the old-fashioned perruque,' out of Mozart's operas. I took 'Batti, batti' and the 'Champagne' song, and afterwards, with an eye to the heroic, Archduke Carl wound up with 'See, the conquering Hero.' In answer to the Emperor's question, 'Wasn't the last the march from the "Vestalin?'" I said, 'Something similar, your Majesty,' and the Empress quickly interposed a question, 'Had I studied in Vienna or Prague?' At 10.30 the Court withdrew, ices were handed round, and I put some sweetmeats in my pocket for the children. Good night."

On the 13th of December Moscheles writes: "It is well that we have made up our minds to this temporary separation, for my stay here seems to me endlessly protracted, as the Archduchess Sophie wants me to play at her concert on the 19th. My improvisation on Handelian themes seems to have impressed her and the Archduke so favorably that they now wish to hear me treat subjects from Gluck's operas. In addition to this, they request me to give a regular 'menu' of my compositions, with the 'Nursery Tale' as dessert. I had a funny conversation with Count Moritz D—, of which I give you a faint outline; it would require a Hoffmann to describe it properly. After some hemming and hawing, he said: 'I have to hand over to you, as a fee for your glorious playing at Court, this small rouleau of ducats; there are sixty of them.' I pleaded for a souvenir instead. He cried down such presents as useless; but I was a match for him, for it ended in his taking back the ducats, and bringing me next day three diamond studs, for which I thanked him. My patience has been sorely tried at a performance of Mendelssohn's 'Lobgesang.' You may imagine how I delighted in hearing that music—I, a fervid worshipper of Mendelssohn—while the public sat listening in stolid indifference; no clapping of hands disturbed my ecstasies. The Chorale, and song, 'Watchman, will the night soon pass?' moved me even to tears. Herr Hoschek, a music-master, came up to me and said, 'Isn't this music very artificially strung together?' My sensations were those of a man pitched head foremost out of a balloon, but I smothered my anger, and said, 'That's as people choose to take it.'"

The next letter is from Prague: "Yesterday, accompanied by my brother and sisters, I visited the grave of my parents; a sweet if sad pilgrimage. On the whole, I feel greatly refreshed by my quiet time here, spent as it is with those near and dear to me, and far away from busy Vienna." The letter concludes with words of affection and advice, addressed individually to each of his children: "My dear Emily, by this time you are beginning to settle down after the harum-scarum life you have led in Vienna. Now I look forward to your devoting more time to yourself, and pioneering your brother and sisters in their studies. You, dear Serena, will regard the meeting with your mother as a happy turning-point, after the crucial time of separation, and enjoy it all the more because you have known what parting means. As for you, dear Felix, if the 'optime' marked under your exercise by your tutor relates to your general behavior, you may feel always certain of my love and gratification; take the 'optime' as a motto to accompany you through life. As for thee, my Benjamina, I expect to find a great big girl, and take care, when you jump up to hug papa, that you don't upset him.'

At Leipzig the meeting with Hauptmann, David, Gade, Joachim, and Frau Frege, has all the old fascination for Moscheles. He writes: "Here I find a genuine artistic atmosphere, where good music seems native to the place. . . . . Yesterday I had a quiet evening with David, who played me the new violin Concerto, which Felix has expressly written for him. It is most beautiful, the last movement thoroughly Mendelssohnian, tripping like a dainty elf. Gade, a young man who conducts the concerts this season, has something in his features that reminds one of Mozart's, judging by the portraits of that illustrious man."

## CHAPTER XXVII.

### 1845.

Dresden—Intercourse with Musical Artists—The Leipzig Conservatoire—Proposed Appointment—Berlin—The Opera House—Jenny Lind—Article in a German Paper, and Reply—Bach's Concertos—Foreign Artists in London—Beethoven as a Conductor—Bonn—Musical Festival—Meyerbeer, Liszt, Chorley, Spohr—Inauguration of Beethoven's Statue—Tumultuous Banquet at the "Stern"—Paris.

MOSCHELES writes to his wife:—

"Leipzig, 1st January, 1845, 7 A. M.

"May every happiness and blessing attend you in the new year! Last night I wrote to you; to-day I will add an important postscript. Schleinitz talked to me about my taking a post in the Conservatoire, and gave me a letter bearing on the matter to the Saxon Minister, von Falkenstein. Of course, I could only answer that, being unprepared for so sudden a proposal, I must take time to consider. . . . . The concert is over; this is my first spare moment. This morning, after rehearsing my Trio with David and Wittman, I heard Bach's glorious Motet (G minor, 3-4), and dined at David's with Gade, Hauptmann, and Joachim. I send you our Gewandhaus programme of this evening:—

Mendelssohn's 95th Psalm.

Overture—Gluck's Iphigenie.

Beethoven's C minor Symphony; the piano passages marvellously done by the orchestra.

Miss Lincoln, a relation of the Dilkes, sang twice, and beautifully. My G minor Concerto very well accompanied, and as well received. After the concert, went to David's with Gade, Schleinitz, and others."

"January 2d.—I went to Dresden—attended Döhler's

concert. He played beautifully, and so did Piatti. After the concert spent a pleasant hour with Hiller."

"January 3d.—Paid interesting visits to Madame Schröder-Devrient, Wagner, and R. Schumann. At 2 o'clock, back to Leipzig, and in the evening played my Trio with Wittman and David."

"January 4th.—Back again to Dresden, immensely pleased with Gutzkow's 'Urbild des Tartuffe;' Emile Devrient excellent in the part of 'Molière."

"January 5th.—My room was as full of visitors as at Vienna, and, there being many 'prodigies' among them, I am glad I had no piano. Hiller gave me a grand Matinée; we played my E major Sonata together; I followed with several solos, all of which were enthusiastically received. In the evening went with Hiller, Lipinsky, and Reissiger to hear Marschner's new opera, 'Adolf von Nassau.' I'm afraid he has helped himself to Spohr and Donizetti."

"January 6th.—I passed a sad hour with Weber's widow; she has my deepest sympathy, for quite recently she has lost a son; poor soul! After such trouble as she has already gone through. My visit seemed to please her."

"January 7th.—My concert to-day was beyond all measure brilliant, Court and audience equally enthusiastic, the 'Nursery Tale' encored; my extempore performance, they tell me, better than ever; recalled after each piece, and one recall here is equivalent to half a dozen in Vienna. Bach's Triple Concerto made a great sensation; Madame Schumann played a Cadenza composed by me, Hiller and I extemporized ours. . . . . Tea at Hiller's. . . . . I forgot to tell you that Minister von Falkenstein, after reading Schleinitz's letter, received me in the most friendly manner, and corroborated everything my friend had said to me about the Leipzig Conservatoire; nothing, he said, was more ardently to be desired than that Mendelssohn and I should take the joint direction of the Conservatoire, only that the funds hitherto raised were inadequate for the proposed appointments. He and Schleinitz would submit the plan for the King's approval. I think that both are well-disposed towards me, so I have the prospect of once more becoming a German artist and ridding myself of the fashionable teacher and all conventionalism."

The next letter is from Berlin: "January 10th, 1845 2 P. M.—To-day I played at Härtel's, before some artists and connoisseurs, my manuscript Studies, which I leave for publication with Kistner; they are intended for the 'Mozart Stiftung.' . . . . I got to Berlin in time for Meyerbeer's opera, 'The Camp of Silesia.' The magnificence of this opera-house defies all description; the house, the piquant music, costumes, dancing, decorations, completely took away my breath. Jenny Lind has fairly enchanted me; she is unique in her way, and her song with two concertante flutes is perhaps the most incredible feat in the way of bravura singing that can possibly be heard; I shall have a great deal to tell you about this. Unfortunately I could not get a word with Meyerbeer, who was forced to hurry straight away from his desk as conductor to the bedside of his daughter Bianca, who was very dangerously ill. All our friends here have received me with open arms, and as usual wish to detain me, but a concert would cost me too much time, and at present the King and all the aristocracy are absent. . . . . . How lucky I was to find Jenny Lind at home! What a glorious singer she is, and so unpretentious withal! . . . . I had an hour with Meyerbeer, who was as kind as ever, and would gladly detain me at Berlin, but cannot clear away the difficulties; I am glad to tell you his daughter is on the way to recovery. He talked with me about Mendelssohn's intimacy and friendly relations with the King. . . . . If railways and coaches suit, I shall be with you all in Hamburg the day after tomorrow."

In pursuance of this plan, Moscheles arrives in Hamburg, where he spends a few days with his family; on their return to London, Moscheles is glad to find that Mendelssohn's music to the Antigone of Sophocles is being rehearsed at Covent Garden.

"My friend Hullah helped me by bringing some of his choir to our house for a performance of some of Felix's music; we actually ventured, too, on some numbers of Bach's Passion music. Sir Henry Bishop is elected permanent conductor of the Philharmonic Concerts. How is it possible to prefer him to Bennett, who is so immeasurably his superior? The experience of such anomalies confirms me in my intention of retiring some time or other to Germany, but for the present I cling in gratitude to Old England. After all, in Germany, too, I have my annoyances! Witness this article which I enclose, although I am afraid it will vex you. As for my detractors I feel towards them like a general, not afraid of small wounds, if only he can keep to the field of battle; nor should I have answered my calumniator, if the Hamburg correspondent had not taken up the wretched gossip. Please send him the article and the reply.*

About this time Moscheles had the misfortune to lose his brother; it was a severe blow, and only by degrees and under the influence of his art, does he recover from it. . . .

* The article alluded to was this: "Moscheles during his last stay in Germany has lost exactly as much as he made on the occasion of his first visit—viz. 800*l*. (9600 florins). This sum has been spent partly in travelling expenses, and partly in unsuccessful concerts. He himself writes to a friend in Prague: 'Liszt costs me a great deal; I couldn't believe that now-a-days people form a different opinion of pianoforte playing; it is unfortunately true. I was in Germany to experience the fact that, since Liszt, I have become "rococo." Happily, I have so much money that the loss doesn't hurt me, and my talent is quite as much as is required for England. What pains me most of all is that I have not succeeded in Vienna; there, where I lived such happy days, I had not contemplated dying.'"

Here is the reply:—

"London, March, 1845.

"When some German friends sent me the above article, I intended to pass it over with that silence which I take to be the most proper reply to such a production; finding, however, that since its first appearance in an obscure paper, it has found its way into other publications, I consider it to be my duty towards all the courts in Germany, which during last autumn and winter received me with so much distinction, as well as to the public of the various towns where I was so kindly welcomed, hereby to declare that the whole contents of the article are untrue. In the course of last September, October, November, and December, I gave concerts at Aix, Frankfort, Darmstadt, Carlsruhe, Stuttgart, Augsburg, Munich, Vienna, Dresden, and Leipzig, and have had as little opportunity of complaining of the damage said to be done to me by my friend Liszt, as was the case some years since, when we gave our concerts in London at the same time. As regards the attack against England, I, as a man of honor, should not be capable of expressing myself so ungratefully towards a country where I have lived and prospered for the last twenty-two years, and I therefore repeat my entire disavowal of the article above named. "I. MOSCHELES."

"The thought of my loss is interwoven with everything I undertake, and yet when I played yesterday at Alsager's I felt the power of art both to soothe and elevate; they made me play four of Beethoven's Sonatas and an Improvisation, and I was glad that my powers did not fail in the B major Sonata. In the Adagio in F sharp minor my feelings were most powerfully moved, but in the fugue it pained me to find so many extravagances. It contains more discords than concords, and Beethoven seems to me all the while to be saying, 'I intend working up a subject in a learned manner, it may sound well or not.'"

Professor Fischhof, of Vienna, sent the promised G minor Concerto of Bach, which (with the Concerto in D major) Moscheles introduces at his Matinée for classical pianoforte music. The duke of Cambridge came to Moscheles' house for the express purpose of hearing Bach's music. "The Duke, accompanied by his groom, rode up to our door, and came in quite unceremoniously. He seemed in great delight with the music, applauded enthusiastically, and behaved so kindly to my children. He asked Felix what profession he was going to follow. The answer was, 'I'm going to be an architect.' The Duke replied, 'Well, you'll be too late to do anything for me, but you can build me a mausoleum.' On leaving us he expressed his gratitude in the most friendly way, adding that it had been one of the most enjoyable hours he had spent for a long time."

Moscheles soon after this receives the Royal command to play at a concert in Buckingham Palace, and shares the honor with other artists. "There is a legion of them here this season," Mrs. Moscheles writes; "you ask me who is best? I don't know; Vieuxtemps is admirable, so is Sivori; Teresa Milanollo is certainly astonishing; as German vocalists, Pischek, Staudigl, and Oberhoffer are rivals, and of pianists, we have two of murderous capacities. Vocal France is represented by Viardot Garcia, Dorus Gras, etc., etc."

Moscheles writes: "I heard Félicien David's 'Désert,' with its piquant original melodies and harmonies illustrative of Oriental life. The 'March of the Caravans,' with its Clarinet Obligato, and the descriptive scene with the sunrise pleased me, but on the whole the subject is treated in the light Frenchified manner. I have heard also a

'Quadrille and Polka Opera,' by Verdi, for voices, key-bugles, trombones, and big drums; it is called 'Ernani.' The next evening, by way of a contrast, we had at the Antient Concert a 'Concerto by Emilio del Cavaliere,' composed in the year 1600, for the violino francese, chitarra, teorbo, arpa, organo, violino, etc. The well known 'Romanesca of the 15th Century' reminded me of hoop-petticoats and powder."

Sir Henry Bishop had directed the first three Philharmonic Concerts, the remaining five were entrusted to Moscheles, who, at the rehearsal, addressed the band to the following effect: "Gentlemen, as we are here assembled together, I should like to compare your performances with the fingers of an admirably trained pianoforte-player's hand. Now, will you allow me to be the hand which sets these fingers in motion, and imparts life to them? May I try to convey to you all the inspirations I feel when I hear the works of the great masters? Thus may we achieve excellence." Another time when a Beethoven Symphony was to be played, he tells the band how he heard this and other great works of Beethoven when they first came out, and how he had kept the traditions of the "Tempi," which at that time were given by Beethoven himself. At last he amuses his hearers exceedingly by imitating Beethoven's movements as a conductor; his stooping down more and more until he almost disappeared at the "piano" passages, the gradual rising up at the "crescendo," and standing tiptoe and bounding up at the "fortissimo." Moscheles does not forget to add: "Inasmuch, however, as I cannot emulate the great man in his works, I abstain from copying him in his attitudes; with him it was all originality, with me it would be caricature."

At the last of these concerts, Moscheles played Bach's "D major Concerto," and is gratified by the marked improvement of the orchestra in the "piano" passages. "In time I should educate these clever fellows to observe even still more light and shade."

Moscheles, at the end of the season, sets off for the Musical festival at Bonn, and writes to his wife from Cologne: "The unsettled and gloomy weather resembled my frame of mind, for the separation had disturbed my equanimity. My philosophy must aid me. . . . . I have visited Meyerbeer here and met him alone with Pischek. Mutual kisses were the beginning and prelude tó a number of inquiries after you, and then we talked of the festival. Meyerbeer is beside himself with the press of business; by to-morrow he must begin the rehearsals of the Court Concerts. The best of the vocal music is to be without orchestra, and only with pianoforte accompaniment; in the interval between the rehearsals, Meyerbeer will go to Bonn to hear the performance there." On the 10th of August, Moscheles comes to Bonn and writes: "I am at the Hotel de l'Etoile d'Or, where are to be found all the crowned heads of music—brown, grey, or bald—all wigged or lackered pates; this is a rendezvous for all ladies, old and young, fanatics for music—all art-judges, German and French reviewers and English reporters, lastly, the abode of Liszt, the absolute monarch, by virtue of his princely gifts outshining all else. Dr. Bacher, from Vienna, offers me a share of his room—no small boon when the streets are crowded with houseless travellers, like the roofless after a great conflagration. Gentlemen and ladies, several English among them, with a whole army of porters and bandboxes, are begging for a shake-down in hotels or private houses; friends and acquaintances meet one another; flags of various colors are waving—such a hurry-skurry everywhere. I have already seen and spoken to colleagues from all the four quarters of the globe; I was also with Liszt, who had his hands full of business, and was surrounded with secretaries and masters of ceremonies, while Chorley sat quietly ensconced in the corner of a sofa. Liszt, too, kissed me, then a few hurried and confused words passed between us, and I did not see him again until I met him afterwards in the concert room. We sat down about 400 of us to dinner, and the first concert took place, under Spohr's direction, in the new Beethoven Hall. The Grand Mass in D major gave me certainly exquisite, although not quite unalloyed pleasure, for occasionally I could not help feeling that the composition diverges from the genuine church style, and thereby loses that unity of color which I prize so highly in other works of the master. The 'Ninth Symphony,' which followed afterwards, was given almost faultlessly, the soprano part in the choruses not only better than in London, but better than I have ever heard anywhere. Staudigl inimitable, but the kettledrums not better tuned than in London. Mr. Jäger a member of the committee, gave me a place of honor among the artists; Liszt behaves to me with marked kindness whenever we meet. I write you these lines after the public supper in the hotel, by way of preparing myself pleasantly for a night's rest, meanwhile I remain con amore languendo, poco a poco agitato, ma sempre Giusto, yours." . . . .

*From the Diary.*

"August 11th.—A new steamer was christened 'Beethoven' with great ceremony. Amid salvos of cannon, the vessel, accompanied by one other, sped merrily to Nonnenwerth, where a cold collation was in readiness. I was capitally placed between Spohr and Fischhof. Pickpockets active. We escaped untouched."

"August 12th.—From eight o'clock this morning the streets were alive with bands of students, guilds, etc. Waited at the Rathhaus, and afterwards managed to get into the Cathedral with the throng. Beethoven's Mass in C gave me exquisite enjoyment. From the Cathedral went to the galleries which are erected around the Beethoven monument. I was exposed for a long time to the burning rays of the sun —a great annoyance—released at last by the arrival of the distinguished guests upon the balcony of the Fürstenberg House. These were the King and Queen of Prussia, Queen Victoria, and Prince Albert, with a numerous suite. Speech by Professor Breidenstein. I was deeply moved when I saw the statue unveiled, the more so because Hähnel has obtained an admirable likeness of the immortal composer. Another tumult and uproar at the table-d'hôtel in the 'Stern' Hotel. I sat near Bacher, Fischhof, and Vesque, Liszt in all his glory, a suite of ladies and gentlemen in attendance on him, Lola Montez among the former. At five o'clock the Concert. Dr. Breidenstein asked me if I would accompany the 'Adelaide' at the morning concert As Madame Pleyel was to play a concerto on that occasion, I thought it infra dig. to perform an inferior service, so I refused."

"August 13th.—Last day of the festival, which began with Liszt's Cantata. It has much that is well thought and felt, as, *e.g.* the introduction of the Andante of the B major Trio, which is cleverly managed; there are also some good instrumental effects; as a whole, however, it is too fragmentary. Liszt, who was vehemently applauded, received an orchestral flourish. The Court arriving late, the Cantata was repeated, and the King made a selection from the programme of the concert, which he staid to hear. Overtures 'Egmont' and 'Coriolan' admirably conducted by Spohr. Violoncello solo, Ganz. Weber's Concert stück, Madame Pleyel. Air from 'Fidelio,' Miss Sabilla Novello. Liszt accompanied Fräulein Kratky in a song.

"Liszt's performance of Beethoven's Concerto in E flat major, almost entirely satisfied one: I can't imagine any one playing the energetic and spirited part of the work better than he did. In other parts I should have preferred a little more warmth and tenderness.

"When the Court had gone, some other pieces were performed, others omitted. At two o'clock banquet at the 'Stern.' Crowd even greater than before. Immediately after the King's health had been proposed, Wolff, the Improvisatore, gave a toast which he called the 'Trefoil.' It was to represent the perfect chord, Spohr the key-note, Liszt the connecting link between all parties, the third—Professor Breidenstein, the Dominant, leading all things to a happy solution. Universal applause. Spohr proposes the health of the Queen of England, Dr. Wolff that of the Professor Hähnel, the sculptor of the monument, and also that of the brass founder. Liszt proposes Prince Albert; a professor with a stentorian voice is laughed and coughed down, people will not listen to him, and then ensued a series of most disgraceful scenes which originated thus: Liszt spoke rather abstrusely upon the subject of the festival. 'Here all nations are met to pay honor to the master. May they live and prosper, the Dutch, the English, the Viennese, who have made a pilgrimage hither!" Upon this Chelard gets up in a passion and screams out to Liszt, 'Vous avez oublié les Francais.' Many voices break in, a regular tumult ensues, some for, some against the speaker. At last Liszt makes himself heard, but, in trying to exculpate himself, seems to get entangled deeper and deeper in a labyrinth of words, seeking to convince his hearers that he has lived fifteen years among Frenchmen, and would certainly not intentionally speak slightingly of them. The contending parties, however, become more uproarious, many leave their seats, the din becomes deafening, and the ladies pale with fright. The fête is interrupted for a full hour, Dr. Wolff, mounting a table, tries to speak, but is hooted down three or four times, and at last quits the room, glad to escape the Babel of tongues. Knots of people are seen disputing in every part of the great salon, and on the confusion increasing, the cause of dispute is lost sight of. The French and English journalists mingle in this fray, by complaining of omissions of all sorts on the part of the Festival Committee. When the tumult threatens to become serious, the landlord hits upon the bright idea of making the band play its loudest, and this drowns the noise of the brawlers, who adjourned to the open air. The waiters once more resumed their services, although many of the guests, especially ladies, had vanished. The contending groups outside showed their bad taste and ridiculous selfishness, for Vivier and some Frenchmen got Liszt among them, and reproached him in the most shameful way. G. ran from party to party, adding fuel to the fire, Chorley was attacked by a French journalist, Mr. J. J. would havè it that the English gentleman, Wentworth Dilke, was a German, who had slighted him: I stepped in between the two, so as at least to put an end to this unfair controversy. I tried as well as I could to soothe these overwrought minds, and pronounced funeral orations over those who had perished in this tempest of words. I alone remained shot-proof and neutral, so also did my Viennese friends. By six o'clock in the evening I became almost deaf from the noise, and was glad to escape; I assure you that a cup of coffee and some music at the Countess Almasy's were very refreshing after the events of the afternoon. I didn't go to the festival ball, preferring to write this account, and to spend a couple of hours with Fischhof, who showed me his 'Theory of Transposing.'"

In an old French poem, the following passage occurs:

"Vous m'envoyez le lendemain un billet daté de la veille." Moscheles was destined to experience a similar fate when the Musical Festival at Bonn was over. He had received no invitation from Meyerbeer or Liszt for the Court Concerts in Stolzenfels and Coblentz, for which many of his art-brethren had been summoned by circulars. He travelled, therefore, on the 14th to Cologne, where he met his family and spent a couple of days, and it was not until the 17th, and consequently after his departure, that the following letter reached Cologne:

"HONORED FRIEND,—His Majesty the King, who has heard that you are in these parts, has commanded me to invite your attendance in the Court Concerts, which the King intends giving in his castle at Coblentz to-morrow evening, Saturday the 16th. Count von Radern has this moment commissioned me to write to you in the name of the King, but it is now midnight, the concert in Stolzenfels is just over, and it is, therefore, impossible to forward the invitation before Saturday. I hope it will not reach you too late. In any case it will show you the friendly remembrance and the hearty esteem the King has for you. Farewell, dear friend.

"Your most devoted,
"MEYERBEER."

Mr. Lefèbre, of the house of Eck in Cologne, had added to this note a few lines expressing regret, for he foresaw that the letter would not reach Moscheles in time. When Moscheles sends his father-in-law copies of these letters, he observes: "I leave to your sagacity the fathoming of the 'why' and 'wherefore' of this transaction. Why, when I was actually in Bonn, did I not get an invitation to the Court Concerts at the same time with the other artists? How was it that the King's command did not reach me at the right time? One might suppose that a Royal messenger, despatched from Stolzenfels at an early hour on Saturday the 16th, would reach me quick enough in Cologne."

Whatever little disappointment Moscheles may have felt at the time, it was soon forgotten in the quiet repose he enjoyed at Lichtenthal, near Baden-Baden. There he met his friends the Rosenhains, and Félicien David, and the pleasure of musical intercourse with them was varied by the enjoyment of frequent excursions in the neighborhood. Of Félicien David's Symphony in E flat, he says: "The music has plenty of flowing melody, it is not commonplace, the instrumentation is richly colored, but the unity of style is not preserved throughout."

From Baden Moscheles goes to Paris, where he composes his "Sonate Symphonique," and is summoned to St. Cloud to play his new composition before the Court. "Accordingly," he says, "the day before we left Paris, Emily and I set off for St. Cloud, and were very graciously received by the Royal family. When we arrived, the Queen, Madame Adelaïde, the Duchess of Orleans, with their suite, were at tea; the King came from an adjoining gallery to hear the Sonata, which Emily played to my entire satisfaction; she had to play a solo too. I improvised à la Grétry, the King's favorite 'genre.' Our Royal listeners were evidently gratified."

In December Moscheles receives an important letter from Mendelssohn, who is anxious to ascertain if his friend intends to carry out the idea of migrating to Germany which they have so often discussed, and settling down at Leipzig to work with him at the Conservatoire. "What grand results for art might fairly be expected if you could make up your mind to accept the post! I don't doubt for a moment that the life here would suit you, as I know in what light you look upon your present professional life. Besides, I candidly own that from all I hear about the doings there, and from what I witnessed myself to a certain extent a year and a half ago, I can well understand how from year to year you get less satisfied with your surroundings, and wish to escape from them. . . . . Now please, if you want in any way to move in the matter, let me know, and give me an opportunity of opening a negotiation, which possibly may become one of the most beneficial in its results that the musical world here has ever experienced."

Moscheles was from the first inclined to accept the post, but wrote to his friend, asking for time to weigh the matter.

# CHAPTER XXVIII.

## 1846.

Leipzig Negotiations — The Appointment Accepted — Benedict's "Crusaders"—Farewell Concert—Marriage of Moscheles' Eldest Daughter—Birmingham Musical Festival—Mendelssohn's "Elijah"—Remarkable Episode—Farewell to London—Reception in Leipzig—Professors of the Conservatoire—Congratulatory Dinner—Attraction of Leipzig—Evening with the Mendelssohns—Examination of Candidates for the Conservatoire.

AS early as the 2d of January Moscheles receives the formal offer of his appointment at the Leipzig Conservatoire, and Mendelssohn writes: "On the day that you accept, I intend drinking my best wine and a glass or two of champagne into the bargain." After giving particulars relative to the cost of living, household expenditure, etc., in Leipzig, he continues: "The universal wish of the people in Leipzig, and their joy at the prospect of your coming, although honorable to yourself, are in no way commensurate with the honor you would confer on them by your settling among them; but such an interchange of feelings must be fruitful of good, and is the earnest of a happy future. In a word, I wish you would come!" Moscheles writes to his father-in-law on the 21st of January: "You will understand, from the enclosed copies of letters just received, the progress of my Leipzig negotiations. I feel more inclined than ever to give up my position here.* . . . Of course, my wife and I fully discuss the all-important point; we are completely agreed in this, that in the matter of material comforts we shall not expect to find London in Leipzig, but these luxuries we shall not miss, if I realize all I anticipate from the art atmosphere, and in my new vocation I shall find some

* As a proof that Moscheles, in abandoning his brilliant position in London, was actuated by his desire to serve the cause of art, it need only be stated that his salary as Professor of the Leipzig Conservatoire was 800 thalers (120*l.*) per annum.

compensation for the many dear and kind friends we leave behind. Parting from them individually, and, indeed, from the English nation generally, will cost us a bitter pang, for twenty-four years of unswerving kindness has laid upon us obligations which we can only pay with life-long gratitude. On the other hand, we shall come nearer to you all—that will be delightful. My acceptance of the post must, however, be weighed well, as I am the father of a family. I beg you will continue your duties as President of the Council on the Moscheles interest, and send me the protocol of each sitting; but don't let us worry ourselves upon the matter, for, whatever fortune may have in store for us, my wife and I are such a happy pair that we should be quite content to live in a cottage, as long as we could educate our children so well that they may never feel the want of great riches. With regard to yourself, I shall ever remain the same in London or Leipzig, "Your faithful son-in-law,

"I. MOSCHELES."

On the 24th of January Moscheles receives a letter from Mendelssohn, which is so satisfactory an answer to all his questions that on the 25th we read in the diary:—"To-day I sent my letter of acceptance to the directing body of the Leipzig Conservatoire. I have crossed the Rubicon." Mendelssohn was not long in sending the expressions of his joy. "When you do come, I'll have some houses painted rose-color, but your arrival alone will give a rose-colored tinge to the old place." Before the news had spread through the musical world, Moscheles received an offer from Birmingham to direct the grand musical festival there in September. Mendelssohn's "Elijah" was to be the only work given under the composer's own direction. Nothing could be more flattering or honorable to Moscheles at the close of his residence in England, and he gladly accepted the offer. He wished to secure the services of Mlle. Jenny Lind and Pischek, but unfortunately they had other engagements.

In the course of this season Benedict's new opera, "The Crusaders," was published. "The music is pleasing, and often dramatically effective; the work gorgeously put upon the stage. Cramer, Beale, and Co. published it, and Benedict wanted me to make a pianoforte arrangement of the most favorite airs. This, however, I declined, seeing they had refused to publish my 'Sonate Symphonique" on the ground of its being too *serious* a work."

Moscheles' "Four Matinées for Classical Pianoforte Music" were brilliantly successful, but before long he was absorbed in the cares and anxieties of preparations for his farewell concert. He wished to show the public on this occasion that to the last he would act consistently with the creed he had adopted throughout his professional career in England—there should be no "concert monstre," with a host of Italian singers and a crowd of rival instrumental players; he would be no slave to fashion; the programme, therefore, was short and pithy. With Madame Pleyel as a coadjutor in his "Sonate Symphonique," and Pischek, and a few vocalists to assist him, he augurs well for the result, and on the 19th of June he writes to his father-in-law:—"The outburst of enthusiasm every time I appeared, the waving of handkerchiefs, the cheering—every one standing upon the benches—all this affected me, and when I came to make my parting bows, I could hardly restrain my emotion; I remained another hour surrounded by friends and acquaintance; really my public farewell could not have taken place under more favorable auspices." "And," adds Mrs. Moscheles, "we are pleased to find that our real friends think Moscheles acts well and wisely in electing to fill a public situation, with his dear friend Mendelssohn for a colleague. Besides this, he needs some repose after his many laborious years in London."

During the summer months, however, Moscheles is busier than ever, for there are the Birmingham programmes to be made, and many public engagements to be attended to. Moscheles gives a farewell party, and over 200 invitations are accepted.

"I usually get to bed about one or two o'clock; thank heaven, my constitution seems made of iron, otherwise I could not stand the day and night work. Yesterday, or rather this morning, I saw the sun rise at four o'clock, as I was going to bed. It is now eight o'clock, and we are up and writing. Our party last night began with music, and ended with dancing. I, old as I am, tripped it lightly with the youngsters. To-day I have six lessons, and at 5 o'clock I must be in the Freemasons' Hall; to-morrow, besides the lessons, I have to conduct a concert a mile long for a pupil.

Mrs. Moscheles writes: "Since the farewell concert, the newspapers never cease trumpeting Moscheles' praises, and deplore the loss that art will sustain by his leaving England. Chorley has used the occasion for suggesting a question which seems to me very near to the point: 'Could not the great City of London, as well as the small burgher-town, offer the great artist an appointment which should be made so advantageous and desirable as to keep him permanently fixed in England?"

This year was an eventful one to Moscheles in more ways than one, for his eldest daughter, Emily, was married to Mr. Roche, who had long been a friend of the family, and had already made a reputation as a Professor of French Literature.

At the end of the season, Mr. Bartholomew, the translator of the German text of Mendelssohn's "Elijah," brought to Moscheles the score of the first part.

"The beauties of the work become more apparent to me each time I sit down to the piano to study it; doubly so at the preliminary rehearsals." The first rehearsal, under Mendelssohn himself, took place at Moscheles' house on the 10th of August, and the two others, with full band, follow shortly afterwards in the Hanover Square Rooms. The lady singers give Mendelssohn some trouble; one finds fault with the song, and insists on its being transposed; Mendelssohn resists with studied politeness, but afterwards, "when we are alone, most unreservedly expresses himself about the 'coolness of such a suggestion.'" The scene now changes to Birmingham, where Moscheles conducts a first rehearsal, but is so unwell that Mendelssohn takes his place at the second. He recovered however so far as to conduct the 'Creation' at the first morning performance, the second part of which consisted of numbers from Rossini's "Stabat Mater," with Grisi, Bassano, and Mario for the principal singers; after that a mixed Italian programme, which took three hours, and "thoroughly satisfied the public. In the evening I had more rehearsals of various pieces." Mrs.

Moscheles writes: "On our arrival we went to the Town Hall; that splendid building greatly impressed me, and, at the overwhelming reception given to my husband by the orchestra, I was deeply moved. After the rehearsal he studied his scores, while I helped Mr. Bartholomew in correcting the text, and so we went on till one o'clock in the morning. The festival promises to be a very profitable one, an unusual number of seats having been sold."

On the following day Moscheles writes: "August 26th. —Mendelssohn achieved his most brilliant triumph in this day's performance of his 'Elijah.' In my opinion this work has more vividness and more dramatic variety than 'St. Paul,' and yet it is written in the purest oratorio style, and places him yet another step higher." Mrs. Moscheles adds: "Yes, Mendelssohn's triumph at yesterday's performance was something quite unparellaled and unheard of. I think eleven numbers had to be repeated, and that too amid a storm of applause and clapping of hands, demonstrations usually forbidden; but on this occasion all attempt at restraint was hopeless, the noisy scene reminded me of the pit in a theatre. Staudigl was a magnificent Elijah, Philip, the bass singer, admirable, and Mendelssohn was particularly pleased with the singing of the two Misses Williams."

In the course of this Festival Moscheles played his "Recollections of Ireland," and with Mendelssohn his "Hommage à Handel." The veteran Braham sang the first recitative and air in the "Messiah," and Mendelssohn gained fresh laurels with his lovely music to the "Midsummer Night's Dream."

On the 28th August Moscheles notes the following episode: "We had a miscellaneous selection; the chief feature consisting of pieces from Beethoven and Spohr. The orchestral parts of a short recitative, the words of which had been printed in the books for the audience, were not forthcoming; we were all in a difficulty, but Mendelssohn came to the rescue. He quietly betook himself to an adjoining room, and there, while the preceding pieces of the programme were being played, he composed the recitative, scored it, and copied the parts, and these were admirably played, with the ink scarcely dry, at first sight, by the band

—the public knew nothing of what had happened—that's the way a Mendelssohn manages."

On the 29th August Mrs. Moscheles writes from London: "Yesterday at four o'clock, with a final beat of Moscheles baton, the great Birmingham Musical Festival came to an end; in the opinion of every one present, it was one of the most brillant and beautiful ever celebrated. The committee has, in the most flattering terms, expressed to my husband their obligation and complete satisfaction. Moscheles' short, but for the time anxious illness, was the only awkward occurrence, but it served to show us Mendelssohn once more in the light of a real friend." "Yes," adds Moscheles, "his sympathy was like that of a brother; his frequent visits when everybody would so gladly have detained him, his attentions to me with such great work before him, were most touching. When he came away from the preliminary rehearsal, which he had conducted for me, he appeared exhausted; Charlotte handed him a glass of champagne, and the effect was magical, for it completely revived him."

The friends soon have to separate, and the Moscheles return to Chester Place, but only to bid it a last farewell. Who can wonder that a feeling of sadness crossed the mind of Moscheles, now on the eve of breaking up a home, the scene of sixteen years of happiness. To a man the master bias of whose mind was always leaning

"To homefelt pleasures and to gentle scenes;"

the nursery where his children played, the study where he passed so many hours of joyful and conscientious labor, the rooms endeared by the memory of birthday festivals, and identified with the presence of beloved friends—to part from all these things cost him a wrench, and, however bright the future, it was a painful task to bid farewell to the old familiar scenes.

At Frankfort the Moscheles had the good fortune to hear the enchanting Jenny Lind, and arrived at Leipzig on the 21st of October. We quote from the diary: "There Felix Mendelssohn and his wife received us most affectionately: owing to their thoughtfulness, we found every arrangement made for our comfort. No courier could have catered so skilfully, none but real friends have acted so kindly." On the 26th of October Moscheles writes: "I have now probably arrived at the final chapter in my art career; sure as I am of your sympathy, I should like to give you the fullest information about my life in this place. It has begun, with God's help, under the best auspices, and if you ask who is the mainspring of our present happiness, we say Mendelssohn, and always Mendelssohn, my more than brother!

On the evening after my arrival, three directors of the Conservatoire came to give me a kindly welcome, and to express a hope that I should find my new duties agreeable; they assured me they would do all in their power to meet my wishes in the Conservatoire. Next day I returned these visits, and in the evening had the great delight of hearing a Gewandhaus Concert. Mendelssohn's conducting was as admirable as ever, the band obeyed his slightest hint. Madame Schumann played Beethoven's 'B major Concerto' to great perfection; I felt this to be a real atmosphere of art. Many of the elder members of the orchestra greeted me warmly, and after the concert we supped very cosily at the Mendelssohns. Yesterday, I talked with Schleinitz about the Conservatoire, and he showed me the following list of the Professors:—

Dr. F. Mendelssohn-Bartholdy—Composition and Solo playing.
Organist—C. F. Becker—Organ Playing, Practice in the Art of Conducting.
David, Klengel, Sachse—Violin Teachers.
Gade—Harmony and Composition.
Hauptmann—Harmony, Counterpoint.
Moscheles—Head of the Department for Playing and Composition.
Plaidy, Wenzel—Pianoforte Playing.
Böhme—Solo and Choral Singing.
Brendel—Lectures on Music.
Neumann—Italian.
Richter—Harmony and Instrumentation.

"Through Schleinitz I heard that Mendelssohn earnestly objected to his name standing first on the list, instead of following the rest in alphabetical order. Yesterday we heard Divine service in the Nicolai Church—a good sermon and admirable organ. Afterwards I attended a dinner given in my honor by the whole body of professors, with Felix at their head. The fête was held in Æckerlein's Cellar. I was greeted cordially on all sides, my place as chief guest marked with a bouquet of flowers, and, after a sumptuous dinner and plenty of champagne, Felix spoke to the following effect: 'Although he had no talent or gift for speaking, on this occasion he must express the feelings uppermost in his mind. It had long been his wish to see me settled in Leipzig, and in active duty at the Conservatoire, and he rejoiced in the sympathy evinced by his colleagues and the public, now that these wishes had been realized. He could never forget the impression which my talent had made upon him, as a boy, how I had kindled the sacred fire within him, and spurred him to higher aims. I had always assisted and cheered him on, and he felt proud of my lasting friendship; he was sure that those present shared his feelings, and would join with him in drinking my health.' Musical cheers were given; I felt much moved, and could only stammer out a few words of thanks in answer to one who, I said, had far outstripped me as an artist, and whom, as a man, I sincerely loved and honored.

"By degrees we dropped the sentimental, and drank every one's health; we blew large clouds of tobacco, and the hours from one till six sped along cheerily. Then I took another long walk with Felix, and, in the course of our confidential talk, asked him why he preferred Leipzig as a residence, while the greatest cities in Europe were ready to do him homage. He explained his preference by saying that the art atmosphere and tendencies of Leipzig had special attractions for him, and that the Conservatoire was a subject so near his heart that, even during the composition of his last Oratorio, he had not neglected his pupils. We spent the evening at the Mendelssohns' in a social quiet way, and were joined by their relatives, Mr. and Mrs. Schunck, who inhabit the same house with us. After supper we amused ourselves on two pianos, and at last had a grand improvisation together, in which Felix was so inspired that in my enthusiasm I almost forgot my own part in listening to him.

"Just imagine, this evening we hardly recognized our good friend Mendelssohn, for his children had painted on his face an imperial and moustache. He had been playing with his children at 'Schwarzen Peter,' and had had to suffer the usual penalty. We live in the second floor in Gerhard's Garten; the Schuncks have the first, and they are charming neighbors."

On the 26th October, we read in the diary: "Felix, with his usual thoughtfulness, had prepared for me a musical performance by his best pupils to be given at the Conservatoire, and I heard some excellent pianoforte-players. Stadtrath Seeburg made a speech in which he alluded to my appointment at the Conservatoire as an important event; I replied that I only regarded myself as a single stone of the beautiful building which rested upon firm foundations," etc.

"October 27th.—Trial of candidates for the Conservatoire. Mendelssohn assisted; his feeling animated both teachers and pupils. In the evening I was at his house, where we talked a great deal about musical matters and household arrangements; he gave me much good advice. I saw a chorus he had lately composed with the title, 'To the Sons of Art.' Joachim played with him the 'Kreutzer Sonata.'" On another occasion Moscheles admires some new and still unpublished "Lieder ohne Worte." He can hardly understand that Mendelssohn should wish, after the performance at Birmingham, to make still further alterations in his "Elijah." "I asked him if that beautiful work is intended to become still more beautiful, and he said, 'Yes,' without being quite clear in his mind what and how much he was going to alter. I replied, 'Your genius is too exacting in its demands, it has already surpassed itself in this "Elijah;" now employ your powers upon new works.' My arguments, however, were ineffective, and he abided by his determination that changes must be made. The violin quintet in B flat major is next examined, Mendelssohn declaring that the last movement is not good; he also shows me the 'Lauda Sion.'" Later on the great composer is full of anxiety about his faithful servant Johann, who lies dangerously ill in his house. Mendelssohn daily visited the sick-room, and read aloud to him; he tended him till the hour of his death, and sincerely lamented his loss.

Moscheles and his wife often take long walks with the Mendelssohns, or meet them at supper at Æckerlein's after the subscription concerts; there they are frequently joined by a third couple, David and his wife; Mendelssohn gives in honor of Moscheles, a grand musical evening; "for a Moscheles," said he, "we take care to make good music; *he* is not everybody."

"November 16th.—Morning rehearsal. In the evening Schumann's Concert. His symphony in C major, conducted in accordance with his wish, by Mendelssohn. Madame Schumann and her younger sister played.

"December 7th.—Mendelssohn paid us a long visit, his first in our new abode, where the Erard, too, had been installed as an honored member of the family; he walked about the rooms, rubbing his hands and muttering, 'Nice, nice,' as he was wont to do when he was pleased with anything. He had once shocked a Leipzig friend whom he met in Switzerland, by applying the word 'hübsch' to the grand scenery before them, but with him that word meant more than any high-flown epithets."

Mrs. Moscheles writes; "We are truly happy in our intercourse with the Mendelssohns; not only he, the amiable, intimate friend, but his wife and their charming children becoming daily more and more attached to us; and what a happy household it is! The abundant means at his command are never squandered upon outward show, but judiciously spent on a well-regulated, comfortable household. Their principles and ideas are entirely in conformity with our own; they, like ourselves, love to welcome friends or interesting guests cordially, but without ceremony."

## CHAPTER XXIX.

### 1847.

Life and Society in Leipzig—Mendelssohn's Birthday—A Forgetful Artist—Chopin's Music—Visit to London—Musical Notes—Jenny Lind—Meeting of Artists—Julius Rietz—Walks with Mendelssohn—Mendelssohn and Queen Victoria—Madame Frege—Illness and Death of Mendelssohn—Excitement in Leipzig—Funeral Ceremony in Leipzig and in Berlin—Mendelssohn's correspondence.

ON their return home from a Christmas visit to Hamburg, the Moscheles are pleasantly impressed by the comfortable appearance of their new home. The house which they share with the Schuncks stands on historical ground. Gerhard's Garden was the scene of the most disastrous episode of the famous battle of Leipzig; it was in the Elster, a small but rapid stream, bounding the garden on one side, that Poniatowsky, in his attempt to cross with the retreating French army, met with his end. The spot is thus memorable as marking one of the greatest disasters in modern warfare. In a little summer-house erected for the purpose in the garden, are preserved many relics of that famous day. This historical site has passed into the hands of Mr. Gerhard, well-known throughout Germany as a man of high literary attainments, and as having been a personal friend of Goethe. His translation of Burns' poems is one of his best works.

Moscheles, speaking of his house, says: "Our friends seem to like it as well as we do. Some object to the small dimensions of our music-room, but I think that good music is to be made everywhere, and I have always belonged to a school which aimed rather at clearness and accent than at loud hammering—at a correct understanding and truthful rendering of music rather than at surprising effects. As for the people themselves, they load us with polite attentions, and the whirl and rush of society hither and thither would be just the same thing as in London, were it not that the earlier hours made the matter easier. I need hardly tell you that the frequent interviews with the Mendelssohns, at their house or ours, are constant sources of enjoyment. On the last occasion Joachim, our favorite, was there; Felix accompanied him in his violin Concerto, and both played the music by heart; afterwards Felix let us hear some 'Lieder ohne Worte,' written by his sister Fanny. Although close imitations of his own, they are interesting, and treated in a genuine musical spirit. He then played us that part of the 'Elijah' where the widow invokes the prophet's help. It has been remodelled, and I must confess that the part of 'Elijah' acquires more dignity and importance than it had at the performance in Birmingham, where I considered the whole work already perfect. The angel trio is now really lovely. We had at our house (besides the Mendelssohns and Madame Frege, whose singing of his songs was indescribably beautiful), Mr. ——, with his deafening 'Fortissimos.' Happily Mendelssohn put an end to the noise by playing the first book of his 'Lieder ohne Worte,' the manuscript of which he has given to me. David's society and playing are never-failing sources of enjoyment. I am beginning to realize my dream of emancipation from professional slavery; in the Conservatoire I am engaged sixteen hours a week, at home I have but eight private lessons to give; what is that after the daily steeple-chase in London?"

On another occasion Moscheles writes: "After dining with Mendelssohn, I went with him to the Berlin pianoforte maker, Schönemann, who has brought here his new invention of octaves. By a pressure of the pedal you can add an octave to each note; a key-board on a diminutive scale can be screwed on to any piano, and enables the player to span two octaves, but this is at the cost of tone, and altogether the invention is yet in its infancy. Still, we amused ourselves alternately by playing octave passages, eight times doubled; what good are D.'s bravuras after this? Soon afterwards Mendelssohn was standing by the conductor's desk in the Gewandhaus, and I had the pleasure of hearing his overture to a 'Calm sea and a prosperous voyage.'

"Mendelssohn took good care not to miss the children's party at Moscheles' house; our conversation was purely on musical subjects, while the others laughed and played with the children. I had to put before him an offer from Chappell, who wanted to have the copyright of an opera which he was to write. The subject proposed was 'The Tempest,' the opera was to be in the regular Italian style, for Lumley. Not a note has been written, and yet the work is already announced for Jenny Lind's appearance in the coming season." Later on Mendelssohn completely abandons the plan of setting music to the subject, and writes to say so, to the disappointment of the Directors.

"We and the Schuncks had combined to celebrate Mendelssohn's birthday. The proceedings were opened with a capital comic scene between two lady's maids, acted, in the Frankfort dialect, by Cécile and her sister. Then came a charade on the word 'Gewandhaus.' Joachim, adorned with a fantastic wig, à la Paganini, played a hare-brained impromptu on the G string; the syllable 'Wand' was represented by the Pyramus and Thisbe wall-scene from the 'Midsummer Night's Dream;' for 'Haus,' Charlotte acted a scene she had written herself, in which she is discovered knitting a blue stocking, and soliloquizing on the foibles of female authoresses, advising them to attend to their domestic duties. By way of enforcing the moral, she calls her cook—the cook was I myself, and my appearance in cap and dress was the signal for a general uproar. Mendelssohn was sitting on a large straw arm-chair which creaked under his weight, as he rocked to and fro, and the room echoed with his peals of laughter. The whole word 'Gewandhaus' was illustrated by a full orchestra, Mendelssohn and my children playing on little drums and trumpets; Joachim leading with a toy violin, my Felix conducting à la Jullien. It was splendid." Such was Mendelssohn's *last* birthday!

On the 17th of February we read: "I fully unburdened my mind to Mendelssohn on the subject of my refusal to play at Gade's Historical Concert, and explained to him my reluctance to appear too frequently before the public. I have played on two occasions lately to please the Directors, and proved I did not consider it a professional matter, by devoting the proceeds to the Orchestral Fund. Compositions must now-a-days have so many inches of Italian phrases, the pieces so many scores of octaves, in order to please; this is most distasteful to me, as it is to him. I could not, however, approve of *his* resolve to take no part in the performance of 'St. Paul,' intended for Good Friday, and I succeeded in persuading him to an opposite view, so that he soon began the rehearsals; but he, as well as I, would not play in the 'Gewandhaus,' and told the Directors so.'

After the second rehearsal of 'St. Paul' we read: "Mendelssohn's strictness with the large amateur chorus was as great as his keeping together the entire force by his pianoforte accompaniment was remarkable." Moscheles attends all the rehearsals, and writes after the Good Friday performance: "I have only now arrived at a perfect appreciation of this glorious work. Here, as in London, I am beset with a host of modern pianoforte players, all writing Arpeggios and octave passages. These gentlemen all belong to the same regiment, and wear the same uniform, the only difference being this, that their epaulettes and gold lace are more or less gaudy.

"We were in a pretty fix the other night at the Pupils' Public Concert, when four young ladies were to play Czerny's piece for eight hands: Miss F. had forgotten her music. Mehdelssohn was up in arms at once. 'What!' he exclaimed, 'forget your music for a public performance, as if it were a mere trifle! This is too bad. There sits the public, and has to wait because you have forgotten your music!' etc., etc. In this dilemma I fetched the tuner out of the corner where he was waiting. 'Sit down,' said I; 'busy yourself with tuning the two pianos, and don't leave off until you see that the messenger who has been dispatched brings Miss F.'s music.' He did as I desired, an awkward pause was filled up, not agreeably, but to the purpose.

"So the youthful G. has gone to Paris in order to learn pianoforte playing in republican fashion, the more so as his master is to be Chopin, who in his Mazurkas and ballads bewails the annihilation of national freedom! Seriously speaking, he may learn a great deal that is good by listening to Chopin's playing, but in his compositions Chopin shows that his best ideas are but isolated; he leaves them fragmentary, and fails to produce a work of complete unity. In his Sonata with the violoncello which has just been published, I often find passages which sound to me like some one preluding on the piano, the player knocking at the door of every key and clef to find if any melodious sounds are at home."

Again: "I amused myself with David by trying over Hiller's six 'Studies' for pianoforte and violin. They are, even as drawing-room pieces, thoroughly piquant and effective. We played also the 'Pensées Fugitives,' by Ernst and Heller." Moscheles composes songs for single and four voices; among the latter "Winternacht" and "Maifeier," among the former, "Freie Kunst," "Die Gespielen," and "Die Botschaft," which has become a great favorite. A "Fantasia" he is writing on some Swedish songs, sung by Jenny Lind, interests him on account of the charming original melodies, as well as the memory of the illustrious songstress, whose characteristics he endeavors to depict in this composition.

The happy event, the expected birth of a first grandchild, called the Moscheles to London, where they had hoped to meet Mendelssohn, who had gone to England to superintend the performance of his "Elijah." He had, however, hurried away to Frankfort, there to hear the sad news of the death of his beloved sister Fanny. This sad event struck him a blow from which he never recovered. "He writes to me from Baden-Baden," says Mrs. Moscheles, "and under this heavy trial shows great fortitude and resignation. It is not certain now whether the Mendelssohns will continue their journey into Switzerland or return to Leipzig; although deeply afflicted, they are, thank God, all in good health."

Moscheles writes: "Musical matters are in no way changed here. Besides Lablache and Madame Castellan, there are heaps of 'inis' and 'ettis,' with their shakes and quavers; but nowhere a full room. By Benedict's desire, I have written a piece for eight hands, expressly for his concert; it went as well as it was received, and yet I feel conscious that the ladies would have preferred a piece upon operatic airs. Besides that, think of an audience wading through nine-and-forty pieces at one concert! There are sinners who perform penance by hunger and fasting; here one does penance by gorging oneself with endless musical menus; and what a sacrifice of time! Benedict wished to play a duet with me at his concert, Willmers and Bennett also at theirs; but I refused to play in public. I heard Spohr's and Mozart's music at the Philharmonic; since my experience of the Gewandhaus, these concerts have lost much of their charm, but Ella's Matinée, where Joachim played, was a real treat to me.

"What shall I say of Jenny Lind? I can find no words adequate to give you any real idea of the impression she has made. Independent of the fact that the language of panegyric is exhausted, this wonderful artiste stands far too high in my judgment to be dragged down by commonplace complimentary phrases, such as newspaper writers so copiously indulge in. This is no short-lived fit of public enthusiasm. Everybody wants to see and hear her, or, having seen her, to see her and hear her again. I wanted to know her off the stage as well as on; but as she lives some distance from me, I asked her in a letter to fix upon an hour for me to call. Simple and unceremonious as she is, she came the next day herself, bringing her answer verbally. So much modesty and so much greatness united, are seldom if ever to be met with, and although her intimate friend Mendelssohn had given me an insight into the noble qualities of her character, I was surprised to find them so apparent at first acquaintance. I had to play her my 'Fantasia' on her Swedish songs. Mendelssohn had chosen the subjects with me; and she said many pretty things about my characteristic treatment of these national airs. We returned her visit in Old Brompton, where she lives, far from the noise of the capital and the arena of her brilliant performances."

Greatly as Moscheles enjoyed his five weeks' stay in his daughter's home and among old friends, he was anxious to get back to Leipzig, although by virtue of his agreement he was allowed three months' absence every year, independent of the regular holidays (the time to be chosen to suit his own convenience); he was always longing to get back to his pupils, and carried out to a nicety his resolve to act conscientiously and laboriously in his new sphere. In July, while at his post at the Conservatoire, he makes a new edition of some classical works and most carefully compares his arrangement of Beethoven's "Symphony in A," with one formerly made by Hummel. We read in the diary: "Hummel, who takes every possible liberty, wishes to improve upon Beethoven's directions to the band, as well as the notes themselves; for instance, in the beginning of the first Allegro, he gives the bass an altered rhythm.

"Towards the end of the movement on the eleventh page, he cuts out ten bars!! On the thirtieth page two-and-twenty bars!!"

In August Moscheles writes: "Ferdinand Hiller's visit to us was a most agreeable diversion; for the rest, I enjoy the quiet, and even the sameness of my life, looking for novelty in books and periodicals. I am much interested in the 'Girondins' and Dahlmann's excellent History of the French Revolution.

"The editor of the local musical journal here has called together a meeting of artists for the 13th and 14th of this month, on which occasion the 'Weal and Woe' of art is to be discussed. I don't expect much good will come of it, but allow my name to figure among them.

"August 13th.—Brendel opened the meeting to day with a speech on the diffusion of classical music; Schumann, in a letter, expresses his wish that the German language may be adopted on the title-pages of music. A wise suggestion was made that some useful guide to pianoforte teaching should be published; I mentioned my 'Méthode des Méthodes.'

"Debate between me and Herr Knorr about his edition

of 'Cramer's Studies,' in which he has substituted his own fingering for that of the author. I defended my opinion that it is best to give the pupil different ways of fingering, as I have done in my 'Studies.'"

Every artist passing through Leipzig made a point of calling on Moscheles, and he received them all with invariable kindness, but he writes: "I must listen to everything, but in return it is my duty to show that one can play the piano without hammering; that such a thing as a pianissimo can be obtained without a soft pedal. The pedals are auxiliaries; whoever makes them of primary importance puts in evidence the incapacity of his own fingers, and he who writes a 'Polka du Diable,' 'Valse Infernale,' 'Menuet à la Démon,' or by way of contrast, 'Moonshine Elegies,' and 'Æolian Harp Sonatas,' seeks to attract by the title, not by original ideas. As for L.'s 'Spring is coming,' I would call it 'Autumn has come,' for the composition is as withered as autumn leaves."

On the 17th of September the Mendelssohn family return home from Switzerland. "In mind dear Felix is the same as ever, but physically he seems altered; he is aged, weakened, and his walk is less elastic than before, but to see him at the piano, or hear him talk about art and artists, he is all life and fire. To his great joy his friend Julius Rietz is just entering upon his duties as Kapellmeister in Leipzig. Of him he says: "Here is another earnest-minded musician, producing much that is good, and capable of guiding the performances of others to the highest pitch of perfection; his conducting must lead to great things at the Gewandhaus Concerts, and what fine music we shall have among ourselves! Rietz is a capital violoncello player, we shall have a glorious winter.' He then fixed on an evening when Rietz and I were to come to his house for music. My new piece for eight hands, written for Benedict's Concert, gave rise to an animated discussion; it was to bear the title of 'Jadis et Aujourd'hui;' Mendelssohn opposed this, and I affirmed 'that the introductory fugues were meant to illustrate the good old times, the lighter movements the music of our own day.' 'But why so?' argued Mendelssohn; 'are not interesting fugues written now-a-days? Surely our time produces still some good things.' 'But the fashionable taste is a vitiated one,' I replied, 'people will only listen to light music and easy rhythms.' 'Yes, they will,' Mendelssohn broke in, eagerly; 'but they shall not. Don't you and I live? Don't we intend to write good music? We will prove that our time is capable of good; so please to give up this title.' This request was not to be withstood, and therefore for 'Jadis et Aujourd'hui,' we substituted 'Les Contrastes,' with which my friend declared he was satisfied."

We read again: "October 3d.—After the Mendelssohns had dined with us, Felix and I amused ourselves at the piano with fugues and gigues by Bach; he then gave us an admirable imitation of the town musicians at Frankfort, whose Polkas he had been condemned to listen to hundreds of times.

"October 5th.—Delightful afternoon at Mendelssohn's, and had much friendly talk about art-matters. He played me his last quartet, all four movements in F minor; the passionate character of the whole, and the mournful key, seem to me an expression of his deeply agitated state of mind; he is still suffering and in sorrow for the loss of his sister. He also showed me some of her manuscript Lieder—everything deeply felt, but not always original.

"October 7th. Mendelssohn came to take me out for a walk, although it rained; we strolled along in the Rosenthal, having such an interesting conversation that the hours flew unheeded by.

"October 8th.—Examination at the Conservatoire. Mendelssohn wrote on a slate, with a piece of chalk, a thorough bass exercise, to test the pupils; while they worked it out, he made some charming pen-and-ink sketches. What a sleepless genius! . . . . In the afternoon and evening we were at his house. He played with Rietz, his D major Sonata with Cello, and the two by Beethoven, op. 102; with me, my 'Sonate Symphonique;' Emily and I played 'Les Contrastes.'

"On the 9th of October Mendelssohn came to see us; we watched him as he walked slowly and languidly through the garden on his way to our house. My wife felt much concerned, and in answer to her inquiry after his health, he replied, 'How am I? Rather shady' (Grau in grau)! She assured him that a walk and the fine weather would do him good, so we—Charlotte, I, and our Felix—went to the Rosenthal, and certainly during our strolls he became so fresh and animated that we forgot his previous words. Charlotte said, 'You have never told us all about your last stay in London,' and this remark elicited from him much about our common friends that interested us. Then he gave us an account of his visit to the Queen. She had received him very graciously, and he was much pleased with her rendering of some of his songs, which he had accompanied; he had also played to the Queen and the Prince. She must have been pleased, for, when he rose to depart, she thanked him, and said, 'You have given me so much pleasure, now what can I do to give you pleasure?' Mendelssohn deprecating, she insisted; so he candidly admitted that he had a wish that only her Majesty could fulfil. He, himself the head of a household, felt mightily interested in the Queen's domestic arrangements; in short, might he see the Royal children in their Royal nurseries? The Queen at once entered into the spirit of his request, and in her most winning way conducted him herself through the nurseries, all the while comparing notes with him on the homely subjects that had a special attraction for both.

"Talking of Cécile's birthday, he told us of a mantle he had bought her for a present; he had a second and priceless gift in store for her, for when he and Klingemann had made a tour of Scotland together, they both joined in keeping a diary, Klingemann jotting down their adventures in verse, Mendelssohn illustrating them. These fugitive pages, arranged and bound, were to be presented to his wife, but alas! he had already been attacked with deadly illness before the next day dawned.

"We parted about one o'clock in the most cheerful mood. That very afternoon, however, Felix was taken very ill in Frau Frege's house; he had gone thither to persuade her to sing in the next performance of his 'Elijah.' 'She is afraid of appearing in public,' Mendelssohn had said some days before, 'and of not being in good voice; but no one can sing at all like her; I must go and encourage her."

We are indebted to Frau Frege for the following account of what occurred in her house on the 9th of October : "These were his words when he entered the room, 'I come to-day, and intend coming every day, until you give me your consent, and I now bring with me again the altered pieces (of the "Elijah") ; but I really feel miserable, so much so that lately I actually cried over my Trio. To-day, however, before we talk of "Elijah," you must help me to put together a book of songs ; the Härtels are pressing me so to publish it.' He brought the book, Op. 71, and as a seventh Lied, the old German Spring Song, 'Der trübe Winter ist vorbei,' which he had composed in the summer of this year, but had not written out until the 7th of October. "I knew pretty well," said Frau Frege, "how he would wish the songs to follow, and arranged them in order, one by one, upon the piano. After I had sung the first, he was very much moved, and asked for it again, adding, 'That was a somewhat serious birthday present for Schleinitz on the 1st of October, but it is quite in accordance with my state of mind, and I can't tell you how melancholy Fanny's still unchanged rooms in Berlin made me. But I have indeed so much to be thankful to God for—Cécile is so well, and little Felix, too' (his youngest son, who was often out of health). He then made me repeat all the Lieder several times, and I still clung to my opinion that the 'Spring Song' was a little out of place in the book. He then said, 'Be it so ; the whole book is serious, and serious it must go into the world.' Although he looked very pale, I had to sing him the first song for the third time over, and he thanked me most kindly and amiably. He continued : 'If you are not tired, let us try the last quartet out of the 'Elijah.' I left the room to order lamps, and on my return found him in the next room on the sofa ; his hands, he said were cold and stiff, and it would be better and wiser to take a turn out of doors, he really felt too ill to make music. I wanted to send for a carriage, but he would not allow me, and after I had given him a saline draught, he left about 5.30. When he got into the air, he felt it would be better to go home instantly ; once at home, he sat down in the corner of the sofa, where Cécile found him at 7 o'clock ; his hands were cold and stiff as before. On the following day he suffered from such violent pain in the head, that leeches were applied; the doctor thought the digestive organs were attacked, and only at a later period pronounced the disease to be the result of an overwrought nervous system. Ever since Fanny's death I had been struck with his paleness when he conducted or played; everything seemed to affect him more intensely than before."

The news of Mendelssohn's illness created quite a panic in Leipzig, but as he seemed so rapidly to recover, all fears were for a time allayed. "On the 15th October," we quote from the diary, "I had to tell Felix a great deal about Hiller's new opera 'Conradin, der letzte Hohenstaufe' the favorable reception of which delighted him heartily. David, Benedict, and I had gone over to Dresden to hear it; Wagner and Tichatschek took the leading parts. The performance was a remarkable one, the music, I thought, full of dignity and passion."

In the course of a few days Mendelsshon so far recovered that his friends find him not only cheerful, but actually making his plans for conducting his "Elijah" in Vienna. To Madame Frege, who visited him, he said: 'Well, I must have given you a pretty fright the other day—a cheerful sight I must have been!" On the 28th he felt so much stronger that he took a walk with Cécile, and felt inclined to go out again. At her persuasion, however, he abandoned the idea; but alas! shortly afterwards he suddenly broke down. It was declared to be an attack of apoplexy. The anxiety of all Leipzig cannot be described. Once more he seems to rally, but only to relapse into a state of feverish excitement; his mind wanders, and he talks in English. On the 3d of November, at half-past two in the afternoon, a third attack supervenes and deprives him of all consciousness.

The bulletin was read again and again by anxious crowds. Thus the 4th of November dawned. We give Moscheles' own words, just as he wrote them in Mendelssohn's house on the morning of the fatal day. "Nature! demandest thou thy rights? Angels above, in heavenly spheres, do ye claim your brother, whom ye regard as your own, as one too high for intercourse with us ordinary mortals? We still possess him, we still cling to him; we hope by God's grace, to keep still longer among us one who has ever shone upon us, a pattern of all that is noble and beautiful, the glory of our century! To Thee, O Creator, it is known why Thou hast lodged those treasures of heart and soul in so frail a tenement, that now threatens to dissolve! Can our prayers win from Thee the life of our brother? What a glorious work hast Thou accomplished in him! Thou hast shown us how high he may soar heavenwards, how near he may approach Thee! Oh! suffer him to enjoy his earthly reward—the blessings of a husband and father, the ties of friendship, the homage of the world!" . .

"Noon.—Drs. Hammer, Hofrath Clarus, the surgeon, Walther, all take their turn by the bedside; Schleinitz writes out a bulletin which gives no hope. Dr. Frege and his wife, David, Rietz, Schleinitz, my wife, and I, are waiting anxiously near the sick room. The doctors say that if no fresh attack on the nerves or lungs supervenes the apparent calm may lead to a happy turn, even to ultimate recovery. This calm, however, was in reality only the utter prostration of all physical power.

"Evening.—From two o'clock in the afternoon, at the hour when another paralytic stroke was dreaded, he gradually began to sink; he lay perfectly quiet, breathing heavily. In the evening we were all by turns assembled around his bed, contemplating the peaceful, seraphic expression on his countenance. The memory of that scene sunk deeply into our hearts. Cécile bore up with fortitude under the crushing weight of her sorrow; she never wavered, never betrayed her struggle by a word. The children had been sent to bed at nine o'clock. Paul Mendelssohn stood, transfixed with grief, at the bedside of his dying brother. Madame Dirichlet and the Schuncks were expected in vain, Dr. Härtel had travelled to Berlin to fetch them and Dr. Schönlein, but they could not arrive in time to witness the closing scene.

"From nine o'clock in the evening we expected every moment would be the last; a light seemed to hover over his features, but the struggle for life became feebler and fainter. Cécile, in floods of tears, kneeled at his pillow; Paul Mendelssohn, David, Schleinitz, and I, in deep and silent prayer, surrounded the deathbed. As his breathing gradually became slower and slower, my mind involuntarily recurred to Beethoven's Funeral March, 'Sulla Morte d'un' Eroe,' to that passage where he seems to depict the hero as he lies breathing his last, the sands of life gradually running out.

The suppressed sobs of the bystanders, and my own hot tears, recalled me to the dread reality.

"At twenty four minutes past nine he expired with a deep sigh. The doctor persuaded the widowed Cécile to leave the room. I knelt down at the bedside, my prayers followed heavenwards the soul of the departed, and I pressed one last kiss on that noble forehead before it grew cold in the damp dew of death. For several hours we bewailed together our irreparable loss; then each one withdrew, to sorrow in silence.

"What poor consolations are funeral honors, however grand and impressive, how miserably inadequate as expressions of grief for the loss of my beloved friend, whose memory will be sacred to me for the rest of my days."

All Leipzig mourned; the Gewandhaus on this 4th November did not give its usual concert; the soul of music seemed to have fled! who would have cared for concerts at such a time? Moscheles, during the next few days, meets with his friends to consult about the funeral, and scores for the sad occasion Mendelssohn's "Lied ohne Worte" in E minor. The body was soon afterwards carried to Berlin; a service takes place on the 7th November, in the Pauliner Church.

The Berlin *Staatszeitung* gives the following account of the funeral in Leipzig: "On the 6th November Mendelssohn's body was brought to the Pauliner (University) Church, preceded by a band of wind instruments, playing Beethoven's 'Funeral March.' The procession consisted of the members of the Gewandhaus orchestra and the pupils of the Conservatoire; the pall-bearers were Moscheles, David, Hauptmann, and Gade. The professors of the Conservatoire, with Mendelssohn's brother as chief mourner, and several guilds and societies from Leipzig and Dresden, followed the coffin. After the pastor's funeral oration in the church, an organ prelude and chorales out of 'St. Paul' and Bach's 'Passion' were played by the orchestra, under Gade's and David's direction. During the service the coffin remained open; the painters, Bendemann, Hübner, and Richard, of Dresden, made drawings of the great man with the wreath of laurel upon his brow. At ten o'clock at night the coffin was closed and carried by the pupils of the Conservatoire to the station of the Berlin Railway. A torchlight procession of more than a thousand persons followed the funeral train through the crowded streets of Leipzig, and similar honors accompanied with funeral music, were paid to the dead at Cöthen, Dessau, and other towns on the road to Berlin, which was reached between seven and eight o'clock in the morning. There the coffin, adorned with ivy leaves and a large wreath of laurel, was carried on a hearse drawn by six horses draped in black, to the churchyard of the Holy Trinity. Thousands of people followed the bier, and Beethoven's 'Funeral March' was again played. Two clergymen and other friends of the deceased pronounced orations at the grave, and a chorus, consisting of six hundred voices, sang a hymn by Groeber, 'Christ and the Resurrection.' It is impossible to describe the mournful scene; the men threw earth, and the women and children flowers, on the coffin when it was finally lowered into the grave. Mendelssohn sleeps near that beloved sister whose death so fatally impressed him."

The King of Prussia had sent Mendelssohn a letter, in appreciation of the "Elijah," the first performance of which he had heard in Berlin; unfortunately, however, this letter reached Leipzig a day after the death of the great master. At the Gewandhaus Concert, on the 11th November, the performance was as follows:—

First part: Overture to St. Paul. Motet, "Lord, now lettest Thou Thy servant depart in peace;" "Vergangen ist der lichte Tag," beautifully and feelingly sung by Frau Frege. Overture to "Melusine."

Second Part: Beethoven's "Eroica."

The dreary sense of isolation, now that Moscheles had

forever lost his art-colleague, made the idea of residence in Leipzig almost intolerable to Mrs. Moscheles; the object of all ambition seemed annihilated; Moscheles, however, argued otherwise: "He invited me to take part in an institution that was so dear to him; to have labored there with him would have been a daily joy and satisfaction, to work on there without him is my duty, which I regard as a sacred trust committed by him to my keeping. I must now work for us both."

Bent on carrying out this resolution, Moscheles once more resumes his classes at the Conservatoire on Monday the 7th of November, and derives from the conscientious performance of his duties some comfort in his deep sorrow. "In spirit, though not in presence, Mendelssohn is with us throughout the dreary winter. The constant visits to Cécile and the dear children, the reading over of his beautiful letters to us both, the perusal of his music, from the 'Kinderstücke' that Clara learns, to the duets that I play with Serena, and his great pianoforte works which I study myself—such are the consolations which he has bequeathed to his sorrowing friends."

The King of Saxony is present at a performance of the "Walpurgisnacht" in the Gewandhaus; the fragments of the "Loreley" are also given. Many sketches of Mendelssohn's life appear, but none represent him so faithfully as his own letters. In these we find reflected the noble mind of the man, and his unswerving devotion to all those that he loved. He regarded art as a gift from heaven, as a glorious possession which he must cultivate and guard, and while so many of his contemporaries wrote for the world and the prevailing taste and fashion of the public, he strove, singly and solely, to clothe his poetical and majestic thoughts in the noblest and loveliest harmonies. He, too, had his detractors—who has not? But none could reproach him with ever having been unfaithful to his art-convictions.

# CHAPTER XXX.

## 1848—1849.

Commemorations of Mendelssohn—Concert in aid of a Pension Fund —Performance of the "Elijah"—Political Agitation—Prague and Vienna—Nestroy the Actor in Leipzig—Change in Musical Taste —The Volunteer Guards—Anniversary of Mendelssohn's Death—A Mendelssohn Foundation—Mark of Royal Favor—Schumann —Mendelssohn's "Athalie"—Madame Dulcken—Lindley—Liszt's Playing—Visit to Prague—Musical Events.

IT would be no exaggeration to say that in Germany and England, if not throughout Europe, Mendelssohn's death was regarded as a public calamity. In Leipzig, the scene of so many of his great achievements, there were famous artists still left to carry on the work of the Conservatoire. There remained such men as Hauptmann, David, Rietz, Cossmann, and Joachim. The mere mention of these names will suffice to show that art, so far from being paralyzed, was sure to develop all its best energies under the care and skill of men of European eminence. Friedrich Schneider, Besker, Reinecke, Griepenkerl, and others, joined in upholding the reputation of Leipzig as a musical centre, and, to crown all, Robert and Clara Schumann gave an historical éclat and interest to the Gewandhaus Concerts of the winter of 1848. "And yet," says Moscheles in one of his letters, "we live daily in the memory of Mendelssohn. We are constantly with his dear children, and Cécile has the courage to be present at all the performances where her husband's works are executed, and to listen to such deeply touching compositions as the last quartet in F minor, and the 'Nachtlied,' sung as only Frau Frege can sing it. On the 3d February, his birth-day, the 'Elijah' was given for the first time here. I have attended all the rehearsals, and Emily and Serena sang in the chorus. A medallion executed for this special occasion by the sculptor Knaur, had been fixed in its place over the orchestra. Behr sang the part of the Prophet with earnestness and energy; Frau Frege, with her clear intonation and fine expression, rendered the music of the widow in her own pure and expressive style, and Fräulein Schloss was an excellent contralto. Gade's conducting, generally speaking, was painstaking and effective, except in certain 'Tempi,' which Mendelssohn had taken differently in Birmingham, where the organ had frequently enhanced the orchestral effects. The concert, given for the benefit of the 'Pension Fund,' was, strange to say, only two-thirds full, and the silence with which the work was received, left it doubtful whether the audience had been duly impressed. Certainly some papers headed what was actually an opposition. We were all indignant at so equivocal a reception, and even my Felix was not to be restrained from writing on the subject to the papers, and protesting against it.

.... "Cécile asked me yesterday to revise the orchestral parts of Felix's A major Symphony, for it may possibly be given at the last Gewandhaus Concert. I have been to the theatre to hear a new opera, which was a complete failure, the music so bad and commonplace that it actually disturbed me in a nap. David, the picture of misery, frequently looked up to me from the orchestra for a sympathetic glance. I pitied him."

The political storm which had so suddenly burst in Paris, the Revolution which cost Louis Philippe his throne, found an echo in several parts of Germany. That Moscheles was no passive spectator of these events, we gather from many passages in his diary: ...." Robert Blum, a Radical, is elected a member of the German Parliament, and gladly accepts. .... Schleswig Holstein is in a most excited state. God forbid there should be a war! I read the sad accounts the newspapers give of petitions, barricades, and tri-colored flags. ....

"It was odd that I should find in the *Wiener Zeitung* an article, taking the King of Prussia to task for refusing civil liberties until he conceded them over the dead bodies of the citizens. And this from Austria! What a state of things we have come to! Do you recollect seeing in the Ballet that quaint old-fashioned gentleman who suddenly turns round and displays a figure all youth and bloom—Austria seems to me as double-sided as that figure !. . . . The States appear to me to be affected with cancer, while a consultation of surgeons is held at Frankfort. Artificial arms, legs, eyes, and noses are being substituted for the decayed members of the mutilated State-body, and our age unhappily is destined to look on at these operations ; it is a hard trial, but God wills it so ! I am not carried away by the hue and cry for liberty. I should like a monarchical 'juste milieu,' without coming under Nicholas' scourge or seeing my neighbors writhing under it. And my old Vienna, with her triumph won over the corpses of her citizens ! My light-hearted, musical Vienna ! it costs me much more of an effort to realize her in a state of fermentation than Berlin, where the tragedy is deepening, and becoming more and more terrible. Heaven preserve us from a repetition of the Reign of Terror ! On Friday evening we and all our friends heard the debates at the patriotic meeting ; Laube, who had just arrived from Vienna, spoke well on the state of things in Austria ; Flathe proposed emigration as the only remedy for a distressed population ; Zestermann defended his fellow-citizens, the people of Zittau, whose patriotism had been suspected. All the discussions were carried on amid clouds of tobacco, rather bad for the ladies, but better anyhow than the smoke of gunpowder." "In the midst of this crisis," Mrs. Moscheles writes, "art and professional avocations are a real comfort, and my husband can be serenely happy in the midst of all the turmoil round him." "Whenever I play, I forget everything," adds Moscheles, "but I certainly cannot now-a-days concentrate my thoughts enough for composing." On a visit to some friends at Lützschena, he moralizes thus : "How beautiful the world is, after all ; this misery will pass, and liberty will dawn upon us ! May we soon see her make her entrance in triumphal procession, as we have seen kings and ministers make their entrance, and—their exit."

Frau Frege, assisted by Moscheles and several artists, gives a very successful concert for the benefit of impoverished artisans. A private gallery of pictures is opened to the public for the same charitable purpose, and the Moscheles try to raise a fund for the members of the orchestra, who have been deprived of their pay owing to the troubled state of the times. Again we read of Moscheles' raptures with the Ninth Symphony: "This work revealed new beauties to me, and this I owe to certain effects and 'nuances' which with all my hearty exertions I could not succeed in bringing out with a London orchestra. The work itself stands relatively to other Symphonies like the Cathedral of Cologne to other churches. Rietz conducted in true musicianly style."

The 30th of May, Moscheles' birthday, evokes the following letter: "Your wishes were doubly welcome to me, at a time when State ties threaten to dissolve, and family ties are loosened by those dreadful politics. Nothing was omitted in my family circle to make me forget the gloom of the present time; accordingly, I allowed myself patiently to be led blindfold by the children to the birthday table. What gave me the greatest delight was a water-color drawing of Mendelssohn's study, painted on the spot by my Felix, exactly as it was left at the time of his death—every detail, even to the most insignificant, faithfully represented. Cécile presented me with an apparatus for striking a light (Zündmaschine), which her husband had used; a precious souvenir, like everything that comes from him."

Nestroy, the famous comic actor from Vienna, comes upon the gloomy days of Leipzig, with his "Freiheit in Krähwinkel," exactly at the right time, to inspirit every one. Moscheles says: "None but a Nestroy could parody government reform and liberty without becoming wearisome or giving offence. Formerly this piece would have given him free admission to the 'Spielberg' (the State-prison); now he can actually introduce Metternich as a comic figure, without any fear of the Censor or police."

At a concert for the destitute artisans, Moscheles plays his E major Concerto, and says: "Germany has my good wishes for such unity as was displayed by the orchestra under Rietz and David. I thank God that I am not now obliged to begin to earn my bread by my art; I should certainly have to turn rope-dancer. . . . . Formes as 'Leporello' the other night was very humorous and powerful, but I was annoyed at his exclaiming in the churchyard scene, 'This sounds like trombones.' The public liked it, but the public, when applauding that kind of thing, is like a will-o'-the-wisp—it leads artists astray. Rietz took several of the 'Tempi' too slowly, which surprised me in a modern Kapellmeister."

There are signs of Leipzig becoming infected with revolution, and as an extra precaution, it is thought necessary to organize a volunteer guard, in which Moscheles is enrolled as a member. He used, however, to joke about his want of taste for soldiering, and having one night mounted guard with Brassin (the bass singer in the theatre), he told his family when he came home that he had been very comfortable, having had a long conversation with his brother-sentinel about "Don Juan;" so that the two amateur soldiers managed to kill time very pleasantly.

"The unpublished music left by Mendelssohn is in the hands of Schleinitz, who is also guardian of the children. One of these works, the 'Reformation Symphony,' was yesterday rehearsed privately. It is in the true ecclesiastical style, and pleased me, however much Felix himself found fault with it. He was as much at home in the sacred style as in the romantic forms of his Lieder, or the fairy music of hobgoblins and dancing elves."

Moscheles mentions in affecting language the commemorative festival at the Conservatoire, on the anniversary of the day of Mendelssohn's death. "Only the professors and their wives were invited, and everybody was dressed in mourning. After preliminary music, one of the Directors, standing before Mendelssohn's bust, made a speech to the pupils, exhorting them to emulate their great model, the founder of the Institution. The ceremony was very imposing, and we were particularly struck with one of the last songs of Mendelssohn, which Frau Frege gave with exquisite pathos. Joachim led the F minor Quartet admirably, and with the correct conception of the work."

Outside the art-world, the political horizon grows darker and darker. Moscheles writes: "All the reforms which the new time is to bring us seem still unripe, and I wish we could put them upon straw, as we do fruit to ripen. Perhaps such a process might obviate the necessity of deluging the soil with human blood; but then eternal peace would be like eternal spring; neither is to be found."

On the 17th December we read: "Unfortunately, in

spite of my ten days' exertions and a great deal of begging, I did not succeed in securing for the blind singer, Miss A. Z., a full room at her Matinée to-day. My warmth on the subject had failed to melt the iceberg which blocked the entrance to the purses of the Leipzigers. Rietz accompanied, Joachim played Bach's 'Chaconne' admirably, and Pelz the pianist appeared for the first time, with an Andante, all embroidery. The poor singer gave her Swiss melodies and some other pieces with much feeling, but after all she only realized twenty-six thalers, twelve of which went to the expenses."

In a letter of the 2d of January, 1849, we read: "There is one piece of news worth telling, as a matter of importance for Leipzig. I allude to the death of an old patroness of art. She had reached her fiftieth year, having flourished in the days of Haydn, Mozart, and Beethoven, and was received on the Continent with honor and distinction. Occasionally she dealt with novelties, and retailed gossip, but her conversation was often instructive. She never travelled with hard cash, but only with notes. Her name was the *Leipziger Allgemeine Zeitung für Musik.* In the farewell number, the editor says that art-productivity is now in such a stagnant state that material is wanting for a musical journal. Schleinitz publishes the statutes for a Mendelssohn Institute, the aim of which is to co-operate with the Conservatoire in assisting art-students; and, by scholarships and other benevolent means, to perpetuate the memory of Mendelssohn. The King has undertaken to act as patron and protector; and I am to be a joint director of the new institute. His Majesty has recently presented me with a gold snuff-box, accompanied by a letter acknowledging my dedication of the 'Contrastes;' but I don't talk about this, or it will go straight into the newspapers. . . . . On a second hearing of Schumann's Symphony in C, I feel more and more that he follows boldly in Beethoven's footsteps, reminding me of him in daring, but scarcely in tenderness. I think his D minor Trio a composition of the most passionate character; it is based less on intensity of ideas than on his power of moving in the most varied keys. The Scherzo is the most piquant movement, the Adagio very gloomy.

'The Schumanns, Frau Schröder, and Frau Frege last

night gave us lovely music, when of a sudden we heard a serenade from the garden ; this was a chorus of men's voices ; the strangers might well appreciate the compliment, for it rained heavily. The one great drawback I feel in Schumann's society is his extreme reticence ; try as I will, I cannot inveigle him into a conversation upon art.

"Paul Mendelssohn asked me, in the name of his sister-in-law, to join Hauptmann, David, and Rietz in editing his brother's posthumous works, a service which I shall render with affection and reverence. The very next evening some movements of the posthumous quartet were tried at David's. One in F minor is, I think, the most valuable ; the Quintet in B major, too, is a great work."

Mendelssohn's "Athalie" is performed, and Edward Devrient recited, between the separate numbers, some lines of his own, written as connecting links to the dramatic scenes. "Felix, when in London, had played me the whole of the music of 'Athalie,' trumpeting—'tuting,' as he called it—every wind-instrument, especially in the 'March of the Priests,' so that I well remembered the most startling modulations. Even then the work pleased me ; now, after attending the performance and rehearsals, I glory in it. In certain passages I was deeply affected, what must he have felt when he wrote it? But, strange to say, the Leipzig public remained cold, as at the 'Elijah' performance."

Family matters take Moscheles for a fortnight to London. The first letter to his wife begins in the following way :

"I remain your faithful and loving husband, I. Moscheles. I begin with the end, just as formerly I began my C major Concerto with the finale cadence, because in both cases my leading idea is expressed :

"Now then about matters here. I was offered an engagement at Exeter Hall immediately on my arrival, but with a gratification bordering on self-complacency, I declared I did not wish any more to play in public. Every one receives me with open arms. . . . .

"The musicians and their publishers are still absorbed in their business; I met a congress of them at Chappell's. Osborne immediately claimed me for his new pianoforte duet in F flat minor; I ventured to attack it, six flats and all, and I think my friend was greatly pleased. Then Dulcken appeared, and told me that his concert on the 20th (he forgot that his wife gave it) would be crowded even if the Hanover Square Rooms were three times the size. 'Why not give it in Exeter Hall?' I asked. 'Because Jenny Lind, whose intimacy with my wife dates from Stockholm days, kindly consents to sing for us, and does not like Exeter Hall.' Subsequently, when I visited Madame Dulcken, she asked me to play a duet with her in the same concert, but for the reasons known to you, I refused.

"Beethoven's Mass in C was a rare treat, and so was Mendelssohn's 'Hymn of Praise.' Costa wields his bâton more in Italian than German style, but he kept the 700 performers admirably together, although the 'Tempi' were not always what I am used to. My neighbor, Mr. Gladstone, asked me several musical questions. When the room was almost empty, I saw the veteran Lindley still sitting by his violoncello. This reminded me of his having been upset in a coach, when he quietly sat down in an open field to see if his instrument had received any injury. . . . . This is a long letter. You shall soon hear more by word of mouth."

Moscheles, soon after his return to Leipzig, writes: "Ernst gave a Matinée which, I grieve to say, was poorly attended. He looks wretchedly ill, but played with great energy and passionate feeling. . . . . We had a novelty in F. Hiller's Symphony in E major, with the motto: 'Es muss doch Frühling werden,' a work in grand style, with excellent points in it. I recognize in all Hiller's music a composer aiming at what is true and beautiful. Liszt played part of a concerto by Henselt, and his Don Juan Fantasia, with all his gigantic power. The tossing about of his hands, which he seems to think a mark of inspiration, I still regard as an eccentricity, although it is no doubt remarkable that he accomplishes the most perilous jumps with scarcely a single mishap.

"'Christus,' the fragment left behind by Mendelssohn, is now being studied by our pupils; it consists of five or six choruses, recitatives, a trio of a dignified kind sung by the three magi, to the words, 'Say, where is He that is born King of Judah?' a chorus, 'Daughters of Zion,' and another of the people, 'Crucify Him'—these are masterpieces, and although fragmentary in character are sure to become famous. . . . . The time of publication is not yet fixed on.

"Yesterday, for the first time, we saw Halévy's 'Thal von Andorra'—music of a genuine dramatic character, which has more flow of melody than his other operas. The subject is cleverly worked up and very expressive. It was so finely given, that the entire body of performers was called forward. I read Berlioz' 'Feuilleton' upon Meyerbeer's 'Prophète.' The libretto is certainly frightful, and contains sensational scenes enough to make one shudder: the music, however, is said to be worthy of Meyerbeer, and I look forward to hearing another work from the pen of my old friend. Lortzing's opera 'Roland's Knappen,' reminds me of the busy bee which sucks its honey out of many flowers."

The winter and spring of this year were saddened by the war in Holstein, and the revolution in Dresden. "A Schröder-Devrient, a Richard Wagner, haranguing the Dresden people! What can it lead to? Alas! we were soon able to answer that question when the barricades were raised in Leipzig, and one of the worthiest citizens, and our excellent friend, was shot dead by a ruffian."

When the storms in the political atmosphere are calmed down, Moscheles takes his children to Prague. "I will show them," he writes, "the birthplace and the house their father was born in, the graves of my own parents, the place on the 'Ring,' where I delighted, as an urchin, to hold the music for the bandsmen, the house of Dionys Weber, nay, the actual corner stone on which I smashed the wine-bottle which I was commissioned by him to carry to his friend, the worthy prelate. Lastly, I want the children to make acquaintance with their relatives." "Returning to Leipzig," he says, "I found Spohr—he played in Voigt's house, that place of rendezvous for good musicians, his Quartet in C major and Double Quartet in G minor, both from the proof sheets, the composition as interesting as ever, but Spohr unchanged; his playing is still noble and fresh. In the Conservatoire we gave him an ovation, and his bust was covered with garlands; he played several things to a delighted audience, and our pupils gave him a serenade afterwards. A short visit from Cécile Mendelssohn, on her way through Leipzig, revived the memory of old days; I had to play to her the march from 'Athalie,' his bust looked down on us, she said but little, but was full of gratitude and tenderness."

Mrs. Moscheles had been summoned to London, where she receives the following letter:

"Leipzig, 12th July.

"Your letter found me at the Conservatoire, it put me into such good humor that from that moment I was all forbearance with false notes and bad fingering. . . . . In to-day's *Times* I read of the triumph of our old, still youthful friend, Henriette Sontag; I hope you will meet her. I have to set to music a song written by our Legationsrath, the 'Schmetterling and Liebchen.' The text is poetical, and touches a sympathetic chord, whether it deserves to be a pendent for the 'Botschaft' you will see. I shall soon join you in London."

Shortly afterwards Moscheles writes from London: "I am determined to hear the 'Prophet;" all the good places are taken, so I must put up with two bad ones, better them than none at all . . . . Madame Viardot is not only an admirable Fides, but she has, as the French say, 'créé le rôle;' she is Kapellmeister, Régisseur, in one word, the soul of the opera, which owes one-half of its success to her. There are fine things in the work, but after one hearing it does not appear to me to come up to the 'Huguenots.' Besides, one listens at times with only one ear; in the awful church scene, in which Viardot is inimitable, the situation is absolutely absorbing. The skating scene made us envious, sitting as we were in oppressive heat."

After a month's stay at Tréport, the Moscheles visit Rouen and Paris. From the latter place Moscheles writes: "I was much interested in seeing Beaumarchais' 'Marriage de Figaro'—the original of the subject which inspired Mozart with his immortal music. The performance was, as formerly, slightly dashed with some interpolated music; instead of the beautiful romance of the Page there was a sentimental vaudeville song, at the wedding a trivial march, anything but Spanish, but as entr'acte we had the genuine Mozart Romance. Roger had re-appeared in the 'Favorita;' he is an admirable singer, with a full-toned voice, but he and all his colleagues here adopt that dreadful 'tremolo,' which they in professional language call 'vibrando;' in addition to that we often hear regular bawling, and the louder it is the louder they are applauded. The last duet was repeated three times, the bawling increased each time, and with it the applause. There was a shower of bouquets on the stage. . . . . We heard, alas! of Chopin's dangerous illness, and on inquiry found our worst fears confirmed. His sister is nursing him: he suffers greatly."

After the dreaded event, Moscheles writes: "Art has lost much in poor Chopin, for if not a classical writer or one who created masterpieces, he possessed the rarest gifts —a depth of feeling, tenderness (Gemüth), and individuality. Jules Janin writes, in the *Journal des Débats*, that shortly before his death he ordered a Polish national song and Mozart's 'Requiem' to be played to him."

From Leipzig Moscheles writes: "How am I to understand this? The very same public which rationally and justly was enthusiastic in favor of Schumann's great work, the B major Symphony, was now completely carried away by a lady-harpist and Parish Alvars' bravura playing! This is your so-called art-enlightened audience! Again I was displeased with the lukewarm reception given to Mendelssohn's works. O Clique! as if in a city where the genius of a Schumann is worshipped, it should be necessary to cry down Mendelssohn as pedantic, and inferior to his brother in art! The public loses all judgment, and subordinates every feeling and musical instinct to one leadership, which cozens it as much as the Radicals do the German people."

# CHAPTER XXXI.

## 1850—1851.

Moscheles and his Pupils—Schumann's "Genovena"—Performance of some of Mendelssohn's Works—Visit to Berlin—The Silver Wedding—Paul David—Brendel—A Musical Quarrel—Bach Society—Joachim—Political Agitation in Germany—Occasional Criticisms—Pianoforte Players—Beethoven's "Mount of Olives"—Lohengrin—Summer Excursion—Reception in Weimar—David—Ferdinand Hiller.

WE are confident that any one of Moscheles' old pupils who happens to read these pages, will call to mind the friendly ways and words of their former teacher, whose wise discipline was invariably tempered with kindness, and who enforced obedience by sympathy. He delighted in organizing small fêtes, where his pupils could meet him on equal terms, where the classical musician would cheerfully put aside Beethoven and Mozart, and play a waltz or polka for the merry dancers. He was a true friend, for to any deserving pupil about to leave the Conservatoire he gave credentials, which were sure to be of value to the recipient. These were honestly and scrupulously worded, and thus became the best of passports for an aspiring artist. How carefully he weighed every word in these certificates, we gather from his numerous notes in reference to the qualifications of the pupils, and from his drafts for the framing of testimonials ; a whole mass of such memoranda was found among his papers after his death. The diary also catalogues with scrupulous accuracy the morning and evening serenades, the tokens of affection, and proofs of gratitude which were matters of constant occurrence.

His health seldom prevented him from attending to his duties at the Conservatoire, but when indisposed and confined to the house, he would have the pupils at home rather than allow them to miss their lesson. If further proof were needed of the warm interest he took in the welfare of those entrusted to his care, we would quote the following note in the diary: "As regards my pupils, I don't allow myself to be trifled with; I have fought a battle for some of them. In the composition of the programmes for the Pupil Concerts, I will not stand any favoritism; each and all shall have their turn, according to their merits."

Moscheles, ever ready to acknowledge rising talent, took great delight in the youthful Wilhelmine Clauss, whose playing at the Gewandhaus he warmly admired. Of Schumann's opera, "Genoveva," he says: "Madame Schumann played it through to me. In dealing with the plot, Schumann is still undecided whether the final reconciliation shall take place in the desert or in the castle. In whatever way he treats the subject, this opera is sure to be interesting to any artist; whether it will be popular, I cannot judge from hearing it once on the pianoforte." In the course of the following summer, after the first performance in the Leipzig Theatre, Moscheles writes: "First impression:—Overture excellent, full of passion; choruses characteristic, the whole vocal part passionately felt, although not strikingly developed. There is a want of intelligible, flowing, rhythmical melody; I am one of Schumann's worshippers, but cannot conceal from myself this weakness. We applauded enthusiastically, and called him forward at the end, but there was not a single 'encore.'"

"At the quartet meetings we had a great variety: In the first place, Schumann's quartet in A major, strongly Beethovenish in character; then back to one of Haydn's, by way of transition to the Mozart school, and lastly, Beethoven's quartet in B major, op. 130. In this work Beethoven storms heaven itself, and yet again what child-like simplicity and passionate grief! Now a reaction for you, worthy of record: 'Our friend Thalberg has played Mozart's concerto at the Philharmonic; there's a triumph for the old school! We had a lovely performance of Mendelssohn's 'The Son and Stranger,' at Frau Frege's. The orchestra was under Rietz, David with Joachim and other great artists assisting. Frau Frege, in the part of a naïve rustic maiden, sang and acted charmingly; Fräulein Buck and Pögner acted the old parents; Widemann was the lover; scenery and decoration charming. We sat next to Cécile,

Paul and Frau Dirichlet, all of whom had come from Berlin to witness the performance. Cécile was alternately moved, interested, and pleased, the other guests were delighted, and all declared that this small idyll would certainly take honorable rank among comic operas on the public stage. The fragments of the opera, 'Lorelei,' in which Mendelssohn shows clearly unmistakable power as a dramatic composer, seemed to intensify our sorrow at his premature death. The passionate strains allotted to 'Lorelei' were superbly rendered by Frau Frege. What a pity that so gifted an artiste should be withheld from the public! I myself may yet have to thank this gifted lady for many a melody, for the style in which she interprets my new songs delights me, and spurs me on to new efforts. We have heard Mendelssohn's 'Œdipus;' the deep pathos of the choral music, the 'ring of ancient days,' acted like magic on my senses, and I felt recalled to the classic times of Grecian poetry." The audience forgot to applaud, whether from ignorance or excess of delight, I cannot say. Cécile attended this performance, and early on the morning of the 26th of February the Moscheles travelled with her to Berlin, and were soon settled in the old house, Leipziger Strasse, No. 3, consecrated by the memory of the happy hours spent there with one now at rest. We read in the diary:—"Cécile received us in her usual charming manner, the dear children were overjoyed to see us; little Felix is well again. I could not help sitting down at the very Erard piano the keys of which had so often responded to the master's fingers, and playing, among other things, his 'Frühlingslied.' It was too much for poor Cécile.". . . .

On the 27th of February the Moscheles go to Hamburg and celebrate there their silver wedding.

On the 1st of March we read: "The all-merciful God has raised me from a bed of sickness, and allowed me to spend this joyous time with all that I love best in the world. I was awoke in the morning by hearing the Chorale 'Nun danket Alle Gott,' then followed the Wedding March out of the 'Midsummer Night's Dream,' a sorrowful reminder of my departed friend, who would have so rejoiced in our happiness."

Moscheles, on returning to Leipzig, hears Paul David,

a promising young pupil of his father, play a Rode Concerto: "He held his own bravely, just like a plucky boy riding on a big horse; he may be thrown once or twice, but he is up again in the saddle in no time. I predict a future for him."

"Spohr is still complete master of his violin, and conducted his 'Seasons' with great precision. The invention in this work is weak, but the treatment and instrumentation are as artistic as ever. The 'Coming of Spring' has a lovely melody, but art and counterpoint outweigh the poetic vein. The music drags on slowly like a cart through deep sand, one wheel creaking and groaning; the 'Autumn' has its share of brightness, and the Rheinlied is cleverly interwoven in the movement. The contrapuntal links of the different subjects interest the thoughtful artist, but fail to elevate him as does the music of a certain Beethoven."

In addition to the sources from which we have hitherto drawn materials for our compilation, we now have Moscheles' letters to his son Felix, who at this time left for Paris. Hitherto the son's classical education had been pursued in Leipzig under the father's eye; this was now to be exchanged for the study of painting, an art to which he intended to devote himself professionally. The correspondence ranges (with some interruptions) over a period of twenty years, and we shall frequently interweave extracts from it in our narrative.

"I went through Neukomm's Mass with him at the pianoforte; he keeps me strictly to the slowest of all tempi; for an 'accelerando' or 'animato' I would have given a kingdom. These are sacrifices which one can make only for an old and tried friend. I endure a trial of patience of another kind, in arranging for four hands Chopin's 'Violoncello Sonata.' I find it a wild overgrown forest, into which only an occasional sunbeam penetrates."

In the Gewandhaus, Otto Goldschmidt played with great success Mendelssohn's "G minor Concerto," a "Capriccio" of his own, and Liszt's "Lucia-Fantasia," with its avalanche of shakes.

"My colleagues are up in arms against Brendel (himself a professor at the Conservatoire), for having inserted an article headed 'Judaism in Music,' in his periodical. In this article the author endeavors in every possible way to depreciate Mendelssohn and Meyerbeer. I say 'endeavors,' for what harm can a malicious article do to such men? Nevertheless, Brendel has given great offence, and Rietz suggests the following letter to the Committee of Directors:—

"'It cannot have escaped the notice of the honorable Directors of the Conservatoire that the *Neue Zeitschrift für Musik* has aimed for some time past at depreciating the state of music and the musical performances at Leipzig, and this in a tone which oversteps the limits of fair criticism. Men are attacked whose merits are recognized throughout the whole musical world, and whose works are precious to every unprejudiced artist and connoisseur. We, the undersigned, would completely ignore these matters if the editor of that journal, Dr. Brendel, was not one of our colleagues at the Conservatoire. As his views are in direct opposition to ours, and we believe they may exercise a bad influence over the pupils of the Conservatoire, we now call on the honorable Directors at once to dismiss Dr. Brendel from his post. Signed: Becker, Böhme, David, Hauptmann, Hermann, Joachim, Klengel, Moscheles, Plaidy, Rietz, Wenzel.'

"The Directors, however, only thought fit to reprimand Dr. Brendel, but much curiosity was naturally excited about the authorship of the article in question. Dr. Brendel, however, very properly refused to divulge the name, and years were to elapse before people ascertained that Richard Wagner was the author."

Moscheles writes:—"Revised, for the engraver, Mendelssohn's seventh book of the 'Lieder ohne Worte,' three songs for a contralto voice, a setting of Goethe's words, 'Ein Blick von Deinen Augen,' which struck me as very curious in rhythm, but I found it was correct when I compared it with the manuscript."

During this winter a Bach Society is formed, consisting of Becker, David, Härtel, Hauptmann, Jahn, Moscheles, and Rietz, and it is determined to bring out as a first publication the B minor Mass.

Joachim, who had already become the great Joachim,

left Leipzig in course of the winter, and went as 'Concertmeister' to Weimar, where he was received with the distinction he merited; Raimond Dreyschock became second Concertmeister and teacher at the Conservatoire. Mrs. Moscheles writes:—"I rejoice to tell you that the composition of the violoncello sonata my husband has just begun, completely absorbs him, and diverts his thoughts from the troubles of the day;" and Moscheles himself says, "I thank you for all the enlightenment which you strive to give me, a dilettante in politics, about the gloomy condition of Europe. I deplore this ceaseless conflict now rife between the upper and lower classes, which unsettles our poor Germany. If you shake a bottle of good old port, the dregs will rise to the surface, and spoil the wine. I read every kind of newspaper, and could almost wish the bad old times back again, when we had only to fight with the foreign foe. But now, German against German! Fie, fie! they ought rather to have their differences settled by diplomatists, or lawyers in wigs and gowns, and write their annals in red ink instead of red blood. Here, as elsewhere, people are desponding, but I cling fast to my art, and lean upon 'Frau Musica' for support.

On the 1st of January, 1851, Moscheles, glancing over the events of the past year, says: "I thank God for the preservation of all those most dear to me, for health and strength, for power of work. . . . . This being my frame of mind, the concert made a great impression on me. We had the Cantata 'Ein' feste Burg,' by J. S. Bach, a grand contrapuntal work; the hautboys, trumpets, and trombones here and there effectively doubled by Rietz; Mendelssohn's beautiful '95th Psalm,' with its pathetic Canon in C minor—the whole performance a worthy inauguration of the year.

"Schubert's Symphony in C has beautiful and well-developed motives, but there is too much repetition; one-half of it would produce double effect. . . . . 'Papa' Haydn's Symphony was as fresh and healthy as ever; nothing of the demon in that. The rehearsal of the 'Antigone' filled me with admiration as far as the music is concerned, but I do not think it very well suited for the Concert-room. Mendelssohn's Finale to the opera of 'Lorelei' is impressive and highly dramatic, every instrument is ennobled, even to the big drum. The general impression was electrical, and even the champions of a new art-system, who hitherto have been pleased to pronounce Mendelssohn and his creations as old-fashioned and out of date, applauded enthusiastically. Should this fragment never be produced on the stage, it will always be a valuable acquisition to the concert-room ; it is a gem from Mendelssohn's posthumous treasures. Beethoven's Ninth Symphony, 'in the whirlwind of its passion,' carried away the audience ; the performers grappled bravely with all the difficulties, and the victory was glorious ; the 'Ode to Joy' found an echo in the hearts of all."

With regard to Litolff, Moscheles writes : "I admire his light-fingered bravura, his weird-like effects and 'verve ;' his execution, although stormy and restless, is always piquant —he at least does not, like so many others, write sickly Italian music, half thunder, half sentiment. Schumann's 'Requiem for Mignon' does not please me so much as his more important compositions. In the 'Waldscenen,' too, which I have lately played, I thought the form too sketchy. I well understand that he, like a good poet, wishes to give an outline, and leave to the fancy of his hearers the filling in of the whole picture ; but I prefer a more definite form and elaboration to that peculiar dreaminess, that irresolution and groping about. In his symphonies he is great. At the Subscription Concerts, Castellan is creating a furore. Handsome and imported from the Italian operas in Paris and London ! No wonder that with such advantages the classical Leipzigers opened their ears and hearts to the airs of all the 'inis' and 'ettis.' The enthusiasm created by the hackneyed roulades of the Rode Variations, proved that genuine Italian music can move even a German audience.

"I have finished my Sonata for pianoforte and violoncello, and have already played it over with Rietz and Grützmacher ; David, who heard it, wishes to arrange it for violin. I do not think of publishing it yet—I like to let my compositions lie by for awhile that they may go through the process of fermentation, that is, I like to give myself the opportunity of using the file after working with the sledge-hammer, as one does in the first heat of composition..... They wanted me to play it at the Quartet Concerts ; I hesitated, but at last took heart, and played it with Rietz, who assisted me valiantly. . . . We have also heard at the theatre Mendelssohn's operetta, 'The Son and Stranger.' Although the idyllic character charmed the connoisseurs and artists, a few hisses were mingled with the applause when the piece was ended; these were like the occasional 'à bas' which are heard among the public cheers for a crowned head."

Moscheles, on being asked whether Beethoven's "Mount of Olives" had not been treated in too secular a vein, answered: "No doubt that objection has been repeatedly made to the work, but even suppose there is some truth in it, who would like to find fault with so great a man! Who, as Gottfried Weber has done in his 'Cäcilia,' would attack Mozart's 'Requiem' on the ground of its not being sufficiently severe in style? In judging such beautiful music, one ought not to draw a hard and fast line between the ecclesiastical and dramatic element."

In the month of May after hearing the opera of "Lohengrin" in Weimar, he remarks: "Liszt directed the admirably trained orchestra; the singers were excellent. From the very first note of the Introduction, with its high violin passages and gradation effects, the instrumentation seemed to me to be strikingly original, in fact rather too original in its harshness. There is much dramatic life in this music, but I do not like the predominance of recitatives; I should prefer more rhythmical melodious phrases or movements in the ordinary form. Wagner's treatment frequently wearied me, from being too monotonous and too overloaded; for one leading theme well worked out, for one well-sustained vein of thought, I would gladly have bartered many of his bright but transient effects; for all that the work interested me extremely. One must have heard it, and one must hear it again, to form a correct judgment.

"My reception in Weimar was of the most cordial description; the Grand-Duke showed me the art-treasures of his palace. A request to write something for the "Schiller Album' in Weimar led to my composing a Fantasia for pianoforte solo on the poem 'Die Erwartung.'

"To-day at the rehearsal of the Pupils' Concert I would have my way. 'Studies' by Chopin and Thalberg for two pianos were to be played by two pupils at once; I opposed this, and successfully. No, the piano is not an orchestral instrument like the violin; mere strictness in keeping time is not enough, and above all it will not do for Chopin's music; all its poetry would be lost if played on two pianos unisono."

For a summer excursion, the Moscheles explore the Hartz Mountains in all directions. He writes:—"Certainly many of the tavern pianos and small organs are afflicted with consumption, but try them I must, and everywhere there is a cantor, an organist, or at least a waiter or a Geheimrath, who listens with due astonishment, not to mention the fair sex, occasionally rather plain." At Alexisbad Moscheles is most cordially received by the Duchess of Bernburg, and meets with a no less friendly welcome at Meiningen. In reference to an excursion to the "Altenstein," Moscheles says:—"As I was alone with the Duke in the carriage, our conversation took a practical turn, and he commissioned me to send him one of our best pupils from the Conservatoire, to teach his youngest daughter. Another good berth for some one."

Shortly after his return to Leipzig, Moscheles writes:—"Few of the pianists appearing at the Gewandhaus this year have found favor with the critical Leipzigers; on one or two occasions their disapproval has been most discourteously expressed. Hisses should be tabooed; have them if you must, in the theatre, but they are out of place in the concert-room. I found Schumann's Overture to the 'Bride of Messina,' at the second hearing, full of power, character, and passion; but the audience, although it numbered many of Schumann's friends, was divided in its appreciation of the work.

"For my own special benefit, and to acquire that particular style, I play Liszt's new Concert solo, the Paganini Studies, and other modern things. As for Liszt I made a fine mistake the other day. Just before he came in, I had received Scudo's book, which had been sent me from Paris. I asked him, 'Do you know this? The first article I see bears your name.' 'Yes; it gives me some very hard raps,' said he, laughing, and began to read aloud the author's attacks. I had expected eulogy, and was at first alarmed, but soon laughed with him."

During the latter part of the year, much uncertainty prevailed among David's friends as to whether he would continue to act as Concertmeister in Leipzig, or would accept an appointment at Cologne. The first létter that Moscheles pens in 1852 mentions the subject: "The best news that the new year could bring is the certainty that we keep our David here. You know he threatened seriously to migrate to Cologne; he has now come to terms with the authorities, who have not only lightened his labors but increased his salary. Ferdinand Hiller, who is at Paris, will, it is said, return to Cologne—another gain for Germany."

# CHAPTER XXXII.

## 1852.

Madame Sontag—The Bach Society—St. Matthew's Passion—Otto Goldschmidt--Complaints About the Conservatoire—Moscheles and his Pupils—Silencing a troublesome Neighbor—The Tannhäuser—Berlioz's Music—Moscheles as Player and Lecturer—Modern Pianists—A Magnificent Gift—Vacation in Saxon Switzerland.

"SONTAG appeared this winter in Leipzig," writes Moscheles; "a little older, a little less sylph-like, but lovely, kind, and unassuming, her voice still well-preserved, and her execution faultless. The growing enthusiasm for her completely upsets the good people of Leipzig—they are quite intoxicated; she is triumphant everywhere, and the students gave her a torch-procession on her way home from the theatre. We have seen her in all her great parts; the voice is still perfectly sufficient for our small Leipzig house. Comparisons are odious, but, charmed as I was, I could not forget, when looking at her quiet lady-like acting, the intense fervor of Jenny Lind, the excessive passion of Malibran. How ungrateful a creature is man! I am delighted when I hear her sing my 'Lieder,' which she does to perfection and 'con amore.' I am now composing a bravura piece for her; it was suggested thus: I frequently play to her, and the other day when she heard my Fantasia on Hungarian airs, she was so pleased with one of the melodies that she said: 'I would like to sing that; do write me some variations on it, Moscheles.' Her wishes are commands, and so I am busy inventing something impossible in the bravura line." Shortly afterwards she left for Dresden, and Moscheles writes: "All Leipzig is still mad about her, people think and talk of nothing else; they nearly forget to start the railway trains and to wind up the church clocks." After she had sung in Weimar, there appeared in the *Neue Zeitschrift für Musik* an article making a furious onslaught on Sontag, who was described as the "Sorceress of Song" (Gesang-Nixe). Jenny Lind also came in for her share of depreciation. This attack brought no good to Weimar; for Count Rossi wrote to the Grand Duke, enclosing the article, and explaining that his wife would never again perform where she had been so misrepresented. She must revoke her promise, lately given, to sing for a charity at Weimar. Sontag took the matter lightly, adding: "They not only cry down my singing, but my personal appearance as well; they give me not only false teeth, but a sham throat into the bargain."

"I cannot always agree with the Bach Society; my proposition to publish the first volume with pianoforte accompaniment was outvoted; I think that village schoolmasters, and ignoramuses unable to decipher a score, ought to become acquainted with Bach by means of the pianoforte edition. . . . . The old music-room, in which Sebastian had his practices with the pupils, has been rebuilt, and I attended the inauguration, where there was four-part singing under Hauptmann's direction—the old portrait of Bach, which has been carefully restored, seemed to preside over our meeting. One of the pupils made an admirable oration. On Good Friday the 'St. Matthew Passion' was performed. I am deeply moved by the work," says Moscheles, "and have published my impressions of this most magnificent music in the *Deutsche Allgemeine*. But what are words? Those double choruses, interspersed with majestic chorales, the moment when Peter 'weeps bitterly' at his own treachery, the air in C minor, 'Ich will bei meinem Jesu wachen'—in fact, one and all of the numbers —how inadequate our praise must be! You must hear it all at the first opportunity. Schneider sang the Evangelist's part admirably, the other singers, with Rietz and David in the orchestra—all were equal to their great task. . . . . When you read this, and see me so deeply immersed in art, you will hardly expect me to give my opinion on bank-shares, government securities, and the like. It is just as if I called on you to give me your opinion upon a score; please act for me in these matters. I gladly put myself into your hands. Talking of our friends, do you know that one of your fellow-citizens, Otto Goldschmidt, has had the good fortune to marry our great artiste, Jenny Lind? He has won a great prize, and she has given her hand to a man of high honor; he is a thorough musician, and aspires to all that is best and purest in art."

Foremost among Moscheles' most loyal and devoted pupils in the Conservatoire were J. O. Grimm, Radecke, the brothers Brassin, Gernsheim, von Sahr, Jadassohn, Mertel, etc.; with such as these he delighted to draw on the past years of his artistic experience, hoping to steep their minds in the traditions of his own school. Always conscientious in his duties as a teacher, he was naturally impatient of interference. "To-day," he says, "I have spoken freely my mind—I must insist on my classes adhering to the readings and 'Tempi' as I give them myself. . . . . What am I to say to this? One of my lady pupils, on the examination day, plays a posthumous manuscript Study in F major by Mendelssohn, a work entirely new to me; on this occasion I learn quite by chance that there still remains among Mendelssohn's papers much that is of artistic value, and yet I and a few others were selected specially by his widow to look through the posthumous works, with a view to their publication. So a favored pupil is allowed the privilege of playing an unheard work of Mendelssohn's before I know even of its existence!"

This year the summer vacation is spent in Saxon Switzerland. "We arrived late in the evening at Tetschen, hungry and tired to death, and ordered supper in our room; but oh, misery! the sound of a piano suddenly breaks upon us! Just imagine, only a thin door between me and Weber's 'Invitation a la Valse,' strummed by an unpracticed hand, and drawled out (to quote Mendelssohn) as 'a slow Presto.' I rang the bell, and frightened the abigail with: 'Who is playing there?' 'Oh, only a young man who, being engaged all day long in business, usually plays for a couple of hours of an evening.' 'A delightful prospect this!' thought I. I tried to eat, but that was impossible, so, without saying a word to my astonished family, I seized my hat, rushed out, and knocked at my neighbor's door. The 'come in' brought me face to face with the innocent delinquent. Assuming an air of feigned politeness, I began the conversation: 'Your playing has allured me, a perfect stranger, and I venture to call. I play a little too and happen to have studied that identical piece; would you like to hear my reading of it?" I went straight to the piano—the young man, quite abashed, made way for me—and without waiting for his answer, I dashed through the piece in the wildest style and at a tearing pace, introducing double octaves wherever I could get them in; this had its effect. 'Alas!' he said, with a sigh, 'I shall certainly never play it like that!' 'Why not?' replied I, 'if you work hard, but—good evening to you!' My object was attained; my nightly tormentor became mute, whether for ever I can't say—at all events, I could eat and sleep in peace. My wife and children, with their ears close to the wall, listened and enjoyed the joke immensely."

In October, Moscheles hears the "Tannhäuser," given in Dresden under Reissiger's direction: "I was often surprised both by the peculiarities of the composer's genius and his original instrumentation; on the whole, however, I still feel as I did after hearing 'Lohengrin.' There are too many recitatives, too much that is fragmentary, in fact monotony, the result of shapelessness. In saying this I bear in mind passages full of genius and surprising effects; but heart and soul are not warmed by being so overloaded with passionate music."

In November Moscheles goes to Weimar, there to make acquaintance with another novelty—Berlioz's music. "Berlioz was very cordially received, his desk was wreathed with laurels; my expectations were not at a high pitch but he certainly has surpassed them. A great deal is no doubt over eccentric and disconnected, but there is much that is grandly conceived and carried out. In the 'Faust,' his introduction of the Rákoczy March is electrifying; this was repeated, as well as the soldier's song, and the waltz. The music given to Queen Mab in 'Romeo and Juliet,' is not only effective and charming, but worthy of being placed by the side of Mendelssohn's works of a similar kind. Berlioz's conducting inspired the orchestra with fire and enthusiasm, he carried everything as it were by storm; I am glad to have made acquaintance with him, both as a composer and conductor."

Next day, Moscheles, Berlioz, and Liszt are invited to

dine with the Dowager Grand-Duchess, and adjourn in the evening to the Theatre, where Liszt conducts a performance of Berlioz's opera of "Benvenuto Cellini." "I was delighted by the flow of melody, and the occasionally very discreet instrumentation; a great deal, however, I find obscure, and the finale, the 'Carnival at Rome,' completely unintelligible. The audience generally was in favor of the music, although there was nothing encored. Berlioz was called for after every act. After the opera, we all met at Liszt's, it was a most interesting evening, and Berlioz was hero of it. I had much conversation with him; he is a great thinker."

At a social union of the Leipzig Professors, Moscheles appeared in the twofold character of player and lecturer. First of all he played Beethoven's Sonata, op. 53, and afterwards prefaced his rendering of the solo Fantasia, op. 77, by some remarks about its origin and character. "This Fantasia," he said, "is rhapsodical, eccentric, and on that account but little known among musical connoisseurs. It seems to me as if Beethoven had wished to represent himself in this work as sitting down unprepared, and perhaps in a very bad humor, to the instrument, and then roving about without a plan in the kingdom of his fancies. I myself occasionally heard him play in such a fashion, and whenever I hear this Fantasia such moments involuntarily recur to my mind."

The winter brings a number of modern pianists. "One plays in a style cold and clear as a bright December night, and just as frosty; another, with his crashing chords, shakes, and arpeggios, is really too merciless on my unfortunate Erard, which is not only beaten out of tune, but somehow or other has been severely injured. I know the culprit; with such handling how could it be otherwise?" The damage could not be repaired in Leipzig, and Moscheles in great straits wrote to the Erards for advice. "Should he send the injured part to Cologne or Paris? How long must he be kept waiting without his Erard?" "Not long," was the obliging answer; "just long enough for one of our best grand pianos to be sent to you; you have had yours for seven or eight years already; since those days we have made great improvements, and you ought to have our very best instrument." Moscheles, all gratitude and delight at receiving this answer, eagerly looked forward to the arrival of the piano, a noble gift, and doubly valued as coming from his old friend, Pierre Erard.

# CHAPTER XXXIII.

## 1853.

The New Erard—The Bach Society—Franz von Holstein—Visit to Italy—Scene in a Church of the Tyrol—Zither and Vocal Concert Residence at Venice—A Musical Adventure—Carl Werner—Serenade Per Canale—Festa di San Rocco—Milan—The Musical Conservatoire—Fumagalli—The Teatro Radegonda—Lake of Como—Visit to Pasta—Zurich—A Musical Treasure—Liszt—Dr. Reclam—Brahm's Compositions.

"THERE are sundry novelties this winter," writes Moscheles. "Gade, conductor of the Gewandhaus Concerts, has produced his Symphony with an obligato part for the pianoforte; the instrumentation of the work is beautiful, but the addition of pianoforte a useless innovation, as the band drowns it. The next new thing is Schumann's impetuous overture to 'Julius Cæsar,' but the newest of the new is my Erard, with which I am intensely delighted. It has the power of an organ and the softness of a flute, with a touch light enough even to satisfy me. As for the lovely case, I think of Schiller's words: 'In dem schönen Körper mus auch eine schöne Seele wohnen'—'In a beautiful body must dwell a beautiful soul.' Really I can act upon it as upon a kindred spirit, and slowly spin out the tone as upon a stringed instrument, and that, too, without using the loud pedal; as for the soft pedal I do not require it to produce a pianissimo, and can rely solely on my touch. No wonder I celebrate the new arrival by inviting all my friends to hear it." Afterwards, when the old instrument is sent back, Moscheles writes in the following lugubrious strain: "My faithful harmonious friend, how sorry I am to part with him! We feel as though some loved being were leaving us. I looked out from my window and saw 'my friend' carted away from our door: did I see a coffin instead of a piano? Cheer up, 'Le roi est mort, vive le roi!'"

With regard to the Bach Society Moscheles writes: "I

have sent in my resignation, because at a conference with the two Härtels, Hauptmann, Becker, and Otto Jahn, a proposal was made by the latter and adopted, that Becker should edit the pianoforte music. Under the circumstances I considered myself of little further use on the Committee, and so I told my colleagues ; all the more zealously, however, have I worked at Bach's newly published Concerto (with violin and flute parts added), for I have been particularly requested to play it with the full band at the Gewandhaus Concert, and not as I had intended previously at the Chamber Concerts. . . . . I examined a new pupil for the Conservatoire, Franz von Holstein, formerly an officer in the army ; his fingers are not flexible, but he seems to have much talent, and wishes to devote himself exclusively to music." *

"Athens on the Pleisse" (as it is often called) is besieged by artists who concentrate their fire on the Hotel Moscheles. "All who fail to secure engagements at the Gewandhaus wish to drag me into the Scylla of their woes, while I try to escape this as well as the Charybdis of their médisance. How refreshing after this to find all our troubles and joys shared by our dear friends the Geibels, in whose house we live, our two families almost merging into one.

The Moscheles this summer carry out their long projected scheme of visiting Italy—taking the Tyrol on their way. An amusing incident occurs at Gries, a village in the Tyrol. One bright Sunday morning they entered the prettily decorated church, and saw a number of neatly-dressed peasants, who were all engaged in devotion ; apparently some "festa" was going on. Moscheles found his way to the organ loft. The organist was in the act of playing the "Kyrie ;" Moscheles slipped behind him, placed his fingers between the organist's, and taking up the organ part at the correct point, quietly ousted the surprised player. However anxious the poor man might at first have been at the intrusion of a stranger, he soon became reconciled, dictating to him what came next in the service, telling him when

* Franz von Holstein has lately achieved great successes throughout Germany with his opera, 'Die Haideschacht,' and other works.

to prelude, when to accompany the "Gloria," etc. At a particular moment the organist had to resume his seat, which the other vacated, bidding him "good-bye." "Do not leave me without telling me who you are," said his newly-acquired friend to Moscheles, who wrote his name on the music. The effect was half comic, half pathetic; our organist, at the sight of the name, was fain to throw himself on Moscheles' neck; his hands, however, were not at liberty to leave the key-board for an instant. Before he had finished his duties Moscheles had disappeared, and was on the point of entering his carriage (all this happening while the horses were being changed), when his enthusiastic friend rushed after him, and gave him the long-delayed embrace. 15th July.—"The constant rain disappointed us yesterday of our intended walk, so we allowed ourselves to be enticed to a 'Zither' and vocal concert, that was said to be national, and was not enough so for our taste. The costume was Tyrolese, the zithers also; but the worm of modern music had gnawed its way into the healthy Tyrolese fruit. We had to endure in the first part some pieces of 'Martha,' all kinds of waltzes, and a 'Strapazier Polka;' we ran off before the second part began."

The travellers are next at Venice, where they stay a month in the Palazzo Mocenigo, once occupied by no less a personage than Lord Byron. The house belongs to the Contessa Mocenigo; portraits of her ancestors, the Doges, are painted by Giambellino on the ceilings. "The Countess is a picture herself; when she steps majestically into her richly-ornamented gondola, and seats herself on her gilded chair, her old servant preceding her with her breviary, we all rush to our balcony to see this embarkation—the scene carries us back to bygone ages. I have a good piano, which probably acquires a fictitious brilliancy from standing on a marble floor. Need I say that the very atmosphere breathed by Byron—the lagoon, the palaces, the moon shining down on St. Marc's, mirrored on the silvery waters—all these bright visions and associations make my improvisations run glibly from my fingers.". . . . . Again Moscheles writes: "I had much wished to make myself acquainted with the state of music and its professors here; but I find on all sides shallowness and mediocrity.

The 'Teatro Fenice' is closed, so also is the 'San Samuele.' The wandering musicians, who play in the Piazza of St. Marc or in eating houses, for small coin payment, are more deafening than animating; the tone, however, of both men and women violinists has often something piquant about it, reminding one of the style of Paganini, by which I mean that the Leipzig Schneckenberg resembles Mont Blanc. At sunset we hear from the Palazzo Foscari (now a barrack) the shrill trumpet signals, which grate harshly on our ears, although the canal lies between us; we hear, too, the gondolieri of the neighboring 'Traghetto' singing with their pretty, soft voices their vapid Barcaroles; we are also favored sometimes with a jingle of guitar and piano, with stale, hackneyed 'fioriture,' which I don't like half as well as good fritture.' The only good music we have is that of the Austrian military band, which plays three evenings in the week on the Piazza of St. Marc. Now let me tell you of my musical adventure. On walking through one of the back-streets I hear some showy pianoforte playing. 'Oho! Oho! that—that is no amateur, but a professional hand.' I pull the bell, and ask boldly if "Il Professore di Cembalo sia di casa?' 'Si, Signore,' is the answer, and I am soon conducted into a room, where a man of some thirty years of age is playing a Bravura Mazurka by Fumagalli, the beginning of which I had heard below; near the player sits a young Abbé. I make him understand by signs that I am anxious not to interrupt him. When he has finished, I ask, 'Will you give me lessons?' and he consents. He now plays Fumagalli's 'Carnovale di Piu,' making all kinds of brilliant skips and octave passages; I repeatedly interrupt him with a 'bravissimo.' After this I am called on to try the instrument, and both teacher and Abbé follow my improvisation with increasing interest; afterwards the pianist in a state of great perplexity, asks, 'Whose pupil are you?' 'Moscheles'!' 'Ah! I know that famous name.' 'Do you also know his compositions?' 'In Venice we don't play such serious music.' 'What music do you choose for your regular art-studies?' 'Generally speaking, the arrangements from favorite operas.' 'I will play to you a study by Moscheles,' said I, and chose the chromatic one in D major. On my rising to leave, he stopped me, 'You don't want lessons from me, that is clear, only I hope you will tell me your name; mine is Carlo Fortunati.' When I gave him my own name, he embraced me with all the impetuosity of a Southerner, and rained kisses and epithets on me; so we parted as musical friends, and shall often meet in that capacity. The Abbé too is a musical enthusiast."

"Fortunati comes, occasionally as a hearer, sometimes, too, as a player. When he brought the overture to Verdi's 'Nabucco' arranged as a pianoforte duet, to try it over with Serena, she lost all patience with his inability to keep time, while at every claptrap rhythm he exclaimed exultingly, 'Oh! che bella sinfonia!'" During their stay at Venice the Moscheles became acquainted with the famous water-color painter, Carl Werner, whose works, and whose studio, with its rich decorations and art treasures, were so celebrated, and he and his gifted pupil Passini became frequent visitors at the Palazzo Mocenigo. . . . . "Yesterday there was a 'Serenata per Canale.' A great wooden vessel, gayly decked with red and white cloth, and illuminated with two pyramids festooned with lamps, floats down the canal when night begins to set in; it is large enough to receive a complete orchestra, two grand pianos, and solo performers; there is singing and flute, fiddle and pianoforte playing, but all in the commonest Italian hum-drum style, nothing for the musically-cultivated ear, everything for the beauty-loving eye; Bengal lights illuminating the canal, a complete scene out of the Arabian Nights. The brilliant vessel is closely surrounded by black gondolas; four gondolas take it in tow, and its course is often impeded by the small craft. We enjoyed the sight, first from our own balcony, then from the Rialto. . . . . On the eve of the 'Festa di San Rocco' a 'Musica a Grand Orchestra' was performed at the church; but how? Pretty waltzes and polkas were played upon the organ, then a fugue full of discordant fifths and octaves, with occasional utterances from a priest's hoarse voice at the high altar, and the tones of a wheezy and discordant organ! The Director marked each rhythm by thrashing his desk as heartily as the poor saint may have been beaten in his lifetime, often drowning the sharp metallic ring of the orchestra, and murdering the effect of the solo, which was sung by a fine tenor, with the usual 'tremolando.' Occasionally the clapping of hands, like castanets, but oftener like the crack of a postillion's whip, was heard in the midst of music. The beautiful marble pillars of the unhappy church were veiled under a covering of red damask, large wax candles dimly lighted up the oppressive atmosphere, and the olfactory nerves suffered from snuff and garlic, which rose in clouds from the dense crowd."

From Venice the Moscheles proceed, viâ Mantua and Brescia, to Milan. There Moscheles visits the Musical Conservatoire, "originally a cloister, now half barrack, half school for young musicians. The Professors show me great respect, my 'Studies' are adopted, that is all they know of my music, of Beethoven or Mendelssohn they know absolutely nothing. I played them my 'Grande Valse' in order to give them a little of our German Bravura. Fumagalli played a song by Gordigiani, 'O santissima Vergine Maria,' very gracefully; afterwards he displayed great powers of execution and novel effects in his 'Carnevale di Più,' which in humor and dash is not inferior to Paganini's. The Teatro Radegonda has a second-rate theatre band, and singers for the most part rough and untrained; the prompter, not hidden as elsewhere, occasionally joins in the fray, the good voices are often shipwrecked in the howling storm of the finales, but at that certain passage where the prima donna steps forward with outstretched arms and rolling eyes, the public applauds vehemently. The opera was 'Luisa Miller' by Verdi; it has no overture, only some hackneyed ideas, screaming noise, and here and there one or two good vocal effects, which barely sufficed to keep me awake."

A visit to Pasta, is next recorded. "This famous 'Cantatrice' lives in a small house adjoining her own villa, on the lake of Como. Close to the door we stumbled on some prosaic matters—dirty saucepans, kitchen utensils, and the like, not to mention the leavings of an early dinner. Amid this debris sat three unkempt girls, not one of them in love with soap and water. At my bidding one of them took in our cards, and the great lady soon appeared. We did not see her at her best, for having just risen from her siesta in which we had disturbed her, she was only half awake. We found her very friendly, and evidently gratified with our visit. Her mouth and teeth are still lovely, the great eyes full of fire, her black hair was in a dishevelled state, and her dress an extremely original medley of oddities. She never ceased talking of old times, and told us she had given up living in the villa, because both her mother and her husband had died there. She afterwards wrote something for our albums, and gave us some beautiful flowers." . . . .

After exploring the Lago Maggiore, etc., the Borromean Islands, etc., Moscheles finds his way to Zurich, where he calls on the son of his old friend Nageli. "He possesses a treasure," says Moscheles, "in the manuscript of Bach's B minor Mass, of which his father became possessed, through Schwenke, in Hamburg. I made him show it to me, and have no doubt of its genuineness. The Bach Society of Leipzig would gladly have purchased it from him, but he stoutly refused to part with it. Besides this he possesses a still unpublished Concerto for four pianos by Bach ; it is in the key of A minor."

Immediately after the return to Leipzig, we find Moscheles receiving Liszt at the Conservatoire. "He seemed satisfied with the performance of the pupils, and spoke kindly and encouragingly to them, but would not play before them ; that was a great disappointment. At David's we heard him play a pianoforte arrangement of his Fantasia on the 'Prophet,' originally written for the organ. Häns v. Bülow played the pedal part in the bass. The first and last movements consist of violent and stormy Fugues ; I prefer the middle one with its quieter subject. He also played his very piquant waltz in A flat major, introducing many overstrained effects by first using the soft pedal, and then suddenly introducing strongly accentuated notes."

In a letter of the 28th Sept. we read: "To-day I write to you during the examination of our 118 pupils, who must one and all be heard in the course of this week! The Directors and Professors sit as judges, the former have their little chat occasionally, the latter, when their own pupils are not playing, while away the time as best they can, David is drawing, I am writing. . . . . I am going through several things: Czerny's op. 800, 'Gradus ad Parnassum' with difficulties well adapted to the hand, but now out of date ; Liszt's 'Rhapsodie Hongroise,' interesting as a faithful transcription of national music; I even try to take off Fumagalli in his 'Carnevale di Più' .... There is some first-rate work in Grützmacher's trio." "Our friend F., with his bumptious ways, is particularly offensive to me; he, like so many others, comes to me for advice, advice meaning praise. How infinitely superior to such professionals are amateurs of the stamp of Frau B.! Her performance of my 'Concert Pathétique' was so good, that I took to playing the piece again myself. To the best of my belief, it is not only in advance of my former compositions in form and style, but a maturer work, and yet it has remained comparatively unnoticed!"

.... "The heavens mourn in sackcloth and ashes; am I to do so likewise, because Eastern affairs seem threatening, or because I am laid up with a bad knee? No, let the contending Powers keep guard over Europe's equilibrium, leave me to my musical nursery, and let Dr. Reclam look out for my knee. I believe that, with his electro-galvanic apparatus, he has hit upon the right remedy to cure me. With my fingers and my advice I can still make myself useful, for the pupils come to my house, and I play a great deal."

Dr. Reclam's treatment rapidly proved effective, he himself became Moscheles' life-long friend, attending him and his family with skill and devotion. Frau Reclam, one of the best interpreters of sacred music in Leipzig, was a frequent visitor at Moscheles' house, and delighted him with her artistic rendering of his songs.

To return to the diary: "Brahm's compositions are of a really elevated character, and Schumann, whom he has chosen as his model, recommends him as the 'Messiah of Music.' I find him, like Schumann, often piquant, but occasionally too labored. Even Beethoven's music was objected to, people say, when it first appeared, as being too far-fetched, and difficult to understand. True it is, that Beethoven's genius lured him away to paths never trodden before, which are not accessible to every one, and yet since that time it has been proved, that he not only sought but found what he wished to express in music. Let us hope that this also may be the lot of the younger composer. B.'s technical powers, his reading from sight, do him and his teacher Edward Marxsen great credit. . . . I have heard a good deal of Berlioz, and give him my closest attention. My opinion of his music remains unshaken, I acknowledge his merit, but cannot always understand him—or is such music as the 'Witches' Sabbath,' not meant to be understood? Curious! one now listens again with pleasure to the simple opera, 'Doctor und Apotheker,' by Dittersdorf, in which Behr and Schneider sing and act so admirably; one forgets, how Rossini, in his 'Tell,' and Meyerbeer in his 'Roberto,' have crammed us with their loaded instrumentation and scenic effects, and how Wagner has gone beyond both. Les extrêmes se touchent."

The end of the year was marked by the happy event of Moscheles' second daughter becoming engaged to Dr. George Rosen, at that time Prussian Consul at Jerusalem. Congratulations from friends contrast sadly with reflections confided to the diary, on the death of Cécile Mendelssohn, the great musician's devoted lover.

## CHAPTER XXXIV.

### 1854—1855.

Madame Lind Goldschmidt—Fritz Gernsheim—Musical Critics—Abortive Works—Asiatic Music—David—Music of the Future—Schindler and Ferdinand Hiller—Summer Holidays—Munich—The Theatre—Fraulein Seebach—Evening at the Schaffrath—Rauch—Pianos in the Exhibition—Egern—Rubinstein—Arabella Goddard—Public Appearances—Mendelssohn's Reformation Symphony.

AN event, that was joyfully welcomed by all of us at Leipzig, was the appearance here of the Lind-Goldschmidts, for the first time since their marriage. Madame Lind-Goldschmidt sang for the 'Pension Fund,' and was our star at the Subscription Concert. She can tone down her glorious voice to a pianissimo whisper, and the sound, however attenuated, is distinctly audible in the remotest corner of the Concert room; she is wonderfully versatile. After astounding every one with her 'fioriture,' and stirring all hearts with her deeply expressive singing, she becomes at once exquisitely naïve and sings a 'Kinderlied' by Taubert, or the 'Sonnenschein,' in a style that makes her hearers feel young again. Goldschmidt played us a great deal of beautiful music; in Chopin's Concerto, Mendelssohn's 'Variations Sérieuses,' a prelude by Bach and some drawing-room pieces, he proved himself a genuine artist, earnest and thoughtful, with no straining for show or effect I was so glad to be able to be of service to him, and to prove my great respect and esteem for him by lending him my Erard piano."

Again we read: "We have passed some delightful hours with the Goldschmidts, meeting them at a family dinner, and at a matinée given by Preusser, where Otto Goldschmidt played his trio, a well-written, clear, and melodious composition, which gave me great pleasure. The Goldschmidts paid us a visit at the Conservatoire, and seemed perfectly satisfied with the performances of the pupils, especially that of the youthful Fritz Gernsheim, who highly distinguished himself in Mendelssohn's Serenade and Allegro. Madame Goldschmidt repeatedly expressed her esteem for an institution to which her husband owed his musical education; and this she did not only in words, but in songs as well, for she sang Mendelssohn's Psalm, 'Hear my prayer,' so exquisitely that none who heard it can ever forget the impression she created."

"I am sorry to say there are many students here who, instead of employing their time in the study of composition, abuse it by writing pungent criticisms for the musical press, a practice which always reminds me of Mendelssohn's words: 'Why on earth do they talk and write so much? let them compose good music instead!' I doubt if he would have found much good music in the pieces so full of splenetic moanings that I am occasionally compelled to listen to. What would he have said of the pupil who ordered music-paper with forty staves to write an opera upon? I failed to discover in the forty lines four thoughts! . . . . Hauptmann, it seems, endorses my opinion; the other day he wrote to the following effect: 'The results of the method of study adopted by Mr. —— are shown in his progressive aptitude for obscurity and confusion!' . . . . A new Sonata, thirty-two pages long! but it does not inspire me. What chaos! Thoughts, ambitious ones, occasionally glimmer through the darkness, but the whole region is as dreary as a churchyard with all its slabs and tombstones turned topsy-turvy by a shock of earthquake. Grinning skulls stare out of the open graves, among them one of a strictly orthodox contrapuntist, who seems to scoff at all the sacrilegious Italian roulades. The corpses of the women begin their witches' howl! When I went to bed I felt completely stunned, and passed a restless night—perhaps I should have done better, if I had sat up all night smoking, and sipping coffee, to recover my equilibrium."

A letter from Mrs. George Rosen, giving her father an account of the state of music in Jerusalem, elicits the following answer: "The unrefined Asiatic music, with its dreamy monotones such as you describe, certainly contrasts strangely with our own fixed canons of art, which are so diametrically opposed to theirs. To the natives I grant this style may be just as interesting as Handel or Mendelssohn is to us; very likely they would be bored by the 'Eroica' Symphony. But even the European ladies who reside near you, and do not get beyond a song or chorale, are characteristic in their way. They will find it a difficult matter to soar up to the regions of Beethoven's latest works, whereas our young Germany already considers this hero as 'rococo,' and spreading its wings, strives to soar to higher regions above."

"I heard 'Don Juan' the other night; Miterwurzer was admirable. I am glad to say that, instead of the dialogues, we had the original Recitatives, and the stupid scene with the messengers of justice was cut out. As often as I hear this opera, and think of the 'music of the future,' I feel as if I had suddenly emerged from a dark wood, where toads and hobgoblins make a hideous concert, and was coming forth into the sunny light of day, and Apollo playing me heavenly melodies. . . . . David withdraws from the direction of the Gewandhaus Concerts, and resumes his duties as Concertmeister. The rude attacks made upon him in the public papers are so irritating that I think he is perfectly justified in declining to expose himself any more to such annoyances. I have a fellow-feeling for him in this matter, and when we discussed the subject yesterday, I handed him Schindler's lately published pamphlet, 'On the Development of Pianoforte playing since Clementi,' in which I am very roughly handled. His egotism is the chief feature throughout; it is '*I*' perpetually; 'Clementi, Cramer, Beethoven, and *I*' worked together for the promotion and welfare of art. 'Hummel and Moscheles have perverted pianoforte-playing. The latter (says he) has actually had the audacity to set to metronome Tempi works of Beethoven, *whom he never heard play*'—he, Schindler, has already paid him out properly for this. He makes a dead set at Liszt, who facetiously prays for a respite of three years, that he may learn to do better, Schindler allows him four, but these having now expired, he announces that he gives him up. . . . Ferdinand Hiller published a letter to Schindler in reply, in which he showed to demonstration the absurdity of his pretending to be the intimate friend of Beethoven, and asked him, "if he ever got so far in his whole life, as to be able to play Cramer's first Study? Can he show him a single trace anywhere of any one composition by Schlinder? or has he, as a conductor, a past history only known to himself? What are his claims to the position of Beethoven's Stadtholder and alter ego?" Hiller concludes with Goethe's words, "Nur die Lumpen sind bescheiden," (None but good-for-nothings are modest), therefore pray discard all modesty, and enlighten on the subject your, so far as possible, humble servant, F. HILLER."

"Meanwhile I employ myself," says Moscheles, "writing Cadenzas for Beethoven's Concertos, which Sneff intends to publish. Of course, self-reliant artists, able to write for themselves, have no need of these; they can follow their own inspirations. I hope, however, to make myself useful to less gifted executants. . . . .

"I have lately seen some remarkable title-pages to pianoforte pieces: 'Le Torrent'—let that pass, because it is a veritable shower-bath of notes; but others, 'From the Highlands,' 'Sunset,' 'Storm,' etc., are mere misnomers. If you give a title at all, let it cap the subject as the dot caps the 'i;' otherwise, I would much rather draw the stroke as through the 't.'"

Moscheles was only too glad to spend his summer holidays in Munich, where his son Felix was pursuing his art studies. "Such a bustle and hurry here!" he writes; "all the world topsy-turvy and Exhibition mad! It rains cats and dogs, as even the visitors to the Exhibition find to their cost, although they fancy they are safe in their promenade under the big glass dome. We have one half-ounce sunshine to a pound of rain—that's about the proportion. In spite of some drawbacks, however, we have great enjoyment; the galleries, museums, etc., are a constant resource, and well may the Munich theatre boast of its 'model performances;' there is a galaxy of all the grand actors in Germany, who condescend by turns to fill the smallest parts in the pieces represented. You can fancy what it is to hear a man like Devrient make something out of nothing, and invest even a third-rate part with dignity. A few evenings since we heard Fräulein Seebach read 'Hamlet' in Kaulbach's house. She is an enthusiastic student of Shakespeare, and every inch an artist. After the reading was over we danced, and I had the honor of a waltz with Madame Kaulbach; it was only due to me because I resigned myself to polka-playing for the universal good."

Moscheles describes an evening at the artists' club-house (Schaffrath): "There was a special ceremony in honor of old Rauch, who was presented with a diploma and greeted with tremendous cheers. In spite of his seventy-one years, he is most dignified and graceful in his ways; amid foaming beer cans and thick clouds of tobacco, I made the acquaintance of all the celebrated painters here. . . . I leave the newspapers to tell you all particulars about the Exhibition; I report only of my special department—the pianos. The Commissioners allow me to try them before the public are admitted, but, however early I come in the building, I find 'their fond fathers' collected together out of the different provinces of Germany. Their name is legion, but I must notice a Klems from Düsseldorf as being marked by Clara Schumann, and André's so-called Mozart-Clavier from Frankfort. The specialties of the different instruments I discover without any difficulty, and endeavor by my treatment to bring into relief all the best points of each. You know my old saying, 'A good rider should be able to sit any horse.'"

To escape the dangers of cholera, which broke out in Munich, Moscheles and his family withdrew to Egern on the Tegernsee, where they were joined by many of their distinguished friends; among them were Baron Liebig, Professor Seibold, Stieler, David, and Bodenstedt, the well-known translator of Shakespeare's sonnets. "That dreadful cholera," Moscheles writes, "has happily as yet not reached this beautiful little spot; it is only a pity that the mountains have the bad habit occasionally, of putting on their cloudcaps and weeping over their own ugliness. To-day umbrellas are no good at all, the puddles more like wells, but in fine weather we boat on the lake, scramble up the mountains, plunge into cow-keepers' cottages, demand pancakes, sing four-part songs, and laugh in unison. If the grasshoppers only knew that we, like them, are musical, they would perhaps give us a little less chirping. . . Mierdel, Jule, and Liese, with their dark head-gear and blonde complexions, and brown feet, do double duty as models for Felix and my teachers of national songs, which I note down as being extremely pretty. Bodenstedt has written some words for me; I have set these to music, and his wife (our prima donna) sings them." This song—"Wenn der Frühling auf die Berge steigt"—has become very popular in Germany.

Leipzig.—"Rubinstein, whom we heard fourteen years ago in London as a prodigy, appeared now as a composer of a Symphony, which he has named 'Ocean.' The clearness of the first movement had the same soothing effect on me as a calm unruffled summer sea; afterwards, however, we had all the storming and roaring that are now the fashion, and the boisterous elements became so hopelessly incomprehensible that my thoughts could find no anchorage in their unfathomable harmonic depths. I fully recognize, however, in Rubinstein a pre-eminent talent for composition. In his Concerto there are true beauties and high flights of imagination; here and there are to be found outrageous extravagances; his shorter movements, generally speaking, are to be commended for their rational form; in power and execution he is inferior to no one. Rubinstein's features and short irrepressible hair remind me of Beethoven; I delight in his simplicity and sincerity; he is always a welcome visitor at our house, and so also is our young friend Arabella Goddard. In her very young days I heard her play in Paris, and prophesied for her at that time a brilliant future; I think events have proved the clearness of my prophetic vision. Miss Goddard conquers enormous difficulties with consummate grace and ease, her touch is clear and pure as a bell. Here, as everywhere, she found that recognition which not even the severest art critic could withhold. . . . . I will spare you the infliction of my politics, which bear the same relation to yours as an engraving to an oil-picture. I will only add that I am pleased with the attitude of Austria, and that the King of Prussia and I are animated with the same feelings for the unity of Germany. May the Emperor of Russia learn to feel that baths in the free mouth of the Danube are more effective than blood-baths! With this wish, I speed the parting year!"

"Spohr's Symphony for double orchestra, 'Irdisches

und Göttliches,' has a subject worthy of a Beethoven; but the artificial construction cramps the free outpour of feeling. . . . . It was remarkable in the Gewandhaus yesterday that, after the stormy overtures to the 'Fliegende Hollander,' not a single hand was raised to applaud, not even a single hiss heard. There is a great deal of 'Geist' in the music, but it is of the scorching kind, and to me such masses of instrumentation and such a piling up of diminished sevenths and discords of all kinds, are distracting and joyless. Gluck, no doubt, has his musical demons, and Mozart his hell in 'Don Juan,' but they do not give one a headache; and yet the papers will maintain that, just as Beethoven's latest works were not immediately understood, so it will take time to become familiar with Wagner. . . . Every performance of Beethoven's overture in C, op. 115, is especially interesting to me, for it reminds me of the old Vienna days, when Beethoven lent it me in manuscript for one of my concerts. Yesterday it went splendidly."

In writing to his relatives, Moscheles alludes to the severe illness of his son Felix, who was confined to the house for several months: "Sickness still hovers over our house like a heavy thunder-cloud, and we are often so depressed that everything seems dark to our eyes. But there is a silver lining to every cloud, and we have never lost our trust in Providence. My time is equally divided between my business and my dear patient; I intend to screw myself up to a public appearance." (He refers to a concert given for a charity, when he played Mozart's A minor Concerto, with his own cadenzas.) "I thank God that the powers of artistic enthusiasm enabled me to suppress many a gloomy thought; I do not think the audience noticed any change in me; nothing could be more flattering than my reception, I was cheered to the echo. I could not help saying to myself over the adagio, 'What divine music!' nor can I wonder at its giving the audience such exquisite pleasure. It gratifies me also to find that there is no necessity as yet for my hanging up my harp upon a willow-tree; publicity, however, has no longer any charms for me. I hope that to my life's end I shall retain enthusiasm and freshness for appreciation of the beauties of Mozart, which have become a part of my very self." A few weeks later he plays again for a charity. "I chose Beethoven's trio in D, and heard for the first time Fräulein Tietjen's glorious voice."

"Such a curious Fantasia I heard to-day. It was a miserably weak commentary on the motto it bore, 'Emotion is only fit for women, man's spirit should strike fire.' Mighty Beethoven! thou couldst make women weep and inspire men, but thy imitators are more diseased in mind than ever deafness made thee!—that Fantasia in three movements, E flat minor, A major, and E flat minor, with twenty-three other keys besides, stormed and whined, and any glimmering of spirit, depth, or poetry, was diluted in the length and monotony, the hopeless want of form and evenness of construction. I don't think the young composer answerable for this; he has talent and judgment enough to do something much better in time. Why not show him, in charity, his faults, and tell him to wait patiently for the ripening of his gifts?"

"I heard Wagner's overture to Faust, whlch I place higher than his other works. The demoniacal element is well worked out, and the better emotions are indicated by clear melodious thoughts. In compliance with the wish of several members of the orchestra, it was proposed to give a posthumous work by Mendelssohn, the 'Reformation Symphony.' Felix himself was dissatisfied with this composition, and did not wish to publish it; his brother, whom we consulted about the performance, left the question to be decided by Rietz, David, Hauptmann, and myself. We tried it at a rehearsal. In spite of many beauties which the work contains, we resolved not to give it, as the whole symphony does not stand on the same high level with Mendelssohn's other compositions, and we were afraid that the work might have to encounter unfriendly criticism. We did not escape some harsh comments in England for having kept back the work of one whose music it was considered, ought to be the heritage of the world.

# CHAPTER XXXV.

## 1856—1860.

Centenary of Mozart's Birth—Programme of the Concert—Julius Stockhausen—Ernst Pauer—Birds of Passage—Behr's Benefit—Louis Brassin—A Charming Present—Max Bruch—Arthur Sullivan—Jubilee of the Prague Conservatoire—Visit to Antwerp—Concours de Chant at Brussels—Schiller Festival—Intercourse with Liszt—Visit to Paris—Rossini.

ON the 27th of January, 1856, the centenary of Mozart's birth was celebrated at the Gewandhaus by a performance, the proceeds of which were to be devoted to the foundation of a Mozart Scholarship, to be competed for by members of the Leipzig Conservatoire. We here insert the Programme, interesting on account of the historical dates:

Overture to the "Re Pastore." Romance and duet out of the same Opera. Composed in 1775 in Salzburg as a Festival Opera, and performed for the first time to commemorate the visit of the Archduke Maximilian to Archbishop Hieronymus.

Concerto for Violin and Viola, composed in the year 1778, played by Herr Dreyschock and David. Overture to Idomeneo. Scene, Air, and March out of the same Opera. Given for the first time 29th January, 1781, in Munich.

March of Priests, Air and Choruses, out of the "Zauberflöte." Performed for the first time in Vienna, 30th September, 1791.

Overture to "Titus." First performance in Prague, 1791.

Last Scene, Second Act, "Don Juan." First performance in Prague, 28th October, 1787.

Symphony in C major, with the Final Fugue. Composed in August, 1788.

It cannot escape observation that, as a composer for the

pianoforte, Mozart was not represented on this occasion, a fact in every way distasteful to Moscheles, who would gladly have shown his devotion to the great master by publicly interpreting one of his works.

"Julius Stockhausen's first appearance here has given us all great pleasure. I can pay him and his singing no higher compliment than to say that he is the worthy son of one whose gifts as a vocalist were of the highest order; his pronunciation and method are faultless. Our public, never over-demonstrative, enthusiastically applauded him."

During the winter of 1856, Moscheles writes the "Humoristische Variationen," which, as we find from the diary, were originated in the hours of a sleepless night. "Unwell and restless as I was, the intellectual employment diverted my thoughts." . . . .

Ernst Pauer is here, a star in our musical firmament; with his light touch and light heart, he is very sympathetic to us. His stay of eight-and-forty hours was much too short for us; but how can a great London professional devote more time to an appearance at the Gewandhaus? In Beethoven's 'Concerto in G,' he developed his full technical powers, and I was much interested to find that Haslinger has allowed him to copy the original Manuscript Cadenzas by Beethoven which he had lent me on a former occasion, although he would never publish them. I do not think them up to the exalted level of the grand Concerto, and discard them in consequence. Pauer played one, without making any marked effect with it, not a soul asked who wrote it; in fact the Cadenzas do not bear the stamp of Beethoven's genius. . . . . We heard Beethoven's 'Men of Prometheus,' a work that certainly reminds one of his earliest time, but is redolent of the noble spirit of the master; then Schumann's overture to 'Hermann and Dorothea,' breathing poetry throughout.

"The influx of pianists is as large as ever. I confess I am annoyed when such birds of passage come pecking sentimentally at my Erard, or boldly smashing a chord or two. They show no curiosity to hear how I would treat the poor thing, in fact to them I am simply dead; they do not see that music is still to me as my own life-blood, and while they are burying me, I am quietly feeding on the Toccatas and Fugues of old Bach, the moderns, too, furnish an occasional meal. I have just fetched the scores of some of Liszt's works; his 'Preludes' and 'Mazeppa' will be performed here, and I must have studied them thoroughly beforehand." The performances alluded to are commented on in the following letter: "The Weimar folk have fought a battle with the Leipzigers; but there were no slain, only a few wounded. Liszt is reported to have said before the concert: 'I suppose they will prepare a defeat for me,' but they did no such thing. He conducted his 'Preludes,' which, although rather obscure, have many grand effects. His stormy 'Mazeppa' music, and his pianoforte Concerto, played with extraordinary power by Bülow, were warmly but not enthusiastically received.

"Behr gave for his benefit the 'Tannhäuser,' under Liszt's direction, some of the Weimar company assisting. My chief objection to the innovators is that they aspire to go *beyond* Beethoven, and altogether dethrone Mozart and Haydn, hitherto the acknowledged keystones to the foundation of music; of course, we lesser lights are to be buried under the ruins of the tottering temples, and I for my part consider myself honored by such sepulture; who knows if we shall not some day or other be dug up like Herculaneum and Pompeii?"

"Yesterday Louis Brassin played in the Gewandhaus my C minor Concerto, with so much roundness of touch and warmth that he earned great applause, although his amazing execution in the last movement made him run away with the 'tempo.' Concertmeister Müller of Brunswick, and Stern from Berlin, who were present, hailed him as a citizen of the musical commonwealth. They would not do as much for S., whose compositions I am just reading through, but the greedy ogres, who require enormous quantities of notes for their daily consumption, will welcome him to *their* commonwealth with open mouths."

"You know how my father *reads through*," adds Felix. "At every not quite orthodox bar he stands stock-still, leaving the guilty chord to do penance in the purgatory of his displeasure; till, after all the tortures of suspense, it is at last released, and may chime in with the loyal and virtuous chords in the Paradise of Harmony."

"New Year's Day (1858) I had a charming present—an original picture of Mozart, taken in the musician's early days in Italy. I at once stored away the treasure in my album, close to the autograph Cadenza of the master.

"We had a new overture by Reinecke, and heard his Trio and Variations on a theme by Bach, which he played at the Quartet Meetings. He is a thorough musician, and we may hope great things of him. A young composer, Max Bruch, showed me a number of Studies he has lately written. His Lieder are finely felt, and the two Cantatas, 'Rinaldo' and 'Jubilate' are fresh and original compositions. Arthur Sullivan, a lad of great promise, has been sent here for his musical education. He has already distinguished himself by winning the Mendelssohn Scholarship recently founded in London, and I feel sure he will do credit to England." We may here state that Moscheles took the liveliest interest in the career of the 'first Mendelssohn Scholar' and treated him invariably with marked kindness. The success of the 'Tempest Music' gave Moscheles sincere pleasure, and he regarded it as the inauguration of a genuine artist-career.

David had conceived the idea of arranging for the violin the "Twenty-four Studies" of Moscheles, who himself wrote the pianoforte accompaniments. Besides this, Moscheles prepared a new edition of the Clementi Sonatas, and the "Gradus ad Parnassum" for Hallberger. "They shall not make blunders for want of a proper system of fingering, or strict marking of the expression and tempi," he used to say, "so I conscientiously consult all previous editions." He also revised the catalogue of his works for publication by Kistner."*

In July the Conservatoire of Prague celebrates its jubilee, and the sister institute of Leipzig sends David and Moscheles with congratulations; we can well realize the feelings of Moscheles on visiting his native city, from which fifty years before he had gone forth full of hope to begin the battle of life, and we can picture to ourselves the pride of his compatriots and the cordial way in which they received him. When the busy days of fêtes and concerts were over, the Moscheles set out for Dresden, on their way to Antwerp.

* We give, at the end of the volume, a translation of the complete catalogue.

"Our journey might have been very unpleasant, for the rain poured in torrents, but what do wandering minstrels care about the weather? There is ever sunshine in art. We managed to get a coupé to ourselves, and David, who never separates from his violin, played all the finer for the obligato steam accompaniment; we had one Concerto after another, and then he tried passages from the 'Studies.' The hours flew past, and before we were aware of it we found ourselves in Dresden."

The summer holidays of this year Moscheles spent at Antwerp, on a visit to his son, and many were the valued friends who welcomed him. He was thoroughly at home among the art-treasures of the old city, and daily associated with such men as De Keyser, Leys, Van Lerius, Jacob Jacobs, Alma Tadema, Lies, Bource, and Heyermanns. At Brussels he was cordially greeted by Fétis, Kufferath, Léonard and others, and proceeding through the Ardennes, pays a short visit to the little town of Huy. Mrs. Moscheles says: "One can scarcely get along in the streets from the flowers, flags, barrel-organs, and festive decorations. It was the septennial 'Fête de la Vierge.' After reading the announcement of a 'Concours de Chant,' and a Concert to be given by the famous royal band, the 'Guides du Roi,' Moscheles sent his card to the Director, to ask for tickets, which, it was said, had been all bought up. Five minutes later this gentleman arrived, and would not leave till Moscheles had promised him to preside over the 'Jury des Concours de Chant.'"

"My duty as a Juryman rather taxed my powers of endurance, as for eight hours we sat on a high platform in the open market-place with the sun scorching us. Round about us was the band, a surging crowd, and a host of fashionables; it was a very animated scene. The Choral Unions, one after another, marched up to the front, banners unfurled, and sang. Not one could be called bad; several were really good."

The Schiller Festival and the King's birthday happening to be solemnized on the same day, Moscheles was asked by the Committee if he would allow his overture to the "Maid of Orleans" to be performed on the occasion. "I refused," he says, "on account of the inferior orchestra, and proposed as a substitute that Mertke, my clever pupil, should play my Fantasia on Schiller's 'Sehnsucht,' and I promised at the same time to write a brilliant piece on Schiller's poem, the 'Tanz.'" The piece composed originally for one performer, he subsequently arranged for four hands, and presented the copyright of the work to the Schiller "Stiftung."

"A grand musical tournament is coming off at Leipzig. The *Neue Zeitschrift für Musik* celebrates in June its twenty-fifth anniversary, and the faction, the principles of which are chiefly represented by this journal, has a grand gathering of artists to commemorate the event. The Riedel Choral Union is studying with great zeal the 'Graner Mass' for the occasion, and I have accepted an invitation to become a member of the Committee of Management. Programmes of the Festival are distributed, and the performances announced in all directions. Liszt, appearing for a short visit to Leipzig in May, persuades Moscheles to join him in playing his 'Hommage à Handel' at the Festival. He says that I, as one of the pillars of pianoforte-playing, am indispensable. I call myself the connecting link between the old and the new school."

Shortly afterwards Moscheles had an opportunity of returning Liszt's visit at Weimar. He writes: "Liszt sat down to the piano, and I heard, to my no small astonishment, my old Op. 42, Variations on the pretty Austrian melody

which I had consigned to oblivion for the last forty years. He played them by heart, and introduced startling effects. He then gave us his own organ Fantasia on the letters B-a-c-h, a piece full of extraordinary combinations, and stupendously played.

The next meeting was again at Leipzig. "I invited several of my colleagues to meet Liszt at dinner; it was a regular artistic gathering. After dinner Liszt, puffing his cigar, rummaged among my music, and found my 'Tanz' and the 'Humoristische Variationen;' he made me sit down there and then and play them with him. It was a genuine treat to draw sparks from the piano as we dashed along together. Liszt's genius seemed to culminate when he played my old 'Variations,' and finally, my 'Sonate Mélancholique.' I wish I could equally admire his style of composition, but there stands the barrier to a perfect artistic intimacy. . . . . A number of our musical visitors, with Liszt at their head, called on me the other day to hear me play; they wanted to take the measure of an old-fashioned pianist; but old-fashioned or not, my relations with Liszt are most cordial, and we know exactly how far we are on common ground; when we are harnessed together in a duet, we make a very good pair; Apollo drives us without whip."

"The crash and din of war have nearly driven out of my head the music of the future. Only last May I wrote my 'Patriotic March,' in which I introduced the Austrian 'Volkslied' and the Prussian air, Lützkow's 'Wilde Jagd,' dealing first of all with each subject separately, and then cordially interweaving the two together. Alas! the union of our two leading states seems more hopeless than ever, so I, an old musician, have reckoned without my host. . . . . Talking of compositions, my dear Clara, I am glad to hear of your zeal and progress in the art of transposing; but do not jump from one thing to another in your attempts at composition. I recommend you always to express some one definite thought, be it serious or gay, cheerful or anxious; when you have succeeded in doing this in short pieces, you may venture upon more important ones, in which a succession of dramatic ideas may alternate. Think always of a scene taken from real life, and despise using merely mechanical means for the purpose of producing an effect. The technical power should only serve as a means to heighten the effect of the principal idea, and give it strength and individuality. Your handwriting is much improved, but I have still to set the heads of many of your notes to rights for the sake of distinctness. Avis au lecteur." . . . . . "You will be sorry to hear that Rietz is going to leave us and take up his abode in Dresden; I do not know what we shall do without him. But what say you to —, who is just arrived from Paris? I asked him if he had ever seen 'Orfeo?' Answer: 'Yes; it is a sparkling little operetta, and has had a long run.' But I mean the real 'Orfeo.' Answer: 'Never heard of it.' And this too after Madame Viardot has sung it already half a hundred times in Paris. You know how strenuously I have always opposed the 'reviewing' in musical newspapers, to which some pupils have lately devoted themselves, also how very averse Mendelssohn was to the practice. The following poem is grist to our mill. I found it in Gutskow's 'Unterhaltungen am häuslichen Heerd':—

DEM ZUKUNFTSMUSIKER VON LUDWIG SEEGER.

Welch tolle Laune plagt den Mann
Beim Handwork nicht zu bleiben?
Wer singen und Laute spielen kann,
Was braucht der Bücher zu schreiben?

Wer zu dem Schwerte greift, der fallt
Durch's Schwert, das merk' sich Jeder,
Wer durch die Feder sündigt, erhält
Ein Urtheil durch die Feder.

Die Zukunftsgrillen verscheuche sie,
Lass Andre sich kritisch befehden!
Dein ist die That, die Melodie,
Die Andern mögen reden.

TO THE MUSICIAN OF THE FUTURE.

BY LUDWIG SEEGER.

Why, hair-brained Cobbler, leave your last?
Why, Carpenter, your hammer?
Ye Singers sing, ye Players play,
Why write a Latin Grammar?

The Bobadils, who cut and slash,
Are felled by their pursuers:
Acritic brains his brother; both
Are "Saturday Reviewers."

Let others "but offend their lungs
By talking" loud detraction,
Find ye in melody your balm,
And happiness in action.

In the summer of 1860 Moscheles spent his holidays in Paris. He writes, "The Erards, Crémieux, and Madame Viardot overwhelm me with kindness, and seem rather anxious to know how the Moscheles of old days adapts himself to the new style of pianoforte-playing. When the people cry me up, I think to myself, 'Rabattez la moitié et marchandez sur le reste.' At my Matinée I translated into correct prose the flowery epithets heaped on me, like bouquets on a ballet-dancer. . . . . For the impending 'Concours du Conservatoire' Herz has given my E flat Concerto to the pupils to study, but alas! in what a broken, fragmentary fashion. Auber, the director, does not allow more than four or five minutes to each pupil for his playing at the 'Concours'; eight bars, therefore, are taken from the 'tutti' and the half of the first solo jumbled together with the second half of the third. How is it possible to test by such a process the capabilities of the performer? I was invited to sit on the jury with Auber, Ambroise Thomas, and others, but declined; now I am beset with troops of fair pianistes about to contend for the prize, who wish me to hear their rendering of my dislocated Concerto. Like jockeys before the race, they all hope to get the first prize, and ask for my protection, as one asks for a vote when canvassing for a seat in Parliament. . . . . I have tried many fine pianos at the different warehouses, among others, those of Pleyel; their quality surprised me, and I am to have an opportunity of further appreciating them, as the firm has most liberally offered to send me one of their finest to Leipzig. George Pfeiffer, one of the partners, is a first-rate pianist, who has already written very excellent things." On one of the earliest days of his stay in Paris, Moscheles drives over with his son to Passy, to visit Rossini.

"Felix had been made quite at home in the Villa on former occasions. To me the 'Parterre Salon,' with its rich furniture, was new, and before the Maestro himself appeared, we looked at his photograph in a circular porcelain frame, on the sides of which were inscribed the names of his works. The ceiling is covered with pictures illustrating scenes out of Palestrina's and Mozart's lives; in the middle of the room stands a Pleyel piano. When Rossini came in he gave me the orthodox Italian kiss, and was effusive in expressions of delight at my re-appearance, and very complimentary on the subject of Felix. In course of our conversation he was full of hard hitting truths, and brilliant satire on the present study and method of vocalization. 'I don't want to hear anything more of it,' he said, 'they scream! All that I want is a resonant, full toned, not a screeching voice, I care not whether it be for speaking or singing; everything ought to sound melodious. He then spoke of the pleasure he felt in studying the piano; and 'if it were not presumption' (he added), 'in composing for that instrument; in playing, however, his fourth and fifth fingers would not do their duty properly.' He complains that the piano is, now-a-days, only maltreated. 'They not only thump the piano, but the armchair, and even the floor.' He then talked of the specialties of the different instruments, and said that the guitarist Sor, and the mandoline-player, Vimercati, proved the possibility of obtaining great artistic results with slender means. I happened to have heard both these artists, and could quite endorse his views. He told me that, arriving late one evening at a small Italian town, he had already retired to rest when Vimercati, the resident Kapellmeister, sent him an invitation to be present at a performance of one of his operas. In those days he was not yet as hard-hearted as he is now, when he persistently refuses to be present at a performance of his works; he not only went to the theatre, but played the double bass as a substitute for the right man, who was not forthcoming. This reminded me of what I once experienced to my cost at York, when the parts of the tenor and the lowest bassoon for Mozart's Symphony in D Major were missing. On the piano I showed Rossini what the effect was. He laughed heartily, and then asked for a little real music: after I had extemporized, he said: 'Is that printed? It is music that flows from the fountain head. There is reservoir water and spring water; the former only runs when you turn the cock, and is always redolent of the vase, the latter always gushes forth fresh and limpid. Now-a-days people confound the simple and the trivial; a motif of Mozart they would call trivial if they dared.' When we talked of the Leipzig 'Conservatoire,' he was delighted to hear that encouragement was given to the serious study of organ-playing, and he complained of the decay of Church music in Italy. He was quite enthusiastic on the subject of Marcello's and Palestrina's sublime creations. Before we parted he made me promise to call on him again before the day fixed upon to dine with him. When I next came, Rossini, yielding to my request, but not without modestly expressing diffidence in his own powers, played an Andante in B flat, beginning somewhat in this style:

in which, after the first eight bars, the following interesting modulation was introduced:

The piece is what we Germans would call tame. He then showed me two manuscript compositions, an Introduction and Fugue in C major, and a sort of pastoral Fantasia, with a brilliant Rondo in A major, which I had to play him. When I added a ♯ to the manuscript, he declared 'it was worth gold to him.' Clara, who was with me, and had already mustered up courage sufficient to sing my 'Frühlingslied' and 'Botschaft,' to Rossini's satisfaction, was obliged to repeat both songs before the singers Ponchard and Levasseur, who had just stepped in. I accompanied, and in answer to Rossini's observation that I had enough flow of melody to write an opera, rejoined, 'What a pity that I am not young enough to become your pupil!' I then had to play from his manuscripts, and that raised me 'to the kingship of pianists.' 'Whatever I am,' I replied, 'is due to the old school, the old master Clementi,' and on my mentioning that name, Rossini goes to the piano, and plays by heart fragments out of his Sonatas.' ". . . .

On other occasions Moscheles plays to the Maestro, who insists on having discovered barricades in the "humoristic variations," so boldly do they seem to raise the standard of musical revolution ; his title of the "Grande Valse," he finds too unassuming. "Surely a waltz with some angelic creature must have inspired you, Moscheles, with this composition, and *that* the title ought to express. Titles, in fact, should pique the curiosity of the public." "A view uncongenial to me," adds Moscheles, "however I did not discuss it. . . . . A dinner at Rossini's is calculated for the enjoyment of a 'gourmet,' and he himself proved to be one, for he went through the very select *menu* as only a connoisseur would. After dinner he looked through my album of musical autographs with the greatest interest, and finally we became very merry, I producing my musical jokes on the piano, and Felix and Clara figuring in the duet which I had written for her voice, and his imitation of the French horn. Rossini cheered lustily, and so one joke followed another till we received the parting kiss and 'good night.' . . . . At my next visit, Rossini showed me a charming 'Lied ohne Worte,' which he composed only yesterday ; a graceful melody is embodied in the well-known technical form. Alluding to a performance of 'Semiramide,' he said with a malicious smile, 'I suppose you saw the beautiful decorations in it?' He has not received the Sisters Marchisio for fear they should sing to him, nor has he heard them in the theatre ; he spoke warmly of Pasta, Lablache, Rubini, and others, then he added that I ought not to look with jealousy upon his budding talent as a pianoforte-player, but that, on the contrary, I should help to establish his reputation as such in Leipzig. He again questioned me with much interest about my intimacy with Clementi, and calling me that master's worthy successor, he said he should like to visit me in Leipzig, if it were not for those dreadful railways, which he would never travel by. All this in his bright and lively way, but when we came to discuss Chevet, who wishes to supplant musical notes by ciphers, he maintained in an earnest and dogmatic tone that the system of notation, as it had developed itself since Pope Gregory's time, was sufficient for all musical requirements. He certainly could not withhold some appreciation for Chevet, but refused to endorse the certificate granted by the Institute in his favor ; the system he thought impracticable.

The never-failing stream of conversation flowed on until eleven o'clock, when I was favored with the inevitable kiss, which on this occasion was accompanied by special farewell blessings.

Shortly after Moscheles had left Paris, his son forwarded to him most friendly messages from Rossini, and continues thus: "Rossini sends you word that he is working hard at the piano, and when you next come to Paris, you shall find him in better practice. . . . . The conversation turning upon German music, I asked him 'which was his favorite among the great masters?' Of Beethoven he said: 'I take him twice a week, Haydn four times, and Mozart every day. You will tell me that Beethoven is a Colossus who often gives you a dig in the ribs, while Mozart is always adorable; it is that the latter had the chance of going very young to Italy, at a time when they still sang well.' Of Weber he says, 'He has talent enough, and to spare' (Il a du talent à revendre celui-là). He told me in reference to him, that when the part of 'Tancred' was sung at Berlin by a bass voice, Weber had written violent articles not only against the management, but against the composer, so that when Weber came to Paris, he did not venture to call on Rossini, who, however let him know that he bore him no grudge for having made these attacks; on receipt of that message Weber called and they became acquainted.

"I asked him if he had met Byron in Venice? 'Only in a Restaurant,' was the answer, 'where I was introduced to him; our acquaintance, therefore, was very slight; it seems he has spoken of me, but I don't know what he says.' I translated for him in a somewhat milder form, Byron's words, which happened to be fresh in my memory: 'They have been crucifying Othello into an Opera, the music good but lugubrious, but, as for the words, all the real scenes with Iago cut out, and the greatest nonsense instead, the handkerchief turned into a billet-doux, and the first singer would not black his face—singing, dresses, and music very good.' The Maestro regretted his ignorance of the English language, and said, 'In my day I gave much time to the study of our Italian literature. Dante is the man I owe most to; he taught me more music than all my music-masters put together, and when I wrote my

Otello' I would introduce those lines of Dante—you know—the song of the Gondolier. My librettist would have it that gondoliers never sang Dante, and but rarely Tasso, but I answered him, 'I know all about that better than you, for I have lived in Venice, and you haven't. Dante I must and will have.' From the sublime to the ridiculous, we came to discuss my drawing of the Sisters Marchisio, and Rossini showed me the title-page of the duet out of 'Semiramide,' on which they are represented. He has at last condescended to receive them; they have sung to him, more than that, he has written a piece for them, and I am soon to meet them at his house. Rossini has in the kindest way composed a piece expressly for my imitation of the French horn, and written it into my album; it is exactly adapted to my voice, or rather to my blowing powers. Above is this inscription:

"Thème of Rossini, followed by two variations and Coda by Moscheles père," offered to my young friend Felix Moscheles.

"G. ROSSINI, Passy, 20th August, 1860."

On receipt of a copy of this piece, which was forwarded to Moscheles, he at once carried out Rossini's suggestion, and after writing the 'Two Variations and Coda,' asked the Maestro's permission to dedicate to him the work in the amended form. The following answer was received:—

"Paris, Passy, 1861.

'MON MAITRE (DE PIANO) ET AMI,—

"Permettez moi de vous remercier de votre aimable lettre. Rien ne pouvait ni ne devait m'être plus agréable, plus flatteur, qu'une dédicace de vous. Ce témoignage de votre affection est d'un prix inestimable à mes yeux, je vous en remercie avec toute la chaleur qui me reste, et qui n'a point encore glacé mon vieux cœur.

"Vous me demandez l'autorisation de faire graver le petit thème que j'ai noté pour votre cher fils;—elle vous est accordée. Rien de plus honorable, cher ami, que d'associer mon nom au vôtre dans cette petite publication, mais, hélas! quel est le rôle que vous me faites jouer en si glorieux mariage? Celui du compositeur vous octroyant à vous, le grande patriarche, l'exclusif du pianiste. Pourquoi ne voulez-vous donc pas m'admettre dans la grande famille un de plus, hein ! quoique je me sois placé très modestement (mais non sans vive peine) dans la catégorie de pianiste de 4ème classe ? Voulez-vous donc, cher Moscheles, me faire mourir de chagrin ?

" Vous y réussirez, vous autres grands pianistes, en me traitant en Paria, oui, vous serez responsables, devant Dieu et devant les hommes, de ma mort.

" Veuillez me rappeler au souvenir de Mme. et des chers enfants, en agréant pour vous l'affection sincère de votre ami de cœur,

"G. Rossini." *

Here is an extract from Moscheles' reply : " Mon cher Maître ! Savez-vous quel est mon numéro favori ? C'est le numéro 4 ; nous lui devons l'harmonie la plus parfaite ; 4 voix humaines, les quatre instruments du Quatuor, le pianiste enfin de 4ème classe, qui en lui seul représente l'harmonie de toutes les voix et de tous les instruments. N'allez pas me dire, cher Maître, que vous détestez le même numéro 4,

* Paris, Passy, 1861.

My Master(of Piano) and Friend,—

Permit me to thank you for your charming letter. Nothing could or would be more agreeable to me, or more flattering, than a dedication from you. This testimony of your affection is of inestimable value in my eyes ; I thank you for it with all the warmth that remains in me, and which has not yet frozen my old heart.

You ask me for authority to print the little melody which I have written for your dear son—it is granted. Nothing could do me more honor, dear friend, than to associate my name with yours in this little publication, but alas ! what is the part you make me play in so glorious a marriage? That of the composer making over to you a monopoly of the titles : "Grand Patriarch and Master of Pianoforte playing." Why on earth will you not admit me one member more in the great family, although I have placed myself very modestly (but not without infinite pains) in the category of pianists of the 4th class ? Or do you mean, my dear Moscheles, to make me die of vexation ?

That's what you will accomplish, all you great pianists, by treating me as a Pariah ; yes, you will be responsible before God and man for my death.

My kindest remembrances to Madame and the dear children, and believe me in all sincerity your affectionate friend,

G. Rossini.

puisque c'est la 4[ème] lettre que je vous écris depuis peu puisque c'est le 4[ème] protégé que j'autorise à frapper à votre porte hospitalière." * . . . .

On his return to Leipzig, Moscheles says: "Reinecke has just entered on his duties as Director of the Gewandhaus Concerts, and begins well by inaugurating his reign with a programme in which the music of the old masters is conspicuous." The Musical Society of London sends a complimentary letter enclosing Moscheles a diploma of honorary membership. He composes a Toccata in F sharp minor for the Mozart album, a two part Christmas song, and observes in a letter to a friend: "I should write music on a larger scale for my instrument, were it not that I am convinced that people now-a-days will not care to play such compositions. Only Beethoven's, Mendelssohn's, Schumann's, and Chopin's Concertos are now the fashion, Mozart and Hummel are completely ignored. Of my eight Concertos, that in G minor is becoming every day a greater rarity as an item in programmes. I flatter myself that my 'Characteristic Studies,' my 'Grande Valse,' and some of my other compositions, might hold their own as Bravura pieces, that my 'Nursery Tale' and my Study in A flat could sing in competition with the modern Notturnos; but not one of my colleagues plays them in public. I no longer appear at concerts, and—to speak with Byron—'I still hold myself too good for the sexton of authorship, the trunkmaker.' Should the rats and mice want such food to gnaw, it shall not be music of mine as long as I am alive. Consequently, at intervals, I compose a piece for a charity concert, or write Lieder and smaller pieces for home use for the grandchildren. I indulge myself in this kind of desultory work, not from loss of power, but from a feeling of pride. The old year (1860) is waning, but let me whisper into your ears this my musical confession."

* MY DEAR MASTER,—Do you know what is my favorite number? It is number four; we owe to it the most perfect harmony, the four human voices, the four instruments of the quartet, and though last, not least, the pianist of the fourth class, who in himself represents the harmony of all voices and all instruments. Do not tell me, dear Master, that you detest that same number four, since it is the fourth letter that I have recently written to you, since it is the fourth protégé that I authorize to knock at your hospitable door.

## CHAPTER XXXVI.

### 1861—1870.

Ovation to Concertmeister David—Sebastian Bach's Preludes—Visit to London—Mazzini—The Goldschmidts—Modern Music—Gounod's "Faust"—A Musical Treasure—Körner—Anniversary of the Battle of Leipzig—War between Austria and Prussia—Handel Festival in London—Wagner's "Meistersänger"—Visit to Belgrade—Illness—Strange Dream—Death of Moscheles.

A WELL merited ovation was given to Concertmeister David, on the 25th anniversary of his appointment at the Leipzig Conservatoire, and the members of the Gewandhaus joined with his pupils and friends to do him honor on the auspicious occasion. "When I congratulated him," writes Moscheles, "he showed me the letter in which Felix Mendelssohn offered him the post of Concertmeister; this, like everything from his pen, is charming both in feeling and expression. Surely his letters breathe as noble a spirit as his works, and how his youthful artistic spirit seems to brighten and expand under the genial influence of his first experiences of Italy! He enjoys everything doubly, keenly alive as he is to the beauties of the sunny south, and grateful for the parental sanction at last vouchsafed to his plans of travel. What a sensation these 'Reisebriefe' will create. I should like to give them the title: 'School for the artist and man.'

"My pupils, Dannreuther, Lienau, and Miss Schiller give me great delight, the Trial Concerts came off brilliantly; Sullivan's music to Shakespeare's 'Tempest' sounded fresh and clear, and the composer was, as he deserved to be, unanimously called forward at the end. . . . I cannot approve of the 'broderies' in Liszt's arrangement of the Mendelssohn 'Midsummer Night's Dream,' they are about as much in keeping as a crinoline would be on the Venus of Milo. . . . At David's I saw six or eight MS. Quartets and Quintets by Beethoven; they belong to Paul Mendelssohn, who lent them to David to edit for Breitkopf and Härtel; they contain a precious mine of inspiration, even in the erased passages or single notes."

It was in this year (1861) that Moscheles became acquainted with Gounod's Violoncello Obligato to the first of Sebastian Bach's famous "Forty-eight Preludes." The idea, so happily treated in this instance, suggested to him the setting of some of the other "Preludes" with melodies for the violoncello; these were subsequently re-arranged with increased effect for two pianos. This work was to Moscheles a labor of love, although he was severely censured by some pianists, who questioned the propriety of making additions to Bach; the majority however of amateurs and art-judges were charmed with the orchestral effects and the contrapuntal treatment of these compositions.

Moscheles thus states his own opinion: "I am praised or soundly rated for my setting of these 'Preludes,' but possibly my Melodies may promote the study of these works among students, who, in the absence of the accompaniments, would find them dry and unattractive. If so, shall I be perfectly satisfied; a deeper insight into Bach's works cannot fail to further the progress of art. While setting these melodies, I am in the same position as our romance writers, who can ventilate an important question of the day more effectively in some fictitious disguise than in a dry treatise."

During the season of 1861, Moscheles once more visits London, and, yielding to the persuasions of his old friends, the Directors of the Philharmonic Society, agrees to play at one of their concerts, giving them to understand that he wished to do so as a friend, and not as a professional. He had not appeared before the English public for fifteen years, and observing an anxious look on his wife's face as she came into the room on the evening of the Concert, he cheered her up with the words: "Surely you feel no misgivings: I intend to play like my former self, and do you honor. At the rehearsal, no doubt, I was rather upset by their affectionate demonstrations, but to-night no amount of fiddle-bow rapping, or the like, shall unnerve me, so pray do not distress yourself." He was as good as his word. The storm of cheers and waving of handkerchiefs, when he appeared, only served to animate him, and he played so finely that his friends eagerly congratulated him on a performance quite on a level with those of his best days.

Notwithstanding the busy life Moscheles led during his stay in London, surrounded as he was by a host of friends, with claims on his time and attention, he found leisure for keeping up his correspondence, a duty at all times pleasant to him. . . . "In answer to a question about Beethoven's sentiments on the subject of religion, I am under the impression that he was a Catholic, but a free-thinker at the same time. Of his piety I have no doubt, for his music speaks to the hearts of all nations, just as the sacred works of a Bach, a Mozart, or Mendelssohn do. Talking of free-thinkers, let me tell you of my acquaintance with Mazzini. Felix is painting a portrait of him, and so I have plenty of opportunities of meeting him. I had formed an utterly mistaken idea in my estimate of one whom I had always heard cried down as a conspirator; he seems to me agreeable and unassuming; his conversation even on the subject of politics is mild and apparently inoffensive; he is keenly interested in the subject of music. As a proof of this, I may tell you that his guitar is his inseparable companion, even in his hiding-places, and Meyerbeer is his favorite composer. Cavour's death, Garibaldi's illness, the *quasi* imprisonment of the Pope—on all these matters he discourses, and ends invariably with an observation of this kind: 'Providence is sure to do all for the best.' He lives in rooms of the plainest description, in Onslow Terrace, and goes by the name of 'Ernesti;' everything about him savors of Republicanism; the only luxury he seems to indulge in is that of smoking cigars *ad libitum.* From Mazzini's rooms to Argyle Lodge, where the Goldschmidts reside, is rather a leap; elegance and comfort rule here; there is no oppressive luxury, and one feels quite at home. And then the music. With Otto Goldschmidt I played my 'Hommage à Handel,' and that too without having in any way to sacrifice my artistic convictions; on the contrary I felt that I was understood, and joined by him in my conceptions. We also played the Bach Preludes, and he warmly expressed his approval of the idea and its execution. Madame Goldschmidt's voice is as fine as ever; if anything could enhance the pleasure her singing gives me, it would be to hear her, as I did the other day, in her own drawing-room. I reminded her of her last appearance at the Gewandhaus Concert, when she electrified us with a certain Cadenza, which recurs three times in one of Chopin's Mazurkas:

"I know many think me old-fashioned, but the more I consider the tendency of modern taste, and the abrupt and glaring contrasts indulged in by many composers of the present day, the more strenuously will I uphold that which I know to be sound art, and side with those who can appreciate a Haydn's playfulness, a Mozart's Cantilena, and a Beethoven's surpassing grandeur. What antidotes have we here for all these morbid moanings and overwrought effects! When I hear one of old Sebastian Bach's glorious fugues in the midst of all these fantasias, I accept it as a kind of musical peace-offering; not that I am completely reconciled, for it is usually taken 'Prestissimo.' Here as elsewhere I miss the right 'Tempi,' and look in vain for the traditions of my youth. That tearing speed which sweeps away many a little note; that spinning out of an Andante until it becomes an Adagio, an 'Andante con moto,' in which there is no 'moto' at all, an 'Allegro comodo' which is anything but comfortable—all such anomalies mar my enjoyment.

"At Boulogne, the other evening, a pianoforte-player brought me a Notturno of so restless a description that it threatened to disturb my nocturnal rest; he calls it too learned for Paris, I call it not learned enough for Germany.

I gladly allow that he and his colleagues have a special aptitude for transferring the melodious Italian element to pianoforte pieces, but such music becomes very wearisome to the genuine musician, and can only be tolerated by those whose ears and feelings are accustomed to the 'dolce far niente.' When he told me he thought the German music was too dry and learned, I played him scraps from Mozart, Beethoven and Mendelssohn ; there I had him. At last he said, 'But those were men of genius,' to which I replied, 'No doubt, and only men of genius ought to compose ; others should study the great masters until a portion of their spirit falls upon them.'

"In Gounod I hail a real composer. I have heard his 'Faust' both at Leipzig and Dresden, and am charmed with that refined piquant music. Critics may rave, if they like, against the mutilation of Goethe's masterpiece, the Opera is sure to attract, for it is a fresh, interesting work, with a copious flow of melody and lovely instrumentation."

In the summer of 1863, Moscheles and his family were at Loschwitz, and found an interesting neighbor in Kapellmeister Dorn, who happened to be the possessor of Mozart's original score of the opera of "Figaro," which was ultimately purchased by the firm of Simrock for the sum of 800 thalers. "He told me that the father of a Mr. Schurig, a music-master in Dresden, had bought this treasure from a wandering operatic company for a mere trifle, and that it had been bequeathed to the son in the ordinary way." There before my eyes were the immortal notes, thrown down off hand upon score-paper with fourteen lines, the Italian text and Recitatives in Mozart's handwriting, the German translation written in by another hand. I longed to be wealthy enough to buy this jewel at the high price put upon it by its present possessor. The pianoforte edition (Simrock's) occasionally differs from the original, as, for instance, in the Cavatina of the page "Non so più." Curiously enough, I have just now had in my hands the manuscript of another immortal work, the autograph score of the 'Zauberflote' which André showed me forty years ago in Offenbach. Count Baudissin asks me to examine it, and vouch for its authenticity to Count Ratzan, who is in treaty for purchasing this treasure. Every bar of the music is evidence of the divine inspiration and truth of Mozart; the alterations are very interesting; two bars of solo in the overture are erased, and in the duet, 'Bei Männern,' the Tempo is changed from 6–8 to 3–8."

Of Moscheles' scrupulous conscientiousness in editing the works of great musicians, we have had many proofs in the course of this narrative; the house of Peters was indebted to him for the loan of a manuscript copy of Bach's Prelude and Fugue in C, as well as that of the Trio in A minor, by the same master, so anxious was the owner of the autograph that the public should have correct versions of the best works. His knowledge of Beethoven's music was extraordinarily accurate; we read in the diary: "Beethoven's Quintet was played the other day in the Gewandhaus; in this passage

I heard an intercalated note, which was strange to me; thus—

I examined the original score, and found that Beethoven added this quaver for the violoncello."

His powers of musical analysis were occasionally put to the test in a less agreeable way. He writes on the 26th of August: "Of course the Körner Festival interests me; it not only appeals to my patriotic feelings, but reminds me of my intercourse with Körner in old Vienna days. I knew him when he was writing his drama 'Toni,' for Fräulein Adamberger. To-day all the Guilds turned out, and I followed the procession as far as the Japanese Palace, where I heard festival songs, festival speeches, and afterwards the anything but festival hodge-podge made by bands of music as they marched away and interlaced each other's tune in the following edifying fashion, waves of sound crossing one another thus—

I was utterly distracted, and pushed my way through dust and throngs of people back to the Altstadt." . . .

Moscheles alludes to the celebration at Leipzig of the fiftieth anniversary of the great battle: "Fortunately we had the best of weather for our fête; all our veterans who had served in the battle were handsomely entertained in private houses; two old Grätz artillery-men were quartered on us, and uncommonly jovial they were. The procession was really a very pretty and touching sight, for each old soldier was attended in his march through the streets by a young girl dressed in white, who walked by his side: spring and winter contrasted beautifully. As the procession came under our windows, the Pauliner and other musical societies did me the honor of waving their flags and calling me out to receive their greetings. Everything was admirably managed, the music in the market-place, the torch-procession, illuminations, etc. . . . . Talking of 'veterans,' I suppose I may speak of my fingers; I do not allow them to take it easy, but set them their daily task of difficult passages and scale-gymnastics. I thoroughly believe in Riehl's words: 'A man of fifty years of age, who allows his physical and mental energies to slacken, is sixty within a couple of years; a man of seventy, who by dint of healthy energetic work has aspired to retain all his youthful vigor, is a man in his best years.' And yet, continues Moscheles, 'I am at issue with him in that part of his excellent letter where he deals with the subject of the Musical Education of the people, since he would have the violin taught before the piano. Organ and piano offer the best opportunity for an understanding of the relations of tones and connection of harmonies; and therefore I think they should be studied first of all."

Moscheles, on the happy occasion of the marriage of his third daughter, Clara, to the advocate, Dr. Adolar Gerhard, was the very embodiment of Riehl's "ideal man of seventy," for he was radiant with happiness, and took an active part in the festive proceedings. Dr. Gerhard had inherited his father's gift for poetry, and some of his verses suggested to Moscheles the melodies of two charming Lieder.

In the summer of 1866 Moscheles was in London. Two years previously he had been painfully interested by the Schleswig-Holstein question; now the absorbing topic of the day was the war between Austria and Prussia. "I will not, I cannot believe, in Germans wishing to take up arms against Germans." The occupation of Leipzig by the Prussians soon undeceived him, and the dreadful miseries that followed prompted him to join with Madame Jenny Lind-Goldschmidt in giving a concert for the wounded soldiers. "For such a purpose I am glad once more to play in public, and will cheerfully put up with hearing myself called old-fashioned, if I, a venerable curiosity, can earn a good harvest of guineas for others. What I could afford out of my own purse is too little for these thousands of unfortunate beings. Therefore—Art *versus* War—and let us see if she, the peaceful one, cannot make head against the destroyer. Let us have harmonies, not the din of battle." Moscheles handed over his half of the proceeds, 1400 thalers, to the Fund for the sufferers by the war.

"We were present at Mrs. Schwabe's, who gave a farewell dinner to the poet Freiligrath. Our great musical episode was the Handel Festival in the Crystal Palace; Costa steered his ship very cleverly through the giant rocks of this locality, and Titiens, with her colossal voice, sang splendidly; the effect at times of the double choruses was so thrilling that I thought to myself, 'Fancy old Handel standing and conducting his gigantic works in this gigantic place!'"

After all the excitement of a London season, Moscheles rejoiced to find himself at the sea side, where, surrounded by his grandchildren, and under the influence of that bright and sunny picture of happy childhood, he composes the "Familienleben!" "These small pieces for four hands are intended as a bequest to the grandchildren; to my own, first of all—after them, to all my grandchildren in art, who, I hope will find amusement in them. Each piece depicts some incident gathered from the little world of children, some story they may listen to with pleasure; and if, while learning to play these pieces, their little minds are active, or their miniature feelings awakened, they will be learning to play well." At a later period he added to the twelve numbers of the Familienleben" three others: "The Little Prattlers," "Grandmamma's Night Thoughts at the Spinning-Wheel," and "The Boy on his Rocking-Horse." Moscheles' playing would often attract a grateful crowd of rustics, who stood outside and listened by the window, and one evening the grandchildren were greatly impressed by the spectacle of a working-man, who, after mounting the shoulders of his companion and peering in at the window, called out in a stentorian voice: "God grant that gentleman for a long time the use of his hands."

At this time Felix painted his father's portrait, an engraving of which forms the frontispiece of the present work, and certainly no more favorable moment could have been chosen to do justice to the original. Moscheles both mentally and physically was at his best, and enlivened the hours of sitting by conversation on the points of comparison between the sister arts; this was always a favorite topic with him.

Moscheles spent his seventy-third birthday at Leipzig, and records that anniversary in language of simple truth and gratitude: "How can I reckon up this great number of years without thanking the Almighty for His having guided me so far under His protection, and that too by the side of my loving and beloved wife! Old age is something of everyday occurrence, but to be old and to feel at the same time young and susceptible of all the enjoyments of life, is a consciousness rarely bestowed." . . . .

The letters as well as the diary of this year testify to Moscheles' full capacity of musical enjoyment. On two occasions he goes to Dresden; on the first he hears a performance of Franz von Holstein's opera, "Der Haideschact;" on the second, Wagner's "Meistersänger" is the attraction. Of the former he says: "I was very much pleased with this music, after playing it on the piano from a copy of the score; the orchestral performance has completely justified all the hopes raised in my mind by that first examination. The music is flowing and melodious, the instrumentation effective, and there is abundance of dramatic force; the artists, one and all, sang 'con amore'—nay, with positive enthusiasm. I think this composer has a great future before him." With regard to Wagner's "Meistersänger," he writes: "I find more unity in this opera than in Wagner's earlier works for the stage, although the composer's views of the relation between orchestra and singers are here, as everywhere in his music, peculiar—the singers with long declamatory recitatives, and often 'parlando,' have to struggle, as best they can, with overwrought orchestral modulations and effects. I thought I caught some echoes of 'Don Juan,' in that scene where Lerporello in a minuet rhythm invites the 'maschere' to the ball. Next day Rietz and I had a long conversation on the subject of the eccentricities, as well as the undeniably great qualities, of the 'Meistersänger;' we examined the printed score too, and admired the well-calculated instrumental effects. The old-fashioned lute, used by Beckmesser in the Serenade, was effectively represented by a small harp with metal instead of the ordinary strings; the effect certainly was very good."

So little had old age begun to tell on Moscheles, that he fearlessly set out on so distant a journey as to Hungary and Servia, on a visit to his daughter Serena, whose husband (Dr. Rosen) had been appointed by the Prussian Government Consul General at Belgrade. From the latter place Moscheles writes: "We certainly move here in European society, and indulge in European music; on the other hand, our surroundings are rather strange and primitive. We have seen the park of Topschidere, where the Prince Michael was insidiously murdered; the market place with people in their national costumes, the Turkish quarter, with Prince Eugene's half-ruined palace, and the gipsies' street, with its squalid, half-naked denizens. Servian tailors, weavers, and shoemakers pursue their trade in open stalls; there is a brisk demand for frippery and second-hand goods of all kinds. Behind a clump of faded oleander trees, you can see people munching fruits, vegetables, and meat, and washing it all down with 'Slibowitz,' their favorite beverage. . . . .

"The other day we saw a Servian wedding procession. I counted twenty open calèches, all the occupants were dressed in different colored costumes, even the horses were decorated with ornamental cloths, part of the wedding presents made to the newly-married couple."

Moscheles, on his return from Belgrade, visits some old friends at Pesth, where a complimentary banquet is given in his honor. At the theatre he was received with an orchestral flourish, by way of prelude to the overture of the national opera "Hunyady," and a performance of that most graceful and charming of all national dances, the "Csardas."

On his return to Leipzig, Moscheles writes: "I have indeed, cause to be thankful, as I look back upon the incidents of my journey. I have travelled many a mile to meet with those dear to me. I have enjoyed art and nature with them, seen a country new and interesting to me, have met with the kindest reception by art brothers and friends, and now I return home hale and hearty."

This he wrote at the beginning of August; yet when, in

the following October, his four children were once more assembled in Leipzig on a visit to their parents, they observed with apprehension symptoms of debility, which, as being so unusual with their father, gave rise in their minds to anxious forebodings. In November he suffered much from want of sleep, and it was not until the following month that the skill of his friends, Professors Reclam and Wagner, gave him any relief. What his friends were to him and his wife, during that sad time, cannot be told in words. May they all, on reading these pages, feel that the poor but imperfect tribute to their sympathy comes from the heart of her who writes them! Under the date of the 6th of December we find these few bars of music with a motto over them, both in his handwriting:

"Auflösung ist das Ziel unseres irdischen Lebens."
("Dissolution is the goal of our earthly life.")

On the 8th December, 1869: For my diary:

"In my feverish restlessness and wretchedness last night, I could not get out of my head Mendelssohn's Capriccio (in A minor, op. 33, No. 1); from the first to the last bar it exactly expresses my condition. That faultless piece has, however, one awkward passage which did not escape me, awkward when judged by the strictly orthodox laws of harmony; it is the sequence of the 263d bar to the next."

On Tuesday, the 20th of December, 1869, he writes in the diary: "Towards morning, after a restless, almost sleepless night, I had the following highly exciting dream. I chanced to hear (I wonder where?) that, since the day of Beethoven's death in Vienna, a couple of old servants were in charge of the room in which he died, and declared that, on each anniversary of Beethoven's birthday, he could be conjured up to appear in bodily form, but only to those with whom he had been personally acquainted in his lifetime. The watchers had had printed a description of his last moments, and sold it to any one for a few kreutzers. I must go there (I said to myself,) and told Charlotte what I proposed doing. She eagerly caught at the idea, and begged and prayed I would take her with me. I was much embarrassed, and explained to her that such a thing was impossible, as she had not known Beethoven personally. She would not be put off, and begged hard I would allow her at least to see the manes of the great departed; surely I could make him understand that *my* wife ought to be pardoned this act of indiscretion. After much hesitation I consented! On the appointed day we came to Vienna, and demanded admission to the room. We sat upon the bed in which Beethoven had pronounced his last words, 'Plaudite, amici, comœdia finita est.' The servants made some mysterious movements with their hands, and soon afterwards Beethoven, in bodily form, arose slowly like a statue of white marble, the body draped in classical Grecian folds. The apparition came near, and stretched out its cold hands towards me; I clasped them immediately and kissed them. Beethoven turned his head towards me in a kindly way, as if he wanted to ask me questions; I intimated to him by signs that he could not hear my answers. He shook his head sorrowfully, withdrew his hands from mine, and vanished into the upper air—then I awoke."

"December 31st, 1869.—My thoughts were turned towards the Creator, who, after my long and laborious career, has brought me to the winter of my existence, and tended by my faithful Charlotte, linked by the chain of love to all my family, I find, although an invalid, quiet and comfort. With these words I take leave of the year 1869—Finis."

In January and February he rallies sufficiently to be able to enjoy music. "It was a great undertaking," he says, "but I have at last realized my desire to hear Cherubini's 'Medea,' with Franz Lachner's Recitatives, but the intense interest with which I followed every note was too much for me." A few days later he gives words of counsel and encouragement to the youthful Emma Brandes, whose musical endowments had a special charm for him, as being in harmony with his own art-creed. When she had played to him, he sat down to the piano to show her his rendering of the "Concert Fantastique," but as he wrote afterwards, "I could only play it "Mezza voce.'"

The 1st of March, 1870, was the forty-fifth anniversary of his wedding-day, and Moscheles, making every effort to take part in the home fête, played, with his daughter and two friends, an overture to "Der Freyschutz," for four performers. The day afterwards, although he was palpably unfit for any physical exertion, he insisted on going to the Gewandhaus Rehearsal. This was to be his last effort.

In his last illness, Moscheles, the best of fathers, husbands, sons, and friends, faced death with calm confidence, and retained his cheerfulness unto the last moment of his life. On the 10th of March, 1870, when the angel of death hovered over the sick man's chamber, Moscheles still had an affectionate smile of recognition for the dear ones around him. His faith failed not when the hour of departure was at hand, and he died, as he had lived, in peace, and in the fear and love of God.

# A COMPLETE CATALOGUE

*OF COMPOSITIONS*

## BY I. MOSCHELES.

---

### A.—*Compositions marked with the Number of the Work.*

Op. 1. Variations on a Theme from Mehul's Opera, "Une Folie." For Piano. Leipzig: Kistner.

Op. 2. Ten Variations on a Favorite Air from the Opera, "Der Dorf Barbier." For the Piano. Vienna: Haslinger.

Op. 3. Polonaise for the Piano. Leipzig: Hofmeister.

Op. 4. New Sonatine, easy and popular. For the Piano. Vienna: Artaria & Co.

Op. 5. Favorite Air, by Weigl, "Wer hörte wohl," with Variations. For the Piano. Vienna: Spina.

Op. 6. Variations for the Piano, on an Austrian National Air. Vienna: Artaria & Co.

Op. 7. Variations on a Cavatina from the Opera, "Trajano in Dacia." Vienna: Artaria & Co.

Op. 8. Ten Waltzes for the Pianoforte. Vienna: Artaria & Co.

Op. 9. Five German Dances for the Pianoforte. Vienna: Spina.

Op. 10. Triumphal March, with two Trios, for four hands on the Pianoforte. Vienna: Spina.

Op. 11. Two Rondos for the Piano, on Themes introduced in the Ballet, "Les Portraits." Leipzig: Kistner.

Op. 12. Introduction and Rondo, for the Piano, on a Venetian Barcarolle. Vienna: Haslinger.

Op. 13. Fantasie Héroique. For the Piano. Vienna: Spina.—New Edition. Leipzig: Hofmeister.

Op. 14. Rondo Brilliante. For the Piano. Vienna: Artaria & Co.

Op. 15. Variations, for the Piano, on a Theme from the Opera, "The Oculist." Vienna: Spina.

Op. 16. Three Love Songs, by E. Ludwig, with Pianoforte Accompaniment (Dream and Reality, The Kiss, The Eternal). Leipzig: Hofmeister.

Op. 17. Introduction et Variation Concertantes. For Piano, Violin, and Violoncello. Vienna: Haslinger.

Op. 18. Three Rondos for the Pianoforte. Vienna: Spina.

Op. 19. Polonaise, preceded by an Introduction. For the Pianoforte. Vienna: Spina.

Op. 20. Grand Duo Concertant. For Piano and Guitar. Vienna: Artaria & Co.

Op. 21. Six Variations for Piano and Flute, or Violin. Vienna: Haslinger.

Op. 22. Sonata for the Pianoforte. Vienna: Spina.

Op. 23. Variations for the Pianoforte, on a Russian Theme. Vienna: Artaria & Co.

Op. 24. Rondo Espagnol. For the Piano. Vienna: Spina.

Op. 25. Caprice. For the Piano. Vienna: Spina.

Op. 26. Triumphal Entry of the Allies into Paris—a descriptive piece. For the Piano. Vienna: Artaria & Co.

Op. 27. Sonata (characteristic). For the Piano. Vienna: Artaria & Co.

Op. 28. Six Divertissements, for the Piano. Vienna: Spina.

Op. 29. Variations for the Piano on a Theme of Handel. Vienna: Spina.

Op. 30. Rondo Brilliant, for Four Hands. Vienna: Spina.

Op. 31. Trois Marches Héroiques, for Four Hands. Vienna: Spina.

Op. 32. "La Marche d'Alexandre," with Variations. For the Piano and Orchestral Accompaniment. Vienna: Artaria & Co. Arranged with Quartet; Piano Solo; Pianoforte Duet. Leipzig: Breitkopf and Hartel.

Op. 33. Six Waltzes, with Trios for Pianoforte Duet. Vienna: Artaria & Co.

Op. 34. Grand Duo Concertant. For Piano and Violoncello, or Bassoon. Vienna: Artaria & Co.

Op. 35. Grand Sextuor. For Piano, Violin, Flute, Two Horns, and Violoncello. Leipzig: Hofmeister. Arranged as a Sonata for Piano, for two Pianos; for Pianoforte Duet.

Op, 36. Variations on an Austrian National Melody. For Piano and Violin. Vienna: Haslinger.

Op. 37. Grand Caprice, followed by a Potpourri. For Piano and Violoncello, or Violin Concertants. Vienna: Spina.

Op. 38. Fantasia (in the Italian style), followed by a Grand Rondo. For Piano. Vienna: Haslinger.

Op. 39. Introduction and Variations, for the Piano, on an Austrian National Air. Vienna: Haslinger.

Op. 40. "Les Portraits"—Ballet Champêtre et Comique. Arranged for Pianoforte. Vienna: Artaria & Co. Overture for Pianoforte Solo and Duet. Three Divertissements for Piano, on Subjects taken from the Ballet "Les Portraits." Leipzig: Hofmeister.

Op. 41. Grand Sonata. For Piano. (Dedicated to Beethoven.) Vienna: Haslinger.

Op. 42. Grand Variations on an Austrian National Melody. For Piano, Two Violins, Viola, Violoncello, and Double Bass, or without Accompaniment. Vienna: Artaria & Co.

Op. 43. Grand Rondeau Brilliant. For Piano, accompanied by Two

Violins, Viola, Violoncello, and Double Bass (*ad lib.*). Vienna: Artaria & Co. For Pianoforte Solo or Duet. Leipzig: Hofmeister.

Op. 44. Grand Sonate Concertante. For Piano and Flute. Vienna: Artaria & Co.

Op. 45. Concert de Sociétê. For Piano, with Accompaniment for small Orchestra. Vienna: Spina.

Op. 46. Fantasia, Variations, and Finale, on the Bohemian National Song, "To Gsau Kône." For Piano, Violin, Clarinet, and Violoncello. Vienna: Haslinger.

Op. 47. Grand Sonate. Piano, for Four Hands (E major sonata). Vienna: Artaria & Co. New Edition, Hamburg: Cranz.

Op. 48. French Rondo. Arranged for Piano and Violin, with a small Orchestra, or without. Vienna: Haslinger.

Op. 49. Sonate mélancholique. For the Piano. Vienna: Artaria & Co. Berlin: Schlesinger.

Op. 50. Fantasia and Variations, on the favorite air, "Au clair de la Lune." For the Piano, with accompaniment for the Orchestra. Berlin: Schlesinger. With Quartet, for Pianoforte Solo.

Op. 51. Allegri di Bravura (La Forza, La Legerezza, Il Capriccio). Leipzig: Peters.

Op. 52. La Tenerezza. Rondoletto for the Pianoforte. Vienna: Spina. New Edition, Hamburg: Cranz.

Op. 53. Colonaise Brillante. For the Piano. Leipzig: Hofmeister.

Op. 54. Les Charmes de Paris. Rondo Brillante. For the Piano, Berlin: Schlesinger.

Op. 55. Bonbonnière Musicale; Suite de Morceaux Faciles for Piano. Paris: Schlesinger.

Op. 56. Grand Concerto in E major. For the Piano, with Orchestral Accompaniment. Leipzig: Klemm. With Quartet, as Pianoforte Solo, Rondo Brillalla Polacca for Pianoforte Duet. Leipzig: Hofmeister.

Op. 57. Fantasia for the Piano, on Three Favorite Scotch Airs. Leipzig: Breitkopf & Hartel.

Op. 58. "Jadis et Aujourdhui," a Gigue and Quadrille Rondeau. For the Piano. Hamburg: Cranz.

Op. 59. Grand Potpourri Concertant. For Piano and Violin, or Flute (By Moscheles and Lafont). Berlin: Schlesinger.

Op. 60. Third Concerto (G minor). For Piano, with Orchestra. Leipzig: Klemm. With Quartet. For Pianoforte Solo.

Op. 61. Rondoletto, on a Favorite Nocturne by Paër. For the Piano. Vienna: Artaria & Co.

Op. 62. Impromptu. For the Piano. Leipzig: Kistner.

Op. 63. Introduction, and Scotch Rondo. Concertante, for Piano and Horn, or Violin and Viola. Leipzig: Kistner. Arranged as Pianoforte Duet.

Op. 64. Fourth Concerto. For the Piano, with Orchestral Accompaniment. Vienna: Steiner & Co.

Op. 65. Impromptu Martial, on the English Air, "Revenge, he cried." For the Piano. Leipzig: Kistner.

Op. 66. La Petite Babillarde. Rondo for the Piano. Leipzig: Kistner.

Op. 67. Three Brilliant Rondos for the Piano, on Favorite Motives from the Vaudeville, "The Viennese at Berlin." Berlin: Schlesinger.

Op. 68. Fantasia and Rondo, on an Austrian March. For the Piano. Leipzig: Kistner.

Op. 69. Souvenirs d'Irlande. Grand Fantasia. For the Piano, with Accompaniment for Orchestra or Quartet. Leipzig: Hofmeister. Arranged as Pianoforte Solo and Duet.

Op. 70. Twenty-four Studies for Advanced Players. Leipzig: Kistner.

Op. 71. Rondeau Expressif, on a favorite Theme of Gallenberg. For Piano. Leipzig: Kistner.

Op. 72. No. 1. Fantaisie Dramatique, in the Italian Style, on a Favorite Air sung by Madame Pasta. For the Piano. Leipzig: Kistner.

Op. 72. No. 2. Bijoux à la Sontag. Fantaisie Dramatique. For the Piano. Kistner.

Op. 72. No. 3. Bijoux à la Malibran. Fantastique Dramatique (two books). Kistner.

Op. 73. Fifty Preludes in the different Major and Minor Keys. For Piano. Kistner.

Op. 74. Les Charmes de Londres. Brilliant Rondo for Piano. Kistner.

Op. 75. Echoes from Scotland. Fantasia on Scotch National Airs. For the Pianoforte, with Orchestra or Quartet. Leipzig: Hofmeister.—Arranged for Piano Solo.

Op. 76. "La Belle Union." Brilliant Rondo, preceded by an Introduction for the Piano. For Four Hands. Leipzig: Kistner.

Op. 77. Allegro di Bravura. For the Piano (Dedicated to Mendelssohn). Berlin: Schlesinger.

Op. 78. Divertissements à la Savoyarde. For Piano and Flute or Violin. Liepzig: Hofmeister.

Op. 79. Sonata Concertante. For Piano and Flute, or Violin. Leipzig: Kistner.

Op. 80. Fantasia on Airs of the Scotch Bards. For Piano with Orchestra (*ad lib*). Leipzig: Kistner. Arranged for Pianoforte alone.

Op. 81. First Symphony in C. For Grand Orchestra. Leipzig: Kistner.

Op. 82 *a*. Rondeau Sentimental. For Piano. Kistner.

Op. 82 *b*. Quatre Divertissements. For Piano and Flute. Kistner.

Op. 83. Recollections of Denmark. Fantasia on Danish National Airs. For Piano, with Orchestra. Kistner. Arranged for Pianoforte Solo.

Op. 84. Grand Trio. For Piano, Violin, and Violoncello (Dedicated to Cherubini). Kistner.

Op. 85. La Gaieté. Brilliant Rondo for the Piano. Kistner.
Op. 86 *a*. Easy March, with Trio. For Pianoforte Duet. Kistner.
Op. 86 *b*. Souvenir de Rubini. Dramatic Fantasia for the Piano, on a Cavatina from the Opera "Anna Bolena." Kistner.
Op. 87. Fifth Concerto (C Major). For the Piano and Orchestral Accompaniment. Vienna: Haslinger. With Quartet for Pianoforte Solo.
Op. 87 *a*. Souvenir de l'Opéra. Dramatic Fantasia for the Piano, on Favorite Airs sung in London by Madame Pasta. Leipzig: Kistner.
Op. 87 *b*. Duo Concertant. For two Pianos, with Orchestral Accompaniment in the form of Brilliant Variations on the Bohemian March, from the Melodrama "Preciosa." Composed by F. Mendelssohn and I. Moscheles. Kistner. For two Pianos without Accompaniment. For Pianoforte Duet.
Op. 88. Grand Septet. For Piano, Violin, Viola, Clarinet, Horn, Violoncello, and Double Bass. Kistner. For Pianoforte Solo or Duet.
Op. 89. Impromptu. For the Piano. Kistner.
Op. 90. Concerto Fantastiqe (No. 6). For Piano. with Orchestra. Vienna: Haslinger. With Quartet. For Pianoforte alone.
Op. 91. Overture, for Full Orchestra, to Schiller's Tragedy, "Joan of Arc." Leipzig: Kistner. Arranged for Pianoforte Duet.
Op. 92. Hommage à Handel. Grand Duet for Two Pianofortes. Kistner. Arranged as a Pianforte Duet.
Op. 93. Concerto Pathétique. For Piano with Orchestra (No 7). Vienna: Haslinger.
Op. 94 *a*. Rondeau Brilliant on Dessauer's Favorite Romance, "Le Retour des Promis." Leipzig: Kistner.
Op. 94 *b*, Hommage Caractéristique to the Memory of Madame Malibran de Beriot, in the form of a Fantasia, for the Piano. Kistner.
Op. 95. Characteristic Studies for the Piano, for the Higher Development of Execution and Bravura. Kistner.
[Passion—Reconciliation—Contradiction—Juno—Nursery Tales—Bacchanal—Tenderness—National Holiday Scenes—Moonlight by the Sea-shore—Terpsichore—The Dream—Anxiety.]
Op. 96. Pastoral Concerto (No 8). For Piano with Orchestral Accompaniment. Vienna: Haslinger.
Op. 97. Six Songs, with Accompaniment for the Piano. Leipzig: Kistner. Stamme Liebe der Schmied. Zuversicht—Das Reh im Herbste—Sakontala.
Op. 98. Two Studies—"Ambition—Enjoyment;" taken from "La Méthode des Methodés." Berlin: Schlesinger
Op. 99. Tutti Frutti. Six new Melodies, For the Piano. Paris: Pacini.
Op. 100. Ballad. For the Piano. Brunswick: Spohr.—Arranged for Piano Duet.

Op. 101. Romance and Brilliant Tarantella. For the Piano. Leipzig: Hofmeister.
Op. 102. Hommage à Weber. Grand Duet for the Piano, on subjects from Euryanthe and Oberon. Leipzig: Kistner.
Op. 103. Serenade. For the Piano. Kistner.
Op. 104. Romanesca. For the Piano. Kistner.
Op. 105. Two Studies for the Piano (written for the Beethoven Album). Vienna: Spina.
Op. 106. Brilliant Fantasia, for the Piano, on a Cavatina from Rossini's Opera, "Zelmira," and a Ballad from Mozart's "Seraglio." Leipzig: Kistner.
Op. 107. Daily Studies in the Harmonic Scale, for Practice in different Rhythms. A Series of Fifty-five Pieces, for Four Hands (Two Books). Kistner.
Op. 108. Two Brilliant Fantasias for the Piano on Favorite Airs from Balfe's "Bohemian Girl" (Two Books). Kistner.
Op. 109. Mélange for the Piano on the "Serenade" and other favorite airs from "Don Pasquale." Leipzig: Hofmeister.
Op. 109 *a*. Brilliant Fantasia, on Favorite Themes from the Opera, "Don Pasquale." For the Piano. Leipzig: Hofmeister.
Op. 110. Gondolier's Song. For the Piano. Rotterdam.
Op. 111. Four Great Concert Studies. For the Piano. Leipzig: Kistner. [Réverie et Allégresse—Le Carillon—Tendresse et Exultation—La Fougue.]
Op. 112. Grand Sonate Symphonique, (No 2) for Four Hands. Berlin: Friedlander.
Op. 113. Album of the Favorite Songs of Pischek. Transcribed for the Piano, in the form of a Brilliant Fantasia. Leipzig: Kistner.
Op. 114. Souvenirs de Jenny Lind. Brilliant Fantasia for the Piano, on Swedish Airs. Kistner.
Op. 115. Les Contrastes. Grand Duo for Two Pianos. Arranged for Four or Eight Hands. Kistner.
Op. 116. Freie Kunst. A Poem, by Uhland. For a Bass or Alto Voice with Pianoforte Accompaniment. Kistner.
Op. 117. Six Lieder, with Pianoforte Accompaniment. [Liebeslaun schen—dem Liebesänger. Warum so stumm—Botschaft—Schäfers Sonntagslied. Frühlingslieder.] Kistner.
Op. 118. Grand Waltz. For the Piano. Kistner.
Op. 119. Six Songs, with Pianoforte Accompaniment. [Abends—Die Zigeunerin—Strenge—Jemand—Der Liebenswündigen—Der dreifache Schnee.] Kistner.
Op. 120. Mazurka Appassionata. For Piano. Kistner.
Op. 121. Sonata. For Piano and Violoncello; for Piano and Violin; for Pianoforte Duet. Kistner.
Op. 122. "Expectation" (after Schiller). Fantasia for the Piano. Hamburg: Cranz.
Op. 123. Magyaren Klänge. Original Fantasia for the Pianoforte. Brunswick: Litolff.
Op. 124. "Longing" (Schiller's Poem). Fantasia for the Pianoforte. Leipzig: Siegel.

Op. 125. Spring Song. For a Soprano or Tenor Voice, with Pianoforte Accompaniment. Cologne: Schloss.
Op. 126. Grand Concert Study. For Piano. Leipzig: Kistner.
Op. 127. Scherzo. For the Piano. Leipzig: Payne.
Op. 128. Humoristic Variations. Scherzo and Variations for the Piano. Leipzig: Kistner.
Op. 129. The Dance.' Characteristic Piece (after Schiller). For the Piano. Leipzig: Breitkopf & Hartel.
Op. 130. Symphonesque-Heroic March on German National Songs. For Piano (Four Hands). Arranged for Two Pianos. Leipzig: Kistner.
Op. 131. Six Songs, with Pianoforte Accompaniment. Kistner.
Op. 132. Four Duets, for Soprano and Alto, with Pianoforte Accompaniment. [Gieb uns teglich Brod—Frühlingsliebe, Schmetrering und Liebchen—Am Meere, Inniges Verstêndniss, Tauz Reigen der Donischen Kosaken.] Kistner.
Op. 133. Reverie Mélodique. For the Piano. Stuttgart: E. Hallberger.
Op. 134. Toccata. For the Piano. (In the Mozart Album).
Op. 135. Pastoral in the Organ Style. Erfürt: Bartholomaüs.
Op. 136. To G. Rossini. "To the Rivulet." Song, with Horn (or Viola) Obligato, and Piano. Leipzig: Kistner.
Op. 137. Studies in Melodious Counterpoint. A Selection of Ten Preludes from J. S. Bach's "Well Tempered Clavier," with an obligato Violoncello part added by Moscheles. Also Arranged for a Second Piano instead of Violoncello. Leipzig: Kistner.
Op. 138. Feuillet d'Album de Rossini. An Original Theme for Piano and Horn; for Piano and Viola; for Two Pianos. Kistner.
Op. 139. "Lied im Volkston," with Variations, on an Original Theme. Leipzig: Klemm.
Op. 140. Domestic Life. Twelve Progressive Piano Pieces for Four Hands. Two Books. Leipzig: Kistner.
Op. 141. March and Scherzo as Rhythmical Exercises. Hamburg: Cranz.
Op. 142. Three Character Pieces for Pianoforte Duet. Leipzig: Kistner.

## B.—*Various Compositions.*

1. Souvenir de Belisaire. Two Fantasias for the Piano. Leipzig: Kistner.
2. Fantasia for the Piano, on Motives from Balfe's "Falstaff." Mayence: Schotts fils.
3. Fantasia on Favorite Themes from the Opera "Oberon." For the Piano. Berlin: Schlesinger.
4. Fantasie à la Paganini. For Pianoforte Solo. Leipzig: Kistner.

5. Fantasia on Motives from Balfe's Opera, "The Siege of Rochelle." For the Piano. Vienna: Spina.
6. Bouquet des Melodies. Fantasia on Favorite Airs. Hamburg: Cranz.
7. The Popular Barcarolle, "Or che in Cielo." Sung by Signor Ivanhaff in Donizetti's Opera "Marino Faliero." Arranged as a Fantasia with Variations for the Pianoforte. London: Addison and Hodson.
8. Pensées Fugitives for the Piano. Vienna: Spina. (Romance—Impromptu—Nocturne—Rhapsodie.)
9. Andante and Rondeau on a German Theme. For the Piano. Leipzig: Kistner.
10. Echo des Alpes. Divertissment for the Piano on three Swiss Pastoral Airs. Kistner.
11. The Tyrolese Family, 3d "Divertissement." For the Piano. Leipzig: Hofmeister.
12. Divertissement on Tyrolese Airs. Sung by the Rainer Family. For the Piano. Leipzig: Peters.
13. Divertissements on Swiss National Airs. For the Piano. Leipzig: Kistner.
14. Rondeau on a Favorite Scotch Melody. For the Piano. Vienna: Haslinger.
15. Rondeau Militaire, for the Piano, on the favorite Duett, "Entendez-vous," from Auber's "Fiancée." Leipzig: Kistner.
16. Farewell March of The Emperor Alexander Regiment. Vienna: Spina.
17. Two Grand Marches for the Imperial Alexander Regiment. Spina.
18. March of the 2d Regiment of Viennese National Guard. For the Piano. Spina.
19. Favorite March with Trio, of the Regiments Kutschera and Max Joseph. For Pianoforte Duet. Spina.
20. Rhapsodie Champêtre. For the Piano. Berlin: Schlesinger.
21. The Departure of the Troubadours. Romance with German and Italian words. Variations by Moscheles, Giuliani, and Mayseder. Vienna: Spina. Czerny's Arrangement for Two Pianofortes, for Pianoforte Duet.
22. Music Composed for the Sledging Party of the Allied Princes. Vienna: Artaria & Co.
23. Three Fashionable Waltzes. For the Piano. Artaria & Co.
24. Twelve German Dances Complete. Vienna.
25. Six Waltzes, for the Piano. Vienna: Spina.
26. Six Ecossaises for the Piano. Vienna: Artaria & Co.
27. Six Waltzes for the Piano. Leipzig: Peters.
28. Concord (words by T. Probald). For Voice and Piano. Leipzig: Payne.
29. Fantasia for the Piano on Airs of Neukomm. London: Cramer & Co.
30. L'Elégante. Rondeau for the Piano. London: Chappell.
31. Variations on Handel's "Harmonious Blacksmith," for the Piano For Four Hands. Leipzig: Kistner.

# INDEX OF NAMES

## MENTIONED THROUGHOUT THE WORK.

**THE END.**